Playing with Fire

Critical Frontiers of Theory, Research, and Policy in International Development Studies

Series Editors: Andrew Fischer, Uma Kothari, and Giles Mohan

Critical Frontiers of Theory, Research, and Policy in International Development Studies is the official book series of the Development Studies Association of the UK and Ireland (DSA).

The series profiles research monographs that will shape the theory, practice, and teaching of international development for a new generation of scholars, students, and practitioners. The objective is to set high quality standards within the field of development studies to nurture and advance the field, as is the central mandate of the DSA. Critical scholarship is especially encouraged, within the spirit of development studies as an interdisciplinary and applied field, with a classical focus on national and global processes of accumulation and structural transformation, and associated political, social, and cultural change. In this manner, the series seeks to promote a range of applied theory and empirics based on the analysis of historical development experiences, as was the methodological and epistemological strength of classical development studies.

Also in this series:

The Aid Lab: Understanding Bangladesh's Unexpected Success
Naomi Hossain

Taken for a Ride: Grounded Neoliberalism, Precarious Labour, and Public Transport in an African Metropolis
Matteo Rizzo

The South Centre

The South Centre is the intergovernmental policy research organization of developing countries established in 1995 to undertake research and analysis on various international development policy areas that are relevant to the protection and promotion of the development interests of developing countries. The South Centre helps developing countries to develop common points of view and to work together on major international development-related policy issues relevant to the countries of the South and the global community in general, such as development policies, sustainable development, climate change, global governance, economic and social development, South-South cooperation, global economic conditions, intellectual property, technology transfer, access to knowledge, health, trade agreements and food security.

Playing with Fire

Deepened Financial Integration and Changing Vulnerabilities of the Global South

Yılmaz Akyüz

OXFORD
UNIVERSITY PRESS

Great Clarendon Street, Oxford, OX2 6DP,
United Kingdom

Oxford University Press is a department of the University of Oxford.
It furthers the University's objective of excellence in research, scholarship,
and education by publishing worldwide. Oxford is a registered trade mark of
Oxford University Press in the UK and in certain other countries

First Edition published in 2017
Impression: 1

Published in the United States of America by Oxford University Press
198 Madison Avenue, New York, NY 10016, United States of America

British Library Cataloguing in Publication Data
Data available

Library of Congress Control Number: 2017935269

ISBN 978–0–19–879717–3

Printed in Great Britain by
Clays Ltd, St Ives plc

To the memory of my mother and father

Preface

The new millennium has brought far-reaching changes in the world economy. The early years were marked by optimism elicited by Great Moderation in the United States and elsewhere in the industrialized world—almost two decades of tranquillity marked by reduced volatility of business cycle fluctuations and increased macroeconomic stability, with better monetary policy seen as the driving factor. Europe moved to monetary union without a major hiccup, promising greater stability and faster growth. Led by China, emerging and developing economies started to surge ahead, many recovering from virulent financial crises and growing at rates that would secure rapid convergence towards the levels of advanced economies, and ready to play the role of locomotives for the world economy. Undaunted by recurrent crises, they hastened their integration into the global financial system, greatly helped by policies in advanced economies.

The picture changed drastically with the onset of the most severe post-war crisis, first in the United States and then in Europe. The Great Moderation in the North came to be displaced by Great Recession and the fear of Secular Stagnation. The Eurozone faced a serious risk of disintegration within a decade of its establishment. After an initial resilience, growth in the South converged downwards towards the depressed levels of advanced economies. The BRICS have come to be seen as part of the problem, leading the world economy into slump. The vulnerabilities resulting from deepened financial integration of emerging and developing countries have become visible even before a significant tightening of international monetary and financial conditions.

This book is a collection of three essays on these themes—crisis, integration, and vulnerability—drawing on papers written in the past three years in the South Centre. Part I combines, updates, and extends two earlier papers: 'Waving or Drowning: Developing Countries after the Financial Crisis', June 2013; and 'Crisis Mismanagement in the United States and Europe: Impact on Developing Countries and Longer-term Consequences', February 2014. It makes a critical examination of the policy response of the United States and the Eurozone to the 2007–08 crisis, and particularly the consequences of unconventional monetary policy for financial integration and vulnerability of emerging and developing economies. Part II is based on a paper written in

January 2015. It reviews the policies and market forces driving global financial integration of emerging and developing economies, examines changes in its depth and pattern, and new sources of vulnerability. While Part II focuses on the size and composition of external financial assets and liabilities of these economies and their linkages with international financial markets, Part III turns to foreign direct investment, based on a paper written in October 2015. It discusses the macroeconomic and developmental impact of foreign direct investment in the South, and the implications of bilateral investment treaties for national policy autonomy. These three parts are preceded by an introduction that blends the main arguments and discusses the policies needed to put the world economy into a decent shape.

The views expressed in this book were presented and discussed in various meetings in the South Centre and the United Nations as well as in academic seminars and conferences in the past few years. I owe a debt of gratitude to their participants for comments and suggestions. My special thanks go to my colleagues in the South Centre, Martin Khor, Humberto Campodonico, Michael Mah-Hui, and Manuel Montes, and in UNCTAD, Richard Kozul-Wright, Joerg Mayer, and Sabri Öncü. I am also grateful to Nathalie Bernasconi and Sanya Reid for helpful suggestions on foreign direct investment regimes and agreements. Comments from referees also helped improve the quality of the volume. I thank particularly Andrew Fischer, the co-editor of the Development Studies Association book series Critical Frontiers in International Development Studies, for his unstinting support and insightful comments and suggestions. Xuan Zhang and Anna Bernardo of the South Centre provided excellent statistical and editorial assistance, respectively. The usual caveat applies.

Yılmaz Akyüz
Bodrum, Turkey

August 2016

Contents

List of Figures

List of Tables

List of Tables

List of Acronyms

ADB	Asian Development Bank
AEs	Advanced Economies
AFCG	American Funds, Capital Guardian
AMECO	Annual Macro-Economic Database, European Commission
BIS	Bank for International Settlements
BITs	Bilateral Investment Treaties
BNM	Bank Negara Malaysia
BOEA	Bureau of Economic Analysis
BPM (BPM5, . . .)	Balance of Payments and International Investment Position Manual
BRIC	Brazil, Russia, India, and China
BRICS	Brazil, Russia, India, China, and South Africa
BWIs	Bretton Woods Institutions
CA	Current Account
CACs	Collective Action Clauses
CEE	Central and Eastern Europe
CIEPR	Committee on International Economic Policy and Reform
CIS	Commonwealth of Independent States
CMIM	Chiang-Mai Initiative Multilateralization
CPIS	Coordinated Portfolio Investment Surveys
CRA	Contingent Reserve Arrangement
EC	European Commission
ECB	European Central Bank
EDEs	Emerging and Developing Economies
EFSF	European Financial Stability Facility
EM ARA	Assessing Reserve Adequacy for Emerging Market Economies
EME	Emerging Market Economies
EMU	Economic and Monetary Union

ERP	Economic Report of the President
ESM	European Stability Mechanism
EU	European Union
FDI	Foreign Direct Investment
FRBNY	Federal Reserve Bank of New York
FRED	Federal Reserve Bank of St. Louis Economic Research Economic Data
FSB	Financial Stability Board
FTAs	Free Trade Agreements
G20	Group of 20
GATS	General Agreement on Trade in Services
GDP	Gross Domestic Product
German DAX	*Deutscher Aktienindex* (German stock index)
GFCF	Gross Fixed Capital Formation
GKOs	*Gosudarstvennoye Kratkosrochnoye Obyazatyelstvo* (Russian Government Short-term Commitments)
GNI	Gross National Income
ICMA	International Capital Market Association
IDB	Inter-American Development Bank
IIF	Institute of International Finance
ILO	International Labour Organization
IMF	International Monetary Fund
IMF BOP	International Monetary Fund Balance of Payments Database
IMF CPIS	International Monetary Fund Coordinated Portfolio Investment Surveys
IMF GFSR	International Monetary Fund Global Financial Stability Report
IMF IFS	International Monetary Fund International Financial Statistics
IMF WEO	International Monetary Fund World Economic Outlook
J.P. Morgan EMBI Global	J.P. Morgan Emerging Markets Bond Index Global
J.P. Morgan GBI-EM	J.P. Morgan Government Bond Index-Emerging Markets
LA	Latin America
LAC	Latin America and the Caribbean
LDC	Least Developed Country
MENA	Middle East and North Africa

MFN	Most-Favoured-Nation
MSCI	Morgan Stanley Capital International
MSCI EM	Morgan Stanley Capital International Emerging Markets Index
M&A	Mergers and Acquisitions
NAFTA	North American Free Trade Agreement
NBS	National Bureau of Statistics of the People's Republic of China
NFA	Net Foreign Asset
NIEs	Newly Industrializing Economies
OANDA	Olsen and Associates
OECD	Organisation for Economic Co-operation and Development
OEM	Original Equipment Manufacturer
OFCs	Offshore Financial Centres
QE (QE1, 2...)	Quantitative Easing
RMB	Renminbi
R&D	Research and Development
SAFE	State Administration of Foreign Exchange
SDDS	Special Data Dissemination Standard
SDR/SDRs	Special Drawing Right(s)
SDRM	Sovereign Debt Restructuring Mechanism
SMEs	Small and Medium-sized Enterprises
SSA	Sub-Saharan Africa
TNCs	Transnational Corporations
TRIMs	Agreement on Trade-Related Investment Measures
TRIPs	Agreement on Trade-Related Aspects of Intellectual Property Rights
UK	United Kingdom
UK FTSE	United Kingdom Financial Times Stock Exchange
UN	United Nations
UNCTAD	United Nations Conference on Trade and Development
UNCTAD TDR	United Nations Conference on Trade and Development Trade and Development Report
UNCTAD WIR	United Nations Conference on Trade and Development World Investment Report
UNECA	United Nations Economic Commission for Africa

UNEP	United Nations Environment Programme
US	United States
USD	United States Dollar
WB	World Bank
World Bank WDI	World Bank World Development Indicators
WTO	World Trade Organization
ZIRP	Zero Interest Rate Policy
ZLB	Zero Lower Bound

Introduction

0.1 Global Economic Landscape and Prospects

Before the world economy can fully recover from the crisis that began more than eight years ago, there is a widespread concern that it may be poised for yet another crisis. In several ways it looks no less fragile now than it did on the eve of the subprime debacle. Global income growth remains well below the levels recorded in the period before the 2009 crisis. The US and European economies have not got back to a decent shape and Japan is still grappling with deflation. Exceptional monetary policy measures introduced to deal with financial instability and recession are still in place. The economic landscape is not much better in the emerging and developing economies (EDEs),[1] which have become increasingly integrated into the world economy, not just in trade and investment but more importantly in finance, rendering them highly susceptible to global boom–bust cycles. The crisis has moved in a third wave to several major emerging economies after having swept from the United States to Europe. The jury is still out on whether the second largest economy, China, will be able to avoid financial turbulence and growth collapse with severe social and political repercussions.

The US acted quickly to resolve the financial crisis resulting from mounting loan delinquencies and asset deflation by bailing out banks and passing the buck to debtors. But the resolution of economic crisis proved to be much harder. The green shoots said to have been seen in 2009 soon froze and the subsequent recovery was sluggish and unbalanced between the rich and the poor, between capital and labour, and between finance and industry. After more than 24 quarters of positive growth, a large segment of the US population feels that the economy is still in recession.

[1] EDEs correspond to what the IMF calls 'Emerging Market and Developing Economies' and emerging economies refer to what the IMF calls 'emerging market economies'.

The Eurozone has not even been able to resolve its financial crisis, let alone economic crisis. It is still engaged in protracted debt negotiations with Greece and its banks are suffering from undercapitalization and bad loans. Income in several periphery countries is below pre-crisis peaks and unemployment rates are at historical highs. Potential growth in the region has been falling even more rapidly than in the US because of lack of productive investment, erosion of skills, and the debt overhang. The region faces political uncertainty and prospects of economic stagnation over the medium term.

The fortunes of EDEs traditionally varied with conditions in international commodity markets because of their dependence on commodity exports. However, global financial conditions have increasingly become a stronger influence. This is not so much because of their success in industrialization as because of their deepened integration into the international financial system, financialization of commodities, and mutually reinforcing impulses between international financial and commodity markets. Indeed there has been a strong correlation between commodity prices and capital inflows to EDEs in the new millennium, and growth in the South has gone up and down with them.

The policies of advanced economies that culminated in the global crisis and strong growth in China as a major consumer of many commodities resulted in a twin boom in capital inflows and commodity prices in the run up to the crisis, and produced a significant acceleration of growth in the South. The recovery of these economies from the crisis was also rapid, thanks to a renewed surge in capital flows resulting from the ultra-easy monetary policy and a strong upturn in commodity prices, mainly due to an investment boom engineered by China in response to fallouts from the crisis. The boom in capital inflows not only added to the growth momentum in the South, but also increased their external vulnerability by deepening their integration into the global financial system.

The acceleration of growth in EDEs relative to advanced economies before the crisis was widely interpreted as decoupling of the South from the North, including by the International Monetary Fund (IMF). After the crisis the combination of rapid recovery of EDEs with stagnation and faltering growth in advanced economies created a belief that major EDEs, notably BRICS (Brazil, Russia, India, China, and South Africa), were becoming the engines of the global economy. However this myth was soon demolished with the collapse of commodity prices, significant weakening of capital flows and economic slowdown in China. Growth in EDEs has converged downward towards the levels of advanced economies from the highs recorded in the run up to the global crisis and its immediate aftermath. Most BRICS economies have come to be seen as part of the problem, pushing the world economy into slump. EDEs have little policy space to respond to destabilizing and deflationary impulses from commodity and financial markets. Their potential growth has been falling more rapidly and their medium-term prospects are bleaker than advanced economies.

This state of affairs owes a great deal to shortcomings in the policies adopted in response to the financial crisis in advanced economies. These policies, notably the ultra-easy monetary policy, have not only failed to bring about a rapid and broad-based economic recovery and stability, but also aggravated many of the underlying systemic problems including inequality, the deflationary gap, and financial fragility. They have created strong destabilizing impulses for EDEs and increased their susceptibility to external financial shocks by helping deepen their integration into the global financial system and leading to new sources of vulnerability as well as reinforcing the traditional channels of transmission of external financial shocks. Continued liberalization of cross-border financial transactions, foreign direct investment (FDI) regimes, and access to domestic financial markets in EDEs has also been a central factor in this process of deepened integration.

These systemic and policy issues have been extensively analysed and debated in the literature. The purpose of this book is to contribute to this endeavour in several ways. First of all, it aims to bring together, assess, and articulate many of the ideas expressed in these areas with a Southern perspective with a view to contributing to a better understanding of what is at stake for EDEs within a wider community of policy-makers and researchers—a perspective that this author has always aspired to maintain throughout his association with the developing world while in UNCTAD and at the South Centre. It offers a significant departure from the common understanding of the rise of emerging economies in the world economy. It provides a comprehensive treatment of global financial linkages of EDEs and the vulnerabilities they entail, based on a rich set of data and information that have not been put together so far in the literature. It gives an integrated treatment of sources of external vulnerability of commodity-dependent developing countries by introducing the notion of commodity-finance nexus and examining the interactions between commodity and financial cycles and the challenges they pose. Finally, it makes a critical assessment of FDI in EDEs, providing empirical evidence and arguments against several myths held in the mainstream literature regarding its nature and macroeconomic and developmental impact. In no way, however, does this book pretend to have the final say on these matters. What is hoped is, rather, to stimulate new research and thinking on these key issues for the South.

The book aspires to do these in three parts. The first part gives a critical assessment of policies adopted in response to the crisis in major economies, notably the US, Europe and China, and their spillovers to developing countries through financial and commodity channels. The second part provides wide-ranging evidence on deepening integration of EDEs into the global financial system in the new century and the vulnerabilities they entail while the third part turns to the so-called real capital flows, FDI. This introduction summarizes the evidence and arguments elaborated and substantiated throughout the book. It is organized around key issues, bringing together various elements treated in different chapters so as to blend them together to provide an integrated treatment. The book concludes with a discussion of what all these could project for development in the new century.

0.2 Misguided Policies in the US and Europe

It is true that recoveries from recessions resulting from financial crises tend to be weak and protracted because it takes time to repair balance sheets—to remove debt overhang and unwind excessive and unviable investments generated during the bubbles that culminate in such crises. However, the recovery from the global crisis that began in 2007 has been exceptionally long. According to historical records, in the 100 worst past financial crises in advanced economies, it took on average around seven years to reach pre-crisis level of per capita income. In the current crisis this is estimated to take nine years. In some countries in the Eurozone it would take much longer, until at least 2023.

The crisis is taking too long to resolve because of two main shortcomings in the policy response in the US and Europe. First, governments have been unwilling to remove the debt overhang through timely, orderly, and comprehensive restructuring. They resorted to creditor bail-outs to resolve financial instability while enforcing austerity on debtors. Second, macroeconomic policies have been ineffective and even at times counterproductive in supporting aggregate demand and employment. Fiscal policy has acted to restrain recovery, resulting in excessive reliance on unconventional monetary policy. This policy mix has not only failed to boost growth, but also aggravated systemic problems including the debt overhang, financial fragility, inequality, and structural demand gap, and generated strong destabilizing spillovers to the South.

As the crisis in advanced economies had been caused by debt-driven property and consumption bubbles, its resolution should have been expected to bring about a significant reduction of debt. Instead, the ultra-easy monetary policy resulted in a renewed debt pile-up both in the North and the South, by some additional $50 trillion since 2008. In advanced economies household debt did not increase much and even declined in the US as a per cent of gross domestic product (GDP). But this is more than offset by higher government and corporate debt in advanced economies and rapid accumulation of corporate debt in emerging economies. The debt overhang is a main reason why the US Federal Reserve is reluctant to abandon the ultra-easy monetary policy even though it is not fuelling growth but adding to financial fragility, thereby making the exit and normalization even more difficult.

In the US, bail-outs contained the financial crisis and allowed the banks first to recover and then reach record profits. But the government has been reluctant to write down mortgages in line with the ability of households to pay. The drop in household debt as a per cent of GDP since the outset of the crisis is largely due to foreclosures and hence reflects a corresponding reduction in household wealth.

In the Eurozone, policy intervention has been premised on the wrong diagnosis that the crisis in the periphery was due mainly to fiscal profligacy, neglecting the role of intra-Eurozone capital flows and private debt build-up. It also ignored the role of policies in the core countries, notably competitive disinflation and exports surpluses in Germany in generating external deficits and debt in the periphery.

The strategy adopted by Eurozone policy-makers in dealing with the debt crisis was very much like that of the failed Baker Plan pursued during the Latin American crisis in the 1980s—official lending to keep debtors current on their payments to private creditors and austerity. Despite the rhetoric about involving creditors in the resolution of the crisis, interventions mainly served to bail out creditors. The debt-restructuring initiatives brought little relief to debtors. Public debt ratios shot up even in countries such as Spain and Ireland which had adhered to Maastricht thresholds better than Germany.

The burden of balance-of-payments adjustment in the Eurozone fell entirely on deficit countries as Germany refused to stimulate growth in the region by expanding domestic spending and halting competitive disinflation it had been engaged in since the beginning of the new century by keeping wages behind productivity. The periphery has been forced into internal devaluation through drastic cuts in wages. Imports have been slashed and unemployment rose to levels higher than those seen during the Great Depression.

Initially, fiscal response was reflationary in both the US and Eurozone, but as soon as the economies started to show signs of life, fiscal orthodoxy reigned, supported by theoretical fallacies and shaky empirical evidence on the magnitude of fiscal multipliers and the impact of public debt on growth. In the Eurozone the periphery countries that made the most strenuous efforts for fiscal consolidation are also the worst performers in terms of growth.

The return of fiscal orthodoxy led to excessive reliance on monetary policy. Central banks resorted to unconventional measures, including zero and negative policy interest rates and liquidity expansion through massive bond purchases in successive rounds of quantitative easing (QE). Initially, monetary reflation was no doubt necessary to address illiquidity in financial markets and overcome credit crunch. However, it came to be increasingly burdened to resolve a crisis which was about solvency rather than liquidity.

The ultra-easy monetary policy was expected to boost growth by lowering long-term interest rates and encouraging investors to shift from government bonds to other assets, including high-risk, high-yielding assets such as stocks and corporate bonds, thereby creating asset bubbles. In the event long-term rates came down significantly and stock markets reached historical highs, but they failed to boost spending. The increased risk aversion that resulted from deflation made the banks in the US and Europe unwilling to lend to households and small businesses while big businesses have had little need for bank loans or appetite for new spending on labour and equipment in view of economic stagnation. Debt issues by corporations increased, particularly in the US, but these were used not to increase capital spending but for mergers and acquisitions (M&A) and stock buybacks. The wealth effect of asset booms on spending has been weak because the gains are reaped mainly by the rich. Ironically, the ultra-easy monetary policy has been more 'successful' in stimulating spending in emerging economies by giving rise to a surge in capital inflows and creating bubbles in the credit and asset markets of these economies, but at the cost of mounting external financial vulnerability.

0.3 Secular Stagnation, Savings Glut and Underconsumption

The failure of historically low interest rates to reignite a strong recovery bewildered many mainstream economists, leading to a search for an explanation within the conventional macroeconomic framework. According to the secular stagnation thesis, first evoked by Larry Summers, because of structural factors such as the slowdown in technical progress and population growth, investment opportunities have been vanishing in the US and most other major advanced economies. As a result, real interest rates would need to be very low, indeed negative, to bring savings and investment into equilibrium at the full employment level of income, but this is not possible because nominal interest rates cannot be negative and central banks are unable to create inflation. Until the Great Recession this chronic demand gap had been masked by private spending driven by financial bubbles created by low interest rates in search of faster growth. Recurrent credit and asset bubbles would be needed to avert secular stagnation, but since these bubbles eventually culminate in financial crises, the structural demand gap creates a trade-off between financial stability and growth.

According to an alternative hypothesis, based on the same theoretical framework, low interest rates and the demand gap in the US are due to a global savings glut resulting from excess savings in surplus countries—China and major oil exporters before the crisis and the Eurozone and particularly Germany after the crisis. These spilled over to the US through capital flows, depressing long-term rates, strengthening the dollar, weakening US exports, creating large trade deficits, and reducing growth. Global excess savings have thus the same effect as reduced investment opportunities on economic activity. However, on this view, the problem arises from policies pursued in surplus countries rather than structural factors.

While there is little dispute that accumulation and growth slowed down and monetary policy has become ineffective, these ad hoc explanations do not stand up to the realities of modern monetary economies. They are both based on the pre-Keynesian Loanable Funds model which fails to distinguish between savings and financing, and to grasp that in a monetary economy loans and investment do not come from pre-existing stocks of savings. Investment is governed mainly by demand and profit expectations and made and financed independently of savings. Excess of savings over investment implies excess supply of goods and services, and sets off a process of adjustment through changes in the level and functional distribution of income, rather than the interest rate. In a monetary economy there is no such thing as a stable natural rate of interest that is compatible with full employment and independent of macroeconomic policy.

A more plausible explanation for the structural demand gap is underconsumption resulting from growing inequalities. There is a secular downward trend in the share of wages in GDP in all major advanced economies as well as China, contrary to the long-standing belief that the share of labour in GDP stays relatively stable in the course of economic growth. Globalization, financialization, and reduced bargaining power of labour resulting from neo-liberal policies rather than technological change are the main reasons.

In advanced economies real compensation of workers has lagged output per worker since the 1980s, reducing the purchasing power of workers over the goods and services they produce. This has also been accompanied by the concentration of wealth in the top 1 per cent and hence the growing inequality in the distribution of incomes earned on assets. These trends in income and wealth distribution imply that inequality is not only a social problem but has increasingly become a macroeconomic problem.

So far there have been two responses to underconsumption. First, creating spending booms driven by credit and asset bubbles, as done by the US throughout the past three decades and China in the aftermath of the global crisis. Second, relying on exports to fill the demand gap—that is, export unemployment through incomes, macroeconomic or exchange rate policies, as done by China and Japan before the global crisis and Germany throughout the new millennium. Neither of these, however, provides a sustainable solution.

Financial bubbles may provide partial and temporary solutions to underconsumption but can in fact aggravate the structural demand gap. First, as seen since 2008, they do not always boost aggregate demand to reduce unemployment and accelerate growth. Second, the boom–bust financial cycles create supply-side distortions, impeding productivity and slowing growth. Third, they also aggravate the deflationary gap by increasing inequality.

Until the crisis China, Germany, and Japan all relied on foreign markets to close the demand gap, with GDP growing faster than domestic demand thanks to a strong growth in exports—more so in Germany than in the others. China's export-led growth came to an end with the crisis, forcing it to turn to domestic demand to sustain growth. However, rather than boosting household incomes and private consumption, China engineered a debt-driven investment boom, creating excess capacity in several sectors and leaving a legacy of a large stock of debt. After the crisis Germany replaced China as the major surplus country, with a current account surplus over 8 per cent of GDP. However, this beggar-thy-neighbour policy is no more sustainable than was the export-led growth of China because it is a problem for everybody, not just for the Eurozone.

Briefly, neither financial bubbles nor export surpluses constitute sustainable solutions to underconsumption in major advanced economies and China. Nor is it possible to stimulate productive investment to fill the demand gap through interest rate adjustments when wages and consumer demand stagnate. The solution is to be found in the reversal of the secular decline in the share of labour in income so as to reignite a wage-led growth.

0.4 The Internationalization of Finance in EDEs

The financial bubbles that culminated in crises in the US and Europe and the subsequent ultra-easy monetary policy have been a significant factor in the acceleration of integration of EDEs into the international financial system. Closer integration had already started in the early 1990s with the liberalization of the capital account in these economies. Despite recurrent crises in the second half of the 1990s and the early 2000s with severe consequences, liberalization continued at full speed and integration deepened significantly in the new millennium, including in countries which had suffered most from financial instability in the past. The pattern of integration has also changed. These economies opened more and more their domestic financial markets to non-resident investors, foreign banks, and other financial institutions and allowed greater freedom to their residents to invest abroad to diversify portfolios and to borrow in international financial markets. These deepened their financial integration and created new vulnerabilities.

In examining the process of integration, attention is focused in Chapter 3 on gross external balance sheets (that is, gross assets and liabilities) rather than net foreign asset positions, and on gross capital flows (that is, non-resident inflows and resident outflows) rather than net capital flows, the difference between the two. It is the gross flows and stocks that determine and define the pace and pattern of integration. While fluctuations in net flows often provoke balance-of-payments instability, gross external balance sheets and the leverage of the national balance sheets are more important in explaining potential vulnerabilities and the incidence and the severity of financial crises than net foreign asset positions or current account deficits (Al-Saffar et al. 2013). Gross flows have never become negative since the 1980s while net flows have undergone wide fluctuations.

The US monetary policy has played a key role in the financialization of the global economy and deepened integration of EDEs. Since the 1980s the US constantly relied on credit and asset bubbles to generate economic expansion; first the Savings and Loans bubble in the 1980s, then the dot-com bubble in the 1990s followed by the subprime bubble in the new century and then by the QE and ZIRP (zero interest rate policy) bubble. As bubbles ended in busts, monetary policy became progressively looser. In the early 2000s the US Federal Reserve brought the policy interest rates to historical lows for fear that the bursting of the dot-com bubble would trigger asset deflation and recession, and kept them at relatively low levels throughout the first half of the decade. Japan also kept policy interest rates almost at zero in an effort to break out of deflation and even the otherwise conservative European Central Bank (ECB) joined in and lowered interest rates to unusually low levels. Easy monetary conditions in reserve issuers, together with strong growth and higher interest rates in emerging economies made the latter increasingly attractive to international lenders and investors looking for yield. Equities of firms in major emerging economies came to be seen as a new asset class for portfolio diversification by international investors. BRIC (Brazil, Russia, India, and China) were identified by international bankers as the 'emerging markets' with the brightest economic prospects and highly profitable venues for investment and lending. All these resulted in a surge in international lending and investment in emerging economies—the third post-war boom in capital inflows to these economies (Akyüz 2011b). The crisis produced a sharp contraction of capital flows but the ultra-easy monetary policy soon triggered a new surge. Although net capital flows started falling after 2010 and became negative in 2014, gross flows remained strong until 2015 when they fell but were still positive.

0.5 External Balance Sheets

The process of integration has produced a rapid expansion of international assets and liabilities of EDEs as conventionally defined—that is, the balance sheet positions of their residents vis-à-vis non-residents. It has not only deepened and strengthened their traditional cross-border financial linkages, but also resulted in an unprecedented foreign presence in their equity, bond, property, and credit markets, exerting a strong influence on their liquidity and valuation dynamics and creating new channels in the transmission of impulses from the global financial markets.

Close to 90 per cent of gross external assets and gross external liabilities of EDEs outstanding at the end of 2015 had been accumulated in the new millennium and their gross balance sheets expanded by more than fivefold during that period. Both gross external assets and liabilities of EDEs increased relative to GDP and grew faster than their trade. Net foreign assets (NFA) position of all developing regions except the Middle East and North Africa (MENA) was negative at the turn of the millennium. Due to strong export performance and rising current account surpluses of China, Asian NFA position became positive in the 2000s while MENA's NFA increased rapidly thanks to the surge in oil prices. However, this upturn came to an end after the crisis with the collapse of oil prices and a steep decline in China's current account surplus. NFA positions of other two major developing regions, Latin America and sub-Saharan Africa (SSA) have been negative throughout.

0.6 Low-yielding Assets, High-yielding Liabilities

A large proportion of gross assets of EDEs are in low-yielding international reserve assets issued by advanced economies, notably the US treasuries. These reserves grew significantly in the new millennium, peaking around $8 trillion in 2014, from $800 billion in 2000. About two-thirds of these reserves were due to current account surpluses of China and fuel exporters. The rest came from capital inflows—that is, they are borrowed rather than earned reserves, matched by an equivalent increase in external liabilities. The share of borrowed reserves in total reserves of EDEs increased after the crisis as their current account surpluses declined.

The unprecedented reserve accumulation by EDEs goes directly against the prognostications of mainstream theory that the need for international reserves should lessen as countries gained access to international financial markets and became more willing to respond to balance-of-payments shocks by exchange rate adjustments. However, capital account liberalization and increased access to international financial markets have produced exactly the opposite result. Private capital flows have led to accumulation of large stocks of external liabilities by allowing running larger and more persistent current account deficits in EDEs beyond the levels that could be attained by relying on the Bretton Woods Institutions or bilateral lenders. Because of pro-cyclical behaviour of international financial markets, EDEs have become highly vulnerable to sudden stops and reversals in capital flows and this has increased the need to keep reserves as self-insurance.

Although direct investment abroad by transnational firms of some major emerging economies has been increasing, the share of FDI in total gross external assets is still low compared to low-yielding reserve assets. Besides, the rate of return on outward FDI from EDEs is lower than the rate of return earned on FDI made in these economies by firms from advanced economies. For these reasons incomes earned on gross external assets held by EDEs is low in comparison to incomes paid on gross external liabilities. For instance, although China has a positive net international asset position, it has been in the red in investment income.

A large proportion of gross liabilities of EDEs are in high-yielding FDI. In the new millennium inward FDI in these economies has increasingly been concentrated in services sectors with little export potentials. Even in export-oriented manufacturing, FDI in EDEs has very high import (foreign value added) contents. Moreover, a large proportion of domestic value added is captured by foreign firms as profits, royalties, licence fees, wage remittances, and interest paid on loans from parent companies. As a result, the export earnings of these firms do not cover their imports and income transfers—that is, they run current account deficits on their operations, making a negative contribution to the balance-of-payments. As shown in Chapter 6, this has also been the case in China since 2010 where foreign firms are more export-oriented than those in most other EDEs. Furthermore, it has become more difficult to extract positive spillovers for industrial development from these firms because they have become increasingly footloose and governments in many EDEs have lost policy autonomy as a result of obligations assumed in multilateral and bilateral investment agreements.

0.7 Foreign Presence in Equity and Debt Markets

The opening of equity markets in emerging economies to non-residents resulted in a surge in portfolio equity inflows and a strong foreign presence in these markets. As the local investor base of emerging markets is not strong enough to make them sufficiently deep and liquid, they remained stagnant until they were increasingly opened to foreigners in the new millennium. Large and sustained inflows created liquidity and excess demand, and a boom in prices which in turn generated additional inflows attracted by prospects of capital gain. An important part of the increase in total portfolio equity liabilities of emerging economies are due to capital gains on the existing stock of equities owned by non-residents, rather than new inflows.

In general non-residents account for a much higher share of emerging equity markets than mature markets, reaching 30–40 per cent and even exceeding 50 per cent compared to 15 per cent in the US. Because of lack of a strong local investor base, the entry and exit of even relatively small amounts of foreign investment into emerging markets tend to result in large price swings. Furthermore, because of increased access to markets abroad, local investors in emerging markets have been acting with a global perspective. Throughout the new millennium, stock prices in emerging economies have been closely correlated with private capital inflows and the correlation between global and emerging-market equity returns has been rising. Even in countries with little foreign presence, equity prices have thus become highly susceptible to changes in the global risk appetite. This is seen on various occasions, notably during the Lehman collapse when equity markets of all major emerging economies, including China, experienced heavy selling pressures. These markets all came under pressure also in May 2013 during the 'taper tantrum', at the end of 2014, and in the second half of 2015.

In the new millennium the share of gross external debt in total gross external liabilities of EDEs fell as a result of a large entry of international capital into their equity markets and the boom in equity prices. There have also been significant changes in the structure of external debt. Bond issues have been growing faster than international bank loans for both public and private sectors. This is partly due to a shift of international banks from cross-border lending to local lending by establishing greater presence in EDEs, particularly outside Latin America, and partly to the impact of the crisis in advanced economies on international bank lending. This shift started in the 1990s and continued with full force in the new century until it was checked by the crisis in the US and Europe. The average market share of foreign banks in EDEs doubled between 1995 and 2009, reaching 50 per cent compared to 20 per cent in the countries in the Organisation for Economic Co-operation and Development (OECD). Most of these banks are from advanced economies. As of 2013, local claims of international banks accounted for almost 60 per cent and cross-border claims for 40 per cent of their total claims on EDEs.

Perhaps a more important development is progressive opening of emerging bond markets to non-residents. This was motivated not only by a desire to deepen these markets and facilitate public borrowing, but also to overcome the so-called original sin problem—that is, the inability of EDEs to issue international debt in their own currencies and to avoid currency and maturity mismatches that had led to virulent crises in Latin America, Asia, and elsewhere in the 1990s and early 2000s. The same considerations also gave rise to the regional Asian Bond Market initiative in the early 2000s.

With the opening of bond markets, governments shifted from internationally issued debt in foreign currency to domestically issued debt in local currency. They also increased domestic currency debt issues in international markets and reduced foreign currency debt issues in domestic markets. At the same time international investors became more willing to assume the currency risk and even to come under local jurisdiction in return for higher yields and large capital gains from currency appreciations. Subsidiaries of foreign-owned international banks have also become important players in local bond markets. Consequently, a growing proportion of sovereign bonds of emerging economies held by foreigners are in local currency and subject to domestic jurisdiction—a development that can have significant consequences for sovereign debt workouts.

There is no comprehensive data on non-resident holding of locally issued, externally held sovereign debt in emerging economies. Such debt is not always reported in external debt statistics. Because of this discrepancy, the external debt of emerging economies is often underestimated. Still, available information shows that because of growing acquisition of locally issued bonds by non-residents, sovereign debt of many emerging economies is internationalized to a greater extent than that of major reserve-issuing countries. While around one-third of US treasuries are held by non-residents, this proportion is higher in several emerging economies. Excluding China and India where access of non-residents to domestic bond markets remains restricted, the average proportion for emerging economies for which data are available is around 30 per cent and in several cases it exceeds 40 per cent. More significantly, the externally held local-currency sovereign debt of emerging economies is not in the hands of foreign central banks and other official bodies, but mostly in the portfolios of fickle investors, including foreign asset managers, making these economies much more vulnerable to changes in global risk appetite and interest rates on international reserve assets.

Opening local bond markets and borrowing from non-residents in local currency have no doubt allowed the sovereign in emerging economies to escape the perennial problem of original sin and pass the currency risk to lenders. However, this, together with increased access of residents to markets abroad, has heightened their sensitivity to shocks to long-term rates in major advanced economies in addition to their susceptibility to changes in short-term policy rates. This could prove equally and even more damaging than currency exposure in the transition of major advanced economies from low-interest to high-interest regimes and normalization of their balance sheets (Sobrun and Turner 2015).

As in equity markets, even where non-resident investment accounts for a small share of the bond market, their entry and exit can have a significant impact on yields because of weak domestic investor base. Domestic holders of long-term bonds are mostly institutional investors that typically hold them to maturity and foreign holdings often reach several multiples of average daily trading volume. Therefore, the capacity of local institutions and market makers to match portfolio outflows is highly limited.

Whether in local currency or dollars, foreign ownership of debt is a key indicator of external vulnerability. This has become more visible during the Eurozone crisis where problems emerged not always in countries with large stocks of debt, such as Italy or Belgium, but large foreign holdings, as in the periphery countries. Increased internationalization of emerging bond markets implies significant loss of autonomy in controlling long-term rates. These markets may no longer be relied on as a 'spare tyre' for local borrowers and provide an escape route at times of interruptions to access to external financing. When global risk appetite and liquidity conditions deteriorate and access of emerging economies to international capital markets is impaired, domestic bond markets too can get crippled due to adverse spillovers, as seen during the Lehman collapse in 2008 and the 'taper tantrum' in May 2013.

0.8 Private External Debt and Exposure to the Currency Risk

The shift of the sovereign from internationally issued debt in foreign currencies to locally issued debt in local currencies is often seen as an important step in reducing the likelihood of external liquidity and debt crises in emerging economies. However, sovereign debt is rarely at the centre of external financial crises. Out of the last eight major external financial crises in emerging economies only two involved sovereign dollar debt: in Argentina internationally issued debt and in Mexico domestically issued dollar-linked debt (*tesobonos*). In Russia the crisis involved domestically issued rouble debt. In no other cases, Thailand, Korea, Indonesia, Turkey, and Brazil, sovereign external debt was the cause, and the crises were mainly due to private external debt.

From this perspective, the current size and structure of external debt liabilities of emerging economies cannot really be said to be less prone to liquidity and solvency crises. While a greater proportion of external sovereign debt has come to be denominated in local currency, both financial and non-financial corporations have become increasingly exposed to the currency risk because of large build-up of debt in reserve currencies. Major emerging economies have accumulated more than $2 trillion external debt since 2008 and much of it is due to non-financial corporations attracted by low dollar interest rates. As a result, the private sector has come to account for a higher proportion of external debt of emerging economies in both international securities and bank loans than the public sector. Their share in total dollar external debt is even higher. The surge in private borrowing is the main reason why the ratio of external debt to GDP has been rising since the crisis after having levelled off and even fallen previously. Many corporations also borrowed in dollars in domestic credit markets with foreign banks playing an important role in renewed dollarization. In major emerging economies such as China and Brazil, corporations also borrowed through their subsidiaries, often in offshore financial centres. Although such borrowing is not considered as external debt as conventionally defined, it has similar impact on corporate fragility.

0.9 External Vulnerability

After recurrent crises in the 1990s and early 2000s, governments in emerging economies sought to reduce the share of debt in external liabilities by opening up equity markets to foreigners and liberalizing the FDI regimes. They also sought to reduce currency mismatches by opening up bond markets to foreigners and borrowing in local currency. These have no doubt brought improvements to the profile of their gross external liabilities and reduced susceptibility to the kind of shocks they had suffered in past crises. However, greater presence of foreigners in bond and equity markets has also increased the potential instability of exchange rates since surges in entry and exit of non-residents affect not only asset prices but also exchange rates. Furthermore such surges are increasingly driven by shifts in global risk appetite and liquidity conditions rather than domestic factors. This is certainly bad news for private corporations with large currency mismatches in balance sheets.

It is also bad news for the sovereign since financial crises caused by private external debt often lead to an explosion of sovereign debt because of bail-outs. In almost all major crises in emerging economies noted in this chapter, an important part of private debt, both domestic and external, was socialized. In a sample of 12 countries hit by currency and external financial crises in the 1990s and 2000s, the average post-crisis public debt ratio was higher than the pre-crisis ratio by 36 per cent of GDP, and in most cases the increase in debt levels persisted several years before governments could roll-back the crisis-induced increases in debt ratios. This is also seen in Spain and Ireland during the Eurozone crisis where public debt rose significantly as private debt was socialized.

These considerations also raise questions about the effectiveness of floating exchange rate regimes in reducing the likelihood of external liquidity and solvency crises. The shift to more flexible exchange rate regimes in emerging economies has no doubt a lot to commend. At times of favourable risk appetite hard nominal pegs offer a one-way bet to international speculators and encourage short-term inflows in search of quick profits. In bad times they can be rarely defended with success. However, it is one thing to allow exchange rates to respond to changing fundamentals in order to facilitate external adjustment, it is another to leave them to the whims of unstable international capital flows. Floating can be effective in absorbing short-term volatility in capital flows, but not gyrations and boom–bust cycles. At times of a boom, floating could generate even greater appreciations than nominal pegs, as seen in several emerging economies before and immediately after the global crisis. If booms are not managed judiciously, floating freely at times of large and sustained outflows would provide little cushion. Indonesia was praised for not trying to defend its currency but letting it float after the Thai baht came under attack in 1997. But this did not stabilize the exchange rate and prevent a free fall.

The changed pattern of integration of emerging economies into the international financial system also necessitates a rethinking of adequacy of reserves. It should now be recognized that the vulnerability to liquidity crises cannot just be assessed on the basis of short-term foreign currency debt, as became fashionable after the Asian crisis. Countries with large foreign presence in domestic equity and bond markets can be highly vulnerable even in the absence of excessive short-term external foreign currency debt. This is particularly true where reserves are borrowed. Again, as seen in several episodes, capital flight by residents can constitute greater potential drain on reserves than external liabilities. Finally, vulnerability to terms-of-trade shocks can rapidly reduce the self-insurance provided by reserves in commodity-dependent countries. Thus, even countries with strong reserve positions and current account surpluses can experience significant drain of reserves and currency depreciations as a result of sharp drops in non-resident inflows, exit of non-residents from domestic securities markets, large and sustained resident outflows, or severe terms-of-trade shocks, as seen in China and Malaysia during 2014–2015 (Akyüz 2015).

0.10 Where Next?

The increased vulnerability of EDEs to external financial shocks resulting from their deepened financial integration is laid bare even before a significant tightening of monetary policy in the US. These economies have been facing strong deflationary and destabilizing impulses from financial markets as well as commodity prices. They are stuck between a rock and a hard place. If the current state of affairs continues, these pressures may lead to growing risk aversion and flight to safety. But they are also damned if the US economy rebounds and US monetary policy swiftly returns to normalcy; this is because higher US interest rates and stronger dollar could exert a downward pressure on commodity prices and accelerate capital flight from EDEs. Their policy space to respond is highly limited.

Policies pursued in several of these economies no doubt made a significant contribution to the build-up of external imbalances and fragility. They did not always manage prudently the twin booms in commodity prices and capital flows. They often stood passively by as their industries were undermined by the foreign exchange bonanza, choosing, instead, to ride a consumption boom driven by short-term financial inflows and foreign borrowing by their private sectors and allowing their currencies to appreciate and external deficits to mount. Hastily erected walls against destabilizing inflows were too little and too late—they were neither wide enough nor high enough to prevent build-up of imbalances and fragility.

The IMF, the organization responsible for safeguarding international monetary and financial stability, failed to anticipate the most serious post-war crisis and to correctly identify the forces driving EDEs, joining the hype about the 'Rise of the South' and underestimating their vulnerability to shifts in global economic conditions. Even when it became clear that capital inflows posed a serious threat to macroeconomic and financial stability, its advice was to avoid capital controls to the extent possible and maintain a financially open economy, and to restrict destabilizing capital flows only as a last resort and on a temporary basis.

Given their significantly deepened integration into the global economy, notably the international financial system, EDEs cannot really restore stability and growth with their own action alone. Major advanced economies that exert a disproportionately large impact on global economic conditions need to reorient their policies and put their house in order. First they need to abandon fiscal orthodoxy. A sizeable public investment in human and physical infrastructure would not only provide the demand stimulus needed for restoring growth but also bring supply-side productivity gains and help raise growth potential. Second, the structural demand gap in major advanced economies should be addressed by reversing the downward trend in the share of labour in national income through significant increases in wages. Since the balance between labour and capital cannot be restored overnight, greater attention would need to be given to redistribution through the budget by increasing taxes on high income groups and cutting taxes and raising transfers for lower ones.

The EDEs have been able to weather the weakening and declines of net capital inflows since 2014 without facing a major liquidity squeeze, partly by using reserves and partly by allowing their currencies to bear the brunt. However, much of the decline in net capital inflows has been due to China, the country with large reserves, while net flows remained positive for many economies, notably in Latin America. They may face severe and persistent liquidity squeeze in the period ahead with the normalization of monetary policy in the US and/or a significant deterioration of the global risk appetite—sudden and sustained stop of capital inflows, rapid exit of foreign investors from equity, bond, and deposit markets, and capital flight by residents. Their response should not be 'business as usual', using reserves and borrowing from the IMF to maintain an open capital account and stay current on debt payments to foreign creditors, socializing private liabilities, and resorting to austere adjustment. Rather, they should seek to bail in international creditors and investors by introducing, inter alia, exchange restrictions and temporary debt standstills. These measures should be supported by the IMF through lending into arrears, but such lending should be designed to maintain income and employment not to finance capital outflows.

Major central banks, notably the US Federal Reserve, as the originators of global financial fragility, should assume full responsibility in counteracting any sharp contraction in international liquidity. First, through a large Special Drawing Rights (SDRs) allocation, larger than that made in 2009 since the scale of the problem is now much bigger. The IMF can designate major central banks to purchase SDRs from EDEs who want to use the SDRs allocated to them. A decision can also be made to allocate SDRs only to EDEs or to non-reserve countries excluding Eurozone members. Secondly, the US Federal Reserve and other major central banks can act directly as a quasi-international lender-of-last-resort to EDEs through swaps or outright purchase of sovereign bonds to shore up their prices and to provide liquidity.

Exchange restrictions, temporary debt standstills, IMF lending into arrears, a sizeable SDR allocation and provision of market support and liquidity by major central banks are no doubt unconventional measures that should be used with prudence. But they are no more unconventional than the measures used by major central banks since 2008. They need to be included in the policy arsenal in order to ensure an orderly response to a severely tightened global financial environment and mitigate the economic and social pains that may be inflicted on EDEs.

There has been no major external debt crisis in emerging economies for over a decade, thanks largely to exceptionally favourable global financial conditions. But the very same conditions have also resulted in significantly increased vulnerability of these economies to external financial shocks by deepening their integration and creating new channels of transmission of shocks. If the global financial conditions tighten and the world economy starts contracting again, an important part of external debt incurred by emerging economies since 2008 could become unpayable. Thus, the international community had better prepare itself for a jubilee by putting in place orderly debt work-out mechanisms.

Such policies and practices are essential for addressing the difficulties facing the world economy and improving its medium term–prospects. They are needed to reduce the deflationary gap in major advanced economies that post-2008 policies have failed to remove and to avoid the temptation to resort to financial bubbles or beggar-my-neighbour policies to reignite growth—issues taken up in Part I. They are also needed to reduce the likelihood of recurrence of virulent financial and balance-of-payments crises in EDEs and to improve their management and resolution, particularly since these economies have become highly vulnerable to shocks from macroeconomic and financial policies in major advanced economies as a result of their deepened integration into the global financial system and investment regimes—issues discussed in Parts II and III, respectively.

Part I

The Financial Crisis, Policy Response, and the Global South

1

Policy Response in Advanced Economies

Neo-liberal Fallacies and Obsessions

1.1 Why Is the Crisis Taking Too Long to Resolve?

In his remarks on the state of the world economy after half a decade from the onset of the subprime crisis in the US, the IMF's chief economist at the time, Olivier Blanchard, is reported to have said, 'It's not yet a lost decade.... But it will surely take at least a decade from the beginning of the crisis for the world economy to get back to decent shape' (Reuters 2012). Indeed, by spring 2016, almost a decade after the beginning of the crisis, the world economy had not got back to decent shape and the policies introduced in response to the crisis had not been normalized.

Even though the US economy was at the origin of the crisis, it has fared much better than other major advanced economies, notably the Eurozone. Since the end of the recession in September 2009, the US economy has had positive growth for 24 quarters, enjoying one of the longest post-war expansions. It has also restored employment to pre-crisis levels. However, the recovery has been unusually slow. The US economy had grown at a rate of around 3 per cent per annum from the 1970s until 2008, including several years of recessions with negative growth rates, and at a rate of 3.6 per cent during the 1991–2001 expansion. In the recovery from the subprime crisis, the average US growth has barely exceeded 2 per cent (see Table 1.1). As a result output has remained well below potential, resulting in significant income and employment losses. More importantly, the crisis has accelerated the decline in potential growth that had already started in the early 2000s (IMF WEO 2015: chap. 3). Investment has been particularly weak with capital spending declining in some key sectors. Although the unemployment rate has been halved from the peak of 10 per cent recorded during the depth of the crisis, it still remains above the lows attained on the eve of the crisis and the improvement is partly

Table 1.1 Real GDP growth in selected advanced economies
(Per cent change)

	2008	2009	2010	2011	2012	2013	2014	2015
United States	−0.3	−2.8	2.5	1.6	2.2	1.5	2.4	2.4
Eurozone (EZ)	0.5	−4.5	2.1	1.6	−0.9	−0.3	0.9	1.6
Germany	0.8	−5.6	3.9	3.7	0.6	0.4	1.6	1.5
Japan	−1.0	−5.5	4.7	−0.5	1.7	1.4	0.0	0.5
United Kingdom	−0.5	−4.2	1.5	2.0	1.2	2.2	2.9	2.2

Source: IMF WEO (2016).

due to a decline in labour force participation—from over 66 per cent in 2006 to 63 per cent in early 2016.

Furthermore, the US recovery has been lopsided. Wages have remained stagnant and income and wealth inequality has increased (Dufour and Orhangazi 2016). And not all segments of the society have recovered. It is found that, as of 2015, only 214 counties out of a total of 3069 had recovered to pre-recession levels on four indicators: total employment, the unemployment rate, size of the economy, and home values (Morath 2016). After six years of recovery, three people out of five polled in May 2015 thought that the US economy was still in recession (Fox News 2015).

On average post-war US expansions ended after about five years, often with overheating and monetary tightening. Although the current expansion has been longer, there are no signs of overheating and the economy still operates below capacity. Thus, short of severe external shocks, such as a drastic slowdown and financial turbulence in China and/or renewed instability and contraction in the Eurozone, the US expansion may still continue for some time to come and prove to be the longest in recorded history. This means that the ultra-easy monetary policy introduced in response to the crisis will remain broadly unchanged and continue to add to financial fragility. This would make the eventual exit even more precarious. But growth is also so fragile that a moderate shock can push the economy into renewed instability and contraction. In such a case the policy-makers would have little ammunition in their existing arsenal, other than doing more of the same.

The Eurozone has barely recovered from the crisis that hit in 2008–09. Its recovery has been much weaker than the US largely because of tighter fiscal policy in the core countries, austerity imposed on the periphery and misguided tightening of monetary policy in 2011. Following a deep recession the region as a whole achieved positive growth in 2010–11, despite continued output and employment losses in the periphery, thanks to a strong recovery in Germany driven by exports. However, as the impact of the crisis spread in the region, the core and Germany in particular could not maintain the momentum. The region had six consecutive quarters of negative growth until the second quarter of 2013 with about half of the countries in recession. The subsequent recovery was weak and uneven. With an average growth of less than 1 per cent since 2010, the region as a whole managed to restore its pre-crisis income only in the first quarter of 2016, five years after the US. GDP was still below the 2008 level in many countries of the region including Italy, Spain, Portugal, Greece, and Cyprus. By 2021, Greek and Italian per capita incomes are estimated to stand at about 14 per cent and 9 per cent, respectively, below their 2007 level (Reinhart 2016). Unemployment fell only moderately, from an all-time high of some 12 per cent in 2013 to 10.3 per cent at the end of 2015, and was still far above the pre-crisis level of 7.2 per cent. It was over 20 per cent in Spain and Greece—higher than the levels seen during the Great Depression.

The output gap in the Eurozone is greater than in the US and the decline in potential growth is more severe, posing the threat of persistent stagnation over the longer term. According to an estimate, potential output losses for 2015 were around 35 per cent for Greece and Ireland, 22 per cent for Spain, and over 13 per cent for Portugal. According to the same estimate the average loss for 2015 in 23 OECD countries was over 8 per cent (Ball 2014).

Although financial stress in the Eurozone has eased considerably, continued austerity and adjustment fatigue in much of the periphery and sluggish growth in the rest of the region could bring it back and even lead to a break-up. The removal of debt-overhang in countries hit by the crisis, notably Greece, is taking even longer than the resolution of the Latin American debt crisis of the 1980s, suggesting that few lessons have been drawn from past experiences. If the Brexit issue is not resolved positively, the damage on both Britain and the rest of Europe could be severe, even impairing further global growth 'that has been too slow for too long' (IMF WEO 2016).

There can be little doubt that recoveries from recessions brought about by financial crises are weak and protracted because it takes time to repair balance sheets—to remove debt overhang and unwind excessive and unviable investments generated during the bubbles that culminate in such crises. Recoveries from such crises also tend to be jobless and generate little investment. This was the case in the US during the early 1990s and particularly the early 2000s when it was recovering from recessions brought about by the bursting of the savings and loans and dot-com bubbles, respectively. In the current recovery, the pre-crisis income in the US had been restored by the second quarter of 2011, but employment was lower by some 6.5 million. Sluggish job and investment growth is also a common feature of recoveries of EDEs from financial crises (Akyüz 2006).

However, this recovery has been long even by the standards of past recessions associated with financial crises. For instance, it has been found that in the 100 worst financial crises since the 1860s it took around seven years, on average, for the advanced economies to reach pre-crisis level of per capita income. In the current global crisis, of the 11 countries affected, only Germany has done better than the historical average while the US recovery has taken a little longer. Using the IMF projections for the coming years, it is estimated that for this group of 11 countries, it would take about nine years to reach the pre-crisis level of income (Reinhart 2016).

It seems that, if ever, it will take much longer than 'a decade from the beginning of the crisis for the world economy to get back to decent shape'. But this is not just due to the nature and the depth of the crisis, but also to ineffectiveness of public interventions. In this respect, there are two major shortcomings in the policy response both in the US and the Eurozone. First, governments have been unwilling to remove the debt overhang through timely, orderly, and comprehensive restructuring and to bring about a redistribution of wealth from creditors to debtors. Instead, they have resorted to extensive creditor bail-outs, creating moral hazard and vulnerabilities in the financial system while enforcing austerity on debtors (Kuttner 2013). Second, there have been serious shortcomings in macroeconomic policy response in support of aggregate demand, growth, and employment. After an initial reflation governments turned to fiscal orthodoxy and relied excessively on monetary means to fight recession. These not only led to unnecessary output and job losses, but also created financial fragility that could compromise future stability and growth.

1.2 The Debt Overhang

The crises in the US and the Eurozone were due to rapid credit expansion and debt-driven property and consumption bubbles. Accordingly their resolution should have called for significant deleveraging and reduction of debt relative to income. Instead, the ultra-easy monetary policy resulted in a renewed debt pile-up both in the North and the South, by some additional $50 trillion since 2008, outpacing the growth of world nominal income. In the US, the ratio of private plus public debt as a proportion of GDP rose by 40 per cent while it more than doubled in the Eurozone periphery. The increase in household debt in advanced economies is moderate compared to debt accumulated in the seven years before the outset of the crisis, but corporate debt saw a significant acceleration (Dobbs et al. 2015; Birds 2015). There has also been a rapid increase in corporate debt in EDEs and an important part of this debt is in dollars (IMF GFSR 2015; McCauley et al. 2015). As of the end of 2015, total non-financial debt stood at 265 per cent of GDP in advanced economies and 185 per cent in EDEs, both up by 35 percentage points since 2007, creating concerns that much of it may become unpayable in the next downturn (White 2016).

In advanced economies government debt has increased without a corresponding build-up of income-yielding public assets through investment in physical and human infrastructure. In the same vein, the increase in corporate debt has not been matched by greater investment. The ultra-easy monetary policy encouraged corporations to issue debt for M&A and stock buybacks, thereby artificially boosting share prices (Durden 2016). In this recovery business fixed investment has been 20 per cent below what would have been expected from pre-crisis trends across advanced economies, including the US (ERP 2016: 92). In 17 of the 20 largest advanced economies, investment growth remained lower during the post-2008 period than in the years before the crisis and five advanced economies experienced declines in investment during 2010–15 (Stiglitz and Rashid 2016). Despite exceptionally favourable financial conditions, real private non-residential gross fixed capital formation remained weak, mainly because of uncertainty about the future state of the economy and depressed profits expectations. As of end 2014, in some countries including France, Germany, and Italy, it had not recovered to its pre-recession level (Banerjee et al. 2015). Investment in EDEs also slowed significantly. In a few cases where corporate debt build-up went hand in hand with investment, the capacity created was in excess of what could possibly be utilized under normal conditions, as in China, or very little of it was in manufacturing, as in India.

In the US the government has been reluctant to bring down mortgages in line with the ability of households to pay by forcing the creditors to write down debt. In particular, the Federal Housing Finance Agency, which regulates government-controlled mortgage financiers Fannie Mae and Freddie Mac, constantly opposed principal reduction.[1] Rather, priority was given to creditor bail-outs. Through the $700 billion Trouble Asset Relief Programme of 2008–09, the US Treasury injected capital into banks whose net worth was moving into the red as a result of loss of asset values. In alleviating the burden of household debt, the government relied mainly on open market operations by the US Federal Reserve through Quantitative Easing (QE), implemented in several rounds, buying US government bonds and mortgage-backed securities to boost their prices and lower long-term rates.

[1] Two voluntary schemes were introduced to help debtors: the Home Affordable Modification Program to encourage lenders to lower monthly mortgage payments of homeowners facing the risk of foreclosure; and the Home Affordable Refinance Program to help homeowners with negative equity to refinance their mortgages. A bill was also introduced in 2012 for debt-for-equity-swaps by allowing the underwater home owners whose home values fall short of their debt to reduce their monthly payments in exchange for a portion of any future price appreciation on the home, known as shared appreciation (Griffith 2012).

Bail-out operations and the ultra-easy monetary policy prevented a banking collapse and hence contained the financial crisis. They allowed the banks first to recover their pre-crisis profitability and then reach record profits. Already by 2013, the four biggest US banks were 30 per cent larger than they had been before the crisis and the too-big-to-fail banks were even bigger (Warren 2013). They continued to post even higher profits during the subsequent years (Leong 2015; Cohan 2016).

However, policy interventions have been much less effective in reducing the household debt overhang and preventing foreclosures. Although there is a sizeable drop in household debt as a per cent of GDP since the outset of the crisis, an important part of this is due to foreclosures and hence reflects a corresponding reduction in household wealth. Because of foreclosures and mortgage delinquencies the home ownership rate fell to a 20-year low in 2015 (FRED 2016). Although the percentage of homes underwater dropped as the housing market recovered, as of mid-2015 there were more than 4 million US homeowners with mortgage debt at least 20 per cent more than their homes were worth and most underwater homeowners were among the homes with the least value (Fottrell 2015). As noted by Bernanke (2013), 'gains in household net worth have been concentrated among wealthier households, while many households in the middle or lower parts of the distribution have experienced declines in wealth since the crisis'.

The failure to act directly on the debt overhang is even more visible in the Eurozone where the policy response was premised on a wrong diagnosis. The periphery was, in effect, facing a balance-of-payments-*cum*-external-debt crisis resulting from excessive domestic spending and foreign borrowing of the kind seen in several EDEs in Latin America and East Asia in the past decades. Contrary to the official diagnosis, this had little to do with fiscal profligacy except in Greece (Lapavitsas et al. 2010; De Grauwe 2010). Spain and Ireland adhered to the Maastricht Treaty much better than Germany—they were both running fiscal surpluses and their debt ratios were lower (see Table 1.2). In fact, Spanish and Irish fiscal balances were better than all other members of Eurozone except Luxembourg and Finland. Portugal had a relatively high deficit, but its debt ratio was not much higher than that of Germany.

As argued by Gros (2011), external debt is the key to the Eurozone crisis and the focus on total public debt is misleading. Belgium had a much higher public debt ratio than Portugal, Spain, and Ireland, but did not face any pressure and in fact enjoyed a relatively low-risk premium because it had a sustained current account surplus and a positive net external asset position. Again, Italy is less affected than other periphery countries because its current account deficit was much smaller and a large proportion of its public debt was held domestically.

Table 1.2 Pre-crisis debt and deficits in the Eurozone
(per cent of GDP)

	Fiscal Balance (2000–07)	Public Debt (2007)	Private Balance (2000–07)	Current Account (2000–07)
Greece	–5.6	107.3	–2.8	–8.4
Italy	–3.0	103.3	+2.4	–0.6
Portugal	–4.1	68.3	–5.2	–9.3
Spain	+0.4	36.3	–6.2	–5.8
Ireland	+1.4	25.0	–3.3	–1.9
Germany	–2.3	65.4	+5.5	+3.2

Source: IMF WEO (2013a) and IMF (2013a).

A common feature of the periphery countries in Table 1.2 is that they were all running larger current account deficits than all other Eurozone members in the run-up to the crisis. In Spain and Ireland, deficits were entirely due to a private savings gap. Even in Greece the current account deficit rose faster than the budget deficit because of a private spending boom. In 2007, the Greek current account deficit was over 14 per cent of GDP while the budget deficit was 6 per cent. Before the outbreak of the crisis, public debt in the periphery, except in Greece, was on a downward trend while private debt was rising. A growing part of the external debt was incurred by the private sector. In Greece only half of the external debt was sovereign and the proportion was even smaller for Portugal and Spain.

Two interrelated factors played an important role in rapid increases in current account deficits and external debt in the Eurozone periphery. First, after the monetary union, wage and price movements diverged sharply between the periphery and the core. During 2000–07 Germany undershot the inflation target and its real labour costs fell while the peripheral countries overshot the inflation target and their labour costs increased. Improved German competitiveness was not always due to a superior productivity growth and wage suppression played a central role. For instance, according to the Eurostat Labour Productivity Data, between 2000 and 2007 German real labour productivity per hour grew, on average, by 1.6 per cent per annum compared to 2.3 in Ireland and 2.6 in Greece. From early 2000 Germany was engaged in a process of what is called 'competitive disinflation' (Fitoussi 2006) or internal devaluation, keeping real wages and private consumption virtually stagnant and increasingly relying on exports for growth (Akyüz 2011c; Palley 2013). By contrast, in the periphery wages went ahead of productivity, leading to an appreciation of the real effective exchange rate and loss of competitiveness (see Figure 1.1). This created a surge in imports, mainly from other EU countries, but also from the rest of the world, notably China (Chen et al. 2012).

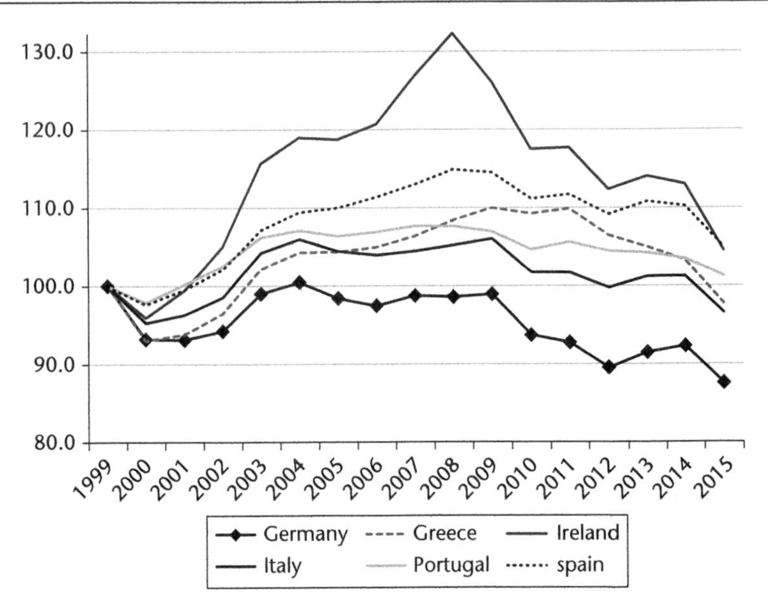

Figure 1.1 Real effective exchange rates in the Eurozone (1999 = 100)
Source: BIS.

The divergence between the core and the periphery was sustained by a surge in capital flows from the former to the latter, triggered by the common currency and abundant international liquidity (Sinn 2011). They fuelled the boom in domestic demand, reduced private savings and widened the current account deficits in the periphery (Atoyan et al. 2013). They also helped Germany to increase exports and hence maintain a higher level of activity than was possible on the basis of domestic demand alone. As in Latin America in the early 1980s, this process of debt accumulation also ended with a shock from the US, this time the subprime crisis, leading to a sharp cutback in lending.

The strategy adopted by Eurozone policy-makers in dealing with the debt problem was very much like that of the failed Baker Plan pursued in response to the Latin American debt crisis in the 1980s—official lending to keep debtors current on their payments to private creditors and austerity (UNCTAD TDR 1988: chap. 4). For this purpose several facilities were introduced and used together with IMF lending. The European Central Bank (ECB) has engaged in sovereign bonds purchases in order to lower borrowing costs to troubled debtors and provided long-term loans to banks at low interest rates to enable them to buy high-yield sovereign bonds and earn large spreads.

Despite occasional references to the need to involve the creditors in the resolution of the crisis, interventions have mainly served to bail out creditor banks. As pointed out by the chairman of the European Banking Authority, Andrea Enria, too few European banks have been wound down and too many of them have survived (Reuters 2013). Public money has been used to bail out banks, leading to increased sovereign debt. The debt-restructuring initiatives have brought limited relief to debtors. Greek workouts in 2012 failed to remove the debt overhang. Because of creditor bail-outs, a very large proportion of Greek sovereign debt came to be held by the official sector, including the ECB, IMF, national central banks, and other Eurozone governments, and the write-down of this debt has been resisted by the ECB and Germany. As of early 2016, Greece was still engaged in protracted negotiations with its official creditors for debt relief.

There were also inconsistencies in the approach to bailing in creditors. In Ireland and Spain, where the crisis originated in the banking system, creditors and depositors of troubled banks largely escaped without a haircut.[2] Ireland gave a blanket guarantee to depositors and Greek workouts also spared deposit holders both at home and abroad. In most of these cases rescue operations involved large amounts of public money to prop up and recapitalize banks. By contrast, in Cyprus the bail-out package inflicted large losses on deposit holders, notably Russians.[3]

Public debt ratios in the periphery shot up significantly because of recession, relatively high spreads and the failure to bail in creditors, to ensure that they took losses on their claims (see Figure 1.2). Indeed, a fundamental dilemma faced in sustaining debt is that when the debt ratio is high and the real interest rate exceeds the growth rate by a large margin, the primary surplus needed to stabilize the debt ratio would be quite high, but cuts made in primary spending to achieve this would create a sizeable contraction in output, making the task even more difficult.[4] Thus, debt ratios of Spain and Ireland rose to 80 per cent in 2015 from 36 per cent and 25 per cent on the eve of the crisis, respectively, and they doubled in Portugal and Greece. Of these countries, as of end 2015, only Ireland managed to reduce its debt ratio from the peak reached during 2012–13. Ireland is also the only crisis-hit country that has maintained positive growth since 2010.

A key problem faced in the Eurozone in debt resolution is destabilizing interfaces between private and public debt. In countries like Spain and Ireland governments had to act to rescue heavily indebted banks and this added

[2] But holders of hybrid debt (securities with elements of both debt and equity) took haircut; see Hay and Unmack (2012).

[3] Ironically, while the operation in Cyprus was meant to penalize 'Russian money launderers', the forced conversion of deposits into shares has led the Russians to take control of Bank of Cyprus—Higgins (2013).

[4] The primary budget surplus needed to stabilize the debt ratio is given by: $p = [(r - g)/(1 + g)]d$ where p is the ratio of primary surplus to GDP; r is the real interest rate; g the growth rate of GDP and d the ratio of debt to GDP (Akyüz 2007). A country with a debt ratio of 100 per cent, a negative growth rate and a real interest rate of 5 per cent would need to generate a primary surplus of at least 5 per cent of GDP in order to stabilize the debt ratio, even in the absence of any negative feedback from fiscal retrenchment to growth.

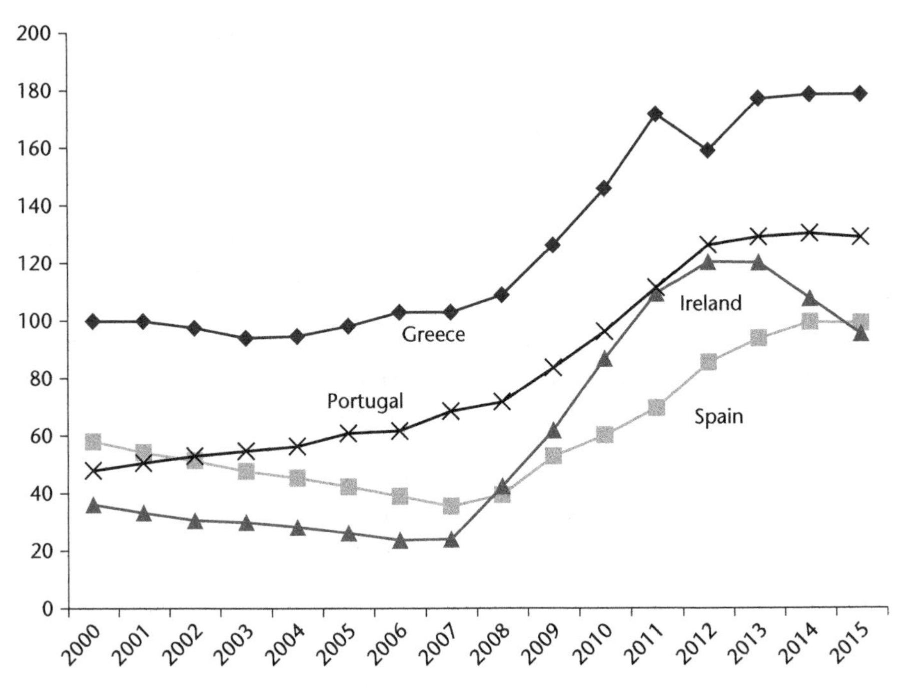

Figure 1.2 Public debt in the Eurozone (per cent of GDP)
Source: IMF WEO Database.

significantly to public debt, increasing its financing needs. However, the very same banks were also expected to play an important role in financing heavily indebted governments. Being unable to print national currency, governments had limited capacity to bail out banks or monetize their own debt. This problem was further aggravated by the tendency of international (intra-Eurozone) lenders to withdraw from crisis-hit countries. A solution to this dilemma could have been to decouple public from private debt by stopping bank bail-outs by national governments and by introducing a Eurozone-wide bank resolution mechanism including bailing-in private creditors, recapitalization, and liquidation.[5]

Not all countries hit by the bursting of the speculative bubble failed to remove the debt overhang. In this respect, Iceland's debt resolution initiatives stand in sharp contrast to the approach pursued in the US and the Eurozone (Hart-Landsberg 2013; Gissurarson 2016). Relative to the size of its economy, Iceland faced the biggest banking failure in economic history. However, it managed to restructure the banking system by letting some of the banks fail and bailing in private creditors, sparing both taxpayers and domestic depositors

[5] For a proposal for such a unified banking framework see, Burda et al. (2012). In June 2012, an agreement was reached to create a Banking Union which is planned to be completed by mid-2017; see EC (2015a).

from paying the price. It imposed capital controls to stem exit and passed an important part of the burden on to international creditors including bondholders and depositors. More importantly, from the end of 2008 until 2013 Iceland's banks wrote off debt for more than a quarter of the population, by some 13 per cent of 2012 GDP. An important part of this is on mortgage debt exceeding 110 per cent of home values. This played an important role in the rapid exit of Iceland from a deep recession in 2009–10 with an unemployment rate of 5 per cent, compared to double-digit unemployment and persistent output losses in the Eurozone periphery.

1.3 Fiscal Orthodoxy

Fiscal policy no doubt gained added importance because of continued debt overhang and the ineffectiveness of monetary policy in lifting effective demand. But both the US and Europe shifted to austerity after an initial fiscal stimulus. In the Eurozone, the core also joined in the austerity imposed on the crisis-hit periphery.

The case for fiscal austerity is premised on two propositions. First, budget deficits add more to public debt than to GDP so that they would raise the debt-to-GDP ratio. Second, high ratios of public debt to GDP are detrimental to growth. It is thus believed that fiscal austerity would not undermine growth and could even stimulate it by lowering the ratio of public debt to GDP—hence, the so-called 'expansionary austerity'.

The first proposition implies that fiscal multipliers are small. This is derived from highly controversial theories that higher public spending would crowd out private spending by pushing up the interest rate and that private sector would start spending less and saving more in order to provide for future tax increases needed to meet higher government debt servicing. These theories make no sense when interest rates are at historical lows and incomes are falling. Still, in the early years of the crisis, the fiscal policy advice of the IMF was premised on the assumption of extremely low multipliers and was invariably pro-cyclical. Because of the underestimation of fiscal multipliers, IMF growth projections turned out to be more optimistic than growth outcomes in several periphery countries with IMF programmes (Weisbrot and Jorgensen 2013). As a result of mounting evidence on fiscal drag, the IMF finally admitted that fiscal multipliers were much greater than had been believed and that they were state-dependent, particularly large under recessions, with the implication that fiscal austerity could in fact raise the debt ratio by depressing income (IMF WEO 2012; Blanchard and Leigh 2013).

The second proposition that high debt ratios could deter growth found support in the finding of an empirical study by Reinhart and Rogoff (2010) that economic growth slows sharply when the ratio of government debt to GDP exceeds 90 per cent. However, it is generally agreed that such an association says effectively nothing about causality—slow growth could cause high debt rather than high debt leading to slow growth. Furthermore, subsequent research by Herndon et al. (2013) found that several critical findings of the Reinhart and Rogoff (2010) study were erroneous and in fact a 90 per cent debt ratio was associated with a much higher rate of growth than was found by these authors.

It is possible for the public sector to add to debt across the cycle without running into sustainability problems provided that it is used to finance productive investment. This implies conducting countercyclical fiscal policy by making a distinction between current and capital spending and adding to public debt over the cycle not to finance current spending but to invest.[6] It is generally agreed that public investment should aim at improving the overall productivity of private activities as well as expanding aggregate demand. Spending on human and physical infrastructure could serve both objectives. Such an approach implies that analysis of fiscal sustainability should not just focus on gross public debt alone, but also consider assets built on the other side of the balance sheet of the public sector that could generate future revenues. When interest rates are at historical lows and likely to remain subdued in the near future, additional revenues needed to service such debt would not be prohibitive.

With the Eurozone unable to reignite growth and growth in the US unable to break into a stride, such an approach is finding advocates even within the mainstream. The OECD (2015) argued that a coordinated expansion of public investment, combined with appropriate structural reforms, could expand output and lower the ratio of public debt to gross domestic product since fiscal multipliers for public investment are above unity, and much higher than multipliers for current spending. In a subsequent simulation OECD (2016) estimated that 0.5 per cent of GDP public investment stimulus in the US and Eurozone would raise GDP by more than 0.5 per cent in the first year and lower the ratio of public debt to GDP. There is considerable scope for increasing public investment not only in the US, UK, and the Eurozone periphery, but also in Germany where the infrastructure has been decaying at an alarming rate.

Spending more, running higher deficits, and financing them with new debt, however, can encounter a dilemma; if public spending is successful in raising economic activity, employment, and prices, it could lead to substantially

[6] In Japan traditionally a second budget was kept alongside the central budget which provided for financing public investment programs, and only the spending financed by bonds issued to cover the central deficits was considered as deficit financing; see UNCTAD TDR (1993: 78).

higher interest rates, which could eventually create debt servicing difficulties. For instance in early 2016, US rates for ten year treasuries were around 2 per cent and interest payments accounted for 6 per cent of all federal outlays. But projections by the Congressional Budget Office show that they could account for more than 13 per cent of all federal outlays in 2026 when interest rates are projected to rise to 4.1 per cent (Wessel 2016).

If and when such a dilemma emerges, other ways would have to be found to finance higher public spending. One way is to combine progressive taxation with increased public spending. This could give a significant boost to economic activity without creating deficits and debt or significantly crowding out private spending. Under conditions of deflation when private spending remains depressed, the so-called balanced-budget multiplier tends to be quite high, particularly if public spending is financed by additional taxes on top income classes. This is particularly true for the US and the UK where income and wealth inequality is much greater than other major OECD countries and taxation is much less progressive. It has been estimated that in such cases the top tax rate on the top 1 per cent income earners could be raised to over 80 per cent without impairing growth and that the potential tax revenue at stake is very large (Piketty et al. 2011). However, the dominant ideology shaping the crisis intervention has sidelined such socially progressive and economically beneficial solutions.

In the US the immediate fiscal response to consumer deleveraging and retrenchment through one-off transfers and tax cuts played an important role in restraining the downturn and initiating recovery. For instance it is estimated that the fiscal stimulus raised 2010 real GDP by as much as 3.4 per cent, held the unemployment rate about 1.5 percentage points lower, and added almost 2.7 million jobs to US payrolls (Blinder and Zandi, 2010). However, as soon as the economy started to show signs of life, fiscal orthodoxy returned. As pointed out by Janet Yellen (2013a: 4) when she was a Vice Chair of the Board of Governors of the Federal Reserve System, 'discretionary fiscal policy hasn't been much of a tailwind during this recovery. In the year following the end of the recession, discretionary fiscal policy at the federal, state, and local levels boosted growth at roughly the same pace as in past recoveries.... But instead of contributing to growth thereafter, discretionary fiscal policy this time has actually acted to restrain the recovery... and I expect that discretionary fiscal policy will continue to be a headwind for the recovery for some time, instead of the tailwind it has been in the past.'

Indeed, fiscal retrenchment continued unabated in the US despite weak recovery. According to Hutchins Center's Fiscal Impact Measure, local, state, and federal governments were a drag on US economic growth over much of the last five years when the economy was still struggling to recover from the Great Recession and it was only after mid-2015 that the fiscal policy started to give a boost to economic activity (Wessel 2015). On another account, however, fiscal policy in the US remained contractionary during 2014–16 (OECD 2016).

The initial fiscal policy response in the Eurozone was also reflationary. Between 2007 and 2009 the budget balance of the Eurozone moved from an average deficit of 0.7 per cent of GDP to 6.3 per cent and according to the European Commission, half of the increase in deficits was due to the conventionally measured automatic stabilizers and half to discretionary countercyclical fiscal policy actions (EC 2011: 15). In Germany fiscal reflation included one-off transfers, tax relief, and spending on transportation and education. From 2010 onwards fiscal policy in the Eurozone became more and more restrictive. Between 2011 and 2013 spending cuts and tax increases amounted to around 4 per cent of GDP and this played a central role in the return of the region to recession during 2012–13 (Rannenberg et al. 2015). Fiscal consolidation continued in subsequent years. According to the European Commission (EC 2015b) the aggregate budget deficit of the region was expected in 2015 to decline from 2.6 per cent of GDP in 2014 to 1.8 per cent in 2016. This is happening at a time when growth in the region is still below par and automatic stabilizers should be expected to widen headline deficits, giving rise to increased calls for a more expansionary fiscal policy to prevent the region from returning to recession (Truger 2015).

In the Eurozone lending to debtor countries incorporated austerity in the form of tax hikes, and cuts in public spending and wages. Much of the burden of fiscal consolidation fell on public investment, with cuts exceeding 2.5 per cent of GDP in Greece, Spain, and Ireland between 2010 and 2013. In a subsequent evaluation of the 2010 Stand-By Agreement with Greece, the IMF (GFSR 2013a) admitted that it had underestimated the damage done to the economy from fiscal austerity imposed in the bail-out programme and that it deviated from its own debt-sustainability standards and should have pushed harder and sooner for lenders to take a haircut to reduce Greece's debt burden. Indeed, as already discussed in this chapter and as subsequently recognized by the OECD (2015), such consolidation efforts can move the economies away from medium-term debt sustainability rather than reducing the ratio of public debt to GDP.

Greece and Portugal made the most strenuous efforts to improve fiscal balances, by around 8 percentage points of GDP during 2010–15. These are also the two countries with the worst growth performance over the same period, with average rates of –4 per cent and –1 per cent respectively. Consequently, both countries saw a significant increase of the ratio of gross public debt to GDP, by around 35 percentage points (Weeks 2016).

While fiscal retrenchment in the periphery widened the deflationary gap (that is, the gap between full employment level of output and actual output) and failed to stabilize sovereign debt, deflation in the core countries made it very difficult for them to make growth-oriented balance-of-payments adjustment based on export expansion rather than contractionary adjustment based on import retrenchment. As the periphery is locked in a currency whose nominal exchange rate is beyond their control, the only way to restore competitiveness would be through cuts in wages. This means that more austerity would be needed to overcome austerity; employment needs to be cut in order to generate external demand.[7] Weak demand in Germany increased the retrenchment needed in the periphery to achieve any given turnaround in external balances.

So far the crisis countries with overvalued currencies have achieved a significant degree of internal devaluation and adjustment in real effective exchange rates through wage suppression (see Figure 1.1). Except Cyprus, all of them moved from current account deficits of 6 to 15 per cent of GDP in 2007 to a surplus in 2015. However, much of this improvement came from economic contraction, cuts in private investment, and imports (Atoyan et al. 2013). Greek imports at the end of 2015 were 40 per cent down from the pre-crisis peak while exports levelled off and fell to pre-crisis levels after a temporary surge in 2012–13. Import cuts were equally sharp in Portugal. In Spain, with more diversified industry, import cuts were less severe while exports showed greater dynamism than Greece and Portugal.[8] This pattern of adjustment is largely shaped by fiscal austerity, sluggish wages, and trade surplus in Germany, which have placed the burden of adjustment disproportionately on debtor deficit countries.

1.4 The Ultra-easy Monetary Policy

The reluctance to use fiscal policy to expand aggregate demand resulted in excessive reliance on monetary policy, particularly as fiscal austerity became self-defeating by restraining growth. Policy interest rates have been cut to historical lows, not only in the US, the UK, and the Eurozone but also many other advanced economies. In several cases, including the Eurozone, Japan, Switzerland, Sweden, and Denmark, central banks have moved to negative rates as the ultra-easy monetary policy proved not as effective as expected.

[7] This problem was encountered by Argentina in the 1990s when it had fixed the peso against the dollar with the Convertibility Plan. In commenting on its prospects, UNCTAD TDR (1995: 90) noted that 'the main question for Argentina is how much unemployment will be needed to improve competitiveness, given that it has excluded the possibility of using what is normally the most potent instrument of policy to that end, namely the exchange rate, and whether such unemployment will be politically acceptable.'

[8] Data from http://www.tradingeconomics.com/.

They have also been engaged in large-scale bond purchases, financed by the creation of reserves in the banking system in order to reduce long-term interest rates and stimulate borrowing and spending.

In the US the targeted federal funds rate was cut to 0.25 per cent in December 2008 and stayed at that level until December 2015, when it was raised to 0.50 per cent. QE1 was started in 2008 for purchases of mortgage-backed securities; QE2 was introduced at the end of 2010 for a purchase of $600 billion of treasury securities and supplemented by the so-called Operation Twist whereby the US Federal Reserve replaced expiring short-term treasury bills with long-term notes and securities; Q3 came in September 2012 followed by an announcement by the US Federal Reserve in December that it would keep buying $85 billion a month in treasuries and asset-backed securities until unemployment fell below 6.5 per cent or inflation rose above 2.5 per cent. The US Federal Reserve started tapering its monthly bond purchases in January 2014 and ended it altogether in October 2014.

In the Eurozone initially monetary policy interventions were less intense, but extended and broadened significantly as the crisis deepened and the region remained in stagnation. The ECB cut its benchmark refinancing rate to 1 per cent in 2009. The two rounds of misguided increases, first to 1.25 per cent then to 1.50 per cent in 2011 were followed by successive cuts, eventually to a record low of zero per cent in March 2016. To expand liquidity in March 2010 the ECB eased collateral requirements in lending to banks, thus accepting low-grade sovereign bonds as well as asset-backed securities. This was followed by the Securities Market Programme in May of the same year with the ECB buying sovereign bonds in secondary markets—an initiative that created controversy regarding the no-bail-out provision of the 2007 Lisbon Treaty. The Long-Term Refinancing Operations were introduced at the end of 2011 for the ECB to provide three-year loans to banks at low interest rates, enabling them to buy high-yield sovereign bonds and earn large spreads, notably in Spain and Italy. As of early 2016, the nominal charge to banks using this facility was set at zero and in fact banks could borrow from the ECB at negative rates (up to -0.4 per cent) if their lending reaches a certain size.

In 2012, soon after its head reaffirmed the pledge to 'do whatever it takes' to save the single currency, the ECB announced that it would undertake outright monetary transactions in secondary sovereign bond markets without ex-ante time or size limits. This was activated in January 2015 with an 'expanded asset purchase' or a big QE programme of €60 billion monthly purchases of euro-area bonds. Originally the QE stimulus was planned to last until September 2016, but in December 2015 the ECB pledged to continue it until March 2017. In March 2016 monthly bond purchases were increased to €80 billion and investment-grade euro-denominated bonds issued by non-bank corporations established in the Eurozone were made eligible for regular purchases under QE.

The channels through which QE programmes were expected to stimulate private spending are not always well understood and there is significant controversy over why they failed to give a significant boost to economic activity, particularly in the US. In QE operations central banks buy bonds from non-bank financial institutions such as pension funds and insurance companies through the banking system. Money supply expands as these institutions exchange their bond holdings with bank deposits while banks acquire reserves at the central bank by a corresponding amount. Since required reserves are a fraction of deposit liabilities of banks, much of these reserves would be excess reserves. The expansion of bank deposits and money supply is not driven by credit expansion as is usually the case in money creation in modern economies.[9]

It is sometimes maintained that the practice of payment of positive interest rates on excess reserves makes the banks unwilling to lend but keep the extra liquidity as reserves at the US Federal Reserve (e.g. Stiglitz and Rashid 2016). However, banks cannot use their reserves at the central bank for lending. In fact QE may even reduce the credit volume if it encourages other means of corporate finance such as bond issues as substitutes to bank credits (McLeay et al. 2014; Coppola 2016; Keen 2016a, 2016b).

Thus, QE operations cannot increase bank lending by providing more reserves to the banking system even though such an impression was created by various commentators, including central bankers. For instance in the early days of bond purchases Bernanke (2009) argued that the 'idea behind quantitative easing is to provide banks with substantial excess liquidity in the hope that they will choose to use some part of that liquidity to make loans'. Rather, they could be expected to stimulate the economy through two channels (Sastry and Wessel 2015). First, they would lower longer-term interest rates. Secondly, investors who sold treasury bonds would shift to other assets, including houses and high-risk, high-yielding assets such as stocks and corporate bonds. This means that in effect QE was designed to stimulate private spending by creating asset bubbles and increasing the demand for corporate debt and reducing its cost.

Even though excess reserves created by QE programmes cannot be used for lending, they allow banks to expand credit without having to borrow from the central bank or in the interbank market. As bank credits and deposits expand, excess reserves would be translated into required reserves (Coppola 2016). However, this would not affect banks' earning on reserves and their lending behaviour if interest is paid at the same rate on both required and excess reserves. This is what the US Federal Reserve has been doing since January

[9] For the money creation process and the nature and effect of QE programmes, see McLeay et al. (2014).

2009 with the rate having been set equal to the targeted federal funds rate. It is argued that the main objective of paying interest on excess reserves is to gain a better control over the federal funds rate. Since rapid growth of reserves made it difficult to reach the targeted federal funds rate by varying the supply of bank reserves, the US Federal Reserve seeks to influence market rates by moving the interest paid on excess reserves (Bernanke and Kohn 2016).

Interest payments on excess reserves in effect constitute a subsidy to banks since the rates they offer to their deposit holders are virtually zero. They also allow reserves and bank profits to grow even in the absence of further QE operations.[10] While the payment of interest on required reserves can be justified for compensation for their opportunity cost to banks, there is no good reason for paying interest on excess reserves at times of recession since the primary purpose of such payments is to prevent banks from lending at lower rates. Indeed, since interest rates on excess reserves establish a lower bound to the federal funds rate, adjustments to these rates are expected to play an important role in the US Federal Reserve's exit from the ultra-easy monetary policy.[11]

Unlike the US Federal Reserve, the ECB and the Bank of Japan apply negative interest to excess reserves while paying positive and zero interest on required reserves, respectively (Bech and Malkhozov 2016). This implies that credit (and hence deposit) expansion could have a positive impact on banks' income from reserves by shifting them from excess to required reserves. However, negative nominal policy interest rates are uncharted waters and there is considerable uncertainty regarding their impact on credit and private spending. As noted by a BIS report 'experience so far suggests that modestly negative policy rates are transmitted to money market rates in very much the same way as positive rates are. However, questions remain as to whether negative policy rates are transmitted to the wider economy through lower lending rates for firms and households, especially in rates associated with bank intermediation' (Bech and Malkhozov 2016: 4). Furthermore, even when they result in lower lending rates, they may not bring faster expansion of credit and private spending than has so far been achieved by massive cuts in policy

[10] According to Stiglitz and Rashid (2016: 2) banks have been 'earning nearly $30 billion—completely risk-free—during the last five years... and as a consequence of the Fed's interest rate hike last month, the subsidy will increase by $13 billion this year'. As Bernanke and Kohn (2016) point out, the money comes from interest received on bonds purchased by the US Federal Reserve. However, as discussed later in this section, since the US Federal Reserve's net income is transferred to the Treasury, these earnings effectively constitute a transfer from public budget.

[11] In explaining the exit strategy, the former US Federal Reserve Chairman pointed out that '[b]y increasing the interest rate on reserves, the Federal Reserve will be able to put significant upward pressure on all short-term interest rates, as banks will not supply short-term funds to the money markets at rates significantly below what they can earn by holding reserves at the Federal Reserve Banks. Actual and prospective increases in short-term interest rates will be reflected in turn in longer-term interest rates and in financial conditions more generally' (Bernanke 2010).

interest rates after the onset of the crisis. In reality negative policy rates can destabilize the banking system rather than expand credits: 'if negative policy rates are transmitted to lending rates for firms and households, then there will be knock-on effects on bank profitability unless negative rates are also imposed on deposits, raising questions as to the stability of the retail deposit base'.[12]

The reasons for the failure of ultra-easy monetary policy in re-igniting bank lending to support spending on goods and services are found in the deflation generated by the crisis. The increased risk aversion made banks in both the US and Europe unwilling to lend to households and small businesses while big businesses have had little need for bank loans or appetite for new spending on labour and equipment in view of sluggish demand. In Europe, in addition, the banking system itself has been in a dire state; it is undercapitalized and impaired by €1 trillion of bad loans (Wharton Finance 2016). As noted, this is in large part because governments chose to rescue rather than force them to restructure in the early days of the crisis. These banks sought to meet capital charges by cutting credit rather than recapitalization even though they were flooded with liquidity. Even the initiative by the ECB to subsidize bank lending under the Long-Term Refinancing Operations was not expected in 2016 to lead to a rapid credit expansion (Münchau 2016; Jones 2016). As put by the Economist (2016), 'increasingly, the markets are doubting the efficacy of overstretched monetary policy'.

The ultra-easy monetary policy has failed to stimulate private spending, but created significant opportunities for fiscal expansion by lowering long-term interest rates and rapidly increasing the central bank holding of government debt, notably in the US. On the one hand, it has resulted in a significant decline in interest payments from the budget. On the other hand, much of the interest payments on debt held by central banks have gone back to the budget as profit remittances.[13] It is estimated that by the end of 2012, total benefits of governments in the US, the UK, and the Eurozone taken together from both reduced debt service costs and increased profits remitted from central banks reached $1.6 trillion (Dobbs et al. 2013). This space was not used effectively for fiscal reflation. In the US alone for 2007–12 benefits from lower interest rates and profit remittances were over $1 trillion compared to a total fiscal stimulus of some $800 billion in the same period (Amadeo 2013). Profit remittances

[12] Bech and Malkhozov (2016: 6). See also Finger (2016) for other unintended adverse consequences of negative policy interest rates. That the initial impact in Japan, Switzerland, and Eurozone is quite opposite of what was expected, see Worthington (2016).

[13] In the US Federal Reserve profits are remitted to the Treasury. In the Eurozone, profits of the ECB are distributed to national central banks of the Eurozone according to their participation in its capital. National central banks also earn profits from other sources. These are transferred to governments. For instance in 2015 ECB profits were around €1.1 billion whereas the profits earned by Deutsche Bundesbank were €3.2 billion, transferred to the Federal Government of Germany.

from the US Federal Reserve alone during 2006–15 reached $600 billion, meeting a large proportion of the deficit created by fiscal stimulus (Sharf 2015; Leubsdorf 2016).

The QE programmes have failed to lift private spending but succeeded in creating asset bubbles. They gave the money not to banks but to non-bank financial institutions which have used it to speculate globally by shifting to high-risk, high-yielding financial assets. They triggered a search for yield in the riskier part of the credit spectrum including high-yield bonds, subordinated debt, and leveraged syndicated loans (BIS 2013: 7). High-yield high-risk corporate debt issuance accelerated in both advanced economies and EDEs and there were significant increases in corporate debt in booming sectors such as energy.[14] Stock markets in most major advanced economies reached historical highs, but the wealth effect of asset booms on spending has been weak because the gains are reaped mainly by the rich.[15]

All these led to an important build-up of fragility in financial markets in advanced economies. The BIS (2013: 1) described the strong issuance of bonds and loans in the riskier part of the spectrum, as 'a phenomenon reminiscent of the exuberance prior to the global financial crisis'. They caused concern even at the US Federal Reserve with Bernanke (2013) issuing a warning that asset prices may get delinked from fundamentals, generating mispricing (see also IMF GFSR 2013a). Similar concerns were expressed by Janet Yellen before becoming the chairman of the US Federal Reserve (Yellen 2013b; see also Fontevecchia 2013).

As discussed in the subsequent chapter, the ultra-easy monetary policy in advanced economies created consumption and property bubbles in several emerging economies by giving rise to a surge in capital flows and booms in credit and asset markets of these economies. In a way, it was more 'successful' in stimulating spending in the South than in the North, but at the cost of creating financial fragility.

There is a growing agreement that it would be difficult to exit from an extended period of ultra-easy money without disrupting global financial stability and impairing growth (White 2012; Stein 2013). QE has created significant fragility in financial markets and increased vulnerability to shocks by producing a combination of macro liquidity and market illiquidity—something which Roubini (2015) calls 'the liquidity time bomb' (see also Lefeuvre 2015). While

[14] An important part of these, around $550 billion, were energy company debt—Idzelis and Torres (2014). In the US alone the junk bond market is estimated to be in the order of $1.5 trillion of which 15–20 per cent consist of energy company debt market; see Snyder (2016).

[15] The Dow Jones industrial average, UK FTSE 100 index and German DAX 30 index all reached historical highs in spring 2015, registering increases between 2 times (UK FTSE) and 3.4 times (DAX 30) from the lows seen in early 2009. The Japanese Nikkei index also rose by 2.7 times during that period; data from http://www.tradingeconomics.com/.

large central bank purchases of safe, liquid government bonds expanded monetary base and macro liquidity, these purchases, together with regulations requiring banks and other large financial institutions to hold large amounts of safe liquid assets, reduced their supply and made them less liquid. For the same reason, the proportion of risky, high-yielding, illiquid assets in private portfolios such as infrequently traded corporate and emerging market bonds increased. A large proportion of these bonds have come to be held in open-ended funds that allow investors quick exit en masse, creating the risk of crash in the event of a shock—something that has caused concern at the IMF and the US Federal Reserve and triggered suggestions to impose exit fees on bond funds (Abramowicz 2014; Durden 2014a).

These imply that unexpected changes in policy or key economic performance indicators such as growth, employment, or oil prices can result in sudden and severe revaluation of asset prices. A hike in policy rates can certainly trigger such a revaluation and this is a reason why the US Federal Reserve is hesitant in normalizing its monetary policy even though it is adding more to financial fragility than to incomes and jobs.[16] But more fundamentally, if growth slows down, the illiquidity of asset markets can burst the booms and bubbles created by QE programmes and zero interest rates, even without a significant tightening of monetary policy.

There were several instances of gyrations in asset markets since 2008 (such as the 'taper tantrum' of May 2013) and early months of 2016 also saw heightened instability. It all started with growth slowdown and reversal of capital flows in EDEs throughout 2015, including in China. As described by the BIS in March 2016, the uneasy calm that had reigned in the financial markets in late 2015 gave way to a turbulent start in 2016, witnessing one of the worst stock market sell-offs since the 2008 financial crisis. Equity prices tumbled worldwide, credit default swap spreads widened, currencies of EDEs fell, especially vis-à-vis the US dollar, and the oil price sank to below the levels seen during the Great Recession. 'Underlying some of the turbulence was market participants' growing concern over the dwindling options for policy support in the face of the weakening growth outlook. With fiscal space tight and structural policies largely dormant, central bank measures were seen to be approaching their limits' (BIS 2016).

Whether or not these stock market developments anticipate an imminent collapse and recession in the world economy, it must be evident that policy-makers lack ammunition to fight another downturn unless they abandon fiscal austerity and give the money to those who would spend it rather than

[16] On the eve of the US Federal Reserve rate rise in December 2015, global bond markets were said to have been haunted by the 'spectre of illiquidity' because the 'levels of secondary market bond liquidity have sunk to perilously low levels'; see West et al. (2015).

speculate with it. However, as problems mount, the ECB is simply promising more of the same thing. As for the US, the only option under the current policy approach would be to join the ECB and re-introduce QE purchases and cut policy rates to negative levels (Bernanke 2016)—but only to make the problems come back with greater force.

1.5 People's Quantitative Easing: The Case for Helicopter Money

Since the large quantities of liquidity provided to financial markets through QE programmes and cuts in policy interest rates to historical lows have failed to expand private spending adequately, a way out could be to make the money available directly to those who are willing to spend but cannot do so because of tight budget constraints and debt overhang they face. Milton Friedman suggested, a long time ago, dropping money from helicopters to avert deflation. In a speech given in 2002 before becoming the chairman of the US Federal Reserve, Bernanke referred to helicopter money as a way of reversing deflation, noting that 'the U.S. government has a technology, called a printing press (or, today, its electronic equivalent), that allows it to produce as many U.S. dollars as it wishes at essentially no cost' and that 'a determined government can always generate higher spending and hence positive inflation'. He then went on to argue that 'the effectiveness of anti-deflation policy could be significantly enhanced by cooperation between the monetary and fiscal authorities' and that 'money-financed tax cut is essentially equivalent to Milton Friedman's famous "helicopter drop" of money' (Bernanke 2002: 4, 6).

In the cooperation for deficit monetization between monetary and fiscal authorities, the Treasury would obtain a credit at the US Federal Reserve by selling sovereign debt and use this credit to finance tax cuts or transfers to households or direct purchases of goods and services in an investment programme. Part of the currency issued would return to the central bank as reserves through increases in bank deposits and a part would be held by the public. Either the US Federal Reserve cancels the treasury bonds or holds them indefinitely. In either case, the sovereign would incur no cost on this debt because the US Federal Reserve's profits are remitted to the Treasury.

At first sight helicopter money looks like a combination of fiscal stimulus plus QE. There are, however, important differences. First, QE is an exchange of assets, newly printed dollars for bonds held by the public through the banking system. By contrast, here the base money and reserves increase as a result of additional spending on goods and services either directly by the government or indirectly by the private sectors through budgetary transfers and tax cuts, not because of asset substitution. Second, the US Federal Reserve's purchase of treasuries in QE operations do not provide the government non-debt creating, interest-free resources unless such debt is monetized indefinitely. In other words, deficit monetization requires permanent QE—an irreversible increase in the nominal stock of fiat money (Buiter 2014). It is true that as long as the bonds acquired by the US Federal Reserve stay on its balance sheet, they do not entail net cost to the government because the US Federal Reserve's profits are remitted to the Treasury. But as soon as the expansion of the US Federal Reserve's balance sheet is reversed and these bonds exit the US Federal Reserve's balance sheet (that is, if they mature without being replaced or if they are liquidated), these profits would dry up. This, together with the return of interest rates to normalcy, would increase debt servicing costs significantly.

The kind of cooperation needed for deficit monetization between the monetary and fiscal authorities is in principle feasible in most advanced economies, including the US.[17] However, in the Eurozone, direct financing of government deficit is explicitly prohibited by the Lisbon Treaty. Unless the relevant provisions of this treaty are reformed, deficit monetization in the Eurozone would have to go through the market—governments would have to issue debt to finance deficits and the ECB would have to buy sovereign bonds from secondary markets but with a commitment to hold them indefinitely. Purchases of sovereign bonds in the secondary markets are already made with the QE programme that started in January 2015.

Thus, permanent monetization of government debt provides an effective answer to deflation and long-term sovereign debt sustainability. The case for overt monetary financing also applies to deficits resulting from debt write-downs and bail-out operations to recapitalize insolvent banks. It would allow stabilizing the banking system without adding to government debt and hence shifting solvency concerns from banks to sovereigns, as has happened in the Eurozone periphery (Turner 2013b).

Should fiscal authorities be unwilling to engage in helicopter money, could central banks do it themselves by sending checks to citizens, dropping money in private bank accounts or in other ways? This is advocated by Wolf (2016): 'If the fiscal authorities are unwilling to behave so sensibly... central banks... could be given the power to send money, ideally in electronic form, to every adult citizen. Would this add to demand? Absolutely. Under existing monetary arrangements, it would also generate a permanent rise in the reserves of commercial banks at the central bank. The easy way to contain any long-term monetary effects would be to raise reserve requirements.' As for the Eurozone, there is nothing in the Lisbon Treaty prohibiting helicopter drops by the

[17] However, in 2011 Bernanke ruled out direct lending to state and local governments, saying that the US Federal Reserve had limited legal authority to help and little will to use that authority, see *Wall Street Journal* 'Bernanke Rejects Bailouts', 8 January 2011.

ECB. Rather, 'one could argue that the Treaty not only permits but demands helicopter money drops from the ECB' in order for the ECB to pursue the objective of getting inflation closer to the 2 per cent target (Buiter 2014: 45).

A possible objection to helicopter drop is that it may not work—that is, money thus supplied may be hoarded rather than spent. However, 'there always exists ... a combined monetary and fiscal policy action that boosts private demand' (Buiter 2014: 1). Under deflationary conditions 'money-financed' spending or tax cuts need be no riskier for financial stability than the ultra-easy monetary policy, since the money thus created would not find its way directly into asset markets. Nor would it endanger monetary instability. If a permanent increase in money supply resulting from deficit financing turns out to be inflationary, it can be sterilized by using bank reserve requirements rather than selling government bonds. As argued by Turner (2013a: 24) the idea that overt money finance of fiscal deficits is inherently any more inflationary than the other policy levers used to stimulate demand is without any technical foundation. Rather, the main challenge is how to 'design institutional constraints and rules that would guard against the misuse of this powerful medicine' (see also White 2013; Turner 2013b; Turner 2015; Wolf 2013).

As monetary policy has increasingly become impotent in dealing with the crisis, the orthodoxy has started to give way to pragmatism. The *Financial Times*, in an editorial entitled 'Helicopter Money: Extreme Money-Printing Should be Openly Discussed' (13–14 October 2012) argued: 'Printing Money—not just temporarily for trading securities in the market, but permanently handing it over to be spent by someone—is the central banker's heresy. Yet it would be irresponsible to rule that option out.' Among the more progressive, helicopter drop has been referred to as People's Quantitative Easing, which occupied a central place in the reform proposal of the new UK Labour Party Leader, Jeremy Corbyn.[18] Some central banks, including the Bank of England, are reported to have given consideration to such a solution (Financial Times 2012).

Since 2008 circumstances have forced central bankers to abandon monetary orthodoxy first by dropping interest rates to zero and then by engaging in QE operations. Regarding the helicopter money, 'all the really important issues are political, since ... the technical feasibility and desirability in some circumstances of monetary finance is not in doubt' (Turner 2015: 1). It is increasingly believed that helicopter money may be unorthodox policy number 3, particularly in the Eurozone which needs more radical measures to save the euro.[19]

[18] See Kaletsky (2012a, 2012b). The Corbyn proposal involves the Bank of England purchasing bonds issued by a yet-to-be established National Investment Bank—see Öncü (2015: 11).

[19] For instance, Bridgewater's fund manager Ray Dalio predicts that circumstances will probably drive them to usher in what he calls 'monetary policy 3' (Wigglesworth 2016). It is suggested that more radical measures that could be taken by the ECB may include intervention in currency

However, this route is unlikely to be taken before economic conditions worsen significantly. Moreover, in all likelihood, central bankers can be expected to try to retain their independence by giving the money directly to private citizens rather than to the government. For, as noted by a Member of the Executive Board of the ECB when asked if the ECB could print cheques and send them to people: 'Yes, all central banks can do it. You can issue currency and you distribute it to people. That's helicopter money. Helicopter money is giving to the people part of the net present value of your future seigniorage, the profit you make on the future banknotes. The question is, if and when is it opportune to make recourse to that sort of instrument which is really an extreme sort of instrument.... So when we say we haven't reached the limit of the toolbox, I think that's true' (ECB Eurosystem 2016a).

1.6 Secular Stagnation

The failure of historically low interest rates to achieve a strong recovery in private spending and growth has bewildered many mainstream economists, leading to a search for a possible explanation within the conventional macroeconomic framework. Much of the debate revolved around the secular stagnation thesis, or what Palley (2016) calls the Zero Lower Bound (ZLB) economics, first evoked by Larry Summers in a speech at the IMF (Summers 2013), and picked up by many others in the same school of thought.[20]

According to this thesis, the subprime crisis uncovered the chronic demand gap that has existed in the US since the 1980s and the risk of secular stagnation. Because of vanishing investment opportunities, the real rate of interest that equates savings and investment at the full employment level of income (the so-called Wicksellian 'natural' rate of interest or the 'equilibrium' rate of interest) has declined significantly and even become negative. Since nominal interest rates cannot be pushed below zero and monetary authorities cannot create inflation, investment remains below the level needed for full employment and income remains below potential. The gap between actual and potential output creates hysteresis, resulting in a decline of potential output and growth; or, in the words of Summers, lack of demand creates its own lack of supply.

markets, purchase of equities, and recapitalization of banks by the ECB as well as helicopter drop—Lynn (2016).

[20] See also Summers (2014) and a collection of subsequent articles and speeches, Summers (2016). For the state of the debate, see a collection of articles in Teulings and Baldwin (2014) and papers discussed in a session on 'The Economics of Secular Stagnation' of the American Economic Association's January 2015 meeting, published in *American Economic Review* 105 (5), May 2015.

According to this hypothesis, until the subprime crisis the chronic demand gap was masked by private spending driven by financial bubbles; Savings and Loans in the 1980s, dot-com in the 1990s and the subprime in the 2000s. These bubbles take place largely because low interest rates in search of faster growth boost asset values and drive investors to take greater risks.[21] Unless the underlying causes of chronic deflationary gap are addressed, credit and asset bubbles would be needed to avert secular stagnation. Since these bubbles eventually burst and culminate in financial crises, this chronic demand gap creates a trade-off between financial stability and growth.

The concept of secular stagnation was elucidated by Alvin Hansen during the great depression of the 1930s who argued that while adequate investment would be needed to attain full employment, investment opportunities would vanish as population growth and technical progress slow down. Summers also refers to these, but at the same time throws in a number of other factors responsible for the decline in the equilibrium rate of interest: the legacy of excessive leverage caused reduction in demand for debt-financed investment; the decline in the relative price of capital reduced investment spending needed to attain a given rate of capacity expansion; and growing income and wealth inequality increased the supply of loanable funds and hence raised the level of investment needed to achieve full employment.[22]

The first line of response to secular stagnation, according to Summers, is to reduce real interest rates as much as possible by operating with a higher inflation target. But this also creates the risk of financial instability by leading to asset and credit bubbles. A more effective way would be to raise aggregate demand by increasing investment and consumption. Appropriate strategies include increased public investment, reductions in structural barriers to private investment, measures to promote business confidence and export promotion through trade agreements, and resistance to protectionism in trading partners.

The Hicksian liquidity trap hypothesis is also invoked to reach similar conclusions regarding the ineffectiveness of monetary policy in stimulating demand (Krugman 2013a, 2013b). According to this view, the deleveraging resulting from the subprime crisis reduced the overall level of demand at any given interest rate and made the natural rate negative, making it impossible for monetary policy to stabilize the economy. To avoid such an outcome, we should not have had debt-driven bubbles in the first place. But if there were no

[21] There is, however, no mention of the role of financial deregulation in the emergence of bubbles, 'the last two of which [Summers] played a huge role in fueling by playing the water-boy for Wall Street's deregulation movement' (Wray 2013: 1).

[22] In the Loanable Funds model underlying this analysis (Keen 2015), population, productivity, and capital good price changes shift the investment curve inwards while distributional changes shift the savings curve outwards.

bubbles, aggregate demand and employment would have remained depressed. Once the current deleveraging is over, demand will shift up, but without renewed bubbles income and employment levels would be subdued. There is also the possibility that the economy may be trapped in a liquidity trap permanently even after the current deleveraging is over and there may be a need for ever-growing debt to stay out of the liquidity trap.[23] Sufficiently large and permanent fiscal stimulus—or permanently bigger government—would be required to avoid this trap. This should be no cause for concern since debt sustainability would be secured as long as the real rate of interest on government debt is below the rate of growth of the economy (Krugman 2015a).

Bernanke (2015a, 2015b) is sceptical that the US faces secular stagnation due to vanishing investment opportunities since at a real interest rate of –2 per cent there would be no dearth of private investment. He also takes issue with the contribution of bubbles to previous recoveries and attributes low interest rates and demand gap in the US to global savings glut. On this view, in the run-up to the crisis, excess savings from China and major oil exporters spilled over to the US through capital flows, depressing long-term rates even as the US Federal Reserve was trying to raise short-term rates, thereby helping sustain the subprime bubble. They also weakened US exports, created a large trade deficit, and reduced US growth by appreciating the dollar. The savings glut persisted after the crisis as the decline in excess savings of Asian EDEs and oil producers was offset by a significant increase in the combined current account surplus of the Eurozone, particularly Germany.[24] It has the same effect as reduced domestic investment on economic activity.[25] However, on this view, here the problem arises from policies pursued in surplus countries rather than structural factors emphasized by the secular stagnation hypothesis. Accordingly, the appropriate response would be to reverse policies that generate the savings glut. With the moderation of global imbalances in trade and financial flows, global real interest rates can thus be expected to rise and the US would be able to grow without bubbles.[26]

This debate among mainstream economists about secular stagnation has elicited strong interest among heterodox economists, particularly since it came from the very same people who had entertained considerable optimism

[23] It seems that differences between Krugman and Summers narrowed as the former moved closer to the position taken by the latter; see Summers (2015b) and Krugman (2015b).

[24] Draghi also joined Bernanke in the savings glut argument—ECB Eurosystem (2016b).

[25] In terms of the underlying Loanable Funds model it signifies an outward shift in the savings curve rather than an inward shift in the investment curve (Keen 2015).

[26] Summers (2015a: 3) conceded the importance of global dimensions of the problem and agreed that during 2003–07 the savings glut abroad was an important impediment to demand in the US and that 'the lower level of interest rates, the greater tendency towards deflation, and inferior output performance in Europe and Japan suggests that the spectre of secular stagnation is greater for them than for the United States'.

about the prospects of modern capitalism, under the rubric of Great Moderation associated with low inflation, reduced volatility of business cycle fluctuations, improvements in economic growth, and the belief that credit risk was a thing of the past (Wray 2013; Palley 2014). Indeed until they changed heart, secular stagnation remained a heretical idea for the mainstream (Backhouse and Boianovsky 2015). They now make no reference to history of economic thought as well as the more recent work done by heterodox economists (e.g. Foster and Magdoff 2009; Palley 2012).

While there is little dispute on the deceleration of accumulation and growth, its causes and the appropriate policy response are highly contentious. From a Marxian perspective, elucidated by Paul Baran, Paul Sweezy, Michael Kalecki, Joseph Steindl, and others, stagnation is the outcome of inherent contradictions in the accumulation process in a capitalist economy (Despain 2015). The mainstream fails to incorporate these or offer a sensible theoretical or a historical explanation of structural changes deemed responsible for the shift of the balance between savings and investment and the relation of secular stagnation 'to the contemporary expansion of finance' (Magdoff and Foster 2014: 2).

Furthermore, both the secular stagnation and savings glut arguments suffer from a failure to distinguish between savings and financing, and to grasp that in a modern monetary economy loans do not come from pre-existing stocks of deposits, and investment from pre-existing stocks savings. Rather, it is credits that generate deposits and investment that generates savings (Palley 2016; Wray 2013; Keen 2014, 2015; Hein 2015). Excess of savings over investment implies excess supply of goods or services. This sets off a process of adjustment through changes in the level and functional distribution of income, rather than the interest rate. Since savings adjust to investment, an 'investment dearth would be matched by a savings dearth' (Wray 2013: 4). Investment is governed by demand and profit expectations and made and financed independently of savings.[27] In a monetary economy the interest rate is a monetary phenomenon and there is no such thing as a stable 'natural' rate of interest that is compatible with full employment: 'Contrary to ZLB economics, not only does a laissez-faire monetary economy lack a mechanism for delivering the natural rate of interest, it may also lack such an interest rate.'[28]

Contrary to the savings glut argument, excess savings in surplus countries cannot exist prior to imports by deficit countries and finance those deficits (Wray 2013). Furthermore, the analysis of international influences over credit

[27] These factors indeed played a greater role in the decline of investment during the global crisis than financial conditions—Banerjee et al. (2015).

[28] Palley (2016:1). See also Borio and Disyatat (2011) for a similar critique of the concept of the natural rate of interest.

and spending booms in deficit countries needs to take into account all kinds of gross financial flows not just net capital flows (current account balances). In these respects there is 'increasing stylised evidence that appears *prima facie* inconsistent' with the savings glut argument: 'the link between current account balances and long-term interest rates looks tenuous'; 'the depreciation of the US dollar for most of the past decade sits uncomfortably with the presumed attractiveness of US assets'; and 'the link between the US current account deficit and global savings appears to be weak' (Borio and Disyatat 2011: 4–5).

1.7 Inequality, Financialization, and Underconsumption

There is little doubt that both demand-side and supply-side factors have been at play in the emergence of a chronic demand gap and slowdown of accumulation and growth in advanced economies. The two key interdependent factors that figure prominently in heterodox explanations of stagnation are growing inequality and financialization. These are mainly the product of neo-liberal policies rather than exogenous influences affecting thrift, accumulation, and productivity.

Declining share of wages in GDP and increasing concentration of wealth in the hands of a very small minority lead to underconsumption and a structural demand gap that cannot be filled permanently by bubble-driven spending. Sluggish wages also reduce inflationary pressures and allow and encourage central banks to pursue expansionary monetary policy. This is all the more so because, with unrelenting fiscal orthodoxy, monetary policy has become the only instrument left for achieving the objective of full employment. In the US, for instance, over the past three cycles the US Federal Reserve pushed its policy rates sequentially lower, cutting it more and more during downturns and raising it less and less during upturns, creating a downward bias in interest rates (Palley 2016: 18). Thus, the 'coincidence of a declining wage share and declining real interest rates is not... accidental' (Goodhart and Erfurth 2014). Easy money generates asset price and debt bubbles, which occasionally but not always produce spending booms. Bubbles create waste and distortions on the supply side, reducing potential growth. They also redistribute to the top, widening the demand gap. When they crash, inequality is aggravated and the economy would need even bigger bubbles to recover and grow. The solution is to be found not in monetary policy and negative interest rates but in reversing the secular decline in wages and concentration of wealth, restraining financialization and assigning a greater role to the public sector in stabilizing aggregate demand.

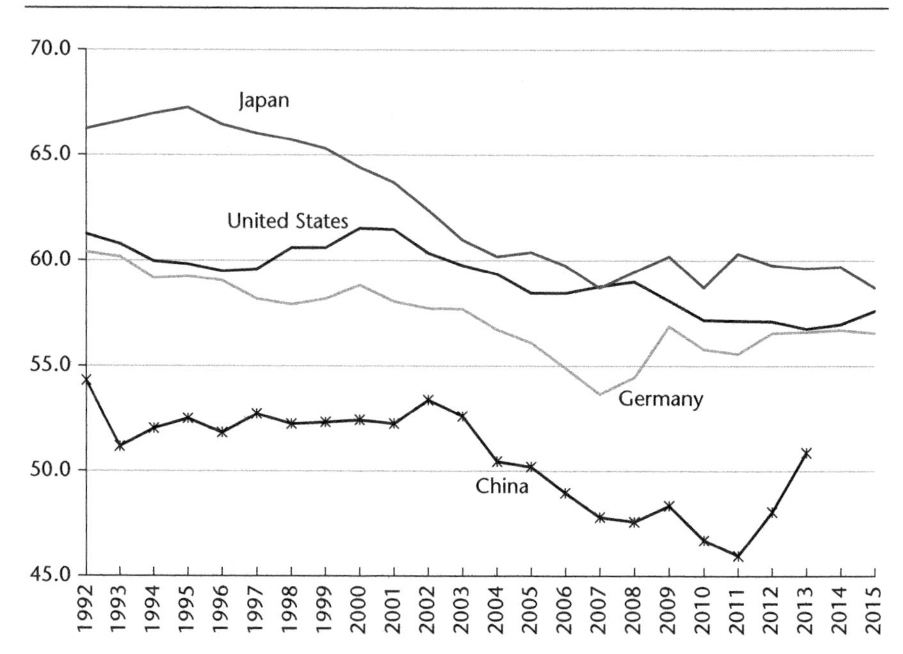

Figure 1.3 Wage share (as per cent of GDP)

Source: AMECO, European Commission and NBS (National Bureau of Statistics of the People's Republic of China).

All major economies, whether in deficit or surplus, suffer from growing inequality and underconsumption. There is a secular downward trend in the share of wages in GDP. Figure 1.3 shows this for unadjusted labour share in the US, China, Germany, and Japan from the 1990s onwards, but the same trend is observed for the adjusted wage share and a wider range of advanced economies including the Eurozone as a whole and the UK from the 1970s onwards.[29] The downward trend is more pronounced in the US and Japan than other major advanced economies. According to the International Labour Organization (ILO) estimates, between 1970 and 2014 the labour share declined by around 10 percentage points in the US and Japan and around 6–7 percentage points in Germany and the UK. This stands in sharp contrast with a long-standing belief that the share of labour in GDP stays relatively stable in the course of economic growth.

Evidence from EDEs is more nuanced, but there is a pronounced downward trend in the share of wages in Asian countries (ILO 2015). A notable example is China where the share of wages in GDP has shown a downward trend since the early 1990s with its growing integration into the global economic system.

[29] See Goodhart and Erfurth (2014: Figure 1) and ILO/OECD (2015). The labour share is defined as the share of net national income that is received by workers in the form of labour compensation. The adjusted labour share increases the unadjusted labour share by the ratio of self-employed.

The wage share in China is also lower than that in major advanced economies, about 50 per cent compared to 55 per cent or more in the latter. However, the downward trend in China appears to have been reversed since 2011 as a result of efforts to establish a strong domestic consumer market.

In advanced economies growth in real compensation of workers has weakened since the 1980s and stayed behind output per worker. According to ILO/ OECD (2015), in ten advanced economies for which data are available, between 2000 and 2013 labour productivity rose by 17 per cent while real wage index rose by some 6 per cent. This means that the purchasing power of workers over the goods and services they produce has been declining. The decline in the share of labour in income is also accompanied by a well-documented increase in the concentration of wealth in the top 1 per cent and hence the growing inequality in the distribution of incomes earned on assets. These trends in income and wealth distribution imply that inequality is not only a social problem but has increasingly become a macroeconomic problem.

Several studies undertaken in the OECD, IMF, and the European Commission suggest that technological changes are the main reason for the decline in the share of labour in income. However, this is highly contentious since the measurement of this effect is fraught with difficulties (Goodhart and Erfurth 2014). Indeed, closer examination has revealed that many of these findings are not robust (Stockhammer 2009). Rather, globalization and financialization as well as reduced bargaining power of labour resulting from neo-liberal policies appear to have played a central role in the downward trend in the share of wages in advanced economies (Palley 2007; Stockhammer 2009, 2012; ILO 2011; Hein 2013; Dünhaupt 2013).

The literature has identified various channels through which financialization aggravates inequality. Financial markets and institutions exert a strong influence on policy-making, thereby promoting the interest of capital vis-à-vis labour. The increased share of the financial sector in the economy reduces the share of wages in aggregate income because finance is less labour intensive than the rest of the economy. Financial boom–bust cycles tend to widen income and wealth inequality. Capital account liberalization reduces the labour share particularly when it culminates in crises (Furceri and Loungani 2015). It widens the options of corporations in investment strategy and enhances their bargaining power vis-à-vis labour. As management remuneration is increasingly tied to profits, their interest coincides with that of shareholders rather than labour. Short-termism associated with financialization raises dividend payments relative to retained earnings. Accordingly the decline in the wage share is reflected mainly by increases in dividends and interest incomes rather than higher corporate investment from retained earnings.

Globalization has also shifted the balance between labour and capital. China's and India's integration into the global system and the collapse of the Soviet Union have added to economically active persons in the world by almost 1.5 billion workers, doubling the global labour force. It is argued that as the new entrants brought little useful capital with them, the global capital-labour ratio has fallen by more than 50 per cent (Freeman 2010). This works against labour not only because labour productivity and pay tend to increase with the capital-labour ratio, but also because it shifts the balance of power towards capital as too many workers chase too few jobs or too little capital to employ them. The emergence of cheaper offshore locations has also raised the bargaining power of corporations, making capital a lot more mobile than labour.

It is also suggested that the glut in the labour market is aggravated by the entry of baby boomers in advanced economies into the workforce after 1970. On this view, the greying population in the advanced economies and demographic shifts in EDEs, notably China, would reverse the downward trend in labour income over the next three decades (Goodhart et al. 2015). However, the glut in the labour market depends on the pace of accumulation which continues to be depressed by underconsumption. Besides, demography is not the only factor influencing distributive trends. Unless financialization and the neo-liberal policies affecting the bargaining power of labour vis-à-vis capital are reversed, it is difficult to see how demographic changes alone could restore the balance.

While technology and globalization tend to have similar effects on countries, the extent of inequality differs significantly in different advanced economies. In terms of the Gini coefficient, the US and the UK come at the top of the list of major OECD countries. This is partly because financialization has gone much further in the Anglo-American world than in major economies in continental Europe. Another reason concerns differences in policies affecting the relative bargaining power of labour and capital. The erosion of labour markets institutions such as declines in union density has had a strong impact on inequality and there are significant differences in this respect between the US and UK on the one hand, and continental Europe, on the other. There are also important differences regarding minimum wage legislation (Jaumotte and Buitron 2015; ILO 2015). Thus, differences in policies with respect to finance and labour markets explain much of the intercountry variations in income and wealth distribution.

So far there have been two responses to underconsumption. First, create spending booms driven by debt and asset market bubbles, as in the US during the subprime expansion and in China in the aftermath of the Great Recession. Second, rely on exports to fill the demand gap; that is, export unemployment through macroeconomic, exchange rate, or incomes policies as done by China and Japan before the global crisis and Germany throughout the new millennium. Neither of these, however, provides a sustainable solution.

Financial bubbles may provide partial and temporary solutions to underconsumption but can in fact aggravate the structural demand gap. First, they do not always raise aggregate demand sufficiently to reduce unemployment and accelerate growth except when they lead to increased consumption or investment through debt accumulation. This happened during the subprime expansion in the US but the contribution of the dot-com bubble to growth in spending was limited in large part because the bubble was in the stock market, benefiting mainly high-income classes with lower spending propensities (Wray 2013). Again, the asset bubbles created by historically low interest rates and QE have not had much impact on aggregate spending because the benefits have gone to the rich and there has been little lending to lower income classes (and to the periphery in the Eurozone) with higher propensities to spend. In effect financial bubbles are more effective when they involve lending to income classes with higher propensities to consume. But this also would heighten financial fragility, rendering much of the debt so accumulated unpayable.

Second, the boom–bust cycles create supply-side distortions, impeding productivity and slowing growth. During booms, cheap credit diverts resources to low-productivity sectors such as construction and real estate services at the expense of more productive sectors such as manufacturing. The financial sector also crowds out real economic activity and more productive sectors (Cecchetti and Kharroubi 2015). Viable companies are held down by zombie companies, sustained by artificially favourable financial conditions. Misallocations created by the booms are exposed during the ensuing crises when the economy would have to make a shift back to viable sectors and companies, but this is impeded by credit crunch and deflation. Such adverse supply-side effects of debt-driven booms are revealed by a BIS study. Examining the link between credit booms, productivity growth, labour reallocations, and financial crises Borio et al. (2015) conclude that labour misallocations that occur during a boom have a much larger effect on subsequent productivity if a crisis follows—when economic conditions become more hostile, misallocations beget misallocations. It is estimated that the cumulative hysteresis effect of lost productivity over a decade long boom-bust cycle amounts to several per cent of GDP.

Third, boom-bust cycles aggravate the underconsumption problem by increasing inequality. Booms favour asset holders, while crises tend to reinforce the long-term trend in inequality. In the US, the crisis impoverished the poor, particularly those subject to foreclosures, while policy interventions benefited the rich. In the recovery period 2009–14, the top 1 per cent captured 58 per cent of total growth as their income grew by 27 per cent against 4.3 per cent growth of the income of the bottom 99 per cent (Saez 2015). In 2010 the households in the middle had lower real incomes than they did

Table 1.3 GDP, domestic demand and current account in main surplus countries
(Annual per cent change unless otherwise indicated)

	2004–07	2010	2011	2012	2013	2014	2015
Germany							
GDP growth	2.2	3.9	3.7	0.6	0.4	1.6	1.5
Domestic demand	1.1	2.9	3.0	–0.9	0.9	1.3	1.4
Private consumption	0.5	0.3	1.3	0.9	0.8	1.0	1.9
CA (% of GDP)	5.9	5.6	6.1	7.0	6.8	7.3	8.5
Japan							
GDP	1.9	4.7	–0.5	1.7	1.4	0.0	0.5
Domestic demand	1.1	2.9	0.4	2.6	1.7	0.0	0.0
Private consumption	1.2	2.8	0.3	2.3	1.7	–0.9	–1.3
CA (% of GDP)	4.0	4.0	2.2	1.0	0.8	0.5	3.3
China							
GDP	12.1	10.6	9.5	7.7	7.7	7.3	6.9
Domestic demand	10.3*	12.1	10.3	7.5	7.8	7.2	6.5
Consumption (total)	8.8*	9.4	11.4	8.2	6.9	6.9	7.1
CA (% of GDP)	7.1	4.0	1.8	2.5	1.6	2.1	2.7

* 2005–07 average.
Source: South Centre estimates based on IMF WEO database; IMF Article IV Consultation Reports with the People's Republic of China.

in 1996 and this was slowing the recovery by holding back aggregate spending (Stiglitz 2013). In every year from 2008 onwards real hourly wages stayed behind hourly labour productivity and the share of wages fell both during the contraction and subsequent recovery (Dufour and Orhangazi 2016).

Until the Great Recession, China, Germany, and Japan all relied on foreign markets to fill the demand gap, with GDP growing faster than domestic demand thanks to a strong growth in exports (see Table 1.3). During 2004–07, exports accounted for about one-third of Chinese GDP growth thanks to their phenomenal expansion.[30] In Japan and Germany export growth was more moderate, but their contribution to growth was much greater than that in China because in both countries domestic demand was sluggish. In other words Chinese export push was accompanied by a much stronger growth in domestic demand than in Japan and Germany, creating an expanding market for many other countries, notably exporters of commodities and manufactured parts and components for consumer goods.

In all three countries, in the period until the global crisis, the shares of wages and private consumption in GDP declined. However, unlike the other two countries, in China the decline in the wage share was associated with a strong

[30] See Akyüz (2011c). In these estimates, imports are allocated between exports and domestic absorption according to their direct and indirect import contents. They thus differ from the conventional estimates of contribution of trade to growth based on net exports—see Akyüz (2011a).

growth in real wages as well as in employment. As noted on p. 29, Germany was engaged in 'competitive disinflation', cutting productivity-adjusted real wages and prices to improve competitiveness. In Japan, too, the gap between productivity and wage growth widened during that period as outsourcing and competition from low-cost EDEs put pressure on wages.

This picture changed drastically with the onset of the global crisis. With the collapse of its main markets in advanced economies, growth in China fell sharply. This in effect gave an opportunity to design a stimulus package so as to address underconsumption. However, rather than boosting household incomes and private consumption, China focused on a debt-driven boom in investment in infrastructure, property, and industry, pushing its investment ratio towards 50 per cent of GDP and credit growth well ahead of GDP. This created excess capacity in several sectors and has left a legacy of a large stock of debt in public enterprises and local governments. The ratio of debt to GDP reached 250 per cent of GDP in 2015.

Chinese policy response thus created an imbalance between domestic investment and consumption while rebalancing external and domestic sources of demand. However, since investment boom could not be maintained over time, China gradually turned its attention to rebalancing consumption and investment. So far the progress made is quite modest, with the share of private consumption rising from around 35 per cent of GDP in 2009 to 37 per cent in 2014, compared to 47 per cent at the turn of the century. The jury is still out on whether and how fast the rebalancing can be done and a large and vibrant domestic consumer market can be created without facing financial turmoil and/or a sharp slowdown of growth.

After the global financial crisis Germany replaced China as a major surplus country with its exports almost rising constantly relative to imports, also helped by the weakening euro. In almost every year since the crisis growth of domestic demand in Germany continued to remain below that of GDP (Table 1.3). The contribution of the public sector to aggregate demand remained below the levels seen before the crisis while stagnant real wages resulted in a decline in private consumption as a percentage of GDP. As a result the German surplus rose from some 5 per cent of GDP to more than 8 per cent after the crisis while China's current account surplus dropped from a peak of 10 per cent to 2–3 per cent. Before the onset of the Eurozone crisis, the region's current account with the rest of the world was in balance and an important part of German surplus was with other Eurozone countries, notably the periphery countries with large current account deficits. Since the crisis, the German surplus increased while the region as a whole moved to a surplus with the rest of the world, by 3 per cent of its combined GDP.

It is not clear if Germany can keep relying on foreign demand to fill the domestic demand gap at a time when growth in the US remains sluggish,

China and most other EDEs are slowing and the rest of the Eurozone is still trying to complete its recovery from the crisis. German surplus is unsustainable because it is a problem almost for everybody (Bernanke 2015c; Tilford 2015). It is sucking demand from the rest of the world while imposing deflationary adjustment on the Eurozone periphery. Given its size and role in Europe, the attempt by Germany to overcome underconsumption by exporting unemployment is no more sustainable than was the rapid export-led growth of China. It is incompatible with economic and political stability in the Eurozone. More generally, for large economies export surpluses cannot provide a viable solution to the systemic problem of underconsumption because they face the problem of fallacy of composition and breed conflict.

To sum up, neither financial bubbles nor export surpluses constitute sustainable solutions to underconsumption in major advanced economies and China. Nor is it possible to stimulate productive private investment to fill the demand gap through interest rate adjustments. The solution is to be found in the reversal of the secular decline in the share of labour in income so as to reignite a wage-led growth (Onaran and Stockhammer 2016; Lavoie and Stockhammer 2012). This is the only secure way to create inflation that many central banks are striving but unable to achieve in order to lower the real interest rate. How this can be best done naturally varies from country to country but should include significant increases in minimum wages as well as across-the-board increases in compensations in both public and private sectors. The spectre of yet another crisis and recession has prompted governments in some advanced economies to move in this direction in order to reflate demand (Sandbu 2016). Whether or not these initiatives will go far enough to meet the challenge remains to be seen.

What role should the public sector play in overcoming underconsumption? Since there is a structural demand gap, the additional public spending needed to fill the gap should be permanent. That means bigger government. But this does not imply that the public sector should run a higher level of debt. As noted, this could be self-defeating by causing higher interest rates and creating sustainability problems. To avoid this, higher levels of public spending should be financed by permanently higher taxes on top income groups rather than by borrowing from them. This would have the same effect on aggregate demand as redistributing income from the rich to the poor. Since the balance between labour and capital cannot be restored overnight, greater attention would need to be given to redistribution through the budget.

2

Spillovers to the Global South

2.1 Decoupling and Recoupling

At the end of the 1990s and the early 2000s, many economies in the developing world were in disarray. East Asia was still recovering from the 1997 crisis while a host of other EDEs were falling into payments and financial crises one after another; Brazil and Russia in 1998, Turkey 2000–01 and Argentina 2001–02. The prospects for the global economy were dimmed by the bursting of the dot-com bubble in the US at the beginning of the decade, coming on top of prolonged deflation in Japan, and uneven and erratic growth and uncertainties produced by the Monetary Union in Europe.

For the entire period from 1990 to 2002, EDEs taken together grew by only one percentage point faster than advanced economies and in per capita terms there was hardly any income convergence. The picture was even worse in the 1980s when a large number of EDEs were suffering from severe payments difficulties caused by a debt overhang and sharp declines in commodity prices. Until the new millennium the only major economy in the South that was able to close the income gap with advanced economies significantly was China, with an average growth rate close to 10 per cent during 1990–2002 compared to less than 4 per cent in the rest of the developing world.

This picture changed in the new millennium. From 2002 until the outbreak of the subprime crisis, the growth difference between the EDEs and advanced economies shot up to 5 percentage points (see Figure 2.1). This was not because of slowdown in advanced economies, but acceleration in EDEs where the growth rate doubled from the 1990s. This was unprecedented. During the post-war golden age EDEs had also grown at a very rapid pace, by some 6 per cent per annum, but growth in advanced economies was also high and the margin was no more than a couple of percentage points.

The acceleration was not just due to China—its growth rate during the 1990s was also very high; 9.6 per cent over 1990–2002 compared to 11.6 per cent during 2003–07. It was broad-based but with significant variations among

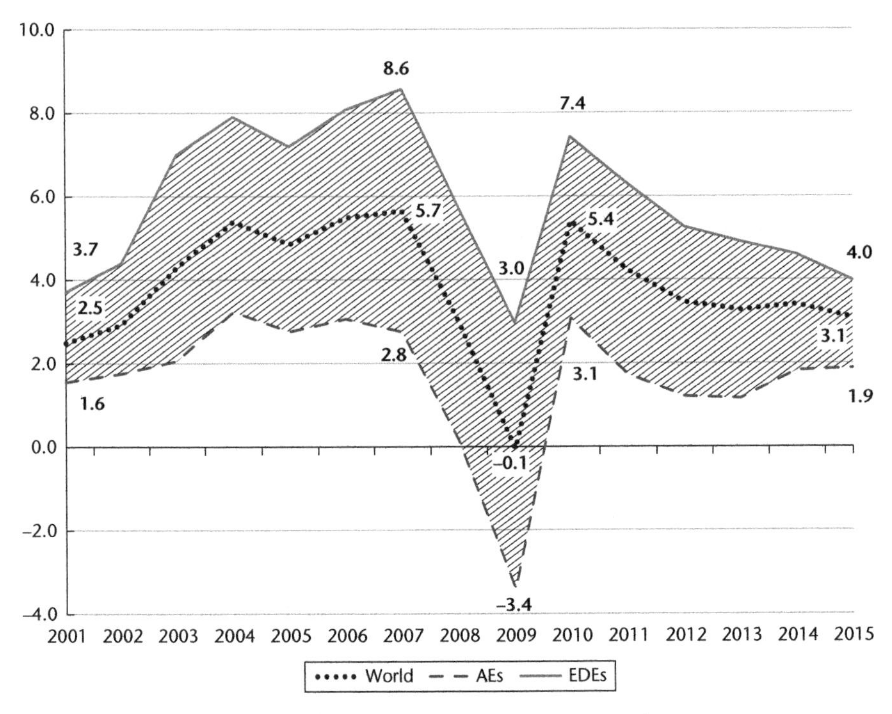

Figure 2.1 Real output growth (per cent)
Source: IMF WEO (2016).

regions and countries. Acceleration was faster in Africa than the two other regions even though African growth continued to remain below Asia. The Western Hemisphere saw only a modest rise compared to the 1990s. Fuel exporters had faster acceleration than either the exporters of non-fuel commodities or manufactures. Acceleration was also rapid in countries recovering from severe crises that had occurred in the late 1990s and early 2000s such as Russia, Argentina, and Turkey.

The global crisis led to a loss of momentum in EDEs, but they still maintained some 3 per cent growth in 2009 while advanced economies went into a deep recession. Their recovery was also much more vigorous than advanced economies. However, they never regained the pre-crisis momentum but started to slow, particularly after 2011. Although advanced economies failed to achieve a strong and sustained recovery after the 2009 recession, the slowdown was more marked in EDEs and their growth converged downward towards the rate in advanced economies. By the end of 2015, the growth differential had come down to 2 percentage points, from a peak of almost 6 percentage points in 2007.

Rapid acceleration of growth in EDEs and relatively weak performance of advanced economies before the crisis was widely interpreted as decoupling of the South from the North. After the crisis the combination of rapid recovery of EDEs with stagnation and faltering growth in advanced economies not only revived the decoupling hypothesis, but also created a widespread belief that major EDEs, notably China and to a lesser extent India and Brazil, would play a key role in taking the world economy out of recession.

Decoupling in the sense that the economic performance of the South has become independent of conditions in the North would be quite implausible in view of increasingly closer global integration of EDEs. Indeed, as discussed in Akyüz (2012), evidence shows that the deviations of economic activity from underlying trends continue to be highly correlated between EDEs and advanced economies. This was also evident during the post-Lehman downturn when a large majority of EDEs experienced a significant slowdown despite a strong counter-cyclical policy response.

A more fundamental question is whether there was an upward shift in the trend (potential) growth of EDEs relative to advanced economies and a secular acceleration of convergence. After examining the role played by domestic and external factors in the acceleration of growth in EDEs in the new millennium and their rapid recovery from the crisis, Akyüz (2012) concluded that even though there were improvements in macroeconomic management in many EDEs after the recurrent crises of the 1990s and early 2000s, their impressive economic performance before and immediately after the global crisis were driven by exceptionally favourable but unsustainable global conditions rather than improved growth fundamentals. It also warned that the failure to make a correct assessment of respective roles of external and domestic factors in the superior performance of EDEs could lead to complacency and increase their exposure to shocks.

Until 2013 the IMF was a major advocate of the decoupling thesis. Its analysis and projections show significant shortcomings in its grasp of growth fundamentals in the South and their global linkages. The IMF did not only underestimate the depth of the crisis, but also its impact on EDEs, maintaining that the dependence of growth in the South on the North had significantly weakened (IMF WEO 2007 and 2008). After 2010 it constantly over-projected growth in EDEs: IMF WEO (2011) projected 6.5 per cent growth for 2012, this was revised downward to 6.1 in September 2011, 5.7 per cent in April 2012 and 5.3 in October 2012. A large proportion of forecast errors pertained to larger EDEs, notably BRICS that had been expected to become locomotives for the world economy (IMF WEO 2014b: Box 1.2).

The IMF 'refined' its position on the question of decoupling in IMF (WEO 2012: chap. 4) under 'Resilience in Emerging Market and Developing Economies: Will it last?' In a quantitative analysis, lumping together more than 100 EDEs with per capita incomes ranging from $200 to over $20,000 and examining their evolution over the past 60 years, it concluded that '[t]hese economies did so well during the past decade that for the first time, [they] spent more time in expansion and had smaller downturns than advanced economies. Their improved performance is explained by both good policies and a lower incidence of external and domestic shocks: better policies account for about three-fifths of their improved performance, and less-frequent shocks account for the rest' (p. 129).

However, when growth outcomes for EDEs continued to frustrate, the IMF (WEO 2013a: 19) recognized the possibility that 'forecast disappointments are symptomatic of deeper, structural problems.' In a subsequent report submitted to the St Petersburg meeting of the G20, the Fund 'dropped its view that emerging economies were the dynamic engine of the world economy' in a 'humbling series of U-turns over its global economic assessment' (Giles 2013). It came to the conclusion that the 'world's economies moved much more in lockstep during the peak of the global financial crisis than at any other time in recent decades...The increased comovement...was observed across all geographic regions and among advanced, emerging market, and developing economies' (IMF WEO 2013b: 81). Finally, IMF (WEO 2015: chap. 3) discovered that while potential growth declined both in advanced and emerging market economies, the decline was more pronounced in the latter, by some 2 percentage points after the crisis, mainly due to lower total factor productivity growth. The decline was also expected to continue in the medium term. There is, however, no indication if and to what extent this was due to a reversal of 'good policies' that the Fund had identified less than three years ago as the main factor in the upturn of the trend growth of EDEs in pre-crisis years.

2.2 The Commodity–Finance Nexus

Changes in conditions in international commodity and financial markets have played a central role in variations in growth performance of EDEs in the new millennium and these conditions are largely shaped by policies in major advanced economies and China. Both commodity prices and capital inflows to EDEs started to rise sharply in the early 2000s; both booms were interrupted briefly by the Lehman collapse in 2008; recovery was quick in both cases; commodity prices started to soften in 2011 and then collapsed while the boom in capital inflows continued until 2014 when they first moderated and then fell sharply (See Figure 2.2 and Figure 2.3).

However, the causality between growth in EDEs and booms in commodity prices and capital inflows ran in both directions. Not only did favourable conditions in commodity and financial markets bring faster growth in EDEs, but faster growth also fed into higher commodity prices by raising demand and into higher capital inflows by increasing profit opportunities for international capital. When commodity prices and capital flows were reversed, a

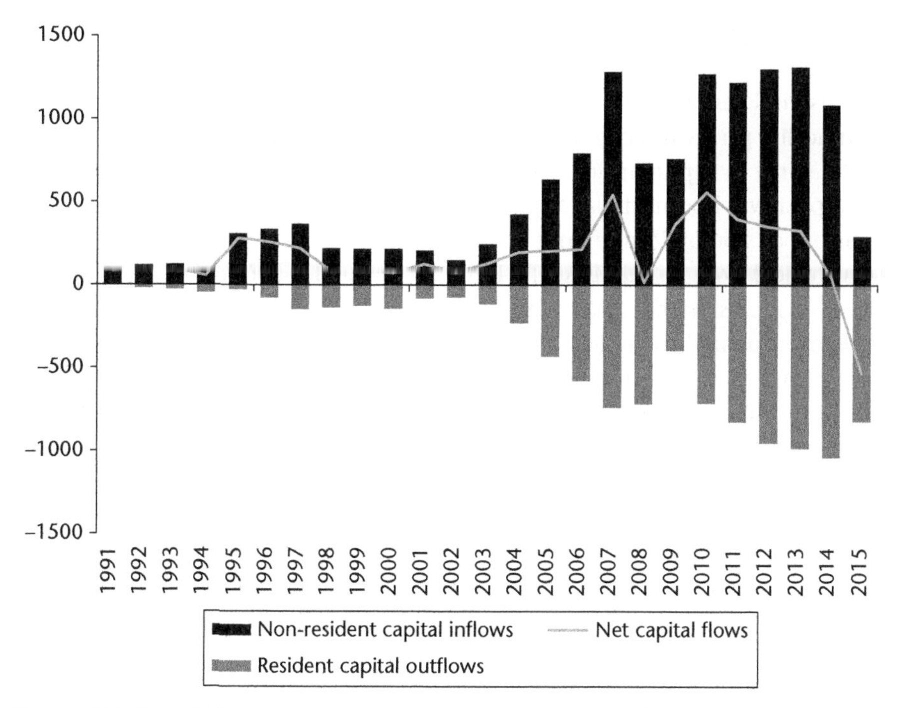

Figure 2.2 Capital flows to emerging economies (in billions of US dollars)

Note: Resident capital outflows exclude reserves.

Source: IIF Capital Flows to Emerging Markets (various issues).

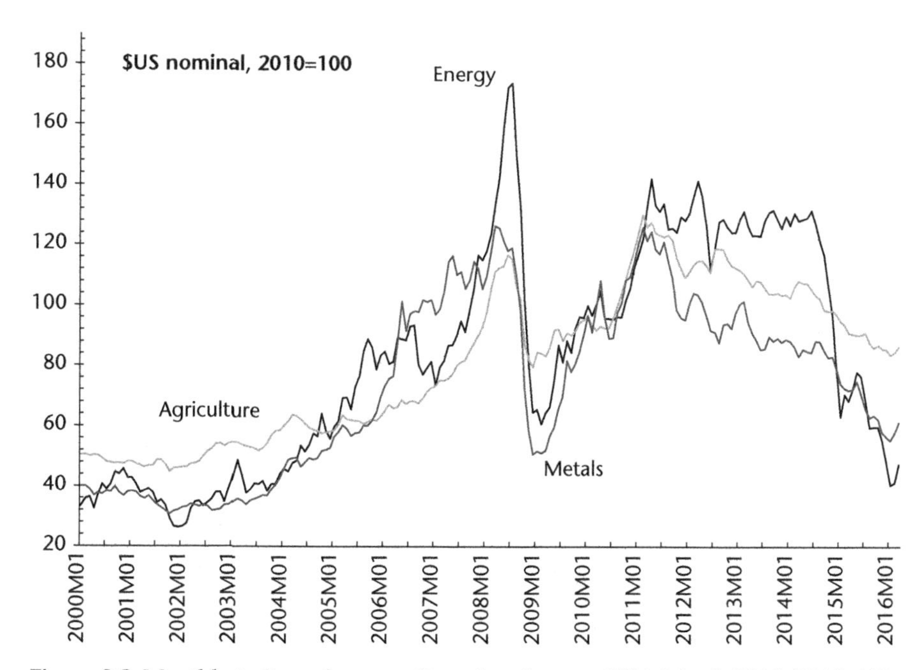

Figure 2.3 Monthly indices of commodity prices, January 2001–March 2016 (2010=100, in US dollars)

Source: World Bank Commodity Price Data.

vicious circle emerged whereby declining growth in the South led to weaker commodity prices and capital inflows which in turn weakened growth further.

The surge in capital inflows to EDEs that started in the early 2000s was the third post-war boom. It was triggered by exceptionally low interest rates and rapid expansion of liquidity not only in the US which had brought policy rates to historical lows for fear that the bursting of the dot-com bubble would lead to a deep recession, but also in Europe and Japan (Akyüz 2011b). The surge was also accompanied by rapidly narrowing risk spreads of EDEs due to a significantly improved risk appetite for lending and investment in these economies. The boom in commodity prices started at more or less the same time. It was widely seen as the beginning of a new commodity super-cycle driven by rapid growth and urbanization in China (Farooki and Kaplinsky 2011).

Although there are specific factors affecting commodity and financial cycles, they are not independent of each other. For several reasons there is a strong positive correlation between commodity prices and private capital inflows to EDEs (see Figure 2.4). On the one hand, the factors that affect capital inflows to EDEs, notably monetary conditions and interest rates in major advanced economies and the strength of the dollar, also have a strong influence on commodity prices (Bastourre et al. 2013). Low interest rates tend to encourage stock piling and discourage rate of exploitation of oil and minerals, thereby

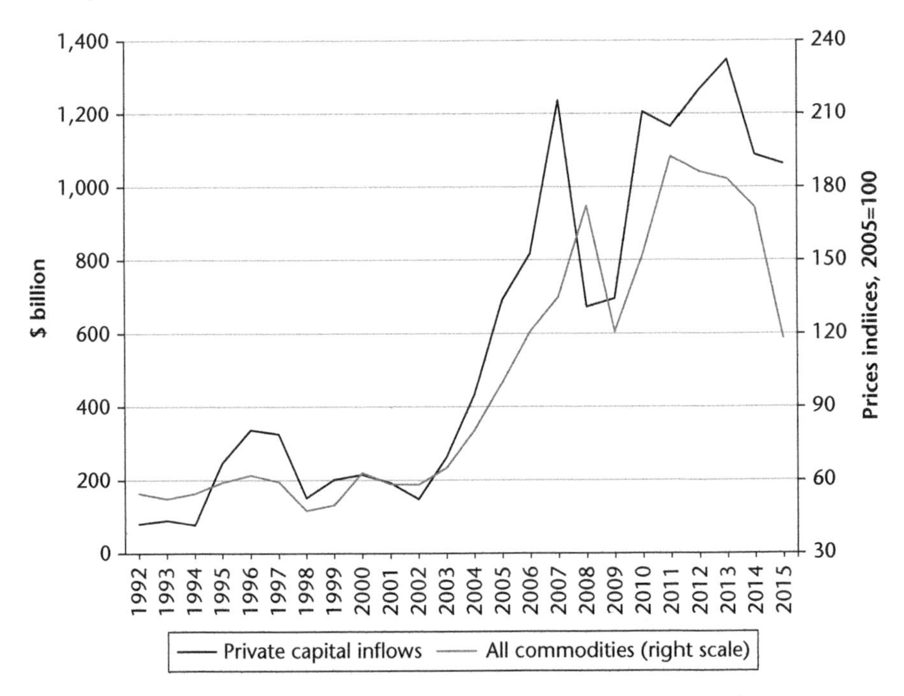

Figure 2.4 Private capital inflows to emerging economies and commodity prices
Source: IIF (2015) and IMF Primary Commodity Prices dataset.

raising demand relative to supply and pushing up prices. An increase in interest rates has the opposite effect, reducing the demand for storable commodities and the incentive for extraction today rather than tomorrow, thereby reducing prices (Frankel 2006).

Interest rates also have a strong impact on prices through trading in commodity derivatives. This has gained importance in the new millennium as commodity markets have become more like financial markets, with several commodities being treated as a distinct asset class and attracting growing amounts of money in search for profits from price movements. Low interest rates encourage speculators to shift into commodity derivatives, particularly when prices are on an upward trend, adding further to the price momentum. This was an important factor in the strength of commodity prices before the crisis. But when sentiments turn sour regarding future commodity price movements and/or interest rates, financialization can also result in rapid and self-fulfilling declines. This was most visible at the outset of the subprime crisis in 2008 when the overall commodity price index rose by 35 per cent in the first six months of the year followed by a decline of 55 per cent in the second half.[1]

The exchange rate of the dollar also has a relatively strong influence on commodity prices. Since a large proportion of commodities are priced in dollars, shifts in the exchange rate of the dollar alter the price of commodities in other currencies, thereby affecting overall demand. There is indeed a remarkable inverse correlation between the nominal effective exchange rate of the dollar and commodity prices in the new millennium (see Figure 2.5).

On the other hand, strong commodity prices tend to lower risk spreads and encourage lending to and investment in commodity economies and sectors. For instance, it is estimated that in 2015 the total debt of the oil and gas sector globally stood at roughly $2.5 trillion, two and a half times what it was at the end of 2006. A substantial part of the increased borrowing was by state-owned major integrated oil firms from EDEs. Between 2006 and 2014, the stock of total borrowing, including syndicated loans and debt securities, of Russian companies grew at an annual rate of 13 per cent. The figure was 25 per cent for Brazilian companies and 31 per cent for Chinese companies (Domanski et al. 2015).

Briefly, commodity and financial cycles reinforce each other in several ways. Expansion of liquidity and low interest rates in advanced economies and a weak dollar trigger surges in capital inflows to EDEs and push commodity

[1] See Akyüz (2011b) for further discussion. According to Filimonov et al. (2013), price dynamics of highly traded future commodity markets, including for corn, oil, soybean, sugar, and wheat, are driven by self-reinforcing mechanisms (short-term endogeneity) rather than novel information about factors affecting supply and demand conditions. It is found that endogeneity increased in the 2000s and that about 60–70 per cent of price changes were due to self-generated activities.

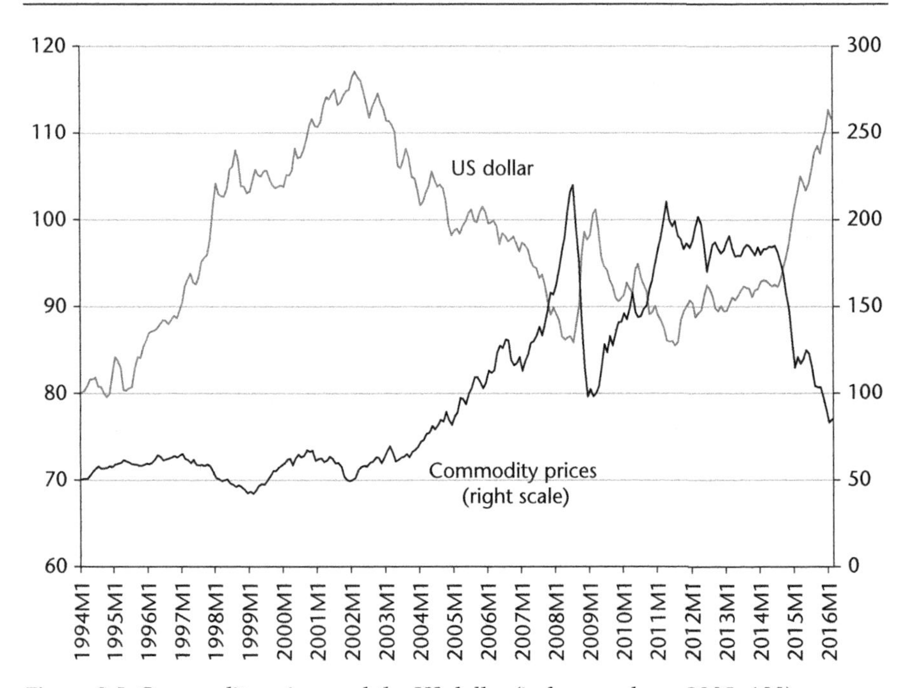

Figure 2.5 Commodity prices and the US dollar (index numbers, 2005=100)
Source: BIS Nominal effective exchange rates dataset and IMF Primary Commodity Prices dataset.

prices upward simultaneously. While rising prices lead to higher capital inflows by reducing risk spreads and increasing lending and investment in commodity-dependent countries, higher capital inflows to EDEs in turn raise commodity demand by generating a boom in domestic spending. This latter effect tends to be particularly strong since the commodity content of growth in EDEs is high compared to that in advanced economies. During downturns this commodity–finance nexus operates in the opposite direction. Declines in commodity price discourage capital inflows, which in turn reduce growth and demand and put further downward pressures on commodity prices.

The combined boom in commodity prices and capital inflows up until the global crisis resulted in a staggering but unsustainable rise of the South (Akyüz 2012). Although these booms were not always prudently managed, they provided significant policy space to EDEs by improving their fiscal, balance-of-payments, and international reserve positions which allowed them to give a strong countercyclical response to fallouts from the global crisis. On the other hand, China's policy response to the crisis through massive investment in infrastructure and property to offset the decline of its exports provided a major boost to commodity producers. Finally, despite occasional protests by emerging economies against the pressures placed on their currencies by the ultra-easy monetary policy in major advanced economies, the impact of that policy on emerging economies was generally reflationary. It was instrumental in the quick recovery of private capital inflows after the Lehman collapse, and this allowed many deficit EDEs to expand domestic demand without facing payments constraints.

These three factors, the countercyclical policy response of EDEs to the crisis, the renewed boom in capital inflows and the sharp recovery in commodity prices thus explain why these economies were resilient to the crisis and could maintain a relatively high growth despite a deep recession and lacklustre recovery in advanced economies. But this soon came to an end with the collapse of commodity prices and a sharp drop in capital inflows, particularly since EDEs no longer enjoyed the policy space they had during 2008–09 to respond to such shocks.

2.3 Financial Spillovers

Although the boom in non-resident private capital inflows to emerging economies that began in the early years of the 2000s came to an end with the flight to safety triggered by the Lehman collapse in September 2008, the recovery was quick thanks to the ultra-easy monetary policy in the US and Europe and shifts in risk perceptions against advanced economies. During 2010–13 in absolute amounts total capital inflows were slightly below the peak reached in 2007, but they were much lower as a per cent of GDP of the recipient countries—around 5 per cent compared to over 8 per cent in 2007. This relative weakness of total private capital inflows was due in large part to sharp drops in inflows to European emerging economies due to fallouts from the Eurozone crisis. By contrast, inflows to Asia and Latin America exceeded the peaks reached before the crisis. But they started falling in 2014 everywhere and took a sharp dive in 2015, to a third of the level recorded in 2009 at the depth of the subprime crisis (IIF 2016).

The period since the crisis has also seen a significant acceleration of resident outflows. Governments not only allowed such outflows by liberalizing the capital account for residents, but also occasionally encouraged residents to invest abroad in order to relieve the pressure exerted by surges in inflows on the exchange rate. Until 2014 non-resident inflows exceeded resident outflows and net capital flows were positive. On average they were above the levels recorded in the run-up to the crisis, but on a downward trend because of a stronger growth in resident outflows. The downward trend in net capital flows was more pronounced as a proportion of GDP.

This picture started to change in 2014 when non-resident inflows fell sharply while resident outflows remained strong. As a result, for the first time in many years, net capital flows became negative. The turnaround in 2015 was even more dramatic when inflows collapsed while the decline in outflows was moderate. Much of the decline in inflows was due to a deep cutback in net international lending. Thus, in 2015 there was a net capital outflow of some $750 billion. A large proportion of these (about $675 billion) were from China, mainly due to dollar debt repayments of its corporations in an effort to avoid losses from declines in the exchange rate of the RMB. There was also an acceleration of capital flight by Chinese residents. In many emerging economies, notably in LA, however, net flows remained positive.

The combined current account of the emerging economies included in Figure 2.2 has been in surplus since the crisis, though on a downward trend. As a result of twin surpluses on the current and capital accounts, until 2014 the international reserves of emerging economies increased but at a declining rate (see Figure 2.6). The increase continued in 2014 even though net flows became negative thanks to a relatively large current account surplus. However, the collapse of inflows in 2015 resulted in a sharp drop in reserves, by some $500 billon, because the combined current account surpluses of these countries were not enough to meet outflows. About two-thirds of this drop was due to China. This was the first decline in reserves in the new millennium—even at the depth of the crisis when inflows fell sharply, emerging economies had continued to add to their international reserves.

Changes in capital flows since the onset of the crisis caused significant instability in asset and currency markets and policies regarding capital flows

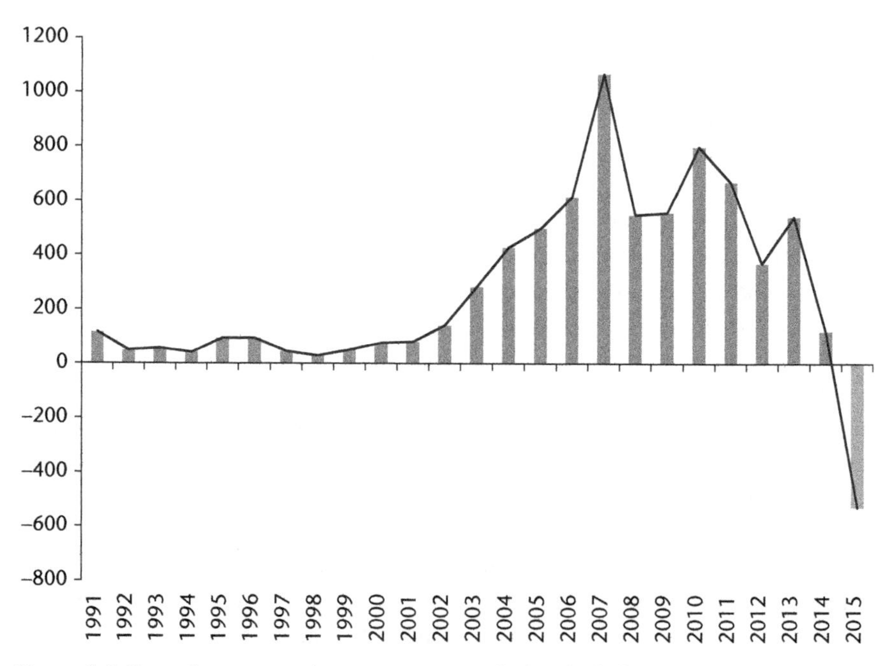

Figure 2.6 Emerging economies reserve accumulation (in billions of US dollars)
Source: IIF Capital Flows to Emerging Markets (various issues).

in emerging economies. The surge in 2010 led to a strong recovery in exchange rates and equity prices in most major emerging economies which had come under severe pressures in the immediate aftermath of the Lehman collapse (see Figure 2.7 and Figure 2.8). Governments generally welcomed the recovery of capital inflows and the boom in stock markets, but many of them, notably in deficit emerging economies, were ambivalent about the strong upward pressure they exerted on exchange rates. The ultra-easy monetary policies in advanced economies came to be seen as an attempt for beggar-thy-neighbour competitive devaluations to boost exports to drive recovery in conditions of sluggish domestic demand. It was described as a 'currency war' by the Brazilian Minister of Finance while the Governor of the South African Reserve Bank alluded that EDEs were in effect caught in a cross-fire between the ECB and the US Federal Reserve (Marcus 2012).

Asian emerging economies generally intervened in foreign exchange markets, adding to reserves and trying to sterilize interventions by issuing government debt, thereby avoiding sharp appreciations and overheating. Others, particularly those pursuing inflation targeting, such as Brazil and Turkey, abstained from extensive interventions and experienced considerable appreciations during 2009–11. As the upward pressure on currencies persisted, however, several emerging economies abandoned the hands-off

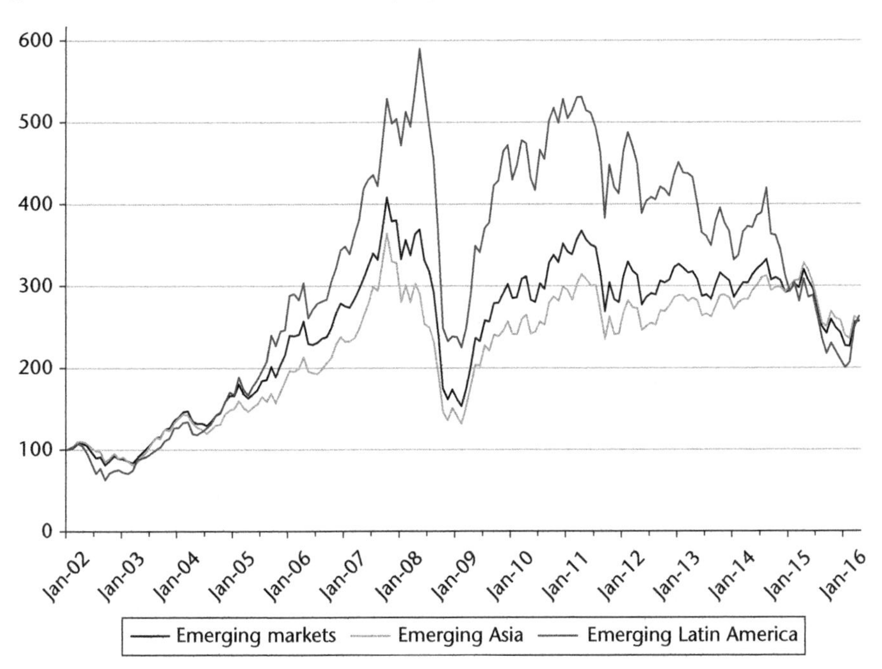

Figure 2.7 Monthly MSCI equity market indices, January 2002–April 2016 (January 2002=100)
Source: MSCI.

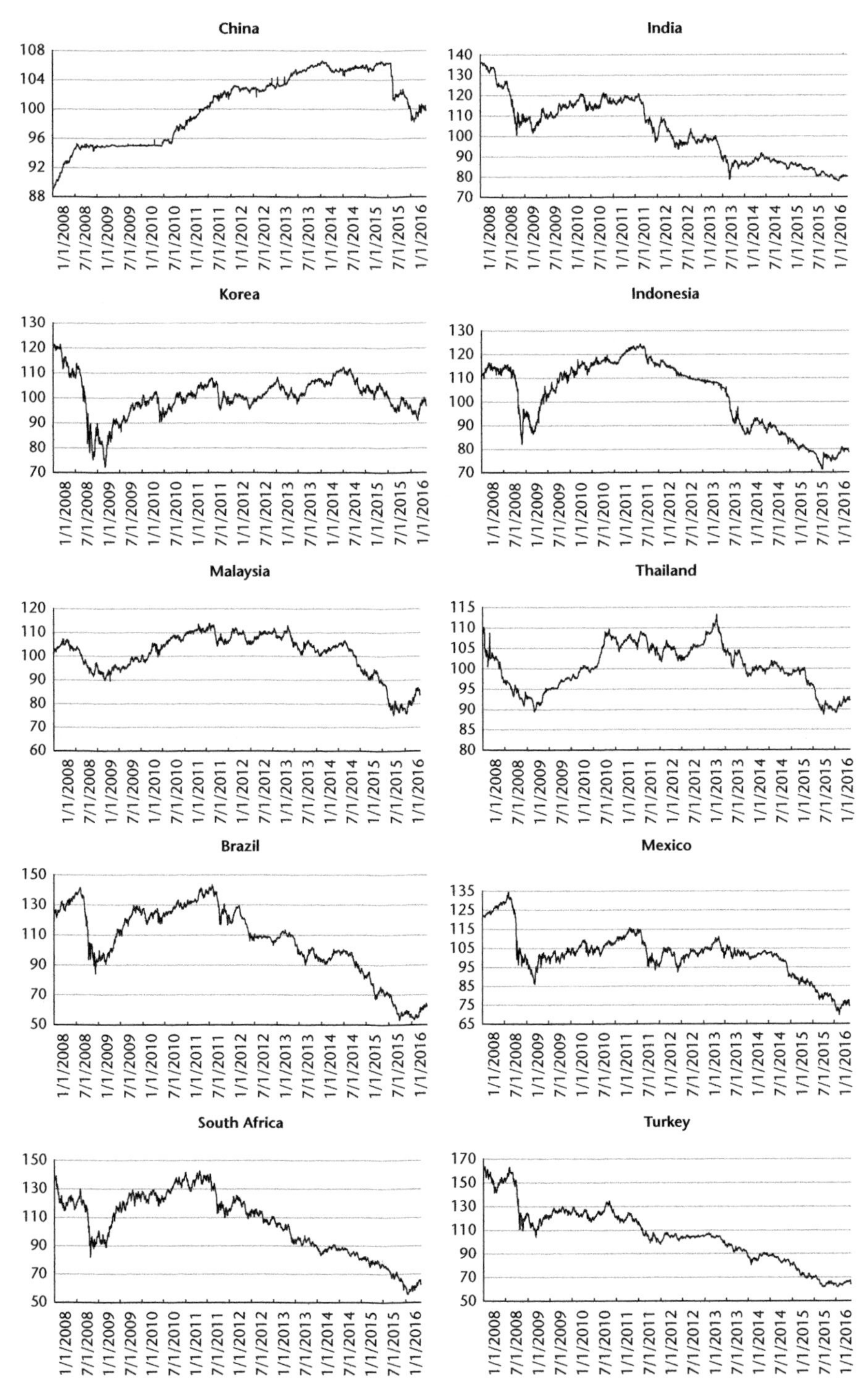

Figure 2.8 Nominal exchange rates in selected economies against the US dollar (period average=100)

Source: OANDA.

approach to inflows and started to control them, generally using market-friendly measures rather than direct restrictions.

Given strong destabilizing impulses generated by capital flows, the IMF also felt obliged to reconsider its position about capital account liberalization. It recognized that there might be circumstances when capital movements may need to be restricted, but such measures need to be deployed only as a last resort and on a temporary basis. 'For countries that have to manage the macroeconomic and financial stability risks associated with inflow surges or disruptive outflows, a key role needs to be played by macroeconomic policies, including monetary, fiscal, and exchange rate management' (IMF 2012: 1–2). This position is highly questionable since there is no strong rationale for an economy to alter its macroeconomic policies when faced with an externally generated temporary surge in capital flows if these policies are judiciously designed to secure stability and growth, and debt and balance-of-payments sustainability. For such an economy, capital controls can indeed be the first best measures to insulate domestic conditions from externally generated destabilizing pressures.

Interestingly the country that made the most frequent recourse to control measures is Korea, a member of the OECD and hence is subject to provisions of its Code of Liberalization of Capital Movements (Singh 2010). It introduced various measures in 2010 to control inflows including ceilings on forex forward positions of banks, a levy on non-deposit liabilities and a withholding tax on interest income from foreign holdings of treasuries and monetary stabilization bonds. The Korean won was one of the weakest currencies in the aftermath of the crisis. Its effective exchange rate never went back to pre-crisis levels, eliciting remarks that, together with the UK, it is the most aggressive 'currency warrior' of the past five and a half years (Ferguson 2013).

Several market-friendly measures were used to control capital inflows in Brazil, Peru, Colombia, India, Indonesia, and Thailand. These included unremunerated reserve requirements; taxes on portfolio inflows and foreign purchases of central bank paper; minimum stay or holding periods for inward FDI and central banks papers; special reserve requirements and taxes on banks' short positions; higher reserve requirements for non-resident local currency deposits; taxes and restrictions over private borrowing abroad; additional capital requirements for forex credit exposure; and withholding taxes on interest income and capital gains from domestic bonds. Some emerging economies such as South Africa liberalized outflows by residents in order to relieve the upward pressure on the currency.

These measures were designed mainly to prevent currency appreciations rather than asset and debt bubbles. Not only did most emerging economies welcome the bubbles in asset markets, but they also ignored the build-up of vulnerability resulting from increased corporate borrowing abroad.

The measures were not always effective in limiting the volume of inflows as exceptions were made in several areas. In many cases the composition of inflows changed towards longer maturities and types of investment not covered by measures. Taxes and other restrictions imposed were also too weak to match arbitrage margins. Implementation capacity was limited in many countries and the sanctions attached to violation did not have a strong deterrent effect.

In any case these measures did not last long. Net capital flows as a per cent of GDP started to fall after 2011 while external financing needs of emerging economies increased. Even though growth in most countries slowed, current account deficits widened as a proportion of GDP. Thus, the need for foreign capital increased just as inflows became weaker and unstable. These led first to an easing and then a reversal of the upward pressure on the currencies and asset markets in emerging economies (Figure 2.7 and Figure 2.8). Capital controls over inflows were dismantled and protests against the ultra-easy monetary policy in advanced economies vanished. Some countries have even introduced measures to attract more foreign capital.

The response to sharp drops in net flows in 2014–15 varied. In general a trade-off emerged between currency and reserve declines. Several emerging economies with large current account deficits such as Brazil, South Africa, and Turkey refrained from interventions in foreign exchange markets and allowed their currencies to take the burden. This limited reserve losses but led to large depreciations, thereby creating difficulties for private debtors with currency mismatches. Others with comfortable reserve positions, notably China, intervened to restrain depreciations. Monetary policy was tightened in Argentina, Chile, Colombia, Mexico, and South Africa despite growth slowdown. Selective controls on outflows have been introduced in Azerbaijan, Egypt, India, Saudi Arabia, Venezuela, and China (Cui 2016; Wildau 2016). However, there has not been a widespread resort to exchange restrictions because it has so far been possible to absorb the shocks through currency depreciations and/or use of reserves.

China's experience in this respect is particularly notable. In an effort to promote the RMB as an international currency and support its inclusion in the SDR basket, in 2015 China accelerated the liberalization of its capital account. On 11 August 2015, the People's Bank of China also allowed greater freedom to markets in the determination of the exchange rate of the RMB, but simultaneously undertook the largest one-day devaluation of the RMB in two decades, followed by another one the next day. However, as outflows started growing and the RMB came under pressure in the latter part of the year, the authorities tried to restrain the depreciation by interventions in the currency market, losing large amounts of reserves. They also tried to restrict outflows through moral suasion, urging banks to limit sale of dollars, by temporarily suspending forex business for some foreign banks, suspending applications for certain outbound investment and implementing a reserve requirement ratio on offshore banks' domestic deposits. China's control over outflows found support from one of its major trading partners affected by weaker RMB. The governor of the Bank of Japan Kuroda is reported to have suggested that '[c]apital controls could be useful to manage [China's] exchange rate as well as domestic monetary policy in a constructive way' (Giles 2016). This is an important change of heart regarding the freedom to be allowed to currency markets in determining the exchange rate—for, when China had intervened in the past to limit the appreciation of the RMB it was accused of currency manipulation.

The trend in capital flows to emerging economies since the crisis has been dampened by instabilities and uncertainties created by a series of events in advanced economies. First, they became particularly sensitive to news coming from the Eurozone. From mid-2011, market sentiments turned sour with the deepening of the Greek crisis, strikes and political turmoil in the periphery, and credit downgrading, leading to downturn in inflows. Global risk appetite improved in the early months of 2012 with the agreement on the European Stability Mechanism (ESM) and austerity packages in Greece and Spain, the implementation of the Long-Term Refinancing Operations, the signing of the Fiscal Compact and increased lending limits from the European Financial Stability Facility (EFSF) and ESM. However, markets became bearish again after spring 2012 when Spain requested assistance for bank capitalization, was downgraded by rating agencies and its yield spreads mounted, and concerns grew over Greece. This was followed by renewed optimism after mid-2012 with the commitment of the ECB to save the euro. However, the mood changed again with the confusion created by the Cypriot bail-out plan in March 2013.

Subsequently, starting in 2013, capital flows became sensitive to statements by US Federal Reserve officials about bond purchases and to economic data from the US. Ironically, weaker-than-expected growth and employment data often led to a rally in asset and currency markets of emerging economies, particularly those dependent on foreign capital, since they implied delays in tapering and normalization of monetary policy. This reflects that these countries were a lot more exposed to financial shocks from tapering and monetary tightening than to trade shock from sluggish growth in the US.

The pronouncements by the US Federal Reserve in May 2013 that it could start tapering in the summer triggered a hike in the ten-year treasury bond yield and a sharp decline in capital inflows to emerging economies. However, subsequent weaker economic data led the US Federal Reserve to postpone tapering and this gave a push to asset markets almost everywhere and to currencies of emerging economies. After relatively strong monthly job figures and increased concerns about the effectiveness and risks of QE, the US Federal Reserve decided in December 2013 to gradually end its monthly purchases in the course of 2014, starting with a modest reduction of $10 billion in January while signalling that the policy rates would not likely be changed much before the end of 2015.

The initial reaction of financial markets to the removal of uncertainty about tapering and the reassurance that historically low policy interest rates would stay two more years was positive. However, capital inflows started falling during the tapering of bond purchases by the US Federal Reserve between January 2014 and October 2014. The sharp fall in inflows in 2015 came before the US Federal Reserve raised the policy rate in December 2015 and was accompanied by double digit declines in the currencies and stocks of most emerging economies. It was caused by a loss of risk appetite and reflected in relatively large increases in spreads on emerging economies' bonds. Events such as the economic slowdown of China, sharp drops in Chinese stocks and devaluation of the RMB, economic and political crisis in Brazil, continued weaknesses of oil prices and, above all, growing mistrust about the ability of central bankers in advanced economies to take the world economy 'back to decent shape' led to a search for safety—the factors that also caused sharp drops in markets in advanced economies in early 2016. Although there is a considerable uncertainty about the direction of the world economy, projections for the period ahead are for continued capital outflows from emerging economies and further pressures in their asset and currency markets (IIF 2016).

2.4 The Global Crisis and Commodity Prices

The financial crisis in advanced economies did not depress commodity prices to the extent seen in previous post-war recessions. The boom that had started in 2003 continued until summer 2008 with the index for all primary commodities rising by more than threefold (Figure 2.3). This was followed by a steep downturn in the second half of 2008, which took the index back to the level of 2004. But like capital flows, commodity prices also recovered strongly from the beginning of 2009, rising until spring 2011 when they levelled off and started to fall, also manifesting increased short-term instability. In the early months of 2016, the index for all commodities was 60 per cent below the peak reached in 2011.

Different commodities that go into the aggregate index are not only linked to economic activity in different ways, but have also important supply-side differences.[2] Still, the co-movement among different commodity sub-categories

[2] Energy, which has the large weight of some 63 per cent in the overall index, is subject to geopolitical risks. Food, with a weight of some 17 per cent, is subject to supply disruptions due to

is greater than in the past and the turning points are broadly synchronized and highly correlated with global economic activity, particularly in EDEs. Rapid growth in major commodity-importing EDEs, notably China played a central role in the pre-crisis boom. Growth in commodity-dependent EDEs also added to the momentum by creating demand for each other's primary commodities. Prices increased along with the share of EDEs in world commodity consumption. Oil demand from EDEs rose to levels as high as that from advanced economies, with China importing as much as the Eurozone and twice as much as Japan. China has also come to account for almost half of global metal consumption.

After the outbreak of the financial crisis in advanced economies, the momentum in commodity prices was kept up entirely by growth in the South, notably in China whose import composition changed from manufactures to commodities as a result of its shift from exports to investment in infrastructure and property for growth. Since such investment is much more intensive in commodities, particularly in metals and energy, than exports of manufactures that rely heavily on imported parts and components, the shift resulted in a massive increase in Chinese primary commodity imports, which doubled between 2009 and 2011 while its manufactured imports rose by some 50 per cent.[3] During the same period the prices of metals rose 2.4 fold, much faster than other primary commodities.

The downturn in commodity prices that started in 2011 coincided with a slowdown in China and other EDEs. IMF (WEO 2013b: 25) finds a strong 'correlation between growth in commodity prices and growth in macroeconomic activity in emerging markets' and concludes that a 'slowdown in economic activity in emerging markets is an important driver of commodity price declines'. In particular the slowdown in China and the shift it started from investment towards consumption and from manufacturing towards services has had a strong impact because these activities are much less

weather conditions or crop infestation. Metals, the most important component of primary industrial inputs with a weight of over 10 per cent, are also subject to supply disruptions, largely due to social and political instability in the producing countries and regions. For a detailed account of the components of the overall commodity price index, see IMF WEO (2012, chap. 1; Special Feature: Commodity Market Review).

[3] UNEP (2013) estimates that in material use (including metal ores and industrial minerals, fossil fuels, construction minerals, and biomass) the Asia-Pacific region overtook the rest of the world by 2005, with China accounting for over 60 per cent of the region's total material consumption, and that during 2008, almost all of the growth in global material consumption was due to the Asia-Pacific region. It is found that material intensity, i.e. consumption of materials per dollar of GDP, is much higher in Asia-Pacific than in the rest of the world and has been increasing. While this may reflect inefficiency in the use of materials, as argued by UNEP, it is also true that material intensity depends on the composition of GDP, which changed in favour of material-intensive activities in China after the crisis.

commodity intensive than investment. This effect has been felt particularly in metal imports and prices.

While the prices for all commodities have been declining, some fell a lot more than others. The decline in energy prices from the peak in 2011 until the beginning of 2016 reached 71 per cent and in metal prices 60 per cent, but declines in agricultural raw materials and food and beverages were much more moderate, of the order of 30–35 per cent. This is mainly explained by supply behaviour. As noted in Section 2.2, the ultra-easy monetary policy in advanced economies encouraged significant borrowing by commodity economies and sectors and much of this money went into investment in highly capital-intensive commodities, notably energy and metals. In metals the investment boom that had started before the crisis continued until 2011. In energy the boom was led by US investment in shale oil and lasted until 2014 followed by sharp cuts. The same policy also generated property and/or consumption bubbles in EDEs and significant increases in commodity demand. However, the supply capacity generated by investment came into effect just as demand from EDEs started faltering. A massive excess supply has emerged as heavily indebted producers have continued to pump out in order to avoid default (Domanski et al. 2015).

Large differences in commodity price declines also imply that EDEs differ in their vulnerability depending on what they import and export. In this respect there are three broad categories of countries. The first category consists of countries which are net importers of fuel and non-fuel commodities, such as China, India, Korea, and Turkey. Clearly, commodity price declines have brought significant benefits to them. As seen in Table 2.1, these countries have had a positive swing in their current accounts since 2011. Although factors other than commodity prices have also played a role, the decline in energy prices on the trade balance has been particularly strong in deficit countries with large energy import bills such as Turkey and India. Again, this group of countries have seen a relatively smaller decline in their growth rates than exporters of fuel and non-fuel commodities.

Table 2.1 Commodity prices and swings in current account balances and GDP growth (2011–15)

	Current account (% of GDP)	Growth
All EDEs	− 2.1	−2.3
Fuel exporters	−14.5	−4.9
Non-fuel commodity exporters	−1.8	−3.2
All non-fuel exporters	1.2	−1.6

Source: IMF WEO database.

The second group consists of net exporters of fuel. Most of these are also net importers of other commodities including food and beverages and agricultural raw materials, as well as manufactures. This group includes MENA, Angola, and Nigeria in sub-Saharan Africa (SSA), and Bolivia, Colombia, Ecuador, and Venezuela in Latin America. They benefit from declines in the prices of the commodities they import, but they lose a lot more from declines in revenues from their fuel exports. Accordingly, this group has experienced the largest deterioration in their current account balance and the sharpest fall in their growth rates between 2011 and 2016.

The last group comes in between the two. They are net exporters of non-fuel commodities but net importers of fuel as well as manufactures. It includes Argentina, Chile, Nicaragua, Peru, and Uruguay in Latin America and Côte d'Ivoire, Malawi, Mali, South Africa, and Zambia in SSA. These countries, particularly exporters of metals such as Chile and Peru, also suffer from declines in the prices of their commodity exports. But they benefit more from fuel price declines, especially where the fuel bill accounts for a large proportion of spending on imports. Consequently, the deterioration in the current account positions of this group is smaller than that of fuel exporters. They have also experienced a more moderate decline in growth.

Naturally, the impact of commodity price declines on commodity-exporting EDEs does not only depend on the incidence of shocks but also on their underlying fundamentals and macroeconomic conditions. In this respect the way the preceding booms in commodity prices and capital flows were managed plays a key role (Adler and Sosa 2011). This is a main reason why growth losses vary significantly even among countries with similar trade structures. For instance two major exporters of fuel in Latin America, Venezuela and Bolivia, are in totally different positions regarding external sustainability and growth even though they suffered from similar terms-of-trade shocks. In the former country between 2011 and 2015 the current account deteriorated by 12.5 percentage points of GDP and growth came down from over 4 per cent to –5.7 per cent. Bolivia, on the other hand, is continuing to grow at a moderately lower rate than that achieved before the price collapse, at some 4 per cent, even though the deterioration in its current account was greater, by over 14 percentage points of GDP.

The booms in commodity prices and capital inflows in the new millennium were not always managed prudently by commodity-dependent EDEs (Akyüz 2012). Before the crisis fiscal policy was generally procyclical and the fiscal space used up during the crisis as a result of countercyclical policies was not rebuilt during the subsequent boom. Only a few countries such as Bolivia, Ecuador, and Botswana managed to increase their share in revenues from the commodity bonanza by successfully renegotiating royalties with transnational corporations (TNCs) and in most cases the benefits were reaped mainly by TNCs. With some notable exceptions such as Chile the stabilization funds set up did not always deliver when the reversal came after 2011. In several countries including Angola, Brazil, Chile, Colombia, Indonesia, Nigeria, Russia, South Africa, Venezuela, and Zambia real exchange rates appreciated, by 50 per cent and even more in some. An important part of the reserves accumulated came from capital inflows rather than current account surpluses. Many commodity economies typically dependent on official lending including Bolivia, Ecuador, Ethiopia, Gabon, Ghana, Nigeria, Rwanda, Senegal, Tanzania, Zambia went to international markets to benefit from low interest rates and improved risk appetite and issued for the first time dollar-denominated bonds while commodity-dependent emerging economies such as Brazil and Russia allowed significant build-up of private external debt in dollars. The current account positions worsened in many countries despite price boom (Argentina, Brazil, Chile, Colombia, Peru, Venezuela, Congo, Ghana, Tanzania, Russia, and Indonesia). Only a few countries managed to improve domestic savings and investment ratios and current account positions, and there has been very little investment in non-traditional sectors to reduce commodity dependence. Some semi-industrialized economies such as Brazil and Malaysia allowed their industries to be undermined by the commodity boom, experiencing significant declines in the share of manufacturing in GDP and exports.

Despite all the rhetoric about industrialization, the growth story in the South, with some notable exceptions such as China, India, and Turkey, still remains a commodity story. The growth cycles of most countries continue to be governed by commodity cycles. In fact this is even more so than 10–20 years ago because of deindustrialization, which had already started in the 1990s before the boom in commodity prices in the new millennium (UNCTAD TDR 2003). The new twist is finance, but as discussed in Section 2.2, it is closely linked to commodities. Consequently, despite the benefits that large commodity importers such as China, India, and Turkey derive from the price reversal, the overall impact of the commodity collapse on the South is severely negative.

Usually declines in commodity prices, particularly oil prices, are expected to be reflationary for advanced economies and for the world economy as a whole because consumers are expected to increase spending while producers are expected to adjust savings (Rogoff 2015). But this has not been the case so far, at least to the extent anticipated. First, producers in the South have been retrenching. This is true even for some richer oil exporters in the Gulf which typically had avoided spending cuts in past downturns. Second, households in advanced economies are not increasing spending by using the savings on the energy bill (Leduc et al. 2016). Third, commodity prices are pushing prices down in advanced economies at a time when central banks are trying to create inflation in order to lower the real interest rates and stimulate private spending. Finally, many commodity producers which accumulated large amounts of debt after 2008 have started deleveraging and cutting investment spending with the decline in prices. Thus, the collapse of oil prices cannot be expected to bring much reflation to the world economy until consumers in advanced economies start spending the large gains from price declines. But this depends very much on the success of policy-makers in these economies to boost consumer confidence.

2.5 Conclusions: Reorienting Policies

Most emerging and developing economies have not only lost their growth momentum but find themselves in a tenuous position with an uncanny similarity to the 1970s and 1980s when the combined booms in capital flows and commodity prices that had started in the second half of the 1970s ended with a debt crisis as a result of a sharp turnaround in the US monetary policy, costing them a decade in development. They have been facing strong deflationary and destabilizing pressures from the reversal of commodity prices and capital flows. In particular they have become highly vulnerable to external financial shocks as a result of their deepened integration into the international financial system—an issue to be examined in some detail in Chapter 3. If global financial conditions tighten significantly in the coming years, those with large external liabilities and deficits and/or a very strong presence of foreigners in domestic financial markets may find it extremely difficult, for the reasons discussed in Chapter 4, to restore 'confidence' and regain macroeconomic control simply by allowing their currencies to float, hiking interest rates or using reserves to finance outflows.

EDEs cannot really restore stability and growth with their own action alone and the responsibility for putting the world economy in a decent shape falls primarily on major advanced economies. They need to abandon fiscal orthodoxy and assume a central role in restoring global growth. The structural demand gap and the problem of underconsumption should be addressed by restoring the balance between labour and capital and increasing the share of lower income groups in national income. Since the balance between labour and capital cannot be restored overnight, greater attention would need to be given to redistribution through the budget by using taxes and transfers. China also needs to accelerate reforms to build a strong domestic consumer market by raising the share of households in income and rebalancing investment and consumption, and resist temptation to reignite strong growth by creating another bubble or to go back to export-led growth.

If global financial conditions tighten significantly, EDEs should not simply go back to business as usual and borrow from the IMF in order to remain current on their obligations to foreign creditors and investors and to keep their capital account open. They should, instead, seek to involve private lenders and investors in the resolution of liquidity and currency crises by introducing, inter alia, exchange restrictions and temporary debt standstills. These measures should be supported by the IMF, where necessary, through lending into arrears, but such lending should be for current account transactions and preventing import compression and contraction in economic activity.

The IMF lacks resources to effectively address any sharp contraction in international liquidity that may result from normalization of monetary policy in the US and/or a massive flight to safety. In any case major central banks, notably the US Federal Reserve, as the main originators of global financial fragility that now threatens the South, should assume responsibility for the provision of adequate international liquidity. This can be done through a large SDR allocation. The IMF can designate major central banks to purchase SDRs from EDEs who want to use the SDRs allocated to them. A decision can also be made to allocate SDRs only to EDEs or to non-SDR countries excluding Eurozone members. In this way, balance sheets of major central banks would be expanding by purchasing SDRs from those who want to use them. Alternatively, the US Federal Reserve and other major central banks can act directly as a quasi-international lender-of-last-resort to EDEs facing severe liquidity problems through outright purchase of locally and internationally issued sovereign bonds of these economies to shore up their prices and to provide liquidity. They could also establish swaps to supplement reserves of non-reserve issuing countries.

Finally, it would be extremely difficult to avoid debt crises after so many years of financial excesses and debt build-up. Should the world economy turn down and incomes collapse, an important part of the debt piled up since 2008 could become unpayable, notably the debt incurred by private residents and sovereigns in EDEs. The international community should not muddle through in resolving international debt crises, as done during the Latin American crisis in the 1980s and more recently in the Eurozone. Rather, they should seek orderly and equitable debt resolution along the lines discussed in Chapter 5 as to whether debt servicing difficulties are due to private or sovereign debt.

Part II

Internationalization of Finance and Changing Vulnerabilities in Emerging and Developing Economies

3

Deepening Integration

3.1 Factors Accelerating Financial Integration

After recurrent crises with severe economic and social consequences in the 1990s and early 2000s, emerging and developing economies (EDEs) have become even more closely integrated into what is now widely recognized as an inherently unstable international financial system.[1] The crisis that hit the US and Europe in 2008 did not slow this process despite initial fears that it could lead to a retreat from globalization (Altman 2009). Widespread liberalization of international capital flows and greater openness to foreign financial institutions in EDEs, together with growing optimism about the growth prospects of several of them, have played an important role in attracting foreign investors and banks to these economies. This process was greatly helped by highly favourable global financial conditions before 2008 thanks to the very same credit and spending bubbles that culminated in a severe crisis in the US and Europe. It has been continuing unabated since then because of ultra-easy monetary policies pursued in these economies, notably in the US, in response to the crisis, discussed at some length in Chapter 1.

A central factor in the acceleration of integration of EDEs into the international financial system is the surge in capital inflows that started in the early 2000s (see Figure 3.1).[2] This was the third post-war boom in capital inflows to EDEs. The first boom had started in the late 1970s and ended in 1982 with a

[1] EDEs correspond to what the IMF calls 'Emerging Market and Developing Economies'.

[2] Here capital flows are used for both inflows and outflows. *Capital inflows* refer to the net acquisition of domestic assets by *non-residents* where sales of assets are defined as negative inflows. *Capital outflows* refer to the net acquisition of foreign assets by *residents*, including foreign companies and individuals that have established residence in EDEs, and sales are defined as negative outflows. *Net capital flows* are the difference between capital inflows and capital outflows. Figure 3.1 is based on data from the Institute of International Finance (IIF) rather than the IMF since the IIF provides data on portfolio equity inflows for the entire period under consideration. These data cover the 30 largest countries which account for a very large proportion of total income and capital flows of EDEs.

debt crisis in Latin America. The second boom came in the first half of the 1990s and took only a few years to culminate in recurrent crises, starting with Mexico in 1994–95 and followed by East Asia, Brazil, Russia, Turkey, and Argentina. The third boom in capital inflows surpassed the first two not only in absolute terms but also in per cent of gross domestic product (GDP) (Akyüz 2011b).

Both push and pull factors played a role. From 2002 onwards, policies pursued in advanced economies generated highly favourable external financial conditions for EDEs. Sharp cuts in interest rates in all major advanced economies and rapid liquidity and credit expansion that led to the subprime bubble in the US and property and consumption bubbles in several European countries also gave a major boost to capital inflows to EDEs. Although the collapse of Lehman Brothers in September 2008 resulted in a rapid deterioration in global financial conditions and sudden reversal of capital inflows to EDEs, these were short-lived thanks primarily to the policy response of the US. The resort to zero-bound policy rates and rapid expansion of liquidity, the so-called quantitative easing, generated a swift recovery of capital inflows to

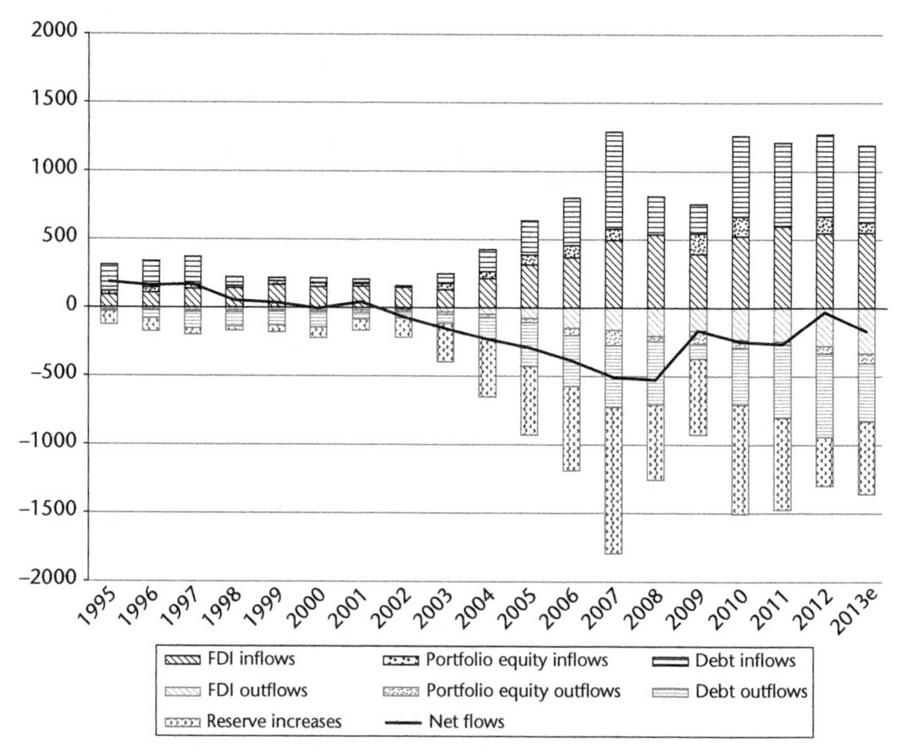

Figure 3.1 Capital flows in EDEs (billions of US dollars)

Note: e: estimates.

Source: IIF (2014).

EDEs, resulting in a new surge in several regions. If the Lehman blip is excluded, the boom in capital inflows that started around 2002 is longer than previous post-war booms, lasting over a decade.

Because of higher interest rates and more vibrant asset markets, several EDEs became more attractive for international investors and lenders from the early years of the 2000s. Risk appetite shifted in favour of EDEs and equities of firms in several major EDEs emerged as a new asset class for portfolio diversification by international investors. BRIC (Brazil, Russia, India, and China) were identified by international bankers as the 'emerging markets' with the brightest economic prospects and came to be seen as highly profitable venues for investment and lending (O'Neill 2001). Again, many economies in the European periphery enjoyed improvements in their credit ratings and falls in spreads thanks to their inclusion in the Economic and Monetary Union (EMU).

As discussed in detail in Chapter 2, significantly accelerated growth in EDEs after the early 2000s was an important reason for the growing interest of international investors. Many EDEs had been in disarray in the late 1990s and early 2000s, facing severe currency, liquidity and debt crises one after another. However, their recovery was rapid and until the crisis in 2008–09 they grew much faster than advanced economies, thanks mainly to an exceptionally favourable global economic environment. Their recovery from the crisis was also much faster. Thus, a virtuous circle emerged whereby rapid growth attracted more capital into EDEs and this in turn added to growth by stimulating private spending in investment in property and consumption, thereby attracting even more capital.

An equally important factor in the deepening of global financial integration of EDEs is capital account liberalization. In some cases this was undertaken as a result of obligations undertaken in the World Trade Organization (WTO) negotiations on trade in financial services. For many others, as discussed in Chapter 7, it resulted from commitments made in Free Trade Agreements (FTAs) and Bilateral Investment Treaties (BITs) with major advanced economies, particularly the US and the EU. Nevertheless, most countries, notably those with chronic current account deficits, including some major emerging economies such as Brazil, India, South Africa, and Turkey, chose to open up their capital accounts and liberalize their FDI regimes unilaterally in order to facilitate the financing of external deficits and accelerate investment and growth.

Local bond markets were opened to foreign investors in order to deepen them and facilitate public borrowing. This was also expected to address the so-called original sin problem—that is, the inability of EDEs to issue international debt in their own currencies (Eichengreen et al. 2003)—and allow them to pass the currency risk to creditors and minimize the impact of currency declines on debt burden and external sustainability. In East Asia the development of regional bond markets was seen as a solution to the problems of currency and maturity mismatches[3] that had devastated the region during the 1997 crisis, culminating in the Asian Bond Market initiative in 2003 (Lim and Lim 2012).

The new millennium also saw a widespread liberalization of inflows of direct and portfolio equity investment. Many private financial and non-financial corporations in EDEs started looking for partners from advanced economies in order to facilitate their access to foreign markets and finance, and this accounts for an important part of foreign acquisitions of equity in EDEs. On the other hand, following China's success in becoming an international hub for manufactured exports to advanced economies, hopes were increasingly pinned on participation in international production networks organized and controlled by transnational corporations from advanced economies for export-led industrialization. Even countries such as India, traditionally quite selective vis-à-vis direct and portfolio equity inflows, relaxed or removed overall limits or sectoral caps. The outcome has been a significant escalation of foreign presence and influence in real and financial sectors of EDEs.

Domestic markets have also been opened to foreign banks, notably but not only from advanced economies, often on grounds that this would improve the efficiency of the banking system, lower the intermediation margin and enhance the resilience of EDEs to external financial shocks. The World Bank has been particularly active in promoting foreign ownership of banking in developing countries (Stein 2010). Some countries have encouraged joint ownership with local partners while others allowed fully owned foreign subsidiaries or branches under the control of parent banks.

As a result of the liberalization of the capital account for residents, both financial and non-financial corporations have come to enjoy greater access to international financial markets flooded with cheap money, particularly since the onset of the crisis in the US and Europe. In major EDEs, including deficit countries dependent on foreign capital such as Brazil, India, South Africa, and Turkey, corporations have been allowed and even encouraged to invest and expand abroad and become global players. In many cases limits on the acquisition of foreign securities and deposits by individuals and institutional investors were also raised or abolished. During the surge in capital inflows, a main motive for outward liberalization was to relieve pressures of strong capital inflows on currencies and avoid costly interventions in foreign exchange markets (Akyüz 2008).

[3] Currency mismatch refers to a situation where assets are denominated in a different currency than liabilities. Maturity mismatches arise when assets and liabilities have different maturities—usually when there are more short-term liabilities than short-term assets and more medium-term and long-term assets than medium-term and long-term liabilities.

Thus, finance in EDEs has become increasingly internationalized in two overlapping dimensions. First, through rapid expansion of international assets and liabilities as conventionally defined on the basis of residence—that is, the balance sheet positions of residents of EDEs vis-à-vis non-residents. Second, as a result of growing assets and liabilities defined on the basis of nationality—that is, the balance sheet positions of nationals of EDEs vis-à-vis foreigners including debt to foreign banks located in EDEs and the external debt of overseas subsidiaries of their corporations.

3.2 Expansion of External Balance Sheets

The evolution of gross external assets and liabilities of EDEs has been shaped by their two principal determinants: current account balances and capital flows.[4] In most of the 1990s the current account of EDEs taken together was in deficit despite occasional small surpluses in East Asia and fuel exporters. As a result, capital inflows provided financing for both current account deficits and acquisition of (gross) assets abroad. However, growth of external balance sheets was slow because when capital inflows were strong, deficits were large, as in the first half of the decade, and when deficits came down, so did capital inflows, as in the second half.

The picture changed in the new millennium when both current accounts and capital inflows improved significantly. For EDEs as a whole, the current account shifted to a surplus thanks to a strong export drive by China and smaller East Asian economies and large surpluses of fuel exporters. In Asia the cumulative current account surplus exceeded $1 trillion during 2002–07 and over 85 per cent of this was due to China. Large inflows of capital and current account surpluses allowed several East Asian EDEs and many fuel exporters to build up sizeable external assets. In the rest of the developing world deficits declined and even small surpluses emerged thanks to a surge in commodity earnings. The combination of improved current account positions and the surge in capital inflows resulted in a significant expansion of their external balance sheets in the period before the crisis. After 2008, China's surplus fell sharply, but Asia and EDEs as a whole continued to run a current account surplus. While many major EDEs started to run large deficits, strong capital inflows still allowed them to acquire assets abroad and to expand their external balance sheets.

[4] In addition, both gross assets and liabilities and net foreign asset positions are subject to valuation effects due to changes in bond and equity prices and exchange rates when they are denominated in different currencies; see Lane and Milesi-Ferretti (2014). This issue will be subsequently discussed in relation to the measurement of the degree of financial integration and the effect of equity price changes on external liabilities.

From the beginning of the millennium until the crisis in 2008 the external balance sheet (that is, gross external assets plus liabilities) of EDEs taken together expanded by threefold (see Figure 3.2). The momentum has continued unabated after the Lehman collapse except for a brief interruption. For the entire period of 2000–13 gross international assets and liabilities of EDEs grew by about 15 and 12.5 per cent per annum, respectively, and their gross balance sheets expanded by more than fivefold. About 84 per cent of gross external assets and 78 per cent of gross external liabilities outstanding at the end of 2013 had been accumulated after 2000.

A conventional measure of the degree of financial integration is the ratio of external assets plus liabilities to GDP—the volume-based measure of international financial integration (Lane and Milesi-Ferretti 2007). However, this measure is subject to distortions due to valuation changes; that is, changes in exchange rates and asset prices, notably bond and equity prices, relative to prices of goods and services that comprise GDP. When external assets and liabilities are denominated in foreign currencies, a real depreciation of the

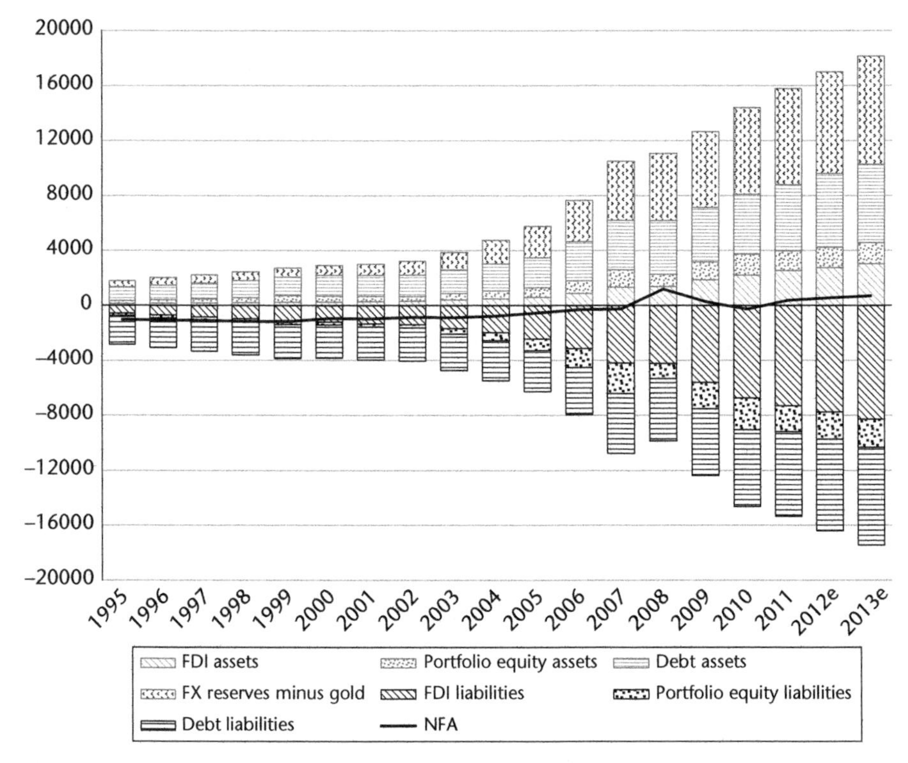

Figure 3.2 External assets and liabilities in EDEs (billions of US dollars)

Note: e: estimates.

Source: South Centre calculations and estimates based on Lane and Milesi-Ferretti (2007), IIF (2014) and IMF WEO (2014a).

national currency would raise their value relative to GDP and vice-versa for appreciations. Similarly, an equity market boom would raise the value of existing foreign holdings relative to GDP even in the absence of an increase in the degree of foreign participation in the market. This effect is particularly important for portfolio equity liabilities which are estimated at market values while direct equity investment is typically reported at book values.

For these reasons it is sometimes argued that a more accurate normalization of foreign holdings (liabilities) should be the size of relevant markets—namely, debt and equity markets. In the same vein, for the foreign assets held, normalization should be based on total portfolio holdings by residents so as to assess the extent of international portfolio diversification (Yeyati and Williams 2011). Such measures will be explored in subsequent discussions on equity and debt markets and the banking system. Nevertheless, it is important to keep in mind that valuation effects cannot always be avoided by taking the size of relevant domestic markets rather than GDP to measure the relative importance of external liabilities as long as these liabilities are denominated in several currencies. This is certainly the case for debt where foreigners hold both hard-currency and local-currency claims. Such valuation effects should and can be accounted for by tracing the movement of the relative prices involved.

The ratio of sum total of gross external assets and liabilities to GDP is shown in Figure 3.3. It was around 84 per cent in the mid-1990s, rising in the second half of the decade but falling subsequently. The upward trend that started in the early 2000s with the boom in capital inflows and the growing current account surplus of EDEs was interrupted by the Lehman collapse in 2008. With the recovery in capital inflows the ratio rose sharply during 2009–10, but fell again as inflows slowed and the current account surplus contracted. At the end of 2013, it was about 125 per cent, well above the levels of the 1990s but below the peaks reached on the eve and the wake of the Lehman collapse.

Changes in external balance sheets relative to GDP are no doubt influenced by movements in exchange rates and asset prices. As seen in Chapter 2, during the early 2000s until 2013, exchange rates and equity prices of EDEs generally moved in the same direction, implying that their valuation effects worked in opposite directions. Until the Lehman collapse, currencies of EDEs mostly appreciated, creating a negative valuation effect on the ratio of external assets and liabilities to GDP while equity prices increased sharply, creating a positive valuation effect. The Lehman collapse triggered sharp declines in both currencies and equity prices, reversing their valuation effects. The strong recovery during 2009–10 was followed by a relative weakening of both currencies and equity prices.

At the end of 2013, the currencies of major EDEs against the dollar were higher by around 20 per cent compared to the levels of the early 2000s in real terms, implying a negative valuation effect. In the same period, the MSCI equity price index registered an increase of about 200 per cent, raising the

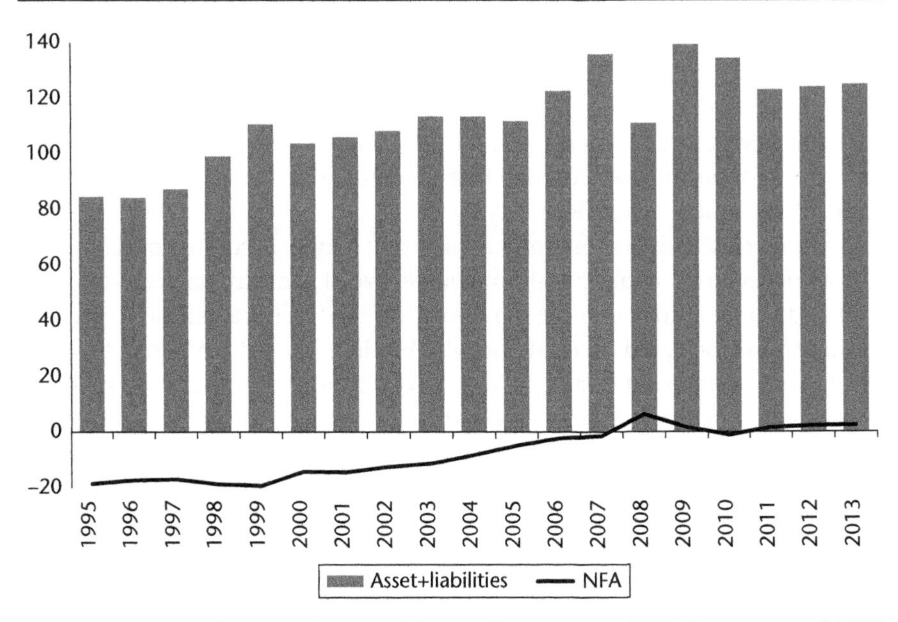

Figure 3.3 External balance sheets and financial openness in EDEs (percentage of GDP)
Source: South Centre calculations and estimates based on Lane and Milesi-Ferretti (2007) and IMF WEO (2014a).

value of foreign equity holdings and hence causing a positive valuation effect. However, the latter was small compared to the negative valuation effect of currency appreciations since external portfolio equity liabilities constituted less than 12 per cent of total liabilities in 2013. Therefore, the valuation effect during 2000–13 is likely to have reduced rather than increased the volume of external gross balance sheets of EDEs as a per cent of GDP, thereby resulting in an underestimation of the degree of integration on volume-based measure.

External assets and liabilities and capital flows of EDEs also grew faster than their international trade in goods and services during 2000–13. Until the onset of the crisis in 2008, both imports and exports of EDEs had grown rapidly thanks to growth of exports of manufactured consumer goods from East Asian EDEs to the US and Europe and the boom in commodity prices and trade. However, this came to an end in 2008 even though commodity prices recovered quickly due to China's stimulus package. For the entire period from 2000 to 2013, in value terms total trade (imports plus exports) of EDEs grew by some 11.5 per cent per annum while growth of their total stock of assets and liabilities in dollar terms was 13.6 per cent. The gap is even wider in terms of capital flows (inflows plus outflows) which grew on average by around 15 per cent per annum.

With assets growing faster than liabilities due to a strong export performance and current account position, the net foreign assets of EDEs as a whole moved from negative to positive territory after the 1990s. At the end of the 1990s, total external liabilities of EDEs had exceeded their total external assets by $1.2 trillion or almost 20 per cent of their combined GDP. Subsequently their net asset position improved and became positive, reaching $1.2 trillion or 6.2 per cent of their combined GDP in 2008. However, after the crisis, as the current account surplus of EDEs fell, their net foreign assets as a per cent of GDP started to decline, hovering around 2 per cent during the period 2011–13 (Figure 3.3).

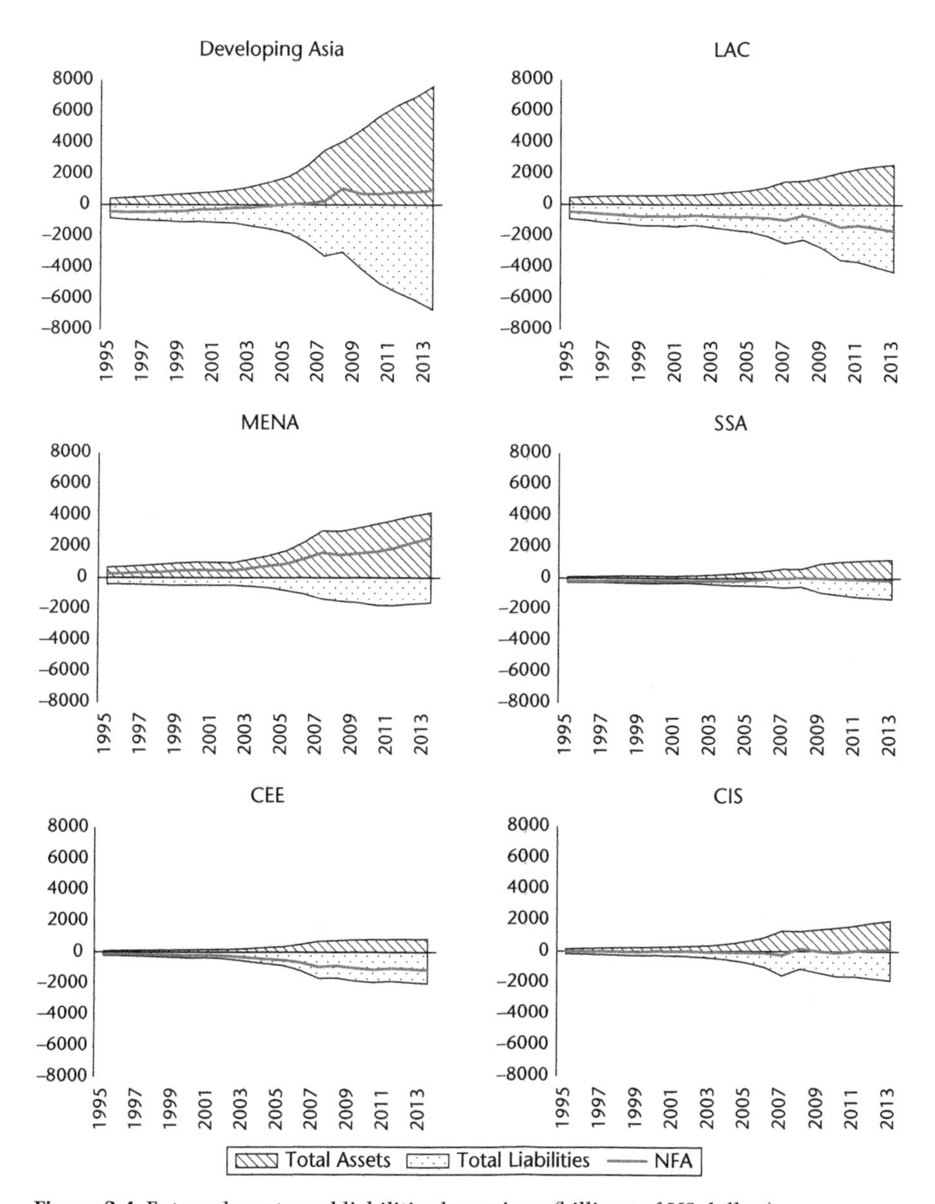

Figure 3.4 External assets and liabilities by regions (billions of US dollars)

Source: South Centre calculations and estimates based on Lane and Milesi-Ferretti (2007) and IMF WEO (2014a).

Table 3.1 External assets (A), liabilities (L) and net foreign assets (NFA)

	A+L (*billions of US dollars*)		(A+L)/GDP		NFA/GDP	
	2000	2013	2000	2013	2000	2013
Asia	1836	14,287	81	106	−13	7
LAC	1935	6880	90	119	−34	−29
MENA	1476	5768	168	170	56	75
SSA	490	2501	141	190	−51	−10
CEE	528	2820	89	147	−38	−60
CIS	524	3801	149	135	3	4

Source: South Centre calculations and estimates based on Lane and Milesi-Ferretti (2007) and IMF WEO database.

This aggregate picture naturally conceals significant diversity among various regions and countries (see Figure 3.4). Given its sheer size, it is not surprising that a large proportion of international assets and liabilities of EDEs are concentrated in Asia, accounting for 40 per cent of the total, followed by Latin America and the Caribbean (LAC) and Middle East and North Africa (MENA) (see Table 3.1). Asia also tops the list in terms of the pace of financial integration since the early 1990s, as measured by the growth of its external asset and liabilities. However, as a proportion of GDP, Asian external balance sheets are smaller than all other regions, including sub-Saharan Africa (SSA), just over 100 per cent in 2013, up from 80 per cent in 2000. At the beginning of the millennium all regions except oil-rich MENA and the Commonwealth of Independent States (CIS), had negative net foreign asset (NFA) positions. Both MENA and the CIS increased their NFA subsequently thanks to strong energy prices while Asian EDEs shifted from negative to positive NFA positions. In 2013 SSA still had a negative NFA position despite a significant improvement after the early 2000s. LAC continued to have a large negative NFA position whereas the crisis-stricken Central and Eastern Europe (CEE) saw a significant deterioration throughout the 2000s.

Figure 3.5 gives the total international balance sheet volumes and Figure 3.6 NFA positions as a per cent of GDP for individual countries. Almost all countries saw their balance sheets expand relative to GDP until the onset of the crisis. After 2007 the picture became more varied according to the combination of capital inflows and current account balances and growth rates. At the end of 2012 all EDEs except China and the Russian Federation had negative NFA positions, with Colombia, India, Mexico, South Africa, and Turkey showing significant deteriorations compared to the beginning of the century.

3.3 Gross External Assets

There is considerable diversity in the growth of different components of gross external assets of EDEs over the past decade. At the beginning of the 2000s external debt assets such as deposits held abroad, loans extended to

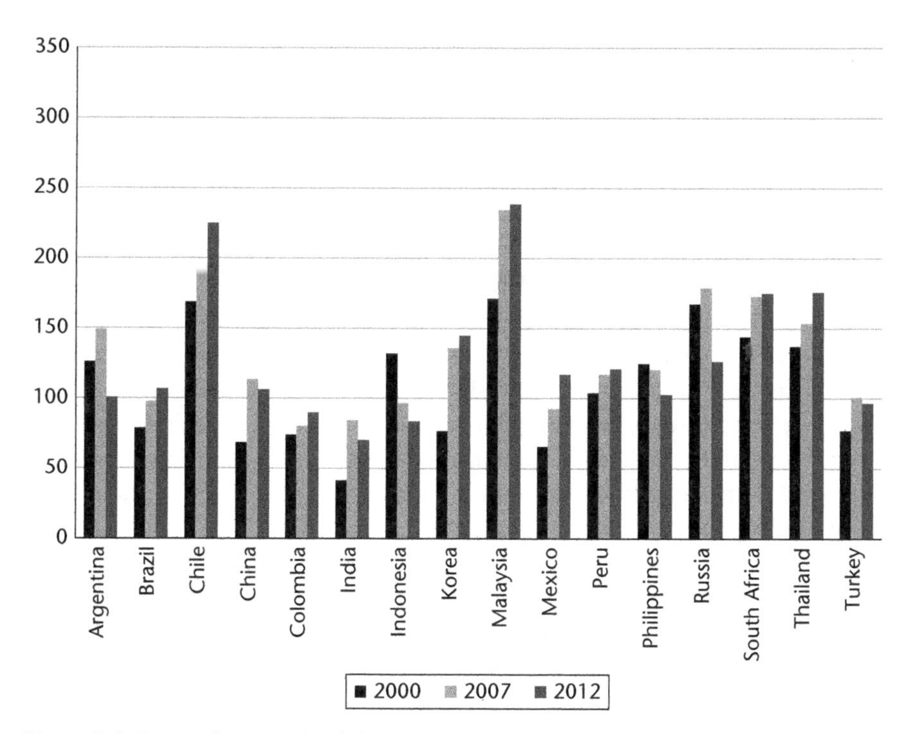

Figure 3.5 External assets plus liabilities in EDEs (percentage of GDP)

Source: South Centre calculations and estimates based on Lane and Milesi-Ferretti (2007) and IMF BOP.

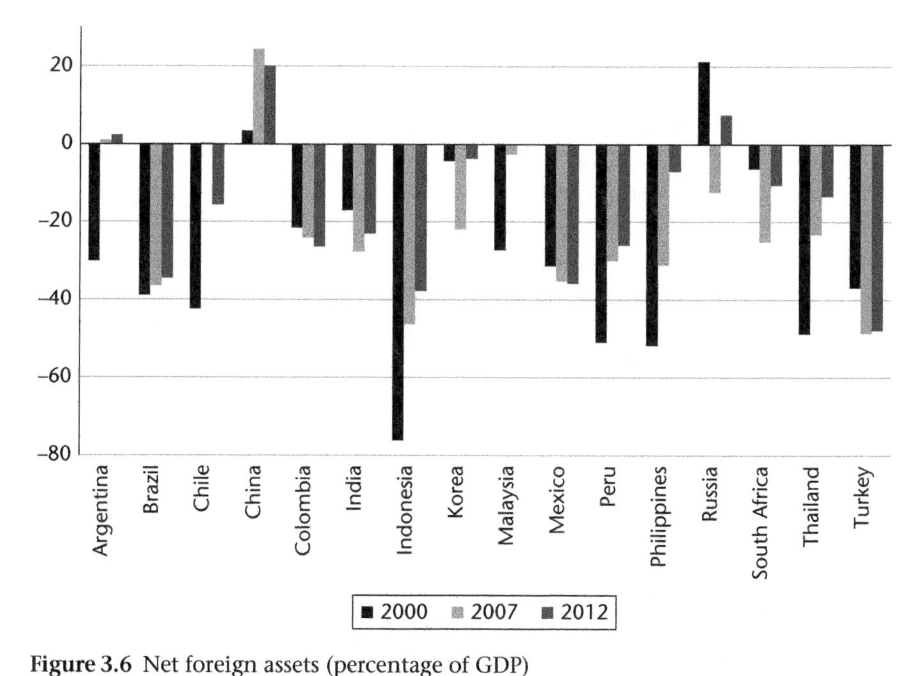

Figure 3.6 Net foreign assets (percentage of GDP)

Source: South Centre calculations and estimates based on Lane and Milesi-Ferretti (2007) and IMF BOP.

non-residents and foreign bond holdings accounted for more than half of total assets of EDEs; by 2013 their share fell to less than one-third. The share of direct equity (FDI) in total assets doubled to reach 17 per cent in 2013 thanks to the emergence of some firms in major EDEs such as Brazil, China, India, South Africa, and Turkey as international investors, particularly in other EDEs. By contrast portfolio equity investment abroad grew slowly and its share in total assets fell from 15 per cent to some 8 per cent during the same period. A main factor is the increased attraction of local equity markets in EDEs compared to those in advanced economies, which offered higher capital gains not only because of a boom in local currency prices but also because of currency appreciations.

But even more striking is the unprecedented growth of international reserves. Excluding gold, which is not a claim on non-residents, their share in total assets increased from less than a quarter in 2000 to 43 per cent by 2013. The increase exceeded by a large margin the total cumulative current account surpluses of EDEs (see Table 3.2). Of some $7 trillion reserves accumulated between 2000 and 2013, almost two-thirds were earned from current account surpluses and one-third were borrowed—i.e., put aside from capital inflows.[5] Over 40 per cent of *total* reserves of EDEs in 2013 were borrowed reserves.[6] This was close to one-half of their total gross external debt in that year.

Of the two major surplus economies, fuel exporters used their current account surpluses partly to add to reserves and partly to use for other forms of investment abroad, often through Sovereign Wealth Funds. In other words, they reinvested abroad all capital inflows plus almost two-thirds of their current account surpluses. In China, about two-thirds of additional reserves came from current account surpluses and the rest from capital inflows. Thus, unlike fuel exporters, Chinese investment abroad, excluding reserves, was less than foreign investment in China. For the rest of the countries, reserves accumulated between 2000 and 2013 were entirely borrowed, coming from capital inflows, as these countries ran, on average, current account deficits over that period. There are, however, some exceptions, notably smaller East Asian countries with sustained current account surpluses such as Malaysia.

Collectively EDEs had net liabilities in both debt (excluding reserves) and equities in 2013. This is also true for a large majority of them individually. There was a relatively large number of EDEs with positive net debt positions including reserves—that is, their debt assets plus reserves exceed their debt liabilities. But many of these countries had negative net external positions in

[5] Borrowed in the sense that their counterpart is increased liabilities to non-residents in one form or another, including equity investment as well as debt, which all generate outward income transfers.

[6] Since before the 2000s the current account of EDEs as a whole was generally in deficit, a large proportion of reserves held at the beginning of the new millennium were borrowed reserves. Adding to this the reserves accumulated from capital inflows during 2000–13 would give around 40 per cent of total reserves in 2013 as borrowed reserves.

Table 3.2 Current account and reserves (billions of US dollars)

	EDEs	Fuel exporters	China	Other EDEs
Reserves				
2013	7774.9	1798.8	3839.5	2136.6
2000	801.1	192.0	168.3	440.8
Increase	6973.8	1606.8	3671.3	1695.8
Current account[a]				
2000–13	4477.1	4572.2	2322.3	–2417.4
Borrowed reserves[b]				
2000–13	2496.7	–	1349.0	1695.8

[a] Cumulative current account balance over 2000–13.
[b] Reserves accumulated from capital inflows over 2000–13.
Source: IMF IFS and WEO databases.

equities. For instance it is estimated that, as of the mid-2000s, 31 of the 39 EDEs with positive net debt positions had negative net equity positions (Lane and Milesi-Ferretti 2007). This means that reserves of these countries came from equity inflows whereas in others with net negative positions in both debt and equity, they came partly from debt inflows and partly from equity inflows.

The unprecedented reserve accumulation by EDEs in the new millennium, including by deficit countries, goes directly against the prognostications of mainstream theory that the need for international reserves should lessen as countries gained access to international financial markets and became more willing to respond to balance-of-payments shocks by exchange rate adjustments. However, capital account liberalization and increased access to international financial markets have produced exactly the opposite result. Private capital flows have no doubt allowed larger and more persistent current account deficits in EDEs beyond the levels that could be attained by relying on borrowing from the Bretton Woods Institutions (BWIs) or bilateral lenders. But this has also meant accumulation of large stocks of external liabilities. Because of pro-cyclical behaviour of international financial markets, EDEs have become highly vulnerable to sudden stops and reversals in capital flows and this has increased the need to keep reserves as self-insurance.

Empirical evidence indeed shows a strong correlation between capital account liberalization and reserve holdings and a growing tendency to absorb capital inflows into reserves rather than using them for current payments (Aizenman and Lee 2005; Choi et al. 2007). The widespread distrust among EDEs against the IMF because of pro-cyclical macroeconomic conditionalities and structural adjustments attached to lending at times of currency and balance-of-payments crises has no doubt reinforced this tendency towards self-insurance.

Since EDEs as a whole had a current account surplus in the new millennium until 2015, net capital flows (that is, net capital inflows minus net outflows, including reserve changes) ran from poor to rich countries. However, this was not the case for market-intermediated or private capital flows. Official reserve accumulation by EDEs as a whole exceeded their total current account surplus and the difference came from positive net private flows (net private inflows minus net private outflows). This is the case even for China which had twin surpluses on its current and (non-reserve) capital accounts and used a sizeable proportion of private capital inflows to add to reserves. In other words, market-intermediated net private capital inflows plus current account surpluses of EDEs were reinvested back by their central banks into international reserve assets issued by governments in major advanced economies and this is why in aggregate money was flowing from poor to rich countries.

3.4 Equity Inflows and Markets

The liberalization of FDI regimes and portfolio equity inflows, together with the increased willingness of foreigners to invest in EDEs, resulted in a 7-fold increase in total equity liabilities of EDEs between 2000 and 2013, reaching almost 60 per cent of their total external liabilities in 2013, up from about 37 per cent at the beginning of the century. Growth in portfolio equity liabilities was faster, albeit more unstable. Equity liabilities also show a significant increase as a proportion of GDP over the same period (see Table 3.3). The increase was due not only to rapid growth in direct and portfolio equity *inflows*, but also to the impact of an upward trend in equity prices on the value of the existing *stock* of foreign holdings in the equity markets of EDEs. This upward trend was triggered by large and sustained foreign inflows from the early years of the century. Substantial foreign presence has become a permanent feature of these markets and led to structural changes regarding their liquidity and valuation dynamics and making them highly susceptible to changes in global financial conditions.

Equity inflows to EDEs have generally been stronger than debt-creating inflows. During the boom in the 1990s, external debt of EDEs grew faster than equity inflows, but this was reversed after the Asian crisis when equity inflows kept up but international lending to EDEs fell sharply. Both recovered after 2002. The Lehman collapse in 2008 led to a much sharper decline in international lending to EDEs than in equity inflows. After the crisis external borrowing shot up once again, almost matching total equity inflows between 2010 and 2013. Still, the increase in total equity liabilities of EDEs during 1995–2013 was 3.5 times the increase in their total gross external debt.

Of the two components of equity, portfolio inflows are generally more pro-cyclical than direct equity. This, together with sharp swings in equity prices, results in a significant instability in the composition of equity liabilities.

Table 3.3 Total equity liabilities (TEL) and portfolio equity liabilities (PEL) (per cent of GDP)

	1995		2000		2007		2012	
	TEL	PEL	TEL	PEL	TEL	PEL	TEL	PEL
EDEs	13.4	3.0	21.6	3.5	40.9	14.2	36.0	7.3
Argentina	15.3	4.5	25.1	1.3	28.6	2.6	20.7	0.7
Brazil	10.2	3.1	24.8	6.9	49.3	26.6	46.6	15.9
Chile	37.3	7.6	64.7	6.0	62.8	5.3	72.4	7.9
China	14.1	0.9	20.5	1.2	33.2	13.1	27.7	4.5
Colombia	8.4	0.6	11.6	0.4	30.3	3.5	30.8	4.3
India	5.0	2.9	7.9	3.6	38.5	29.4	22.1	10.8
Indonesia	11.8	2.8	14.4	3.6	37.8	19.0	33.6	12.4
Korea	6.2	4.4	13.7	7.3	42.1	30.5	36.9	25.1
Malaysia	56.4	25.5	50.9	14.9	74.3	35.2	59.7	21.9
Mexico	19.4	7.2	23.7	7.0	42.6	14.9	41.0	11.0
Peru	13.2	3.0	25.0	4.3	42.8	17.8	38.2	12.8
Philippines	16.5	7.2	16.0	3.9	31.4	17.7	20.4	9.1
Russia	6.1	0.2	16.7	4.3	61.5	23.8	31.4	8.8
South Africa	18.2	8.3	49.7	17.0	77.2	38.5	62.7	27.3
Thailand	25.8	14.6	32.0	6.6	62.2	23.1	60.1	19.0
Turkey	5.6	1.0	10.0	2.8	33.8	9.9	22.7	5.0

Note: EDEs refer to IMF classifications of 'emerging markets and developing economies'.

Source: South Centre calculations and estimates based on Lane and Milesi-Ferretti (2007), IIF (2014), IMF WEO (2014a) and IMF BOP.

Indeed, the share of portfolio equity in total equity liabilities doubled between the early 2000s and 2007 to reach 35 per cent as portfolio inflows accelerated and equity prices increased sharply. The Lehman collapse had a much stronger impact on portfolio inflows than direct equity. Despite a rapid recovery after 2009, at the end of 2012 portfolio equity liabilities as per cent of GDP were below the peaks reached on the eve of the crisis in most countries in Table 3.3. But they were still well above the levels recorded at the beginning of the millennium and their share in total equity liabilities of EDEs was also higher by 5 percentage points.

In interpreting these numbers it should be noted that there are several problems in the way portfolio and direct equity investments are defined and reported in international statistics. This is discussed in detail in Chapter 6. First, the division between FDI and portfolio equity is quite arbitrary. Second, in FDI statistics retained earnings are imputed as being payable to the owners to be reinvested as an increase in their equity. However, it is generally not possible to identify if this is really the case. This problem of identification of the use of retained earnings is particularly important because they constitute a significant part of statistically measured FDI inflows. Finally, loans and advances from parent companies to affiliates are also treated as part of direct equity rather than debt, on grounds that such debt is strongly connected to direct investment relationships. However, in practice it is not possible to identify the nature and effects of lending and borrowing between parents and affiliated corporations. For all these reasons, an important part of what is recorded in international statistics as direct equity investment may very well behave like portfolio flows.

International capital flows into equity markets of EDEs have come to play a central role in their price dynamics. The movement of prices in these markets depends on net inflows of equity capital, both domestic and foreign, relative to new issues through initial public offerings and issues by the companies already listed. Foreign direct investors do not generally issue equities in EDEs or list their companies in local stock markets. In fact evidence suggests that FDI tends to be positively correlated with the migration of capital raising, listing, and trading to international financial centres, and FDI inflows to EDEs have almost no effect on stock market depth (market capitalization) in these economies (Claessens et al. 2001; Doytch 2013a, 2013b).[7] By contrast, large and sustained inflows of portfolio equity can add considerably to demand for equities. This is also true for foreign acquisition of equities of existing firms classified under direct investment, but the way data on equity inflows are reported does not allow this to be identified.

A sudden price boom after a prolonged period of relatively sluggish markets could only happen as a result of large and sustained net inflows. These create liquidity and excess demand and raise prices which can in turn generate additional inflows as investors are attracted by prospects of capital gain. Price rises continue until excess demand is eliminated by new issues or an autonomous exit from the market. Historically, the rise of institutional investors is seen to have triggered such a boom. International capital flows into equity markets of EDEs in the new millennium appear to have been playing a similar role.[8]

During the second half of the 1990s until 2002, both portfolio equity inflows and prices fluctuated without any discernible upward trend (see Figure 3.7).[9] They shot up from 2003, rising constantly and reaching peaks on the eve of the crisis, by which time prices had increased by 2.5 times and portfolio equity inflows by 7.5 times in comparison with 2002. As net inflows became negative after the Lehman collapse in 2008, prices took a dive, falling by almost 50 per cent. With the subsequent recovery in portfolio equity

[7] Indeed the number of companies from BRICS countries listed in the US and UK stock markets rose significantly before the onset of the crisis in advanced economies, from 180 to over 300 between 2005 and 2009; see Chandra (2010).

[8] Toporowski (2002) calls this process 'capital market inflation' and links it historically to the creation of funded pension schemes. Bonizzi (2013) uses the same approach to explain price dynamics in the equity markets of Brazil and the Republic of Korea in recent years by a historical jump in the presence of foreigners.

[9] Figure 3.7 on the link between portfolio equity inflows and prices uses IIF data on inflows valued at entry prices rather than changes in portfolio liabilities based on the data from Lane and Milesi-Ferretti (2007) since the latter include the impact of valuation changes which the inflows contribute to.

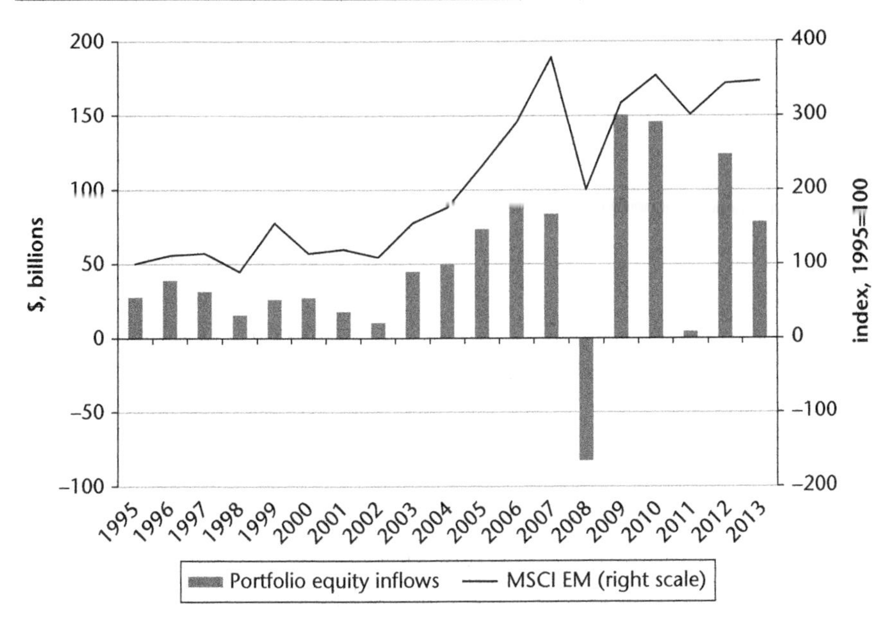

Figure 3.7 Portfolio equity inflows and MSCI in EDEs
Note: MSCI index in local currency.
Source: MSCI and IIF (2014).

inflows, prices made a sharp upturn, almost matching pre-crisis levels. The drop in inflows in 2011 was also reflected in a downturn in prices, followed by recovery in both.

In the entire period from the beginning of the boom until 2013, cumulative portfolio equity inflows amounted to $760 billion for the sample of countries in Figure 3.7, resulting in a significant increase in foreign presence in their equity markets, despite the instability caused by a series of adverse external shocks including the Lehman collapse, the Eurozone crisis and tapering by the US Federal Reserve. During the same period the increase in external portfolio equity liabilities of the countries in Table 3.3 was in the order of $1.8 trillion. Although a direct comparison is not possible because of differences in coverage between these two sets of data, it can still be concluded that an important part of increased external portfolio equity liabilities of EDEs since the early 2000s is due to price increases and represents a significant capital gain for foreign holders.

Market capitalization—the market value of outstanding shares—also moved closely with equity prices, starting to rise rapidly after 2002, reaching a peak on the eve of the crisis and recovering after the Lehman collapse (see Figure 3.8). It also increased as a per cent of GDP, thereby resulting in a significant degree of financial deepening. Except a few countries such as Chile, Malaysia, and South Africa, market capitalization as a per cent of GDP was low in the 1990s in comparison with advanced economies (see Table 3.4).

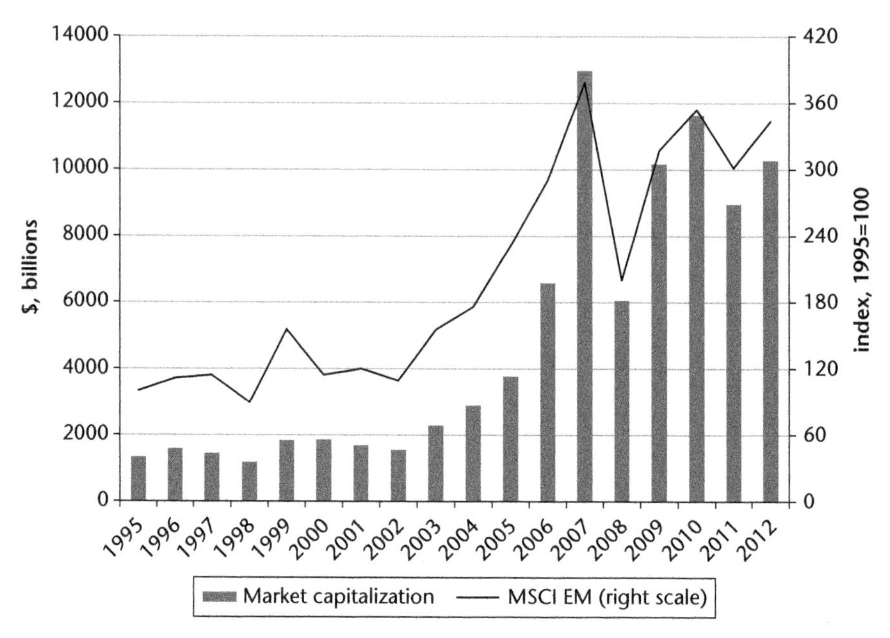

Figure 3.8 Market capitalization and MSCI in EDEs

Note: MSCI index in local currency.

Source: World Bank WDI and MSCI.

By 2007 it was considerably higher in almost every country. In that year, in half of the EDEs in Table 3.4, its ratio to GDP was close to or higher than the levels in advanced economies. Subsequently, notably after 2010, the capitalization ratio fell almost everywhere with the weakening of prices, but in 2012 it was still much higher than the levels seen in the 1990s and early 2000s.

Country-specific evidence on stock market inflows, share issuance and foreign purchases of equity from Brazil and the Republic of Korea also shows a similar process of 'capital market inflation' (Bonizzi 2013). In both countries equity prices were relatively stable and stock market capitalization kept pace with new issues until 2002 when prices and capitalization started to rise rapidly because of the surge in foreign inflows. Between 1995 and 2010, valuation changes accounted for 78 per cent of the increase in market capitalization in Brazil and 85 per cent in the Republic of Korea. Price hikes were responsible for a large proportion of the increase in portfolio liabilities in both countries, bringing significant capital gains to foreign holders.

There are no comprehensive and consistent data on the share of foreign holdings in equity markets of EDEs. Table 3.5 is based on external equity liabilities compiled from the IMF's Coordinated Portfolio Investment Surveys (CPIS). As noted by Lane and Milesi-Ferretti (2007: 8), 'the equity liabilities of a country derived from the *CPIS* provide a lower bound on that country's stock of liabilities' largely because of underreporting. Still the figures in the

Table 3.4 Market capitalization (per cent of GDP)

	1995	2000	2007	2012
EDEs	32.2	35.6	110.8	48.2
Argentina	14.6	58.4	33.2	7.2
Brazil	19.2	35.1	100.3	54.6
China	5.8	48.5	178.2	44.9
Chile	103.5	76.1	123.0	116.1
Colombia	19.3	9.6	49.1	70.9
India	34.7	31.1	146.9	68.0
Indonesia	32.9	16.3	49.0	45.2
Korea	35.2	32.2	107.1	104.5
Malaysia	250.7	124.7	168.3	156.2
Mexico	26.1	18.1	38.1	44.6
Peru	22.0	19.8	98.6	47.5
Philippines	79.5	32.0	69.1	105.6
Russia	4.0	15.0	115.6	43.4
South Africa	185.6	154.2	291.3	159.3
Thailand	84.2	24.0	79.4	104.7
Turkey	12.3	26.1	44.3	39.1
Memo: Advanced Economies	*64.7*	*112.0*	*118.9*	*86.7*

Note: EDEs refer to low and middle income countries as defined by the World Bank.
Source: World Bank WDI.

table show that in a very large majority of countries (13 out of 16), the share of non-residents in equity markets increased between the early 2000s and 2012. According to another estimate, on the eve of the crisis in 2008, the share of foreign holdings in total equity reached or exceeded 25 per cent in Brazil, Mexico, the Republic of Korea, the Russian Federation, and Turkey (Psalida and Sun 2009: Figure 7). In Asia, the average foreign share during 2003–07 was close to 20 per cent; in Indonesia, the Republic of Korea and Thailand it was higher (ADB 2011). Bonizzi (2013) estimates that in Brazil foreign stock holdings fell from a peak of more than 40 per cent of the market in 2006 to less than 30 per cent in 2010, but recovered subsequently to reach almost the pre-crisis peak in 2012 while in the Republic of Korea they hovered between 30 and 40 per cent of the market during the same period. In Turkey too, the share of foreign portfolios showed significant swings after the crisis, but generally remained well above the levels reported in the IMF's CPIS (Elmas 2010).

It is notable that in many of the so-called 'emerging markets', the share of foreign portfolio holdings is above the levels in some 'mature' markets, such as the US where it is around 14 per cent and Japan where it is 27 per cent.[10] In Table 3.5, in 10 EDEs in 2012 it was higher than the share of foreigners in the US market, even allowing for the underreporting. In 2009, in six Asian EDEs, total foreign holdings of equity as a per cent of total market capitalization was equal to or greater than foreign shares in Japan (ADB 2011).

[10] See FRBNY (2013) for the US and Seguchi (2012) for Japan.

Table 3.5 Non-resident holdings in stock markets (per cent of market capitalization)

	2001	2007	2012
Argentina	1.4	5.7	8.2
Brazil	18.2	21.2	23.4
Chile	6.1	5.4	8.0
China	2.5	6.6	13.5
Colombia	2.3	2.1	4.3
India	12.1	18.1	19.8
Indonesia	15.6	19.0	19.9
Korea	23.6	23.8	25.3
Malaysia	10.5	20.8	17.0
Mexico	32.2	29.9	22.1
Peru	9.4	3.1	6.7
Philippines	8.3	18.5	10.8
Russia	14.4	12.4	16.7
South Africa	9.3	10.2	19.7
Thailand	27.8	29.0	27.0
Turkey	9.4	17.0	20.2

Source: World Bank WDI and IMF Coordinated Portfolio Investment Survey (CPIS).

3.5 External Debt

As a result of the significantly faster growth in equity liabilities, the share of debt in total external liabilities of EDEs fell from more than 60 per cent at the beginning of the 2000s to some 40 per cent in 2013.[11] It also declined as a share of GDP, particularly before the onset of the crisis (see Table 3.6). Although external borrowing by EDEs grew rapidly from the early years of the 2000s until 2008, these economies also enjoyed unprecedented growth. Furthermore, in several EDEs, currency appreciations supported by the surge in capital inflows pulled down the external debt ratio. After the crisis, external debt started to rise faster than GDP in several EDEs due to growing current account deficits and increased private sector borrowing abroad. Currencies also weakened and growth started to falter after 2011 and both these factors contributed to the rise in the external debt ratio. In two-thirds of the countries in Table 3.6, it was higher in 2012 than the levels seen on the eve of the crisis.

A very large proportion of external debt of EDEs is commercial debt, with the share of official debt remaining under 20 per cent of the total in recent years. International debt securities and bank loans constitute its two principal

[11] In this chapter external debt is used, unless stated otherwise, as debt to non-residents, the definition officially adopted by institutions compiling data on debt. It does not include debt to foreigners resident in the debtor country. It consists of debt not only in foreign currency but also local currency and includes debt issued both at home and abroad. However, as noted by Dell'Erba et al. (2013), in practice developing countries are often unable to identify the ultimate holders of their bonds and report figures on external and domestic debt by using information on the place of issuance and governing law. For various definitions, see also Roubini and Setser (2004).

Table 3.6 Gross external debt

	1995	2000	2007	2012/13
EDEs (billions of US dollars)	2087.2	2433.1	4333.3	7129.3
EDEs (per cent of GDP)	38.1	37.2	27.6	24.9
Argentina	33.8	52.9	18.9	7.3
Brazil	27.4	34.0	21.2	29.0
Chile	29.0	40.9	29.2	37.0
China	13.4	12.2	10.8	14.4
Colombia	26.8	35.9	25.4	29.2
India	25.8	21.3	19.1	21.4
Indonesia	93.8	89.6	44.9	34.4
Korea	24.4	26.7	43.3	33.0
Malaysia	49.7	48.5	44.2	56.7
Mexico	31.7	24.8	19.8	27.2
Peru	66.7	52.4	29.4	32.9
Philippines	53.8	72.1	46.2	39.8
Russia	43.2	56.4	58.8	50.8
South Africa	28.4	25.5	20.6	27.9
Thailand	67.8	60.3	28.7	34.2
Turkey	23.5	47.0	47.0	52.6

Note: 2013 for EDEs and 2012 for individual countries.

Source: South Centre calculations and estimates based on Lane and Milesi-Ferretti (2007) and IMF BOP.

components.[12] During the first post-war boom in capital inflows in the late 1970s and early 1980s, much of the external debt accumulated was in syndicated bank loans, largely to private borrowers. During the Latin American debt crisis an important part of this debt ended up with the public sector and was subsequently replaced by Brady bonds. Similarly in the second boom in the 1990s a very large proportion of the debt incurred in Asia was in bank loans to private borrowers, and after the 1997 crisis much of this also ended up in public hands.

International bank claims on EDEs as defined by the BIS, including cross-border claims and local claims in foreign currencies, barely increased in the late 1990s after recurrent crises while bond issues kept up (see Figure 3.9a). The strong recovery of international bank lending during the subprime expansion was followed by a cut-back after the Lehman collapse and the Eurozone crisis (Van Rijckeghem and di Mauro 2013; Avdjiev et al. 2012; He and McCauley 2013). With sustained liquidity expansion and historically low interest rates

[12] As defined in the IMF's Balance of Payments Manual (IMF 2009: chap. 5), debt securities include bills, bonds, notes, negotiable certificates of deposit, commercial paper, debentures, asset-backed securities, money market instruments, and similar instruments normally traded in the financial markets. External debt includes all financial liabilities recognized by the 1993 System of National Accounts, except for shares and other equity and financial derivatives that are owed to non-residents. In addition to bank loans and debt securities, it includes currency and deposits held by non-residents, trade credits extended directly by the supplier of goods and services, and other payables such as liabilities for taxes, pensions and related entitlements, wages, salaries, and dividends that have accrued but not yet paid.

in advanced economies, cross-border lending and total international bank claims both recovered, but lagged behind security issues which picked up vigorously after the crisis (see Figures 3.9a and 3.9b).[13] Between 2008 and 2013, the outstanding external debt of EDEs in securities almost doubled while international bank claims increased by around 50 per cent and cross-border claims even less.

There are also large shifts in the relative shares of the public and private sectors in the external commercial debt of EDEs. After falling in the second half of the 1990s, the share of the private sector in outstanding external debt securities started to rise in the new millennium, overtaking public sector issues. The private sector's share in international bank claims was already very large in the mid-1990s and it has increased further in the new millennium (see Table 3.7). At the end of 2013 the private sector accounted for the bulk of external commercial debt of EDEs both in international bank loans and securities.[14]

The currency composition of *total* external debt of EDEs has shifted towards local currencies for three main reasons. Firstly, there is a sharp increase in the share of local-currency bonds and notes in international issues by both governments and corporations (see Table 3.8; see also Tovar 2005; Gruić and Wooldridge 2012; Hale et al. 2014). In 2000 such debt was around 2 per cent of total international securities issued by EDEs; at the end of 2013 it reached almost 17 per cent (see Figure 3.10). In China, South Africa, Thailand, and Turkey, the share of local-currency bonds and notes in total international issues reached or exceeded one-third in 2013.

Second, domestic securities issued in foreign currencies or linked to the exchange rate have become much less important. In the 1990s when inflation was high, inflation-indexed or forex-linked local debt securities were quite widespread in EDEs, like Mexican tesobonos in the mid-1990s. However, forex-linked bonds and notes have almost disappeared with a widespread shift to flexible exchange rates. They also lost their attractiveness because of currency appreciations in several EDEs.[15]

[13] Figure 3.9a uses international bank claims on EDEs including local claims in foreign currencies whereas Figure 3.9b uses cross-border lending, available only from 2005. Data in Figure 3.9b thus correspond to the conventional definition of external debt based on residency.

[14] Table 3.7 does not give sectoral shares in *external* debt as conventionally defined since international bank loans include local claims of international banks in foreign currencies as well as cross-border lending. To differentiate, it is called *international* commercial debt. During 2005–13, the share of local lending in foreign currencies in total international bank claims on EDEs varied between 10 and 16 per cent, somewhat higher after the crisis than before. This means that 80–90 per cent of international banks claims on EDEs in foreign exchange are cross border claims. Accordingly, figures in Table 3.7 closely track the changes in public and private sectors' shares in external commercial debt of EDEs as conventionally defined.

[15] But several EDEs still continue to have relatively large amounts of inflation-linked bonds and notes, including Argentina, Brazil, Mexico, South Africa, and Turkey—see, BIS Debt Securities Statistics Table 16C.

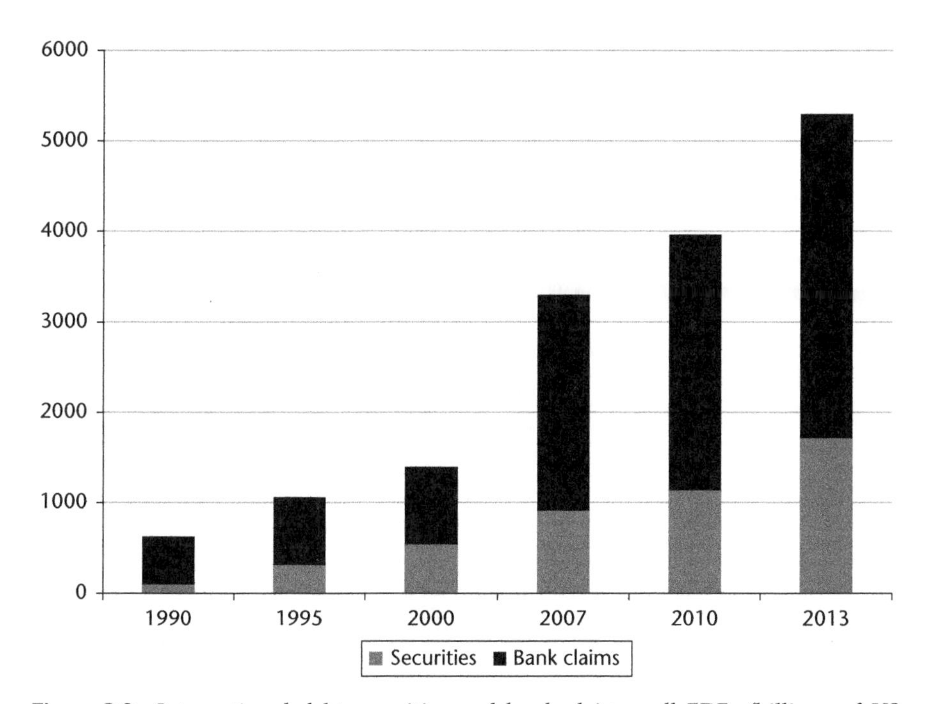

Figure 3.9a International debt securities and bank claims—all EDEs (billions of US dollars)

Note: Includes all EDEs reported by the BIS. Bank claims data are on immediate borrower basis; include cross-border claims and local claims in foreign currencies.

Source: BIS International Financial Statistics database.

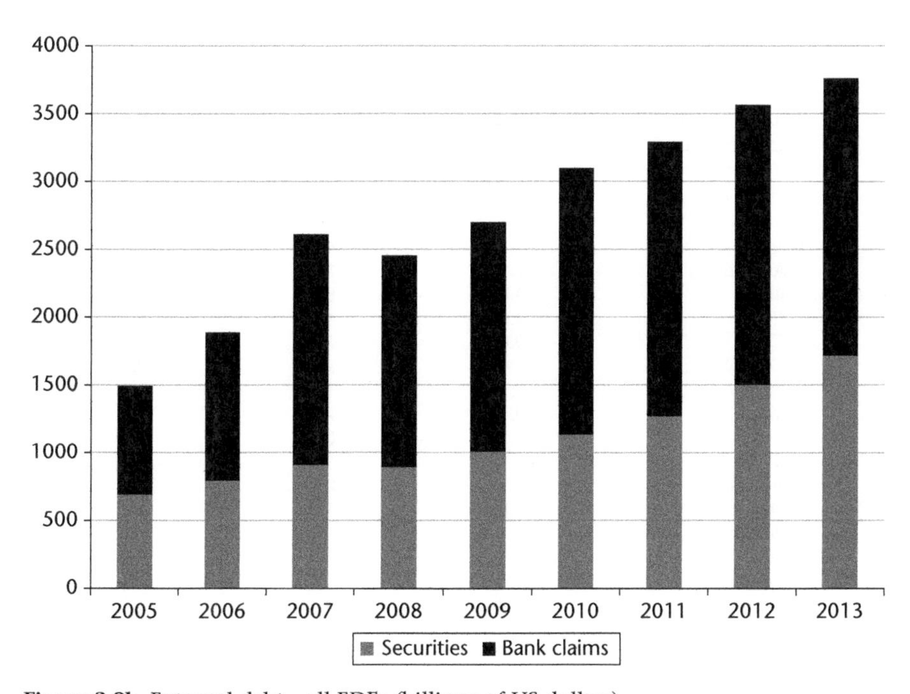

Figure 3.9b External debt—all EDEs (billions of US dollars)

Note: Includes all EDEs reported by the BIS. Bank claims data are on ultimate risk basis; include cross-border claims only.

Source: BIS International Financial Statistics database.

Table 3.7 Shares of private and public sectors in international commercial debt (per cent)

	1995		2000		2007		2013*	
	Private	Public	Private	Public	Private	Public	Private	Public
EDEs	68.6	31.4	64.5	35.5	75.1	24.9	76.8	23.2
Argentina	44.5	55.5	43.3	56.7	32.3	67.7	28.8	71.2
Brazil	47.5	52.5	53.9	46.1	62.4	37.6	71.7	28.3
Chile	80.4	19.6	93.5	6.5	88.7	11.3	91.3	8.7
China	79.8	20.2	83.4	16.6	90.7	9.3	94.5	5.5
Colombia	63.8	36.2	49.3	50.7	38.1	61.9	59.5	40.5
India	79.4	20.6	80.7	19.3	95.8	4.2	96.6	3.4
Indonesia	85.5	14.5	80.6	19.4	65.1	34.9	68.1	31.9
Korea	93.7	6.3	90.3	9.7	85.1	14.9	87.8	12.2
Malaysia	82.5	17.5	82.2	17.8	80.2	19.8	81.3	18.7
Mexico	45.9	54.1	50.2	49.8	62.0	38.0	69.4	30.6
Peru	85.1	14.9	71.4	28.6	57.1	42.9	68.5	31.5
Philippines	53.4	46.6	62.9	37.1	45.8	54.2	54.2	45.8
Russia	93.2	6.8	45.5	54.5	85.2	14.8	78.8	21.2
South Africa	80.5	19.5	71.2	28.8	71.6	28.4	72.3	27.7
Thailand	94.8	5.2	89.4	10.6	89.7	10.3	87.4	12.6
Turkey	46.3	53.7	51.5	48.5	60.3	39.7	66.2	33.8
Memo (all EDEs): Share in								
Debt securities	*40.6*	*59.4*	*35.6*	*64.4*	*48.3*	*51.7*	*57.2*	*42.8*
International bank claims	*80.4*	*19.6*	*82.7*	*17.3*	*85.3*	*14.7*	*86.0*	*14.0*

Note: Numbers include international debt securities and international bank claims as defined by the BIS.
* Q3 numbers.

Source: BIS International Financial Statistics database.

Table 3.8 Share of local currency bonds and notes in total international issues (per cent)

	2000	2007	2013
EDEs	2.2	14.0	16.8
Argentina	2.6	1.5	0.4
Brazil	0.0	18.4	16.9
Chile	4.5	4.5	6.5
China	0.0	12.7	32.3
Colombia	0.0	19.5	19.9
India	0.1	1.4	3.3
Indonesia	0.1	7.2	15.8
Korea	0.2	0.6	0.3
Malaysia	0.0	5.3	9.2
Mexico	0.3	20.7	18.8
Philippines	0.8	1.0	8.8
Russia	1.3	7.2	12.3
South Africa	70.1	73.8	51.5
Thailand	6.4	21.1	32.0
Turkey	0.0	33.1	33.7

Note: EDEs include 15 countries covered in this table.

Source: BIS International Financial Statistics database.

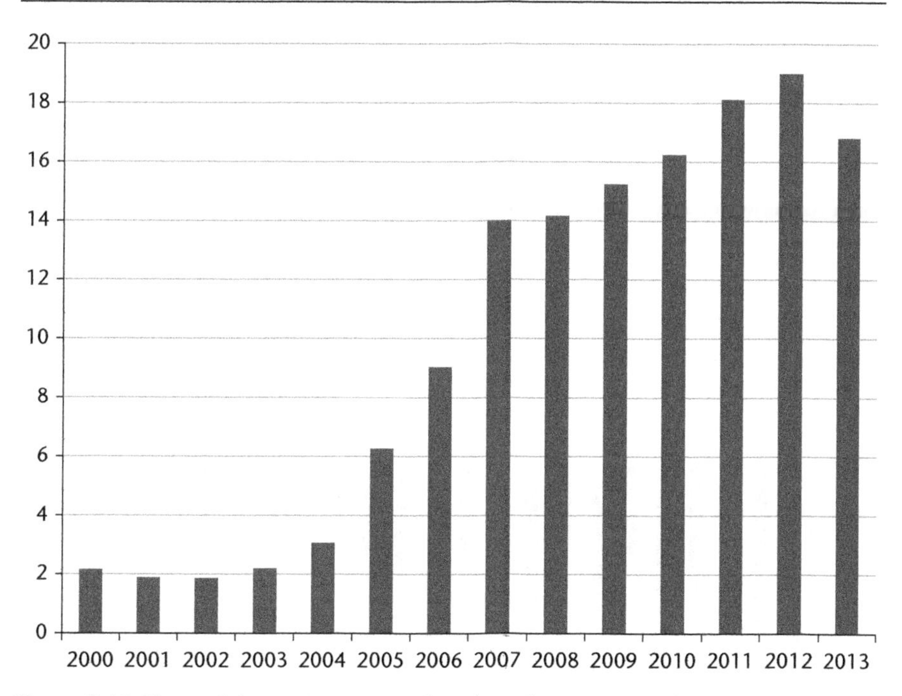

Figure 3.10 Share of domestic currency bonds and notes in total international issues by EDEs (percentage)

Note: EDEs include all the countries in Table 3.8.

Source: BIS International Financial Statistics database.

Third, as taken up in the subsequent section, many governments in EDEs have shifted from international debt in foreign currency to domestic debt in local currency and opened domestic debt markets to foreigners, benefiting from increased willingness of international lenders to assume the currency risk and come under local jurisdiction in return for higher yields and large capital gains. This, together with growing private sector issues in local markets, led to a rapid expansion of domestic debt securities relative to international debt securities (see Table 3.9 and Figure 3.11) and raised the share of local currency in *total* bonds issued by EDEs (see Table 3.10).[16] It also resulted in a large increase in the locally issued debt held by non-residents. According to the World Bank (2013), at the end of 2012 the share of non-resident

[16] The BIS now defines international debt securities as those issued by non-residents in all markets while domestic debt securities are those issued by residents in their local markets–see Gruić and Wooldridge (2012). Here, the external debt of EDEs in securities is defined as issues by their residents in markets abroad in all currencies, foreign and local, plus domestic issues in all currencies held by non-residents. Some residents of EDEs (e.g. local banks) may also hold securities issued in foreign markets by other residents of the same country (e.g. bonds of their own governments). In principle these should be deducted from external debt defined as claims of non-residents over residents, but available data do not always allow identifying this.

Table 3.9 Outstanding total debt issues in EDEs by sectors (billions of US dollars)

	1995	2000	2007	2013
Domestic (all issuers)	317.4	702.6	5528.4	10580.2
General government	247.5	520.4	2954.2	5452.5
Financial corporations	37.0	115.4	1990.6	3247.8
Non-financial corporations	32.0	66.8	583.6	1878.6
International (all issuers)	271.3	464.3	698.2	1298.9
General government	146.5	284.3	304.2	393.2
Financial corporations	69.4	97.0	226.3	555.7
Non-financial corporations	55.0	114.2	171.3	362.4

Notes: 2013: Q3 numbers.
EDEs include 16 countries covered in this paper.
Source: BIS International Financial Statistics database.

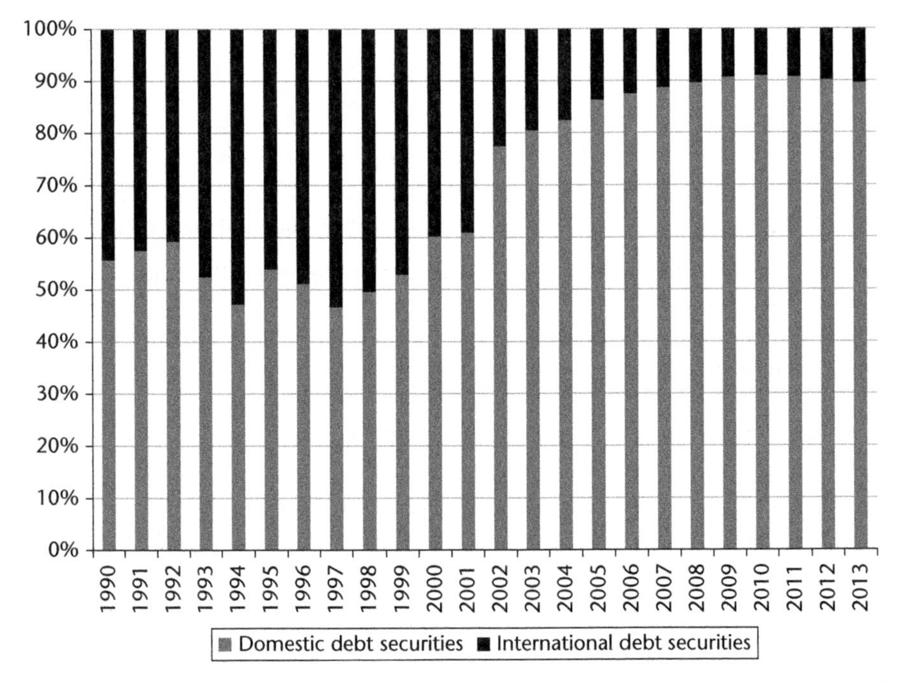

Figure 3.11 Structure of total debt securities outstanding in EDEs (percentage of the total)

Note: Includes 20 countries reported by the BIS 2013: Q2 numbers.

Source: BIS International Financial Statistics database.

holdings in $9.1 trillion local debt market of EDEs reached an unprecedented 26.6 per cent and this proportion exceeded 40 per cent in some economies.

Despite the rapid increase in the share of local currency in *total* external debt issued by EDEs in the new millennium, for many countries the bulk of *total gross external debt* is still in foreign currencies since bank loans account for a large proportion of total external debt and these as well as the official debt of

Table 3.10 Share of local currency in total bonds (per cent)

	2001	2008	2013
EDEs	70	85	82
Argentina	29	49	...
Brazil	59	79	...
Chile	77	73	80
China	95	99	...
Colombia	31	37	76
India	97	92	89
Indonesia	96	80	...
Korea	91	88	88
Malaysia	77	86	85
Mexico	59	81	79
Peru	60	67	...
Philippines	48	53	67
South Africa	87	84	88
Thailand	81	95	95
Turkey	78	81	79

Notes: For 2001 and 2008 EDEs refer to IMF classifications of 'emerging markets and developing economies'; for 2013, they include 11 countries for which data are available.
Bonds with original maturity over one year.

Source: Burger et al. (2010) and BIS International Financial Statistics database.

Table 3.11 Share of local currency in total gross external debt (per cent)

	2003	2008	2013
Argentina	1.1	7.2	5.9
Chile	0.8	3.4	5.0
Colombia	0.0	6.6	6.0
India	...	15.3	20.9
Korea	8.5	18.4	28.7
Peru	0.0	2.8	1.0
Philippines	...	...	4.0
South Africa	26.4	41.0	55.7
Thailand	11.2	23.8	31.8
Turkey	0.1	5.9	6.9

Note: 2013: Q3 numbers.

Source: World Bank Quarterly External Debt Statistics/SDDS.

EDEs are mainly in foreign currencies (see Table 3.11). This is true particularly for poorer countries dependent on official lending, countries with rudimentary domestic debt markets or with too low a credit rating to be able to attract foreign investors to domestic debt markets or to issue local-currency denominated international bonds. As noted in Chapter 2, a growing number of such countries, notably in SSA, have been issuing eurobonds and many of them for the first time, taking advantage of expansion in global liquidity, lower interest rates, and improvements in global risk appetite, but assuming significant currency and refinancing risks. These first-time issues between 2009 and 2013 reached almost

$9 billion. While the average size was small, at some $450 million, it reached 10 per cent of GDP in some of them (Guscina et al. 2014).

3.6 Public Commercial Debt

There are three important developments in public debt of major EDEs in the new century. First, in 2013 in most countries total and external public debt as a percentage of GDP stood below the levels seen in the early 2000s, notwithstanding their tendency to rise after the 2008–09 crisis. Second, a greater proportion of public debt is now in local currencies. Finally, there is an extension of maturity and a shift from variable or indexed debt to fixed interest rates in domestic debt markets.

Public sectors' finances in EDEs improved significantly before the onset of the crisis. On average, general government budgets were in deficit by some 3–4 per cent of GDP at the beginning of the 2000s. By 2007–08 they had moved to a surplus, at around 1 per cent of GDP. This decelerated public borrowing and the ratio of public debt to GDP in EDEs taken together fell from around 50 per cent to less than 35 per cent during that period (see Figure 3.12). The decline was particularly impressive in MENA, SSA, and CIS. In Asia where public debt had been already lower than other regions, the debt ratio declined further in the first half of the 2000s. Even in highly indebted Latin American countries, the drop was significant, from over 60 per cent of GDP to less than 50 per cent. In several countries which had suffered from severe crises in the late 1990s and early 2000s, including Indonesia, Thailand, Russia, and Turkey, the public debt ratio went down by as much as 20 percentage points and even more (see Table 3.12).

There can be little doubt that the lessons drawn from recurrent crises in previous decades led to efforts by governments to improve their debt profiles and reduce their vulnerability to crises. However, improvements in public debt profiles and the resilience of EDEs to fallouts from the crisis in the US and Europe cannot be explained by improvements in macroeconomic policies and public debt management alone.[17] As discussed in Chapter 2 these owe a great deal to favourable global economic conditions resulting from the policies that generated consumption and property bubbles in the US and Europe, their policy response to the consequent crisis and the emergence of China as a major commodity importer. This is particularly true for deficit EDEs dependent on capital inflows and commodity exports.

[17] See, e.g., Anderson et al. (2010) which explains the resilience of EDEs to financial shocks from the crisis primarily in terms of better macroeconomic and debt management and improved fundamentals prior to the crisis and policy response to shocks. The same view in fact underlined the so-called decoupling thesis discussed in Chapter 2.

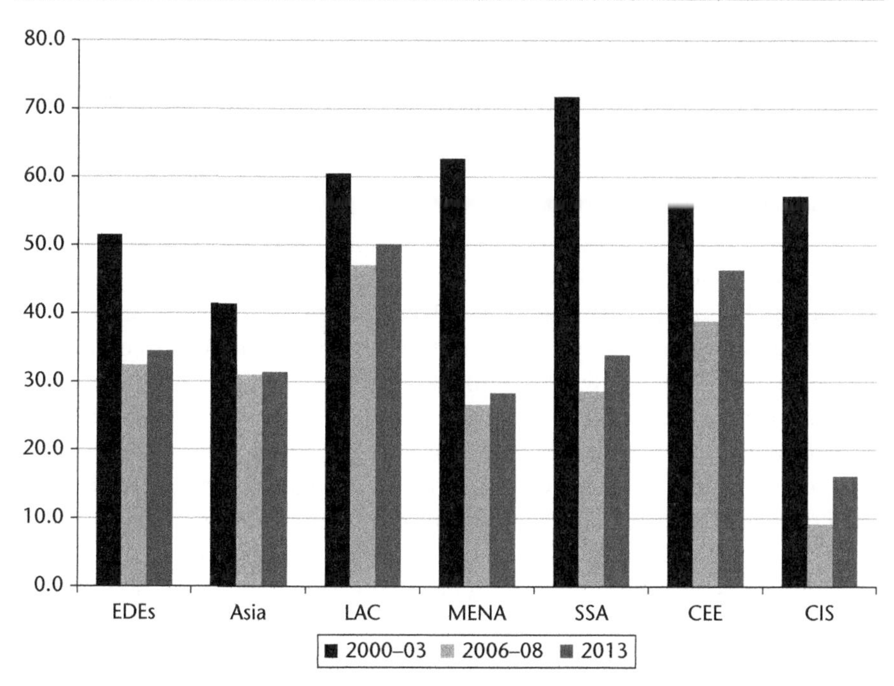

Figure 3.12 General government gross debt: regions (percentage of GDP)

Note: 2000–2003: highest; 2006–2008: lowest.

Source: IMF WEO (2014a).

Table 3.12 General government gross debt (per cent of GDP)

	2000–02	2007–08	2013
EDEs	51.5	34.6	34.5
Argentina	165.0	58.5	46.9
Brazil	79.4	63.5	66.3
Chile	15.1	3.9	12.2
China	18.9	17.0	22.4
Colombia	43.9	30.5	31.8
India	82.9	74.0	66.7
Indonesia	95.1	33.2	26.1
Korea	18.7	30.1	36.7
Malaysia	43.1	41.2	58.2
Mexico	43.5	37.6	46.5
Peru	43.2	26.8	19.6
Philippines	63.3	44.2	38.3
Russia	59.9	7.9	13.4
South Africa	43.5	27.2	45.2
Thailand	57.8	37.3	45.3
Turkey	77.9	39.9	35.8

Note: Highs for 2000–02 and lows for 2007–08.

Source: IMF WEO (2014a).

Starting in the early 2000s, most EDEs enjoyed significant improvements in the terms and conditions of borrowing. At the beginning of the millennium, sovereign spreads had come down from the peaks reached on the wake of the Asian crisis, but they were still hovering between 600 and 800 basis points (see Figure 3.13). They dropped further after 2002, falling below 200 basis points in 2007 and hitting a historical low of 170 bps in the middle of that year. The Lehman collapse caused a temporary hike in spreads. The subsequent decline, together with exceptionally low long-term rates in the US, resulted in a sharp drop in yields on internationally issued US dollar sovereign bonds (see Figure 3.14).

Yields on local-currency government bonds also remained at exceptionally low levels from 2002 onwards thanks largely to increased foreign holdings resulting from a search-for-yield triggered by exceptionally low US Treasury yields (Ebeke and Lu 2014; Turner 2014). Currency appreciations also encouraged foreign holding by creating sizeable capital gains. Success in bringing inflation under control, together with improvements in current account and reserves positions in many EDEs, kept the currency risk down. After the Eurozone crisis, returns on local-currency bonds started to move more closely with those on international assets regarded as 'safe' (Miyajima et al. 2012).[18]

The external trading environment was equally benign for commodity exporters. In Latin America, an important part of the decline in budget deficits after 2002 was due to rising commodity prices, with revenues from commodity taxes, profits and royalties accounting for as much as 50 per cent of the total increase in the fiscal revenue ratio in some countries (Cornia et al. 2011). The fiscal record in Latin America was less impressive in terms of structural balances since several governments in the region pursued pro-cyclical expansion in spending (IMF 2007; IDB 2008; and Jiménez and Gómez-Sabaini 2009). African commodity exporters also benefited from rapidly expanding Chinese imports generated by massive investment stimulus. Every percentage point increase in China's domestic investment growth is estimated to have been associated with a 0.6 percentage point increase in SSA countries' export growth and the impact was larger for resource-rich countries, especially oil exporters (Drummond and Liu 2013).

With the outbreak of the crisis in advanced economies, the fiscal space gained during the subprime expansion allowed an unprecedented countercyclical policy response in many EDEs to adverse fallouts. Consequently, fiscal and external deficits started to rise, aggravated by the weakening of commodity prices, capital inflows, and currencies. After a strong recovery in 2010, growth slowed

[18] On average, countries issuing local-currency bonds have higher credit ratings than those relying mainly on US dollar bonds and this tends to narrow the average margin between local-currency and US dollar bonds. For instance, for several non-investment grade first-time sovereign bond issuers in dollars, the spread during 2009–13 exceeded 500 basis points (Guscina et al. 2014). The dollar bond market is heavily exposed to low-rated Latin America which accounted for 43 per cent of the dollar bond index but some 25 per cent of the local bond index in 2012; see AFCG (2013).

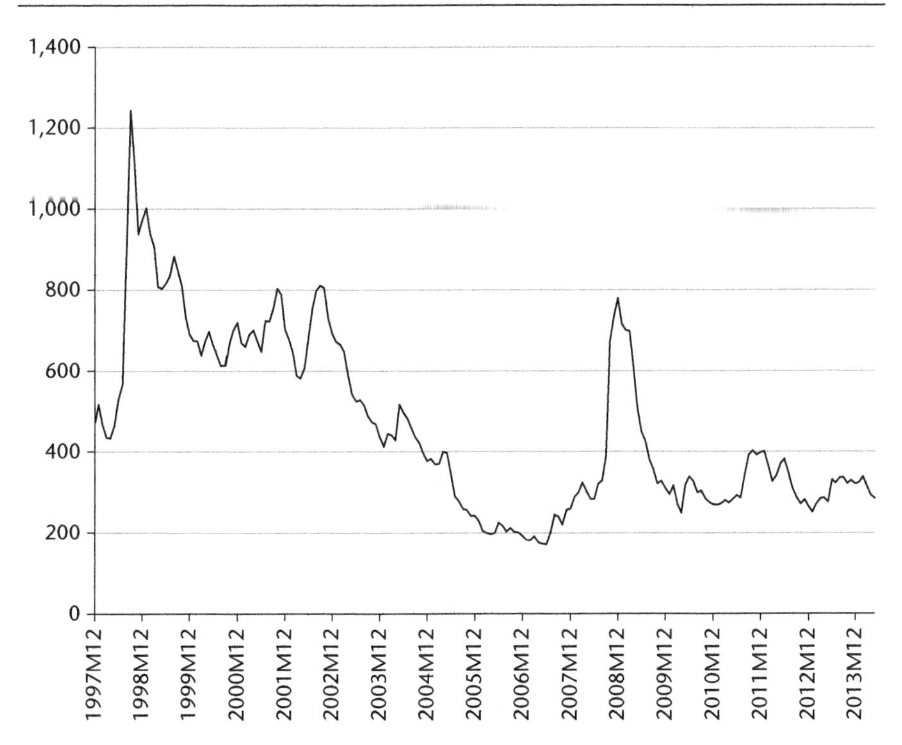

Figure 3.13 Sovereign bond interest rate spreads in EDEs (basis points over US treasuries)

Note: Monthly average data.

Source: World Bank Global Economic Monitor.

down almost everywhere in EDEs, including BRICS (Brazil, Russia, India, China, and South Africa) creating cyclical deficits. During 2012–13 general government deficits reached 4 per cent of GDP in several countries and exceeded 7 per cent in India. At the end of 2013, government debt ratios were higher than the lows attained on the eve of the crisis in all developing regions (Figure 3.12) and in the majority of countries individually (Table 3.12). In China, Malaysia, Mexico, the Republic of Korea, and South Africa, they were also above the levels seen during the turbulent times of the late-1990s and the early 2000s.

There are also important structural changes in public debt. Debt securities still account for the bulk of public borrowing in EDEs compared to bank loans.[19] Due to the shift of governments to domestic debt markets, the share of local issues in outstanding sovereign debt securities shows a significant increase since the beginning of the century (Table 3.9). As a result domestic debt markets is dominated by the public sector while the private sector

[19] A notable exception is China where less than 30 per cent of general government debt is in securities.

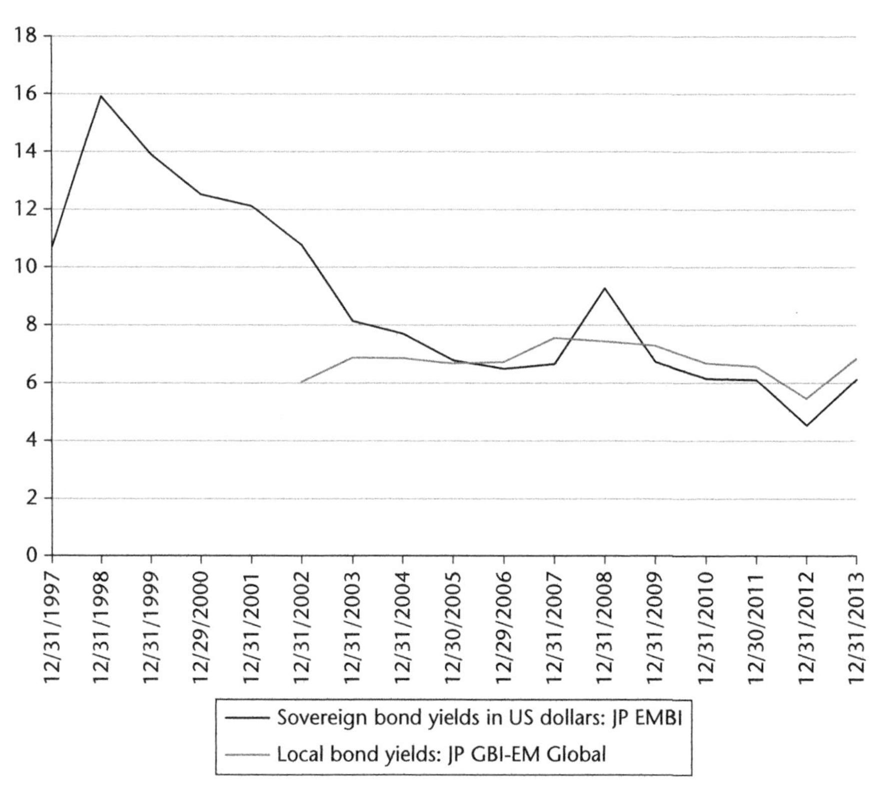

Figure 3.14 Government bond yields in emerging markets (percentage)
Note: Year-end data.
Source: J.P. Morgan.

accounts for a higher share in international issues—around 70 per cent in 2013, up from less than 40 per cent in 2000.

The shift of governments to domestic debt markets and opening them to non-residents has also resulted in a concomitant increase in non-resident participation in local government bond markets in many countries. There is no comprehensive data on non-resident holding of locally issued, externally held sovereign debt in emerging economies. Figure 3.15 gives data only for a few countries. At the end of 2013, in Indonesia, Malaysia, Mexico and Peru non-residents accounted for more than one-third of locally issued government bonds. Almost all of these bonds are in local currencies. Subsidiaries of foreign-owned international banks in EDEs also hold local government bonds, but these are not considered as external debt as conventionally defined.

Domestically issued debt held by non-residents is not always included in external debt statistics. Because of this discrepancy, the external debt of emerging economies is often underestimated. For instance when Bank Negara of Malaysia started using a new definition of external debt recommended by the

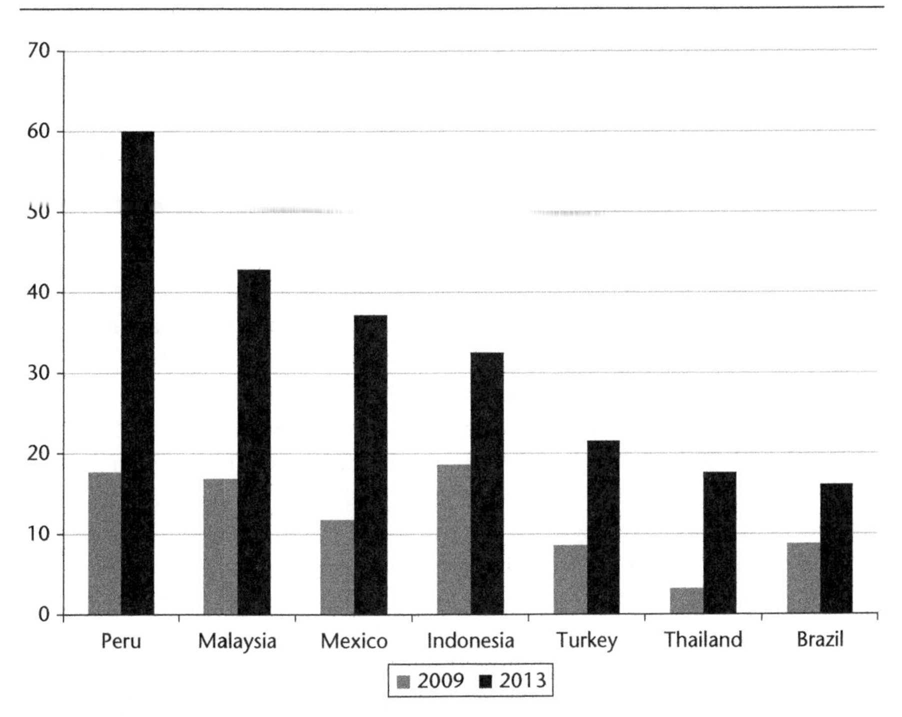

Figure 3.15 Non-resident investor participation in domestic markets for government bonds (percentage of total outstanding)
Source: J.P.Morgan (2013).

Guide for Compilers prepared by the IMF and eight other organizations in the Inter-Agency Task Force on Finance Statistics in 2013, including all debt owed to non-residents irrespective of currency and place of issue, total external debt of Malaysia went up from 30.5 per cent of GDP to over 60 per cent (BNM 2014).

As a result of increased non-resident holding of locally-issued sovereign debt, a higher proportion of sovereign external debt in bonds is subject to domestic jurisdiction. At the end of 2013 this proportion was over 93 per cent in Malaysia and Thailand which barely issued any sovereign debt in international markets in recent years but opened up their domestic debt markets to non-residents. It was over 70 per cent in Brazil and Mexico. Even in countries with a large stock of international bonds, a growing proportion of externally held sovereign debt has come under domestic jurisdiction. This was between 35 and 45 per cent in Indonesia, Peru, and Turkey at the end of 2013.[20] As discussed in Chapter 5, this has important consequences for sovereign debt restructuring.

[20] These estimates are based on the data for non-resident participation in local bond markets given in Figure 3.15 and outstanding domestic and international bond issues as given by the BIS in its International Financial Statistics database, namely Tables 16B and 11E.

International investors were attracted also by internationally issued local-currency government debt because of high yields and currency appreciations. Table 3.13 gives the share of non-residents in local-currency central government securities, including both domestically and internationally issued bonds and notes. In China and India where there is no significant international issuance of local currency debt by governments and access of non-residents to domestic debt markets remains restricted, non-resident shares in local-currency public debt are very low. In most others, after the crisis the share of non-residents in local-currency bonds increased while the exposure of domestic banks to sovereign debt fell as a per cent of total assets, notably in Asia and Latin America (Arslanalp and Tsuda 2014). In 2013, outside Argentina, China, and India, the average share of non-resident holdings of local-currency government debt securities was close to 30 per cent for the countries in Table 3.13.

A significant implication of growing acquisition of locally issued public debt by non-residents as well as the increase in the share of local-currency in international issues is the shift of the currency composition of *external* and *total* sovereign debt towards local currencies. According to figures on outstanding sovereign external debt of a selection of emerging economies, dollar-denominated debt was far greater than local-currency-denominated debt at the beginning of the 2000s (see Figure 3.16).[21] The latter started growing vigorously and steadily, overtaking the dollar issues in mid-2000s. The Lehman collapse had a much stronger impact on local-currency issues than dollar-denominated issues, but after the dip in 2008–09 local-currency issues recovered, albeit showing considerable instability compared to pre-crisis years. In 2013, at over $1 trillion, the local-currency debt market was twice the size of the US dollar debt market (Polychronopoulos and Binstock 2013).

According to IDB (2008), for 7 major Latin American borrowers, the share of local-currency debt in total public debt increased from 35 per cent in the late 1990s to 62 per cent in 2007. Another study for a sample of 11 EDEs estimates that the share of local currency debt in total sovereign debt increased from around 24 per cent in 1995 to almost 80 per cent in 2005.[22] According to the World Bank (2014a) at the end of 2012, the domestic currency component of the central government debt of developing countries reporting to the Public Sector Debt Database averaged 57 per cent of the total. This figure excludes Brazil and China which raised, on average, about 98 per cent of central government financing in domestic markets (see Figure 3.17).

[21] That is, J.P. Morgan EMBI Global for US dollar debt and J.P. Morgan GBI-EM for local currency debt, respectively. The former includes dollar-denominated global bonds, loans and Eurobonds with an outstanding face value of at least $500 million. The latter includes local currency bonds issued by 16 emerging market governments.

[22] See Fried (2013), which also gives a brief survey of empirical research on the currency composition of sovereign debt in EDEs and the factors affecting it.

Table 3.13 Non-resident holdings of local currency denominated central government debt securities (per cent of total)

	2004	2007	2010	2013
Argentina	34.4	18.9	13.7	2.7
Brazil	1.0[a]	5.1	11.4	14.5
China	0.0	0.0	0.0	0.7
India	0.1	0.6	1.0	1.6
Indonesia	2.7	16.4	30.5	31.8
Malaysia	7.3	14.2	21.6	30.9
Mexico	7.1	10.8	19.9	36.1
Peru	0.0	26.7	42.5	56.3
Philippines	0.0	0.0	9.2	14.7
Russia	2.1	1.5	4.0	24.6
South Africa	6.5[b]	10.4	21.8	36.7
Thailand	1.9	0.9	7.3	17.9
Turkey	7.2	14.1	12.3	24.5

Notes: 2013: Q2 numbers.
a: 2005 Q4
b: 2006 Q1.

Source: IMF Sovereign Investor Base Dataset for Emerging Markets (30 December 2013 version).

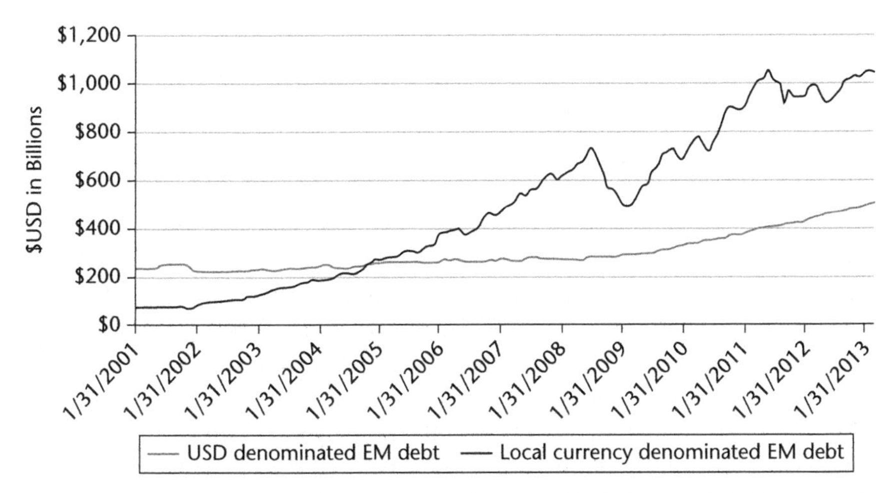

Figure 3.16 Emerging market debt outstanding in US dollars and local currencies (billions of US dollars)

Source: Copyright 2013, Research Affiliates. Originally published on www.researchafiliates.com. Reproduced and republished with permission. All Rights Reserved.

Increased foreign access to domestic debt markets has also resulted in a shift in the holder profile of government debt towards non-residents in several EDEs. It is estimated that non-residents held $1 trillion of government debt of EDEs at the end of 2012, not counting official loans, and about half of this debt was incurred during 2010–12 (Arslanalp and Tsuda 2014). The share of non-residents in *total* gross public debt shows an increase in several countries

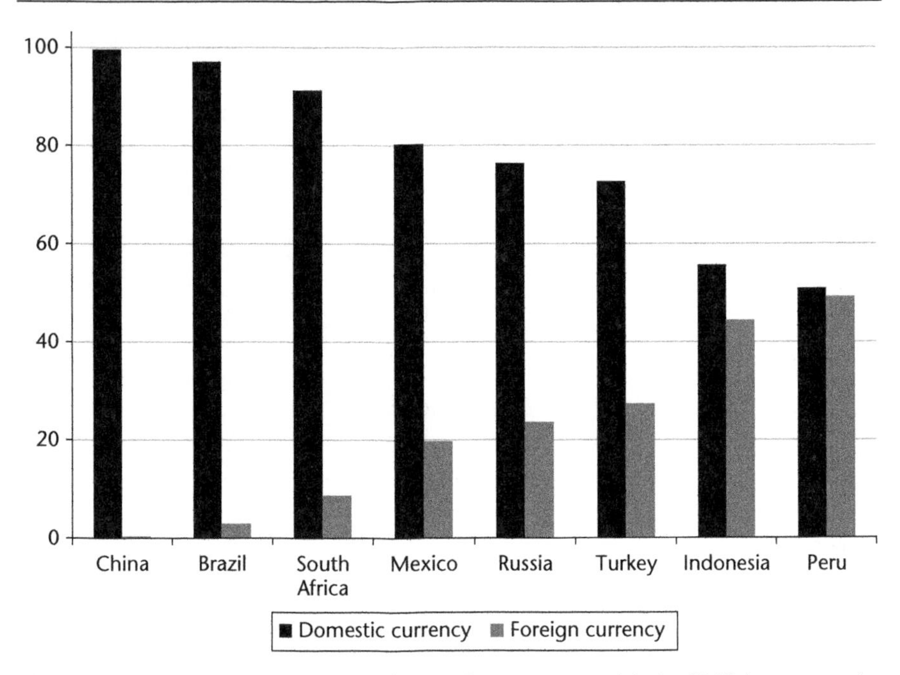

Figure 3.17 Currency composition of central government debt in 2012 (percentage)
Source: World Bank Public Sector Debt Statistics.

including Indonesia, Malaysia, Mexico, South Africa, Thailand, and Turkey (see Table 3.14). The increase in non-resident holdings is much more pronounced and widespread for public debt securities than bank loans. In more than half of the countries in Table 3.15, the share of non-resident holdings in public sector *debt securities* in all currencies was higher in 2013 than in 2004. The increase was particularly rapid after the onset of the crisis. In Brazil, Mexico, and the Russian Federation where the share of non-resident holdings had declined before the crisis, there was a rapid increase after 2007, notably after 2010.

The share of non-residents in total government debt is generally lower in EDEs than in advanced economies. However, the difference is quite small with advanced economies outside the Eurozone (Arslanalp and Tsuda 2014). In fact, public debt in many EDEs is internationalized to a much greater extent than that in some major reserve-issuing countries. On some estimates, about 30 per cent of gross public debt of the US is held abroad, and this proportion is around 20 per cent for the UK and less than 5 per cent in Japan (Weisenthal 2011).[23] For several EDEs the share of public debt held abroad is much higher. This is true not only for public securities denominated in all currencies as in

[23] This ratio is around 50 per cent for German public debt, but a large proportion of it is held within the Eurozone.

Table 3.15, but also for those denominated in local currency (see Figure 3.15 and Table 3.13). In most countries in Figure 3.15 the share of non-residents in *domestically issued local-currency* government bonds exceeds the share of non-residents in sovereign bonds of Japan, the UK, and the US. This is also true for *total* (domestically and internationally issued) *local-currency* central government securities (see Table 3.13).

More significantly, the externally held local-currency government debt of EDEs is not in the hands of foreign central banks and other official bodies, but mostly in the portfolios of fickle investors, including foreign asset managers. It is estimated that as of the end of 2012, foreign central banks held only between $40 billion and $80 billion of government debt of EDEs out of about $1 trillion held by non-residents. And out of a total of 24 EDEs, government debt of only seven countries is included in central bank reserve assets (Arslanalp and Tsuda 2014). Except for a few EDEs with large official debts, foreign official holdings, including official loans and central bank holdings as reserve assets, fall far short of private holdings.

3.7 Private Debt

The evolution of private external debt in EDEs shows important differences in some respects but similarities in others with the evolution of public external debt since the early 2000s.[24] First, as already noted, in EDEs taken together and in several countries individually, private external debt has been growing faster than public external debt in both international bank loans and securities. Second, unlike public debt, there has been no tendency for private external debt to decline as a per cent of GDP. Third, as for public debt, in several EDEs a growing proportion of private debt is held by non-residents. But, unlike the public sector, the share of foreign-currency debt securities in total debt issued by corporations, including domestic issues, has been rising. Overall, a much greater proportion of private external debt is denominated in foreign currencies than public external debt. Finally, there is a renewed tendency towards dollarization in domestic loan markets whereas in most major EDEs the public sector has effectively stopped issuing forex-linked domestic debt.

Private international debt of EDEs grew by about 10 per cent per annum during 2000–13, faster after the onset of the crisis in advanced economies than

[24] It should be noted that some of the corporations included in the private sector data are state-owned enterprises. These are often run on the same commercial basis as privately-owned enterprises. This is true not only for China where state ownership is widespread, but also in some major EDEs such as Brazil and India.

Table 3.14 Holders of general government debt (per cent of total)

	Non-residents				Domestic central banks				Domestic banks			
	2004	2007	2010	2013	2004	2007	2010	2013	2004	2007	2010	2013
Argentina	45.0	43.4	38.5	30.0	15.7	13.2	22.2	34.4	24.7	18.8	24.0	23.8
Brazil	15.9	10.3	12.0	13.8	23.5	21.1	29.0	30.8	25.3	27.7	25.9	24.1
Chile	42.4	50.9	20.6	19.0	43.3	2.0	0.0	0.0	6.4	20.1	22.8	17.4
China	5.0	2.5	1.3	1.1	5.3	15.7	8.0	5.9	80.0	77.9	87.5	91.2
Colombia	41.3	30.6	31.2	29.5	0.8	0.9	0.6	0.0	21.3	15.7	18.6	19.9
India	7.5	5.9	6.0	6.3	3.3	2.9	7.3	10.0	26.9	26.6	29.5	31.3
Indonesia	50.3	52.0	57.1	55.5	21.1	20.1	16.6	17.3	25.0	22.8	14.4	13.8
Malaysia	27.7	22.5	24.2	31.8	0.1	0.9	0.5	0.4	16.0	12.3	25.8	21.6
Mexico	37.7	25.9	32.1	49.3	0.0	0.0	0.0	0.0	9.9	12.1	11.9	8.9
Peru	76.4	66.2	63.1	62.7	0.0	0.0	0.0	1.6	6.6	7.2	7.8	7.9
Philippines	43.1	38.6	45.3	42.7	4.2	11.3	7.0	6.9	24.5	26.4	31.8	30.8
Russia	55.9	29.6	19.1	22.6	9.5	12.0	6.4	4.6	17.0	29.3	36.1	35.3
South Africa	16.9	21.4	25.0	35.8	6.6	2.0	1.1	0.6	19.7	19.3	27.5	23.2
Thailand	12.5	3.6	7.5	17.2	5.7	4.3	7.5	7.8	24.6	28.8	27.9	21.2
Turkey	28.9	29.4	29.9	42.7	7.0	5.1	2.2	2.0	37.5	51.3	61.9	48.0

Note: 2013: Q2 numbers.

Source: IMF Sovereign Investor Base Dataset for Emerging Markets (30 December 2013 version).

Table 3.15 Non-resident holding of government debt securities (per cent of total)

	2004	2007	2010	2013
Argentina	57.2	51.7	37.8	30.7
Brazil	12.8	8.7	10.7	12.5
Chile	71.5	43.7	16.2	16.6
China	2.3	1.0	0.4	0.9
Colombia	30.5	21.5	21.8	22.6
India	0.1	0.6	1.0	1.6
Indonesia	5.5	25.3	43.4	46.7
Malaysia	16.5	18.3	23.7	32.5
Mexico	37.7	26.2	33.3	53.7
Peru	49.2	46.9	53.3	60.4
Philippines	23.6	23.4	31.0	30.9
Russia	47.4	27.2	20.8	32.2
South Africa	14.4	17.9	23.5	35.0
Thailand	3.8	1.1	7.4	17.9
Turkey	15.3	21.6	21.0	36.5

Note: 2013: Q2 numbers.

Source: IMF Sovereign Investor Base Dataset for Emerging Markets (30 December 2013 version).

before (see Table 3.16).[25] However, in the run-up to the crisis it registered a small decline as a percentage of GDP because of rapid economic growth and currency appreciations. It started rising after 2010 as growth slowed but private borrowing abroad kept its momentum. Its ratio to GDP was slightly higher in 2013 than the levels recorded during the surge in international lending in the mid-1990s. Several major EDEs including China, India, Mexico, the Republic of Korea, and Turkey recorded sizeable increases in private external indebtedness between 2000 and 2013 (see Table 3.17). Turkey had the fastest increase in private indebtedness. Bank borrowing in that country grew by almost three-fold between 2008 and the first quarter of 2014, encouraged by the so-called reserve option mechanism (Fitch Ratings 2014).[26] There were also significant increases in China, India, and Brazil, but from a relatively low base. In these countries private international debt-GDP ratios in 2013 were below the average for the EDEs as a whole.

A large proportion of private debt to international banks is due to borrowing by local banks. In the 1990s they accounted for almost 60 per cent of total international bank claims on the private sector in EDEs (Table 3.16). After

[25] Table 3.16 does not give private *external* debt as conventionally defined since international bank loans include local claims of international banks in foreign currencies as well as cross-border lending. Thus, to differentiate, it is called private *international* debt. This is also the case for Table 3.17. However, as noted earlier, the evolution of private *external* debt closely follows that of private *international* debt.

[26] This mechanism allows banks to hold required reserves in foreign currency. It encourages them to borrow abroad in dollars to release local currency for lending in domestic markets at higher interest rates. Domestic credit (deposit) expansion thus leads to increased borrowing by banks abroad, which, in turn, raises domestic lending.

Table 3.16 Private international debt in EDEs (billions of US dollars)

	1995	2000	2007	2010	2013
International bank loans	620.9	695.3	1370.5	1756.7	2540.9
Banks	360.4	287.5	571.4	757.1	1137.5
Non-bank private	260.6	407.8	799.1	999.6	1403.4
International debt securities	124.4	211.2	397.6	518.0	918.1
Financial corporations	69.4	97.0	226.3	296.9	555.7
Banks	*49.7*	*61.3*	*125.7*	*155.5*	*305.3*
Other financial corporations	*19.7*	*35.7*	*100.7*	*141.4*	*250.4*
Non-financial corporations	55.0	114.2	171.3	221.1	362.4
Total (*billions of US dollars*)	745.3	906.5	1768.1	2274.7	3459.0
Total (*per cent of GDP*)	15.2	15.6	14.4	13.3	15.6

Notes: 2013: Q3 numbers.
EDEs include Argentina, Brazil, China, Chile, Colombia, India, Indonesia, Korea, Lebanon, Malaysia, Mexico, Pakistan, Peru, Philippines, Russia, Saudi Arabia, Singapore, South Africa, Thailand, and Turkey.

Source: BIS International Financial Statistics database.

recurrent crises in the latter half of the decade, this proportion fell to almost 40 per cent with a concomitant increase in the share of non-bank corporations. The shares of banks and non-bank corporations in total private debt to international banks remained relatively stable during 2000–13.

There is a visible shift in the composition of private international debt from bank loans towards debt securities. International bank lending to the private sector in EDEs barely increased during the second half of the 1990s while corporate bond issues showed a relatively strong growth. There is an acceleration of corporate bond issues in the new millennium, particularly after the onset of the crisis when corporations shifted to low-interest debt in reserve currencies, assuming currency and interest rate risks (IMF GFSR 2013a; Oprita 2013). Between 2007 and 2013 corporate international security issues grew much faster than international bank loans. They shot up after 2010, with outstanding securities rising by almost 80 per cent in a matter of three years, reaching almost $1 trillion in the third quarter of 2013. Two-thirds of these belonged to non-bank corporations. By contrast, banks in EDEs continued to rely mainly on loans from international banks, but their outstanding external debt securities almost doubled between 2010 and 2013.

The post-crisis shift from bank loans to security issues was particularly rapid in Mexico and the Republic of Korea where securities accounted for a large part of corporate international debt in 2013 (Table 3.17). In Brazil, Indonesia, Malaysia, the Russian Federation, South Africa, and Turkey too, corporate international security issues accelerated after the onset of the crisis, but in these countries bank loans still accounted for a larger proportion of corporate external debt. This is even more so for China and India. In fact in China corporate borrowing from banks abroad expanded much faster than security

Table 3.17 Private international debt (billions of US dollars)

		1995	2000	2007	2010	2013
China	*Bank loans*	38.8	50.2	189.7	298.2	780.3
	Securities	9.2	7.4	13.1	17.8	36.4
	Total (% of GDP)	6.6	4.8	5.8	5.3	8.9
India	*Bank loans*	11.5	16.8	131.3	190.6	194.8
	Securities	3.7	4.4	27.9	28.5	23.1
	Total (% of GDP)	4.2	4.5	12.9	12.8	11.6
Korea	*Bank loans*	71.3	52.8	170.4	166.4	144.6
	Securities	26.2	41.9	97.2	123.1	168.4
	Total (% of GDP)	18.4	17.8	25.5	28.5	25.6
Indonesia	*Bank loans*	37.8	32.3	35.6	51.3	85.5
	Securities	3.5	2.1	3.2	4.7	19.7
	Total (% of GDP)	20.4	20.8	9.0	7.9	12.1
Malaysia	*Bank loans*	14.6	17.2	35.2	38.0	56.7
	Securities	4.8	12.0	20.5	23.5	32.0
	Total (% of GDP)	21.8	31.1	28.8	24.8	28.4
Brazil	*Bank loans*	40.6	54.7	89.9	143.0	163.7
	Securities	15.5	27.3	29.5	66.0	98.2
	Total (% of GDP)	7.3	12.7	8.7	9.8	11.7
Mexico	*Bank loans*	33.8	47.8	68.4	77.1	87.1
	Securities	20.0	24.6	25.3	47.7	120.9
	Total (% of GDP)	15.6	10.6	9.0	11.9	16.5
South Africa	*Bank loans*	13.9	14.8	26.3	25.2	26.1
	Securities	1.5	2.5	13.7	15.7	21.0
	Total (% of GDP)	10.2	13.0	14.0	11.2	13.4
Russia	*Bank loans*	48.3	34.4	177.4	132.5	163.4
	Securities	1.1	0.4	28.5	34.3	78.6
	Total (% of GDP)	15.8	13.4	15.8	10.9	11.4
Turkey	*Bank loans*	13.4	31.6	94.4	98.5	139.5
	Securities	1.1	1.4	1.9	4.3	30.9
	Total (% of GDP)	6.3	12.4	14.9	14.1	20.6

Source: BIS International Financial Statistics database and IMF WEO (2014a).

issues, particularly after 2010, whereas in India outstanding securities fell while borrowing from international banks grew moderately.

The proceeds of international debt issues by non-financial corporations in foreign currencies appear to have been used in several ways. Some firms in China borrowed in foreign currencies to fund acquisition of foreign assets (He and McCauley 2013). Chinese firms also used foreign borrowing for the acquisition of domestic assets such as property, thus assuming the currency risk. In Latin America, high rates of issuance of foreign currency debt by non-financial firms, including those in non-traded sectors, appear to have been behind the rapid growth of their deposits in the region's financial system. When global conditions tighten, a rapid withdrawal of these deposits could result in a significant contraction of domestic credit. In the event of sharp declines in local currencies, these firms could also incur large losses and face solvency problems (IDB 2014).

Corporations in EDEs also borrowed from international markets through issuance by their overseas subsidiaries, including financial vehicles established in Offshore Financial Centres (OFCs). As seen in Table 3.18, the amounts involved are by no means trivial. While on conventional residency basis, between 2010 and 2013, total bond issues by corporations of EDEs amounted to $480 billion, on nationality basis the figure reached $940 billion, with the difference being bonds issued by overseas subsidiaries. In other words, during that period corporations in EDEs issued almost as many bonds through their subsidiaries as they did directly. On nationality basis, the BRIC countries account for over 50 per cent of total corporate issues in EDEs, including by their overseas subsidiaries.

According to an estimate, as of mid-2013, one-quarter of all international debt securities outstanding of corporations of EDEs had been issued in OFCs compared with 22 per cent in advanced economies. This surge is primarily due to China and Brazil. Total issues by Chinese corporations in the 12 months ending in mid-2013 reached $51 billion, up from less than $1 billion during 2001–02, and constituted 70 per cent of all international debt securities issued by Chinese firms. Although Chinese corporations also issued renminbi-denominated securities in OFCs to take advantage of lower cost than domestic issues, these accounted for only 16 per cent of their outstanding issues in 2013 while the bulk (77 per cent) was in US dollars. In the same period, issuance by Brazilian firms in OFCs reached $20 billion or more than 40 per cent of their total international issuance (McCauley et al. 2013; Pinto 2014). In June 2013, the stock of Brazil's external liabilities on a nationality basis was 137 per cent larger than its liabilities on residency basis (IDB 2014).

Since external debt is defined on the basis of cross-border liabilities, issues by transnational corporations from EDEs through their overseas subsidiaries are not included in external debt and balance-of-payments statistics as long as the proceeds are kept abroad. Nevertheless, since the risks they entail impinge directly on the corporations involved, liabilities defined on the basis of

Table 3.18 International emerging market corporate bond issuance (billions of US dollars)

	2010	2011	2012	2013
Total: nationality basis	151.5	167.1	284.0	335.6
BRIC	81.5	89.2	159.4	165.3
Brazil	33.8	33.9	54.9	23.6
China	23.6	42.8	48.3	97.4
Russia	20.7	6.2	51.0	27.7
India	3.4	6.3	5.2	16.6
Total: residence basis	80.4	98.9	143.5	161.3
Issues by overseas subsidiaries*	71.1	68.2	140.5	174.3

* Differences between nationality and residence basis issues.

Source: P. Turner (2014).

nationality rather than residency constitutes a 'better measure of risk exposures' of such corporations (Turner 2014: 5; see also IDB 2014). To what extent and in what form funds borrowed by overseas subsidiaries enter the home country is not always clear. If they enter as inter-company loans, they would be recorded as FDI rather than debt. If global financial conditions tighten and corporations find themselves unable to roll over debt issued by their subsidiaries, payments might have to be made by parent companies. This could result in large withdrawals of corporate deposits from local banks, credit contraction and large claims on international reserves.

The increase in international debt issues of corporations of EDEs since the onset of the crisis, notably since 2010, becomes more pronounced if debt issued by their overseas subsidiaries is taken into account. This suggests that, as in public debt in several EDEs, a growing proportion of corporate debt securities are held by foreigners, although in public debt this is because of increased acquisition of domestic sovereign bonds by non-residents rather than growing international issues. Since a very large proportion of corporate international issues are denominated in reserve currencies, this also implies that, unlike public debt, the composition of corporate debt securities has been changing in favour of foreign currencies. Since the local-currency component of external debt in securities is greater for the public sector than for corporations and since a much higher proportion of corporate external debt is in forex-denominated bank loans, it follows that foreign-currency debt accounts for a higher share of total corporate external debt than total public external debt.

This difference between private and public sectors in terms of their reliance on domestic-currency *versus* foreign-currency debt also reflects how international investors may be differentiating between them in terms of exchange rate and default risks. It is argued that international investors overwhelmingly demand that corporate issuers from EDEs float debt in major currencies in order to hedge against foreign exchange risks (Delikouras et al. 2013). By insisting on lending in foreign currency, investors would be hedging against the currency risk and passing it onto borrowers, which in turn raises the probability of default; that is, investors are substituting currency risk for default risk. By contrast, in lending to the public sector in local currencies, they are substituting default risk for currency risk. This implies that, *ceteris paribus*, international investors assign a higher probability to sovereign default than to private default. This may well be because the corporations that are able to borrow in international markets are often important enough for governments to bail them out.

In contrast to rapid growth of foreign-currency denominated external private borrowing in EDEs, in domestic loan markets dollarization is now less than in the 1990s, particularly in Latin America where the share of foreign currency loans had reached and even exceeded 50 per cent of total domestic loans in several countries. This proportion came down to less than 20 per cent in recent years (Hake et al. 2014; Didier and Schmukler 2013; IMF GFSR 2012). Still some countries in the region such as Peru and Uruguay continued to have high shares of foreign currency in domestic loans. Relatively large volumes of bond issuance in foreign currencies by banks in several Latin American countries also suggest a renewed trend towards loan dollarization (IDB 2014).

Loan dollarization is also widespread in Eastern Europe and Central Asia. In Russia and Turkey despite declines after the early 2000s, the share of foreign-currency loans remained quite high and much of these were loans to non-financial corporations (Kutan et al. 2012 for Turkey and Ponomarenko et al. 2011 for the Russian Federation). According to Moody's (2014), more than 80 per cent of the total debt outstanding for rated Turkish corporates was denominated in foreign currency.

Similarly, in several EDEs in East Asia, the combination of low interest rates on reserve currencies and appreciation pressures on exchange rates resulted in a rapid expansion of foreign-currency credit relative to local-currency credit (Borio et al. 2011). The dollars acquired by Chinese financial corporations through debt issuance abroad were partly used to fund domestic lending in dollars. While they are a small proportion of aggregate credit, they have been growing rapidly since the exceptional easing of global credit conditions. For instance during 2012–13, foreign currency loans in China grew twice as much as renminbi loans, at a rate of 35 per cent for the 12 months ending in March 2013 (He and McCauley 2013).

Exceptionally low interest rates in advanced economies tend to generate conflicting influences on dollarization in EDEs and the incidence of the associated risks. On the one hand, they create incentives for banks to engage in international arbitrage by borrowing abroad in foreign currency and lending at home in local currency while assuming the currency risk. On the other hand, they, together with appreciation pressures, tend to increase the demand for dollar-denominated loans by local borrowers while reducing the attractiveness of dollar-denominated deposits. Thus, banks would be more willing to lend in local currency while borrowers would prefer dollar loans. Again, banks would prefer dollar-denominated liabilities while local-currency deposits would become more attractive to depositors.

The balance of these forces, shaped very much by the nature and effectiveness of rules and regulations regarding foreign currency lending and currency mismatches in the banking system, determines the extent to which appreciation pressures and interest rate differentials affect loan dollarization. Where currency mismatches in the banking system are successfully restricted, loan dollarization and external borrowing by banks can be expected to increase. In that case the currency risk would migrate to ultimate borrowers, but this, in turn, would result in greater credit risk for the banks. By contrast, where banks can engage in international arbitrage, increased external borrowing would be associated with faster growth of loans in local currency than in dollars. In this case, loan de-dollarization may well be an indication of increased exposure of the banking system to the currency risk.

3.8 Foreign Banks: Cross-border and Local Lending

Cross-border bank lending to EDEs fluctuated sharply during the past three decades but there is a long-term decline in its share in total external commercial debt of EDEs. This is due to two main factors. First, the growing reliance of EDEs on security issuance. Second, the shift of international banks from cross-border lending to local lending by establishing commercial presence in EDEs.

This shift started in the 1990s and continued with full force in the new millennium until the crisis in the US and Europe. Initially, in the 1990s, privatization of state-owned banks was an important factor in the growing presence of foreign banks in EDEs. Subsequently, joint ownership with local private banks and fully owned subsidiaries gained importance. As noted by Stein (2010), in this process the World Bank did not only push for privatization but also promoted foreign ownership as the missing component that would deal with the downside risks of financial liberalization.

The presence of foreign banks in EDEs is much stronger than in advanced economies. Claessens and van Horen (2012: 3) observed that 'in terms of loans, deposits and profits, current market shares of foreign banks average 20 percent in OECD countries and close to 50 percent in emerging markets and developing countries'.[27] Between 1995 and 2009 the share of foreign banks as a percentage of the total number of banks doubled in both emerging markets and developing countries (see Table 3.19). A large majority of these banks are from advanced economies. Despite the growing importance of EDEs in the world economy, the share of OECD in foreign banking barely declined, remaining roughly at three-quarters of the total. However, the crisis in advanced economies resulted in a certain degree of withdrawal of their banks from foreign activities, including declines in the number of foreign subsidiaries (Buch et al. 2014).

In LAC foreign banks had a high share of the market already in the 1990s and this increased further until the onset of the global crisis. Eastern and

[27] The definition of 'emerging markets' used by these authors include all countries that are included in the Standard and Poor's Emerging Market and Frontier Markets indices and that were not high-income countries in 2000. Thus, it contains some current OECD countries from Central and Eastern Europe.

Central European and Central Asian countries experienced the fastest growth of foreign banks, due to their rapid integration into the global economy after the fall of the Berlin Wall. South Asia also saw a rapid increase, albeit from a low base. The share of foreign banks is typically higher in poorer and smaller countries than in major EDEs, reaching 100 per cent in some. Among the major EDEs there are considerable variations of foreign bank presence (see Table 3.20). The Republic of Korea, which had no foreign banks before it joined OECD in 1996, saw the fastest increase in their presence in the past two decades even though their share is still lower than the average for other countries in Table 3.19. Three of the BRICS, China, India, and South Africa, also have lower degrees of foreign bank presence than other major EDEs. This is true not only in terms of number of banks but also their shares in total banking assets. Several national banks of these countries have themselves become global players.[28]

In addition to joint ownership with local partners, foreign banks enter into host countries by establishing branch offices or full subsidiaries. Foreign branches are unincorporated banks or bank offices located in a foreign country. They are integral parts of the parent banks and not independent legal entities with separate accounts and capital base. They cannot incur liabilities and own assets in their own right. Their liabilities represent real claims on parent banks. They provide globally funded domestic credits. By contrast foreign subsidiaries are stand-alone legal entities created under the law of the host country. They have separate accounts and capital base from those of the parent company and are financially independent. They have to comply

Table 3.19 Share of foreign banks: regions (per cent of total number)

	1995	2000	2009
East Asia and Pacific	18	19	25
Eastern Europe and Central Asia	15	28	47
LAC	25	35	39
MENA	18	23	36
South Asia	7	9	14
SSA	31	37	54
Emerging economies	18	27	36
Developing countries	24	32	46
OECD	19	21	24
Memo: Share of banks from AEs	*75*	*74*	*72*

Source: Claessens and van Horen (2012).

[28] In China the share of foreign banks in total assets of the banking system is a bare 1 per cent, in India 5 per cent and South Africa 22 per cent. In China they are quite small in comparison with the giants such as the Industrial and Commercial Bank of China, China Construction Bank, Agricultural Bank of China, and Bank of China which have been expanding globally in recent

Table 3.20 Share of foreign banks in selected EDEs (per cent of total number)

	1995	2000	2009
Indonesia	26	33	52
Mexico	32	49	48
Turkey	11	15	43
Brazil	23	35	38
Argentina	22	37	35
Korea	0	6	24
South Africa	18	14	22
China	13	9	19
India	6	8	12

Source: Claessens and van Horen (2012).

with the host country regulations and supervision and are covered by the host country deposit insurance schemes.

Branching provides greater freedom in transferring funds across borders and entails lower funding costs and hence is more attractive for international banks with wholesale operations serving large clients. By contrast, international banks prefer subsidiaries for retail banking involving considerable local intermediation (Cerutti et al. 2005; Fiechter et al. 2011). In several Asian countries including India, the Philippines, the Republic of Korea, Singapore and Thailand, with the notable exception of China, branching is more widespread than subsidiaries. This is also true for several countries in Africa, including South Africa. By contrast, with the exception of Argentina, subsidiaries are the main form of entry of foreign banks in Latin America.

The increased penetration of international banks in the markets of EDEs has resulted in a significant shift in the composition of foreign banks' claims. According to the BIS classification, total foreign claims of international banks consist of local claims in local currency and international claims. The latter includes not only cross-border lending but also local lending in foreign currencies. Thus, the BIS concept of foreign claims of international banks corresponds to external bank debt of EDEs defined on *nationality* basis. On the other hand, the distinction between local claims in local currency and international claims provides a measure of currency composition of foreign bank claims on EDEs.

At the beginning of the 1990s local currency claims of international banks on residents of EDEs barely reached 10 per cent of their total claims while the rest was mainly in international claims (see Figure 3.18). Starting in the second half of the decade local claims in local currency shot up rapidly, reaching 45 per cent of the total foreign bank claims by mid-2000s. This upward trend

years. This is also true, to a lesser extent, for India and South Africa. On the rise of banks from major EDEs as global banks, see van Horen (2012).

came to an end with the onset of the crisis in the US and Europe. There is a moderate decline in the share of local currency claims after 2009. This reflects, in part, the increased attractiveness of foreign-currency loans for private borrowers in EDEs and in part the withdrawal of certain banks from international business after the onset of the crisis, particularly in the Eurozone.[29]

The evolution of local and cross-border lending by international banks to EDEs since mid-2005 is given in Figure 3.19. Here local claims include claims in both local and foreign currencies while cross-border claims correspond to the conventional measure of external debt to international banks defined on residency basis. Local lending in all currencies became more important than cross-border lending, accounting for almost 60 per cent of total foreign bank claims in 2013. A comparison of Figures 3.18 and 3.19 shows that since the onset of the global crisis, a growing proportion of local lending by subsidiaries of international banks in EDEs is in foreign currencies; the share of such claims rose from around 12 per cent of total local claims in 2007 to almost 20 per cent at the end of 2013.

3.9 Summary and Conclusions

The deepened integration of EDEs into the international financial system in the new millennium has involved not only growing cross-border capital flows, but also a significantly increased foreign presence in the equity, property, bond and credit markets of these economies, exerting a strong influence on their liquidity and valuation dynamics and heightening their susceptibility to international financial conditions. Gross assets and liabilities and external balance sheets have expanded rapidly almost everywhere. More importantly, the structure of external balance sheets has undergone important changes, particularly on the liabilities side, bringing new vulnerabilities:

- The share of direct and portfolio equity in external liabilities has increased. However, an important part of the increase in equity liabilities is due to capital gains by foreign holders rather than new inflows. In many EDEs the share of foreign investors in equity markets is greater than that in some advanced economies such as the US and Japan.
- In external debt, bond issues have been growing faster than borrowing from international banks both by the public and private sectors, particularly since the crisis. International banks have been shifting from cross-border lending to local lending by establishing commercial presence in

[29] For instance, international assets held by German banks through subsidiaries abroad fell to some 10 per cent of their total assets whereas they were over 15 per cent before the crisis (Buch et al. 2014).

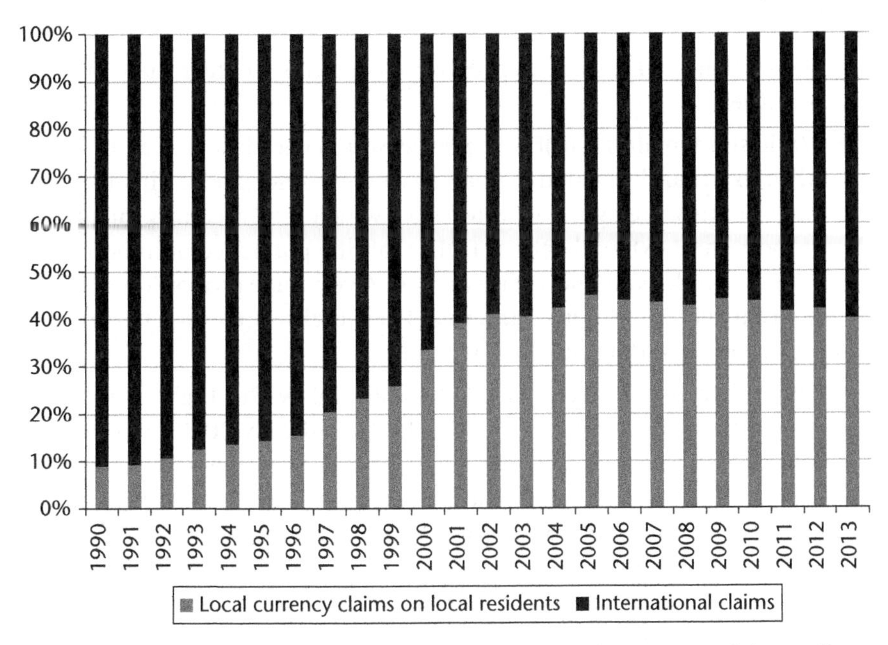

Figure 3.18 Structure of foreign bank claims in EDEs (percentage of the total)

Note: 2013:Q3 numbers.

Source: BIS International Financial Statistics database.

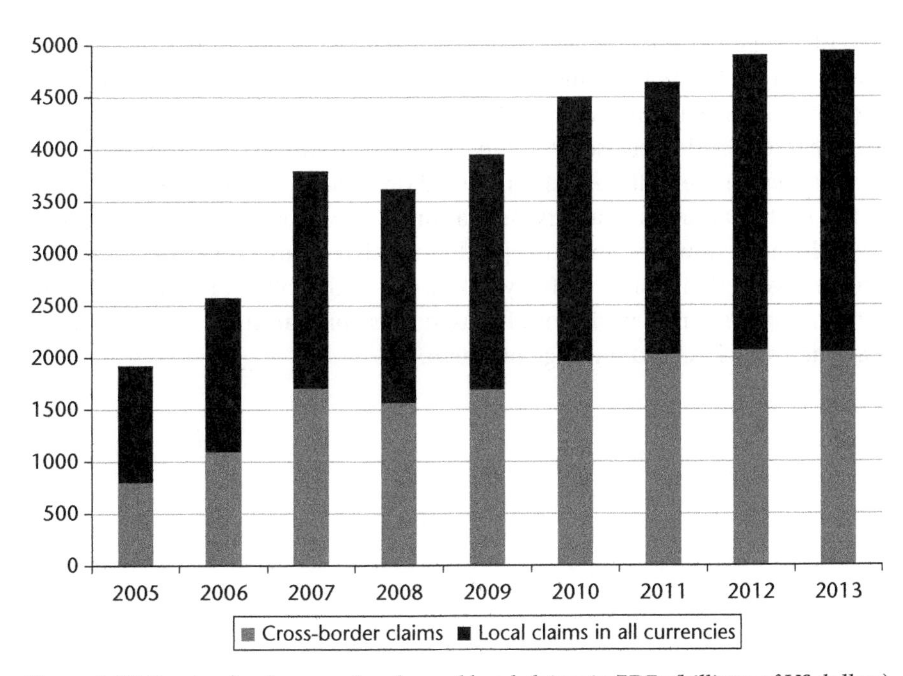

Figure 3.19 Foreign banks: cross-border and local claims in EDEs (billions of US dollars)

Note: Ultimate risk basis.

Source: BIS International Financial Statistics database.

EDEs. Their market share in EDEs is more than twice their share in OECD countries.

- While still remaining below the levels seen a decade ago as a per cent of GDP, external debt build-up has accelerated since 2009. This is mainly due to borrowing by the private sector which now accounts for a higher proportion of external debt of EDEs than the public sector in both international bank loans and security issues. A very large proportion of private external debt is in foreign currency. There is also a renewed tendency for dollarization in domestic loan markets.
- Public debt as a percent of GDP stands below the highs seen in the aftermath of recurrent crises in the 1990s and early 2000s, but in many countries it has started to rise since 2009. Governments in most EDEs have shifted from international to domestic bond markets and opened the latter to foreigners. Much of sovereign external debt is now in local currency and under local jurisdiction. The participation of non-residents in local bond markets has been growing. The proportion of local-currency sovereign debt held by non-residents is greater in many EDEs than in reserve-issuers such as the US, the UK, and Japan. Furthermore, the sovereign debt of EDEs is held by fickle investors abroad rather than by foreign central banks as international reserves.

With deepened and changed pattern of financial integration, new channels have emerged in the transmission of financial shocks from global boom–bust cycles to EDEs. The internationalization of domestic equity, bond and property markets and increased foreign presence in the banking system have created new vulnerabilities, adding to old ones due to interruptions to access to international capital markets. As examined in the following chapter, almost all EDEs have now become susceptible to global financial cycles and shocks irrespective of their balance-of-payments, external debt, net foreign assets and international reserves positions although these play an important role in the way such shocks could impinge on them.

4

External Vulnerabilities

After three decades of recurrent financial turmoil in the world economy, it has become increasingly evident that a close and unfettered integration into the global financial system could severely expose EDEs to shocks and crises. Still, in the new millennium, many of these countries have sought deeper integration, liberalizing international capital flows and allowing greater room for foreign investors and banks in their markets. This, together with the rapid expansion of international liquidity, historically low interest rates and greater risk appetite has resulted in a significant build-up of financial imbalances and fragility in many of these countries, including unsustainable currency appreciations and payments deficits, growing private indebtedness and currency and maturity mismatches in private balance sheets, and bubbles in credit and asset markets. This is particularly the case since the beginning of the crisis in advanced economies. The monetary expansion resulting from the policy response of the US to the crisis accelerated the search for yield in EDEs that had already started in the early years of the 2000s, giving rise to large and sustained inflows of capital and growing presence of foreign investors in EDEs as well as a large build-up of domestic and external private debt well beyond the levels seen during previous financial booms.

As noted in Part I, in the period since the onset of the crisis the international financial markets have seen several instances of heightened volatility, attesting to susceptibility of international financial stability to sudden changes in sentiments and/or policies in major reserve issuing countries, notably the US. These have had significant impact on asset and currency markets in all emerging economies without exception. These were all hit by 'taper tantrum' in May 2013 when the US Federal Reserve revealed its intention to start reducing its bond purchases. In mid-October 2014 there was a dramatic upswing in volatility involving a large sell-off in stocks and bonds, including in emerging economies, triggered by fears over global growth and the impact of an eventual rise in US interest rates. Again, the tension in financial markets developing in late 2015 on the eve of the increase in policy rates in the US for the first time in seven years led to a massive global stock market sell-off in the early months of 2016, leading to sharp declines in equity prices and currencies in all emerging economies.

These bouts of instability were temporary dislocations caused by shifts in market sentiments without any fundamental change in the underlying monetary policies and conditions in major advanced economies. These notwithstanding, the conditions in financial markets since the beginning of the experiment with the ultra-easy monetary policy have generally resembled to what Minsky (1977) described as periods of tranquillity which typically encourage excessive risk taking, thereby sowing the seeds of future instability. Often, they were divorced from underlying economic fundamentals, eliciting such remarks that 'it is hard to avoid the sense of a puzzling disconnect between the markets' buoyancy and underlying economic developments globally' (BIS 2014: 3). Thus, despite the sell-off in the early months of 2016, stock prices have remained at historical highs in the US. They have also stayed relatively strong in the Eurozone despite deflation and financial fragility. Markets have continued to price risky assets as if they are safe, bringing down risk premia to unusually low levels. The UK experienced a property boom which caused concern even before the decision on the Brexit (Osborne and Monaghan 2014). From early 2016, property market conditions in the US started to resemble those prevailing on the eve of the subprime debacle with prices moving towards the highs recorded on the eve of the crisis.

While currency and asset markets of emerging economies have been hit hard by declines in capital inflows after 2014 and, in many cases, by the sharp downturn in commodity prices, these shocks did not reach the proportions seen in the immediate aftermath of the Lehman collapse, in large part because monetary policy in major advanced economies has been highly accommodating. These economies remain extremely vulnerable to an accelerated exit of the US from the ultra-easy monetary policy, including the normalization of the Federal Reserve's balance sheet—that is, a significant contraction of its size and a large shift of its assets back to short- and medium-term treasuries. These would imply not only hikes in short-term rates, but also a tightening of bond markets, possibly pushing the global long-term rates well above the levels seen since the crisis, resulting in significantly tightened financial conditions for emerging economies.

Sharp declines in capital inflows to emerging economies, an exodus of non-residents from domestic financial markets and sustained capital flight by residents triggered by an accelerated exit from the ultra-easy monetary policy in the US could aggravate the difficulties that they have been experiencing since 2014. These could produce a further weakening of currencies and asset prices and tighter domestic credit markets, since capital inflows have been a main driver of credit expansion in these economies since the crisis.[1] They could thus lead not only to external instability but also banking instability.[2] They could also force a severe deleveraging in countries where private debt as a percentage of GDP grew at double digit rates after the 2008 crisis, including Brazil, the Republic of Korea, Turkey, South Africa, Indonesia, Malaysia, and Thailand (IMF GFSR 2014; Colombo 2014a, 2014b, 2014c) possibly leading to widespread defaults and economic contraction.

It is often argued that for several reasons EDEs are now more resilient to external financial shocks than they were in previous decades. First, they have moved away from fixed exchange rates, allowing currency movements to absorb part of the shocks and facilitate balance-of-payments adjustment. Since they are also less exposed to the currency risk, the destabilizing impact of currency movements on balance sheets would remain limited. Second, most EDEs have accumulated large amounts of reserves as self-insurance against capital flow reversals. Third, the likelihood of sovereign external debt crises has diminished considerably because of improved fiscal posture and the shift of governments from international to domestic debt markets. Finally, greater presence of international banks from advanced economies could improve the resilience of the banking system in EDEs to external financial shocks.

It is not clear if and to what extent these could protect EDEs against a severe tightening of global financial conditions. This will be discussed in the subsequent sections of this chapter, taking into account the differences in the way countries have managed their exchange rates, capital flows, balance-of-payments, external balance sheets, and foreign entry into their domestic securities and credit markets during the surge in capital inflows. Generally, in countries with weak external positions, a severe tightening of global financial conditions could be expected to lead to both external instability and turbulence in domestic credit and asset markets. Others with strong payments and net foreign asset positions could avoid external financial turmoil but would be susceptible to instability in domestic credit and asset markets.

[1] What is involved here is not a flow-of-funds-like process critically assessed in Chapter 1 above—that is, capital inflows adding to loanable funds and hence raising the *capacity* of banks to lend. Rather, arbitrage margins due to interest-rate differentials and currency appreciations increase the *willingness* of banks to increase lending by funding abroad.

[2] That gross international capital flows have a tendency to amplify domestic credit cycles; see Borio et al. (2011). There is also growing evidence that rapid domestic credit growth plays a dominant role in predicting subsequent crises and that banking crises are more likely when capital inflows accompany a domestic credit boom. For a review of the link between external debt and domestic credit, see Al-Saffar et al. (2013).

4.1 Exchange Rate Flexibility, Capital Flows, and External Vulnerability

The shift to more flexible exchange rate regimes in financially open EDEs has no doubt a lot to commend. At times of favourable risk appetite hard nominal pegs offer a one-way bet to international speculators and encourage short-term inflows in search of quick profits, resulting in real appreciations and deterioration of the current account, particularly in countries with relatively high inflation rates. In bad times such pegs could rarely be defended with success. Experiments with fixed pegs often end up with balance-of-payments and currency crises with severe adverse effects on the real economy.

However, the recipe is not to move to the other corner and let the currency float freely. It is one thing to allow exchange rates to respond to changing fundamentals in order to facilitate external adjustment; it is another to leave them to the whims of unstable international capital flows. Floating can be effective in absorbing short-term volatility in capital flows, but not gyrations and boom–bust cycles. At times of a boom, free floating could generate even greater appreciations than nominal pegs. When capital inflows are strong, such a regime could lead to nominal as well as real appreciations even as current account deficits are widened—that is, it could generate unsustainable exchange rates and current account positions which could be exposed with sudden stops and reversals. A period of persistent currency misalignments, which often fuel bubbles in non-traded sectors could also produce significant distortions in the structure of production and trade, increasing foreign penetration of domestic markets and creating pressures for deindustrialization which could compromise the ability of the economy to respond to an eventual correction of the exchange rate.

Indeed, if capital flows and the exchange rate are not managed judiciously during the boom and external deficits and debt are allowed to pile up, floating freely at times of capital reversals would provide little cushion for the economy. Indonesia was praised for not trying to defend its currency but letting it float after the Thai baht came under attack in 1997. But this did not help stabilize the exchange rate and prevent a free fall. In most EDEs, notably those dependent on commodities, such currency declines do not provide a significant boost to exports to secure an expansionary balance-of-payments adjustment. Even in economies with robust industries, an increase in exports could be impeded by disruptions to the credit system resulting from the reversal of capital flows and currency declines as seen during many episodes of payments crises in emerging economies. As a result, the immediate balance-of-payments adjustment often takes place by retrenchments of imports and income.

To the extent that there are large currency mismatches in balance sheets, sharp declines in the exchange rate could increase the debt burden, thereby causing bankruptcies and reducing effective demand. Currency mismatches in the private sector tend to be particularly damaging. At times of capital reversals, private borrowers often attempt to close their open positions by purchasing foreign currency in order to avoid further losses from depreciations and this in turn accelerates the fall of the currency. It is true that with the opening of domestic bond markets to non-residents and increased international issuance of debt in local currencies, the exposure of most EDEs to the currency risk has significantly declined compared to previous decades. However, reductions in currency mismatches are largely limited to sovereign debtors while private corporations have been building up debt in low-interest reserve currencies both at home and abroad. In any case, in many EDEs a very large proportion of external debt, including sovereign debt, is still in reserve currencies. Taken together, EDEs have accumulated more than $2 trillion foreign currency debt since the beginning of 2008 (BIS 2014). Thus, they face significant currency risks, particularly where misalignments were tolerated for an extended period.

There is a growing recognition that a viable alternative to corner solutions is managed floating, using a judicious combination of monetary policy, currency market interventions, prudential regulations and capital controls. Looking back at the recent experience, however, the record is not very encouraging. During both pre- and post-Lehman booms in capital inflows, with the exception of a few East Asian countries, most EDEs, particularly those pursuing inflation-targeting such as Brazil, South Africa, and Turkey, experienced sustained currency appreciations. During the pre-Lehman boom many of them nevertheless managed to maintain viable current account positions thanks to a favourable international trading environment, but they started running large deficits during the post-Lehman boom as the international trading environment worsened and they had to turn to domestic demand for growth.

Most EDEs welcomed the strong recovery in capital inflows after the Lehman collapse and the boom in asset prices, ignoring the build-up of vulnerability resulting from increased corporate borrowing abroad and growing foreign presence in domestic securities markets. However, as discussed in Chapter 2, as upward pressures on their currencies persisted, several of them attempted to control capital inflows using market-friendly measures. Still, with the exception of a few countries, these were not very effective in preventing appreciations in large part because they were too timid to meet the challenge. These measures were dismantled after 2011 as capital inflows weakened and became unstable, and the currencies of most EDEs faced downward pressure at a time when they began to have a growing need for external financing in view of their widening current account deficits.

To sum up, in the new millennium many EDEs have allowed their exchange rates to go up and down with international capital flows, driven in large part by policies in advanced economies and the risk appetite in financial markets, rather than their own fundamentals. They have also succumbed to the highly accommodating global financial conditions in allowing asset and credit bubbles to develop and ignored the vulnerabilities resulting from growing external liabilities, notably through private borrowing abroad and increased presence of foreign investors in domestic securities markets. It is no wonder that three of the five BRICS that had been identified at the beginning of the millennium as the 'emerging markets' with the brightest economic prospects, Brazil, India, and South Africa, were subsequently listed among the countries dubbed 'fragile five' with the addition of Turkey and Indonesia, again countries among the rising stars of the new millennium (Lord 2013).[3]

4.2 Reserve Accumulation: How Much Self-insurance?

The large amounts of reserves built up by EDEs in the new millennium, including both surplus and deficit countries, are expected to serve two purposes: to prevent and mitigate balance-of-payments and currency crises by boosting confidence among creditors and investors and reducing the risk of liquidity-driven panics on the one hand, and by providing international liquidity against sudden stops and reversals of capital inflows, on the other. A key question is the extent to which these would really allow EDEs to weather a sharp turnaround in global financial conditions.

Traditionally international reserves were seen as an insurance against current account shocks and amounts needed to cover three months of prospective imports were considered as adequate. After the Asian crisis of 1997, attention increasingly turned to capital account shocks, and vulnerability has come to be assessed on the basis of short-term external debt. The so-called Greenspan–Guidotti rule stipulated that in order to significantly reduce the likelihood of liquidity crises, international reserves should cover short-term external debt in foreign currencies, defined as debt with a remaining maturity of up to one year. While this is the most widely used indicator of external sustainability, empirical evidence does not always show a strong correlation between pressure on reserves and short-term external debt. Often, in many countries suffering large reserve losses, sources other than short-term foreign-currency debt played a greater role (IMF 2011).

[3] The list of fragile emerging economies has constantly changed. The 'fragile 5' became 'fragile 8' with the addition of Argentina, Chile and the Russian Federation. Subsequently, India came to be seen as a 'one-eyed king in the land of blind' in the words of Reserve Bank of India Governor Rajan, as reported in the press in April 2016.

Indeed, vulnerability to liquidity crises is not restricted to short-term foreign currency debt. What matters is the liquidity of external liabilities, including those denominated in local currencies of EDEs. Countries with extensive foreign participation in equity and bond markets could be highly vulnerable, even in the absence of high levels of short-term foreign-currency debt. This is particularly true where reserves are borrowed. But even where reserves are earned from current account surpluses, currencies can come under stress if there is a significant foreign presence in domestic securities markets. To the extent that foreign entry enhances market liquidity, individual investors can exit without incurring large losses, but when sentiments sour, a bandwagon effect may develop, leading to sharp declines in both asset prices and exchange rates, as seen during the Lehman collapse. A rapid and generalized exit could create significant turbulence with broader macroeconomic consequences, even though losses due to declines in asset prices and currencies fall on foreign investors and mitigate the drain of reserves. Financial turmoil could be aggravated if foreign exit is accompanied by resident capital flight. Indeed resident outflows rather than exit by foreign investors may well play a leading role in the drain of reserves and currency declines as seen in some previous episodes.

These sources of drain on reserves are now widely recognized. After the onset of the crisis in advanced economies, the IMF has developed a framework for assessing reserve adequacy for emerging market economies, the so-called 'EM ARA Metric', for determining the level of reserves needed for precautionary purposes (IMF 2011, 2013e). The metric includes four potential sources of pressure on reserves; short-term, medium-term, and long-term debt and equity liabilities, broad money as a potential source of capital flight by residents and export earnings to capture the risk of potential shortfall in foreign exchange earnings due to collapse of foreign demand and terms-of-trade shocks. FDI liabilities are not included as a potential source of drain because of lack of evidence of exit by direct investors at times of stress. Different risk weights are assigned to these sources of drain, based on observed outflows from EDEs during periods of currency pressures. Reserves in the range of 100–150 per cent of the composite metric are considered to be adequate. It is found that while reserves of most countries were above the ARA threshold in 2012, there were around 20 countries that fell below 100 per cent of the ARA metric and bringing these above the threshold would add to global reserves by around $700 billion. It is also recognized that the risks associated with portfolio liabilities and commodity dependence may not have been fully captured by this algorithm.

As an illustration Table 4.1 provides information for 2013 on the level of reserves for a sample of major EDEs and some of the most important potential sources of drain; that is, current account deficits, short-term external debt, and

Table 4.1 Reserves and foreign claims: 2013 (per cent of GDP)

Country	Reserves	Current Account	Short term international commercial debt[a]	Non-resident holdings of local government debt[b]	Non-resident holdings of equities[c]
Argentina	5.8	–0.9	1.8	...	0.6
Brazil	15.9	–3.6	4.4	9.2	10.3
Chile	14.8	–3.4	9.6	...	7.7
China	41.8	2.1	7.6	...	4.7
Colombia	11.2	–3.3	3.4	...	2.4
India	14.8	–2.0	6.7	0.5	8.5
Indonesia	11.1	–3.3	6.2	3.0	8.6
Korea	28.0	5.8	10.2	...	19.8
Malaysia	42.7	3.8	12.5	20.7	28.4
Mexico	14.0	–1.8	3.7	11.4	8.2
Peru	31.2	–4.9	10.1	3.7	2.0
Philippines	27.9	3.5	5.0	...	11.2
Russia	22.3	1.6	3.4	...	5.5
South Africa	12.9	–5.8	4.0	...	27.3
Thailand	41.7	–0.7	5.2	4.3	28.1
Turkey	13.5	–7.9	11.4	4.9	6.1

Note: [a] Short-term international commercial debt does not include international money market instruments for Chile, India, Indonesia, Malaysia, Peru, Philippines, Russia, and Thailand.
[b] Shares of non-resident holdings in local government bonds (see Figure 3.15).
[c] June 2013 numbers.

Source: IMF IFS, WEO and CPIS databases; BIS International Financial Statistics database; and J.P. Morgan (2013).

non-resident holdings of local-currency public debt and equity portfolios. Short-term external debt issued by overseas subsidiaries of corporations in EDEs is not included although it can be a major source of drain on reserves in some countries. Data on foreign participation in local bond markets are readily available only for a few countries. As discussed in Chapter 3, non-resident holding of equities as reported by the IMF's CIPS database underestimates foreign participation in equity markets and figures from national sources for some countries suggest much higher levels of holding. FDI holdings are not included as a potential source of drain even though some of the recorded direct investments are not really distinguishable from portfolio equity holdings. Nor does the table include any potential source of capital flight by residents.

With these considerations in mind, Table 4.1 suggests three broad categories of countries in terms of vulnerability to an interruption of access to international capital markets and sudden stop of capital inflows as of end-2013. The first category includes countries where reserves do not cover the current account deficit plus short-term external debt. Turkey falls in this category. In the event of a sudden stop of inflows, Turkey could not both finance its current account deficit and remain current on its external debt payments even in the absence of exit of non-residents from domestic bond and equity markets and capital flight by residents. This means that unless short-term debt is rolled over and/or international liquidity support is provided by the IMF or bilaterally, Turkey could not continue to run such a high level of deficit and would have to drastically retrench to accommodate a significantly worsened external financial environment. The risk that an interruption to access to international financial markets could directly destabilize the banking system is also high since a large part of external debt is due to banks and their corporate creditors with large currency mismatches.

The second category includes countries where reserves cover current account deficits and short-term debt without leaving much room to accommodate a sizeable exit of foreign investors from domestic securities markets, capital flight by residents and/or trade shocks. It includes Argentina, Chile, Indonesia, and South Africa, which all have narrow margins to respond to a reversal of capital flows by deploying reserves. Indonesia and South Africa have a relatively high degree of foreign presence in domestic securities markets while Argentina, Chile, and South Africa are vulnerable to commodity shocks. Brazil, India, and Mexico have more room, but they are both vulnerable to a large scale exit of foreign investors from securities markets. Brazil is also vulnerable to current account shocks because of its dependence on commodity exports and financial shocks because of short-term external debt issued by overseas subsidiaries of its corporations.[4]

A third category includes EDEs which run current account surpluses and hold reserves higher than the levels needed for precautionary reasons, including China, Malaysia, the Republic of Korea, the Russian Federation and Thailand. Foreign presence in domestic securities markets is limited in China and the Russian Federation so that foreign exit would not be expected to cause external payments and currency problems. But China has a domestic debt overhang due to investment (property) bubbles and the Russian Federation is vulnerable to commodity and political shocks and capital flight. Foreign presence in domestic securities markets is strong in Malaysia, the Republic of Korea, and Thailand so that a generalized exit from domestic securities by non-residents could place strong pressure on the exchange rate despite a very high level of reserves.[5] Indeed, when hit by fallouts from the crisis in advanced economies in 2008, the Republic of Korea lost some $60 billion in reserves and was given a swap line by the US Federal Reserve.

[4] Indeed, subsequently, Brazil's current account moved from a surplus in 2013 to a deficit in 2015, making a swing of over 10 per cent of GDP while Turkey, as a net importer of energy, saw a sizeable decline in its external deficit in the same period.

[5] This indeed happened subsequently in Malaysia where foreign exit placed significant downward pressure on the currency; see, Akyüz (2015).

International reserves held by central banks are not the only assets that EDEs could draw on in the event of sudden stops and reversal of capital flows. Assets accumulated abroad by the private sector are often seen as an additional safeguard in the event of an interruption of their access to international financial markets. However, such assets are often leveraged. Furthermore, they could help only if they are liquid and held by corporations with open foreign exchange positions, rather than other residents such as institutional investors who might not be able or willing to sell them to close the funding gap (Al-Saffar et al. 2013). Liquid assets of Sovereign Wealth Funds may also be deployed. However, such funds are important mostly in surplus countries with strong external payments and reserves positions—that is, those with no significant vulnerability to external instability. Again, swap arrangements with central banks of major reserve-currency countries may be of some help. However, such arrangements are highly politicised and unreliable, and do not constitute reasonable substitutes for international reserves.

Greater hopes are also pinned on South–South cooperation for contingency financing. There are two main arrangements—the Chiang-Mai Initiative Multilateralization (CMIM) of East Asian countries and the Contingent Reserve Arrangement (CRA) of BRICS. The CMIM had started as bilateral swaps to complement, rather than substitute, the existing international facilities before it was multilateralized at the end of 2009. The initiative has never been called upon; during the Lehman collapse, the Republic of Korea, and Singapore approached, instead, the US Federal Reserve and Indonesia secured finance with a consortium led by the World Bank. CMIM has several shortcomings making it almost unusable. It does not have a common fund, but is a series of promises to provide funds, with each country reserving the right not to contribute to the specific request by a member; its size is too small, some 1.5 per cent of total GDP of the countries involved; and access beyond 30 per cent of quotas is tied to an IMF program (Lim and Lim 2012; West 2014).

The CRA is widely praised as a strong political sign of solidarity among EDEs. While it is too early to pass judgement on it, it does not look very much different from the CMIM. It is designed to complement rather than substitute the existing IMF facilities. Its size is even smaller than the CMIM, less than 1 per cent of the combined GDP of BRICS, and access beyond 30 per cent is tied to the conclusion of an IMF programme.[6]

[6] Another arrangement among EDEs is the Latin American Reserve Fund established in 1978 by seven Andean countries to provide balance-of-payments support and improve investment conditions of reserves held by member countries. It has been operating without linking liquidity provision to IMF programmes—see UNCTAD (2011).

4.3 Sovereign Debt and Financial Stability

For two main reasons a recurrence of the kind of international debt crises that devastated many EDEs in the past is now seen much less likely. First, in several countries fiscal discipline has improved significantly with public debt stabilizing and even falling as a proportion of GDP. Secondly, a growing proportion of sovereign external debt of many EDEs is now in local currencies because of the shift from international to domestic debt markets.

This view is in part a reflection of a long-standing belief that fiscal imbalances are at the origin of liquidity and debt crises so that budgetary discipline holds the key for external sustainability. A particular formulation of this was offered by the so-called Lawson Doctrine developed in the late 1980s that a large current account deficit is not a cause for concern if the fiscal accounts are balanced—that is, if the external deficit has its origin in the private sector.[7] Even though this doctrine was discredited by several instances of currency and balance-of-payments crises in economies with sound fiscal positions, it appears to continue to influence the mainstream thinking. Indeed fiscal profligacy and sovereign debt were presented as the root causes of the Eurozone crisis even though this was true only for Greece.

Sovereign debt is rarely at the centre of external financial crises and internationally issued bonds are even less so. In the last eight major external financial crises in EDEs (that is, Mexico, Thailand, Indonesia, the Republic of Korea, the Russian Federation, Brazil, Turkey, and Argentina, in the order of occurrence), sovereign debt was the central problem only in three cases (Argentina, Mexico, and the Russian Federation) and in only one of them (Argentina) it was the internationally issued debt. In Mexico, the crisis originated in domestically issued dollar-linked debt (*tesobonos*) while in the Russian Federation difficulties emerged in rouble-denominated domestic debt (the so-called GKOs). In Asia (Thailand, the Republic of Korea and Indonesia), the crisis was due to excessive short-term cross-border borrowing by local banks and non-bank corporations while in Turkey banks holding domestic sovereign debt came under pressure and difficulties emerged in rolling-over short-term external bank debt (Truman 2002; Akyüz and Boratav 2003).

In almost all these cases, an important part of private debt, both domestic and external, was socialized through government bail-outs, often through recapitalization of insolvent banks, raising sovereign debt. In Indonesia, for instance, bail-outs raised public debt by more than 50 per cent of GDP, creating problems of sustainability despite its good track record in fiscal

[7] Originally the IMF had promoted this doctrine during the Southern Cone borrowing in the late 1970s and early 1980s– an experiment which ended up in a crash. For a discussion and critical evaluation see, UNCTAD TDR (1998: Annex to chapter III); see also Reisen (1998).

discipline (IMF 2003b). For Thailand and the Republic of Korea corresponding figures are 42 per cent and 34 per cent respectively (Hoggarth and Saporta 2001) and for Turkey 33 per cent (World Bank 2003). In a sample of 12 countries hit by currency and external financial crises in the 1990s and 2000s, the average post-crisis public debt ratio was higher than the pre-crisis ratio by 36 per cent of GDP, and in most cases the increase in debt levels persisted several years before governments could roll-back the crisis-induced increases in debt ratios (de Bolle et al. 2006).

This is also observed in Spain and Ireland during the recent Eurozone crisis. As discussed in Chapter 1, on the eve of the crisis public debt was around 36 per cent of GDP in Spain and 25 per cent in Ireland, much lower than the ratio in the core Eurozone countries. In fact these countries had adhered to the Maastricht Treaty much better than Germany where the debt ratio was over 65 per cent. They were running current account deficits in the order of 6 per cent and 2 per cent of GDP, respectively, but these were entirely due to a private savings gap. A growing part of the external debt was incurred by the private sector. The crisis originated in the banking system, and while depositors and creditors, both domestic and foreign, of troubled banks have largely escaped without a haircut, a large part of unpayable private debt has been socialized through bail-out operations. As discussed in Chapter 1, this, together with the impact of the crisis on public finances, produced significant increases in sovereign debt in Spain and Ireland.

The standard framework for the assessment of debt sustainability and vulnerability to external shocks fails to account for such contingent liabilities even though in reality they are an important source of public debt accumulation—on some account even more important than budget deficits (Campos et al. 2006). Likewise, private external debt and domestic credit expansion are at the origin of current vulnerabilities to liquidity and solvency crises in several EDEs, and in the event of turmoil, sovereign debt problems could well emerge even in countries with strong fiscal postures.

Contingent liabilities apart, on standard measures many EDEs have comfortably met the conditions for sovereign debt sustainability since the early 2000s.[8] The interplay of three principal determinants of fiscal sustainability, namely economic growth, interest rates on foreign-currency and local-currency debt and exchange rates have generally been very favourable in large part because of favourable global conditions. These not only boosted growth and improved budget balances in the EDEs in the run up to the 2008 crisis, but also helped achieve a swift recovery after 2009. For several EDEs, until 2013, real interest rates on foreign-currency debt were generally negative because of low

[8] For sovereign debt and fiscal sustainability conditions, see Akyüz (2007).

rates in major advanced economies, increased risk appetite and pressures for currency appreciations.[9] Since yields on local-currency debt also remained low, some 5 per cent in nominal terms and 1 per cent in real terms, governments did not have to make much effort to stabilize or lower their debt ratios. They could even run primary deficits without facing an increase in the ratio of debt to GDP. As capital flows weakened and currencies came under pressure after 2012, real interest rates on foreign-currency debt started to edge up despite historically low rates in major advanced economies.

Although increases in non-resident holdings of local-currency sovereign bonds played an important role in lowering their yields, particularly in the post-Lehman period, international investors in local bonds of EDEs earned a large return because of currency appreciations (AFCG 2013). For the same reason, the bond index in local currency terms outperformed the index in US dollars throughout the period 2008–13, implying a persistent positive return to speculation in the currencies of EDEs (see Polychronopoulos and Binstock 2013).[10] Thus, a win–win situation developed between international investors and sovereign debtors. As foreign investors added to their bond holdings in EDEs, yields came down but currency appreciations generated significant capital gains for them. On the other hand, lower yields and stronger currencies reduced the borrowing cost for governments and improved the sovereign debt profile.

However, these are reversible, particularly in countries with weak fiscal and external positions (Jaramillo and Weber 2013). Indeed, since 2007, bond markets in emerging economies dropped sharply at least on two occasions when the risk sentiment went sour and external financial conditions tightened; during the Lehman collapse in 2008 and the 'taper tantrum' in May 2013. Although the sell-off was much smaller during the latter episode than the Lehman shock, it produced a similar impact on yields (IMF GFSR 2013b). In both periods, currencies also came under strong pressure, notably in deficit EDEs.

As in equity markets, even when non-resident investment accounts for a small share of the bond market, entry and exit can have a significant impact on yields. This is because in EDEs the domestic investor base is not strong enough to make these markets sufficiently deep and liquid. Domestic holders of bonds on the longer end are mostly institutional investors that typically hold these bonds to maturity so that 'even the small amount of foreign investment going into the long end of the yield curve can have a large

[9] Real interest rate on external debt is given by: $[(1 + i)(1 + \acute{\epsilon})/(1 + \pi)] - 1$, where i is the nominal dollar interest rate, $\acute{\epsilon}$ the rate of change of the exchange rate (positive for depreciation) and π the rate of inflation. This expression would be negative when i is low relative to inflation even in the absence of currency appreciation; see Akyüz (2007).

[10] Turner (2012) finds persistent positive returns to speculation by comparing returns on hedged and unhedged portfolios both for 2002–06 and 2007–09.

marginal impact' (Pradhan et al. 2011: 15–16). Foreign holdings reach several multiples of average daily trading volume in the issuing country bonds, and this creates '"a systemic liquidity mismatch" between the potential for portfolio outflows from emerging market economies and the capacity of local institutions and market makers (in particular international banks) to absorb these flows' (IMF GFSR 2014: 36–7 and Figure 1.25). The present risks are more emphatically stated by Morgan Stanley (2014: 3).

> The Achilles' heel of emerging market economies [EM] is the foreign ownership in the domestic bond markets. The spread of local bond yields over Treasuries used to be, but is now likely no longer wide enough to absorb interest rate shocks from the US. This combination has already proved to be near-fatal to EM last summer, and there's no reason to think it won't hurt again. As US interest rates rise, compressed risk premia mean that EM interest rates will have to rise too. As bonds sell off but cannot be sold, we think that foreign investors will sell other asset classes and even assets in other EM economies to protect capital.

By shifting from international issuance in reserve currencies to domestic debt market in local currencies, EDEs have sought to escape the perennial problem of original sin, passing the currency risk onto international lenders. However, they have become highly exposed to interest rate shocks which could have serious consequences for financial stability in the transition towards the normalization of monetary policy in the US (Sobrun and Turner 2015). While the incidence of exchange rate shocks depends very much on external liquidity positions, even countries with strong payments and reserve positions are vulnerable to shocks to bond markets as long as there are sizeable foreign holdings and the domestic investor base is weak.

The shift from international to local debt markets has not just reduced the currency mismatch but also increased the proportion of public debt held by non-residents in several EDEs (Table 3.14). The increase in foreign holdings is even greater if bonds held by the subsidiaries of international banks located in EDEs are included. Whether in local currency or dollars, foreign ownership of debt is a key indicator of external vulnerability. As discussed in Chapter 1, this has become more visible in the Eurozone crisis where problems emerged not in countries with large stocks of debt but large foreign holdings (Gros 2011). Belgium had a much higher public debt ratio than Portugal, Spain, and Ireland, but did not face any pressure and in fact enjoyed a relatively low-risk premium because it has sustained a positive net external asset position. Again, Italy is less affected than other periphery countries because a large proportion of its public debt is held domestically.

The increased foreign presence in domestic bond markets of EDEs implies that these markets may no longer be relied on as a 'spare tyre' for private and public borrowers and provide an escape route at times of interruptions to access to external financing. When global risk appetite and liquidity conditions deteriorate and access of EDEs to international capital markets is impaired, domestic bond markets too can get crippled due to adverse spillovers. An exodus of foreign investors would expose domestic bond-holders. Institutions such as pension funds may not be very much affected because they tend to hold bonds to maturity. But domestic banks, as major holders of sovereign local debt, could come under severe stress because of maturity mismatches in their balance sheets between long-term bonds and short-term liabilities. They could thus join in the sell-off, as seen during the Lehman collapse and the 'taper tantrum', pushing bond yields up further. Governments may then become unable to refinance debt at reasonable interest rates. They could be tempted to solve the problem by forcing banks or pension funds to absorb sovereign bonds and, in the extreme case, pushing them onto the central bank.

The closer global integration of local bond markets in EDEs thus entails a significant loss of autonomy in controlling long-term rates in domestic debt markets. This can have more serious consequences for financial and exchange rate stability than loss of control over short-term rates since capital flows through bond markets have gained added importance relative to international bank lending. It also means further loss of monetary policy autonomy since, as seen in the last two episodes of bond market turmoil, bond prices and exchange rates in EDEs are now intrinsically linked.

The development and internationalization of bond markets of EDEs are widely seen as a recipe for enhancing the resilience of the financial system to external shocks as well as improving the volume and allocation of capital. Similar considerations have also encouraged major EDEs to develop offshore bond markets in local currency in order to have access to even larger and more diverse funds, thus enjoying the benefits of greater liquidity that such markets offer relative to domestic bond markets. However, the risks associated with the internationalization of bond markets before establishing a sound and stable domestic investor base through strong and sustained growth of income and accumulation of wealth may have been seriously underestimated.[11]

The acid test for the wisdom of deep global integration of bond markets in EDEs may well arrive with the normalization of monetary policy in the US. It is sometimes argued that measures taken by governments to address the root causes of the last crisis often become the new sources of instability and the causes of the next crisis. This may well be the case with the internationalization

[11] On the risk of offshore markets in local currency bonds drawing liquidity away from the domestic market in EDEs, see Black and Munro (2010). On a critical assessment of the benefits claimed for a well-developed bond market in the context of the Asian Bond Initiative, see Lim and Lim (2012).

of local bond markets in EDEs; it may turn out to be as big a sin as the original one, rather than a path back to Eden.

4.4 Foreign Banks and Financial Stability

Much has been written on the pros and cons of foreign banks in EDEs. According to the orthodox view, vigorously promoted by the BWIs, foreign banks from advanced economies would not only bring efficiency gains, improve competitiveness, reduce intermediation costs, and generate positive spillovers to local banks in EDEs, but also enhance their resilience to external financial shocks (Stein 2010). At the same time, however, it has been widely recognized that these banks could cream-skim the banking sector, picking the best creditors and depositors and leaving smaller and marginal customers, including SMEs, to local banks. They tend to focus on more lucrative activities where they have a competitive edge, notably trade financing where they enjoy a cost advantage compared to local banks in being able to confirm letters of credit through their head offices, and international financial intermediation rather than domestic intermediation, often obliging the best customers using such services to move all of their business to them. They are also better able to benefit from regulatory arbitrage by shifting operations back and forth between the home and host countries. They can easily avoid the cost of legal reserves by moving large deposits to offshore accounts and this also enables them to offer higher interest rates. Since local banks cannot easily avoid these costs, they would bear an unfair competitive burden.[12]

Since the onset of the global financial crisis, it has been increasingly recognized that extensive presence of foreign banks in EDEs can aggravate their vulnerability to financial shocks, including in an IMF Staff Discussion Note:

> The activities of cross-border banking groups can generate trade-offs between efficiency and financial stability. These groups can lower intermediation costs and improve access to credit by households and firms, facilitate a more efficient allocation of global savings, assist in the development of local capital markets, and make possible the transfer of risk management, payments, and information technology. At the same time, these groups are highly interconnected internationally and may expose individual countries to the risk that shocks in other countries will spill over into their domestic financial systems (Fiechter *et al.* 2011: 5).

Indeed, because of their close international linkages, foreign banks in EDEs act as conduits of expansionary and contractionary impulses from global

[12] For a review of the pros and cons of foreign banks and some evidence from India, see Sarma and Prashad (2014). See also Stein (2010), and Claessens and van Horen, (2012).

financial cycles. As a result, their increased presence, together with the liberalization of international financial transactions, can be expected to intensify global financial spillovers to EDEs. When global liquidity and risk appetite are favourable, foreign banks can contribute to the build-up of external financial fragility. When global financial conditions become stringent, they can exacerbate their destabilizing and deflationary impact on host countries. Both of these influences were observed in the run-up to the global crisis and subsequently.

Foreign banks intermediate between international financial markets and domestic borrowers much more easily than local banks, funding local lending from abroad, including through their parent banks. They have greater room to do this when they operate as branches in EDEs which can escape the prudential and other regulations designed to manage the capital account. In the run-up to the Eurozone crisis, foreign banks were instrumental in the rapid accumulation of debt and build-up of mismatches in private balance sheets in the periphery, particularly where they lacked adequate domestic deposit base, funding local lending from their parent banks. Again during the pre- and post-crisis surges in capital inflows to EDEs, foreign banks were extensively engaged in carry-trade-like intermediations, benefiting from large interest-rate arbitrage margins between reserve-issuing advanced economies and EDEs and currency appreciations in the latter. This has no doubt played an important part in the unprecedented increase in local claims of international banks in local currency discussed in Chapter 3.

Foreign banks can also act as a conduit of financial instability in advanced economies, transmitting credit crunches from home to host countries, rather than insulating domestic credit markets from international financial shocks. The shift of international banks from cross-border to local lending implies that at times of stress in the home country, deleveraging by parent banks could result in credit contraction in host countries. This was seen in Asia during the Eurozone crisis where lending by local subsidiaries and branches was a substantial part of overall European bank claims (Aiyar and Jain-Chandra 2012; He and McCauley 2013). Several other studies also found that foreign subsidiaries cut lending more than domestically owned banks during the global crisis (Claessen and van Horen 2012; Chen and Wu 2014). This is particularly true where they funded a large proportion of their lending from abroad rather than from local deposits (Cetorelli and Goldberg 2009). At the height of the crisis in 2008, in China and Brazil, foreign bank credit growth lagged behind that of domestic banks and 'foreign banks in one EME [Emerging Market Economies]—apparently on instructions from their parent banks—withdrew earlier than domestic banks from the interbank market' (BIS 2010: 3). During both the Asian crisis in 1997 and the crisis in advanced economies in 2008, foreign banks were slower than domestic banks in adjusting their lending to changes in host country monetary policy, thereby impairing its effectiveness (Jeon and Wu 2013 and 2014).

During the Eurozone crisis not only shocks to parent banks were transmitted to their subsidiaries in emerging economies, but the response of the latter amplified the impact on the banking system in host countries. While some global banks gave support to their foreign affiliates, subsidiaries in many European emerging economies acted as conduits of capital outflows in support of their parent banks in the Eurozone core, leading to depletion of reserves and putting pressures on currencies of European emerging economies (BIS 2010; Cetorelli and Goldberg 2011).

Strong adverse fallouts from parent banks in the European core to the CEE, where a small number of subsidiaries of banks from the core dominated the financial sector, necessitated international official intervention, the so-called Vienna initiative launched at the height of the first wave of the global financial crisis in January 2009, involving the European Development Bank, the IMF, and the European Commission (Pistor 2012). The initiative was designed to prevent large-scale exit from Central and Eastern Europe (CEE) and ensure that parent banks maintain exposure to their subsidiaries and the support given by core governments to parent banks, notably through recapitalization, could also benefit their subsidiaries. However, an important part of the burden of supporting the pan-European banking system fell on host countries. Foreign banks effectively avoided large losses while governments of host countries incurred new debt. A number of locally owned banks in CEE failed but there were no failures among foreign-owned banks. More importantly, the agreement between banks and the international financial institutions were conditioned on pro-cyclical macroeconomic policies, including sharp cuts in wages in some countries such as Romania, mainly at the insistence of home countries and their transnational banks, which formed a 'vociferous creditor coalition' (Lutz and Kranke 2010).

In what way the subsidiaries of banks from advanced economies could affect the transmission of destabilizing impulses to EDEs from the normalization of monetary policy in the US remains to be seen. The ultra-easy monetary policy has given rise to an important build-up of financial fragility in advanced economies themselves by triggering a search-for-yield in 'the riskier part of the credit spectrum' including high-yield bonds, subordinated debt and leveraged syndicated loans, 'a phenomenon reminiscent of the exuberance prior to the global financial crisis' (BIS 2013: 1, 7).[13] Indeed, there is evidence that the

[13] Two senior economists from the US Federal Reserve also warned that '[v]ulnerabilities, such as compressed risk premiums, and excessive leverage or maturity and liquidity transformation in the financial system, can increase the probability of a financial crisis and severe recession in the future' (Adrian and Liang 2014: 4).

medium-term credit risks of banks in advanced economies have increased while risk premia fell (Lambert and Ueda 2014). Thus, the end of ultra-easy monetary policy could create destabilizing impulses for these banks, again with adverse spillovers to EDEs through their affiliates.

Experience suggests that local subsidiaries of foreign-owned international banks are unlikely to act as stabilizers of interest rate shocks to local bond markets of EDEs. During the bond market collapse in 2008, rather than increasing their exposure to offset the impact of the exit of foreign investors, these banks joined them, reducing their holdings of local government bonds and scaling back their market-making activity (Turner 2012). Nor can they be relied on to deploy their greater access to diversified sources of liquidity in international markets and reduce the pressure on reserves and play a stabilizing role in the event of a capital reversal. Parent banks are not legally obliged to support subsidiaries during funding stress and other international creditors cannot be expected to increase their exposure to a country through foreign subsidiaries when they are exiting on a large scale.

5

Crisis Management and Resolution

In terms of build-up of financial fragility in recent years, there are two broad categories of EDEs. The first one combines weak external positions with bubbles in domestic credit and asset markets. In the event of a significant tightening of global financial conditions, these could face not only the problem of external financial sustainability but also the risks of domestic credit crunch and asset deflation. The second group comprises mostly East Asian countries with strong external positions. These may not face external turbulence but run risks of domestic financial instability because of credit and asset bubbles generated by the combination of global financial conditions and their own domestic policies. Accordingly, any financial turmoil in the first group would, in all likelihood, require international action for crisis management and resolution, but this would not be the case for the countries in the second group.[1]

In a typical external financial crisis, an emerging economy finds its access to international financial markets interrupted and faces a sudden stop in capital inflows. Its reserves get depleted by short-term debt payments and current account deficits and its currency and asset markets come under stress. All these are aggravated if the sudden stop translates into a capital reversal as a result of exit of foreign investors from deposit, bond and equity markets, and capital flight by residents.

In a typical international intervention in a typical external financial crisis, liquidity is made available by the IMF, often well in excess of the country's normal access limits. The more the IMF has failed in crisis prevention, the more it has become involved in crisis lending. After almost every major financial crisis it has sought a new role and there has been a proliferation of crisis lending instruments in the past two decades. The central objective is to

[1] Even in this latter case international action may be needed to prevent contagion. The third group noted in Chapter 4.2, that is, countries with strong external positions but excessive foreign presence in domestic markets, may eventually fall in one of the two categories above as the events unfold.

keep debtors current on their payments to private international creditors and to maintain an open capital account. As a result, obligations to private creditors are translated into debt to the IMF which is much more difficult to restructure in the event of an eventual default because the IMF enjoys de facto, though not de jure, seniority; that is, priority in repayment of debt over private creditors. Austerity is imposed by means of hikes in domestic interest rates, fiscal retrenchment, and wage cuts in order to achieve a sharp turnaround in the current account, mainly through import compression, and to restore confidence among international creditors and investors. Sometimes, when the crisis is one of liquidity and the IMF lending proves insufficient, a concerted rollover of short-term debt is sought. This is easier to do when debt is owed to banks, as seen during the crises in the Republic of Korea, Indonesia, Brazil, and Turkey, than when it is held by widely dispersed bond-holders. It is often hoped that the liquidity crisis is temporary and the IMF lending and programme would encourage private creditors to resume lending. But when it turns out to be a solvency crisis, the outcome is more often than not a messy default, as in Argentina, since the international system lacks arrangements for orderly debt workouts.

It has been increasingly agreed that this approach to the management of external financial crises in emerging economies is inefficient and inequitable. First, the austerity imposed intensifies the impact of the crisis on incomes, jobs, and poverty in debtor countries. Second, lending by the IMF to keep countries current on their debt payments creates creditors' moral hazard, as it often helps the latter to avoid assuming the full consequences of the risks they have taken and been paid for in risk premia. These result in significant inequality between debtors and creditors in the incidence of the burden of a crisis. Inequalities also emerge among creditors. In the event of default and restructuring those who exit first could escape without a haircut, leaving the others to take the full brunt of debt write-offs. Profit opportunities are also created for vulture funds, at the expense of genuine creditors as well as the debtor, as seen in the case of Argentina.

5.1 Sovereign Debt Workouts

Various proposals have been made for an orderly and equitable resolution of external financial crises. They mainly concentrate on sovereign debt and seek to involve private creditors in crisis resolution. UNCTAD is the first international organization which made such a proposal during the Latin American debt crisis in the 1980s, drawing on chapter 11 of the US bankruptcy code, noting that the absence of a clear and impartial framework for resolving international sovereign debt problems trapped many developing countries in situations where they suffered the stigma of being judged de facto bankrupt without the protection and relief which come from de jure insolvency (UNCTAD TDR 1986).[2]

The application of these principles entails imposition of temporary standstills on debt payments by both private and public sectors, accompanied by exchange restrictions to prevent capital outflows. They need to be sanctioned by an impartial international authority to stop litigation and asset grabbing by creditors. These measures would be necessary whether external payments difficulties are perceived to be as one of liquidity or solvency. This is often difficult to identify with a reasonable degree of precision ex ante. But if it is found necessary to impose restrictions not only on debt payments and capital outflows but also on income transfers, including interest payments and profit remittances, this could be taken as a reasonably good sign that the debtor country may have in fact been engaged in Ponzi financing and hence may not be solvent. In principle such measures would be subject to the Fund's Article VIII jurisdiction and prior approval because they concern current account convertibility (IMF 2013b).

Second, any external financing provided to the debtor country in distress should be used for current transactions in order to maintain imports and the level of economic activity, rather than for repaying debt or maintaining capital account convertibility. This would involve the so-called debtor-in-possession financing which grants seniority status to new debt contracted after the sanctioning of the standstill. The task could be assumed by the IMF. Needless to say, there should be limits to IMF lending during capital account crises if the purpose is to secure private sector involvement in crisis resolution. If the terms of new loans are attractive, private creditors may also become willing to lend since they would be enjoying seniority in the event of an eventual debt restructuring.

The third stage would be debt restructuring. In liquidity crises, standstills may need to be accompanied by extension of maturities of existing obligations and in some cases this can be negotiated between the debtor and creditors. In the case where debt can no longer be paid according to original terms and conditions, write-down would become necessary. The introduction of rollover clauses and collective action clauses (CACs) in debt contracts could facilitate but would not guarantee voluntary restructuring. There would then be a need for impartial arbitration in order to overcome creditor holdout and secure an orderly and equitable restructuring.

[2] The proposal was revisited after the East Asian crisis (UNCTAD TDR 1998). For the application of Chapter 9 of the US insolvency law dealing with debt of public agencies, see Raffer (1990). For the debate around mandatory debt-workout mechanisms, see Akyüz (2002).

During the earlier episodes of crises the IMF (1999, 2000a) recognized the need for 'involving the private sector in forestalling and resolving financial crises', but insisted on voluntary mechanisms, notably CACs and automatic rollover clauses in debt contracts and informal negotiations between debtors and creditors. However, as these proved ineffective and some advanced economies started to oppose bail-outs, the IMF Board agreed that 'in extreme circumstances, if it is not possible to reach agreement on a voluntary standstill, members may find it necessary, as a last resort, to impose one unilaterally', and that since 'there could be a risk that this action would trigger capital outflows...a member would need to consider whether it might be necessary to resort to the introduction of more comprehensive exchange or capital controls'. The Fund could also signal its acceptance of a standstill imposed by a member by lending into arrears to private creditors (IMF 2000b).

The Fund staff went further and proposed a formal Sovereign Debt Restructuring Mechanism (SDRM) to facilitate sovereign bond workouts for countries whose debt is deemed unsustainable by bringing debtors and bond-holders together irrespective of the existence of CACs in bond contracts, and by providing a mechanism for dispute resolution. This mechanism would also 'allow a country to come to the Fund and request a temporary standstill on the repayment of its debts, during which time it would negotiate a rescheduling with its creditors, given the Fund's consent to that line of attack' and to impose exchange controls (Krueger 2001: 7).

However, the SDRM proposal did not fundamentally address the problems associated with IMF bail-outs. It was designed for countries facing insolvency while those experiencing liquidity problems were to continue to rely on IMF lending. The provision for statutory protection to debtors in the form of a stay on litigation was subsequently dropped. Creditor permission would be required in granting seniority to new debt. Even after significant dilution the proposal could not elicit adequate support and had to be withdrawn.

Recently the Fund turned its attention once again to sovereign debt restructuring, particularly after misjudging the sustainability of Greek debt, very much in the same way it had done with Argentina about a decade earlier, pouring in money to bail out private creditors.[3] This time it has been less ambitious than the SDRM, focussing not so much on how to restructure sovereign debt as how to involve the private sector in the crisis resolution so as to 'limit the risk that Fund resources will simply be used to bail out private creditors' (IMF 2013c: 26).

[3] In a subsequent evaluation of the 2010 Stand-By agreement for Greece, the Fund admitted that it had underestimated the damage done by austerity imposed in the bail-out and that it had deviated from its own debt-sustainability standards and should have pushed harder and sooner for lenders to take a haircut (IMF 2013d).

However, although the central idea is to secure some kind of creditor bail-in, to ensure that private creditors make some concessions and take some losses on their holdings as a condition for Fund lending, it is not clear how this is to be done, particularly as the IMF shies away from statutory arrangements and throws the ball to the debtor country. The sovereign approaching the Fund for assistance would be asked to find ways of 'reprofiling' its debt, rolling over all bonds and commercial loans falling due within the life of the Fund programme.[4] The decision for reprofiling would be taken by the IMF based on its debt sustainability analysis.[5] The reprofiling should be market-based wherein creditors are expected to voluntarily agree to reschedule existing debt through rollovers and bond exchanges. This was in fact tried during the debt crisis of the 1980s under the Baker plan when much of the sovereign debt was in bank loans. At the time banks were not all that willing to add to the debt of what turned out to be insolvent sovereigns and the plan failed (UNCTAD TDR 1988). Such concerted lending is more difficult when debt is held by widely dispersed bond-holders. If voluntary reprofiling fails, the debtor has no option but to default on its obligations to private creditors as long as the IMF is not prepared to lend without private sector involvement. The IMF proposes no statutory arrangements to provide protection against litigation in such a case.[6]

If the debt is successfully reprofiled but still proves not to be fully payable, a restructuring would be necessary. This is also supposed to be done on a voluntary basis. Again the central problem is how to overcome holdouts. Standard CACs in bond contracts are no panacea. Holdouts have become even more difficult to prevent after the court rulings in the US on Argentinian restructuring (UNCTAD 2014). Briefly, although this new thinking may be taken as a shift in the IMF's approach to bail-outs, it does not present a workable model for orderly workouts for sovereign external debt.

Various proposals have been advanced to address the holdout problem and protect debtors against litigation in market-based restructuring. A proposal made in a joint study by the Bank of England and the Bank of Canada is to introduce provisions in bond contracts to automatically extend maturity when a country receives IMF emergency liquidity assistance (Brooke et al. 2013). A Brookings report on sovereign debt restructuring argued that 'whereas CACs can be helpful, they do not—at least in the variety that is

[4] The Fund issued another paper in June 2014 proposing to incorporate its new approach to bail-outs into its Exceptional Access Framework established in 2002 by combining lending with upfront reprofiling in cases where debt is deemed sustainable but not with a high probability while continuing to require upfront restructuring when it is judged unsustainable (IMF 2014a).

[5] On the track record of the IMF in debt sustainability analysis see Akyüz (2007).

[6] In its operational guidance on the management of capital flows the Fund also recognized the need for temporary restrictions on capital outflows in debt-distressed countries, but without offering statutory protection (IMF 2013b).

most common in sovereign debt contracts today—eliminate holdouts' (CIEPR 2013: 19) and went on to propose strong aggregation clauses, legislative changes in major financial centres to immunize payments and clearing systems and a Sovereign Debt Adjustment Facility in the IMF to coordinate debt restructuring and official lending, backed up by changes in its Articles to block holdouts.

The International Capital Market Association, a group representing several banks, debtors and investors, agreed to a plan in August 2014 to include new clauses in future bond contracts to make it possible to bind all creditors with a single vote across all bonds, with a 75 per cent voting threshold in order to avoid repetition of Argentina's predicament (ICMA 2014). This could deter holdouts for large debtors because in such cases it would be difficult for vulture funds to acquire a blocking majority. The group has also proposed to modify the *pari passu* (equal footing) clause in bond contracts in order to prevent it from being used by holdout hedge funds to block restructuring. To come into effect, these changes would have to be adopted by governments.[7]

Given their deep-seated misgivings about the governance and policies of the IMF and concerns about systemic repercussions of the US court ruling on the Argentinian restructuring, developing countries have taken the matter to the United Nations with a resolution titled 'towards the establishment of a multilateral legal framework for sovereign debt restructuring processes' (United Nations 2014). This was adopted on 9 September 2014 by a large majority of the members of the UN, with 124 voting in favour, 11 against, and 41 abstentions. Even though the original resolution had been revised and the call for *convention* was changed to *framework*, the initiative was opposed by some major advanced economies including the US, Germany, Japan, and the UK who hold key positions in international finance. Later in the month the UN Human Rights Council also adopted a complementary resolution, placing debt restructuring in the context of human rights and condemning vulture funds. This was also opposed by major advanced economies.

The fate of these resolutions may turn out to be no brighter than several others voted and adopted by a large majority of members of the UN in order to promote global public goods—peace, security, stability, development, and so on. However, what is significant about this initiative is that the developing countries have demonstrated an unprecedented unity and solidarity in calling for a fundamental change in a key aspect of the international financial architecture and in placing the UN at the centre of the debate on sovereign debt restructuring.

[7] IMF (2014b) also put forward proposals for strengthening CACs and modifying the *pari passu* clause in new bond contracts to reduce the likelihood of holdouts, very much in line with those made by the International Capital Market Association.

5.2 Domestic Sovereign Debt

Important as it is, sovereign international debt is not the only potential source of external vulnerability and instability of EDEs. In several emerging economies, domestically issued sovereign debt and internationally issued corporate debt are now more important. In fact, as already noted, private external debt and domestically issued public debt, rather than sovereign international bonds, were at the origin of the majority of the last eight most important crises in emerging economies. These have gained added importance as financial and non-financial corporations in emerging economies have increasingly replaced the sovereign in international debt markets while governments have turned to domestic markets but allowed their locally issued debt to be internationalized and become highly susceptible to conditions in the debt markets of major advanced economies.

We are no longer in a world where external and domestic debts are clearly differentiated in terms of their holders, currency denomination, and governing laws. The empirical evidence examined in Chapter 3 suggests the broad taxonomy of sovereign debt in EDEs today according to place of issue and holders presented in Table 5.1.

This categorization excludes local-issues in foreign currency which is no longer practised in most major EDEs. Existing conventions for the collection of debt statistics do not always allow precise identification of holders of sovereign debt, particularly resident holdings of internationally issued debt as in (B) and internationally issued debt held by non-resident nationals of the issuing country under (A).[8]

The conventional *economic* definition of external debt is based solely on residency and hence includes debt held by non-residents regardless of place of issue, as in categories (A) and (C). The definition of external debt based on nationality includes all foreign (non-national) holdings regardless of the residency of the holders and place of issue. By contrast, *legal* definition of external debt is based on governing law and includes all categories of debt that are issued internationally and hence subject to foreign (external) jurisdiction regardless of nationality and residency of their holders and currency denomination—that is, categories (A) and (B). Legal and economic definitions diverge in two respects. First, internationally issued but locally held debt (B) is external debt in legal terms but not in economic terms.[9] Second, locally issued

[8] In this categorization cross-border bank lending would fall under (A) whereas local loans in local-currency by foreign subsidiaries would fall under (D).

[9] Such debt was particularly important in Argentina on the eve of its default as large amounts of international-law debt had been placed with domestic banks and pension funds (Roubini and Setser 2004).

Table 5.1 Taxonomy of sovereign debt in EDEs today according to place of issue and holders

	Internationally issued—all currencies	Locally issued—local currency
Non residents	A	C
Residents	B	D

but internationally held debt (C) is external debt in economic terms but not in legal terms.

International debt workouts are needed to resolve the collective action problem for internationally issued debt. For debt governed by domestic law and subject to the exclusive jurisdiction of the domestic courts, often the sovereign has the power and the means to resolve this problem. Indeed, the SDRM did not include local-law debt. According to the IMF (2002), foreign investors preferred domestic debt to be excluded from the SDRM as they thought holders of domestic debt should not be subject to the same legal framework as holders of external debt. Thus, although it was recognized that in 'some circumstances, it may be necessary to restructure sovereign domestic debt if the overall burden is to be reduced to a sustainable level,... domestic debt would not be restructured under the SDRM, since governments typically have at their disposal tools for restructuring domestic debt that are not available in the case of external debt' (IMF 2003a). Indeed, it would be extremely difficult to devise a statutory international debt workout mechanism that overrides the domestic law of debtor countries because, inter alia, this would come into considerable conflict with national sovereignty.

A key question is how to treat domestic (local-law) debt relative to internationally issued debt in a sovereign debt crisis. Quite apart from legal prerogatives, there are strong economic reasons for separating domestic from external debt in sovereign debt restructuring and giving a differential treatment in favour of domestic debt. A sovereign external debt crisis is not simply a fiscal crisis that could be fixed through domestic transfers from private creditors. The turmoil caused by the crisis and the adjustments needed already create serious hardship in the economy even when international debt is reprofiled and restructured, and the treatment of domestic debt on par with international debt could aggravate the impact of the crisis by deepening economic contraction and endangering the stability of the financial system, thereby making the debt even less payable. Similarly, if the domestic bond market is expected to play the role of spare tyre to provide an alternative financing channel, it would need to be treated more lightly than non-resident bond-holders. Indeed, many of these economic rationales for differentiation in the treatment of domestic debt were recognized during the deliberations on the SDRM (IMF 2002).

In the developing world default and restructuring is less common for local-law debt than for internationally issued debt even though the sovereign has legal means to address the holdout problem on locally issued debt and it is difficult for the holders of foreign-law debt to block restructuring because payments are made inside the country. As argued by Keynes in writing on what he called 'progressive and catastrophic inflations' in Central and Eastern Europe during the early 1920s, outright default on domestic debt is socially and politically problematic because it 'is too crude, too deliberate, and too obvious in its incidence' and the 'victims are immediately aware and cry out too loud'. Instead, governments often attempt to seek relief through monetization and inflation because it is anonymous in its incidence; 'it follows the line of least resistance, and responsibility cannot be brought home to individuals. It is, so to speak, nature's remedy, which comes into silent operation when the body politic has shrunk from curing itself' (Keynes 1971: 53).

There are only a few instances of outright default on domestic debt in EDEs in the past two decades.[10] They involved mandatory bond exchanges at discounted values or conversion of par value bonds at lower-than-market interest rates. The most notable examples include Russia in 1998 and Argentina in 2001. In the former case where eurobonds were excluded from restructuring, an important part of losses from domestic debt default was incurred by non-residents which held about one-third of locally-issued rouble-denominated treasury bills (GKOs). In Argentina residents took a major hit from default on internationally issued bonds because they were large holders. In conventional economic terms this was a default on domestic debt since they were being held by residents even though they had been issued internationally.

While there are strong reasons for giving a preferential treatment to domestic debt in sovereign debt resolutions, it should also be kept in mind that in several EDEs an increasing proportion of locally issued debt is now held by non-residents. This means that any restructuring of external debt as conventionally defined in economic terms should involve locally issued, externally held debt. This calls for a differentiation between resident and non-resident holders of local-law debt. Again there are strong economic reasons for this, notably differential impact of restructuring of debt held by residents and non-residents on economic activity, social welfare, and financial stability due to differences in their behaviour. There may also be a need to differentiate among various local investors in local-law sovereign debt, such as banks and

[10] Defaults are not limited to EDEs. From the 1920s to the 1960s there were several episodes of domestic and external debt defaults, restructuring and conversions in advanced economies; see Reinhart and Rogoff (2013).

non-banks, so as to minimize the financial disruption and instability that may be caused by restructuring.

In practice sovereigns use considerable leverage to facilitate and shape restructuring of domestic-law debt. Greece was able to introduce retroactively a collective action mechanism on its local-law debt stock in a way that minimized the threat of holdout even though an important part of that debt was held by non-residents.[11] Considerable flexibility is also provided to national governments even in the new crisis resolution mechanism of the Eurozone, the European Stability Mechanism, which requires CACs to be included in both domestic and international law bonds, to be governed by the same law as the underlying bonds (see Haworth 2012; Hofmann 2014).[12] While it is difficult to offer different terms of restructuring to holders of the same international debt instrument, it is possible for the sovereign to impose different terms to non-resident and resident holders of the same domestic-law debt. This was done by Russia for the holders of GKOs. Similarly, Argentina was able to treat local holders of its debt differently after the exchange of eurobonds for a new domestic instrument (Roubini and Setser 2004). Sovereign can also differentiate in restructuring among local holders of local-law debt, notably between banks and non-banks.

However, the power of the sovereign vis-à-vis the holders of its local-law bonds is not absolute. Some countries such as the US have constitutional barriers against default on public debt. Again, as seen in Chapter 7, many others have undertaken obligations under Bilateral Investment Treaties (BITs) with advanced economies that restrict their ability to impose losses on foreign investors in local-law bonds, thereby increasing their leverage in domestic debt markets of EDEs.

Restructuring involving partial debt cancellation or imposition of below-market ceilings on interest rates on existing stock of public debt is not very much different in their effect from a capital levy on bond-holders—the solution favoured by Keynes to remove a debt overhang. There are no doubt serious difficulties in introducing such a tax. But it may meet less serious legal handicaps than default, restructuring and conversion because taxation is a universally recognized sovereign discretion—notwithstanding that some countries have tied their hands in this area too in BITs. Where there is scope, taxes can also be differentiated among various bond-holders so as to minimize

[11] A key role in Greek restructuring was played by cash sweeteners to incentivize participation (CIEPR 2013). This rescue money had to come from abroad because Greece could not print it. In this respect EDEs have much greater scope to sweeten restructuring of their local-currency, local-law debts.

[12] The Brookings report on sovereign debt restructuring noted above argued that the new Eurozone regime would not be adequate for the task and went on to make a number of proposals to fill the gaps (CIEPR 2013).

their adverse impact on economic activity and financial stability. This is well worth considering as a complement or alternative to domestic debt restructuring when, as put by Keynes (1971), the piled-up debt demands more than a tolerable proportion of the fruits of work of the active and working elements of the community, to be handed over to the *rentier* or the bond-holding class.

5.3 Banking Crises and Restructuring

If external financial vulnerability in most EDEs today has its origin in private debt, why focus on sovereign debt restructuring? In what way could a sovereign debt restructuring mechanism help address the problems caused by corporate external debt? One answer is because corporate over-borrowing could cause external liquidity problems for the economy at large. When corporations cannot roll over or refinance their external debt, the economy could face a liquidity crisis in the absence of adequate reserves or access to international liquidity to allow financial and non-financial corporations to meet their obligations. Under these conditions, a statutory sovereign debt workout regime incorporating temporary debt standstills and exchange controls and stay against litigation could play a key role in averting the collapse of the currency and widespread defaults of private debtors.[13]

Another reason why a sovereign debt workout mechanism is needed even though the main problem is external private debt is that, as discussed, the latter is often socialized at times of distress, causing problems for fiscal sustainability. Sovereign bail-out of private debt occurs often in banking crises, but non-financial corporations also get bailed out with public money when they are deemed to be strategically important or because their default could hurt the banking system. This implicit guarantee leads to under-pricing of risks and over-borrowing. To prevent moral hazard and avoid using public money, it is necessary to involve both shareholders and creditors in the resolution of private sector debt crises.

However, in most debt crises in EDEs with international dimensions, one of the first things that the governments do is to guarantee all liabilities of the banking system, including not only those that come under deposit insurance but also non-secured liabilities and debt to non-residents. The objective is to

[13] In arguing for a statutory mechanism UNCTAD TDR (1986) indeed referred to a case where three Costa Rican banks suspended payment in 1981 on a loan from a 39-bank syndicate under orders from the central bank of the Republic because of foreign exchange shortage. The US court first ruled in favour of Costa Rica but reversed its decision after intervention by the US government.

stem bank runs and create confidence among foreign creditors in order to prevent exit. However, this rarely succeeds in regaining access to international financial markets and halting capital outflows.

The European crisis is no exception. As pointed out by the chairman of the European Banking Authority, Andrea Enria, too few European banks have been wound down and too many of them have survived (Reuters 2013). In Ireland and Spain where the crisis originated in the banking system, creditors and depositors of troubled banks largely escaped without a haircut. Ireland gave a blanket guarantee to its bank depositors and Greek workouts also spared deposit holders both at home and abroad. Most bond-holders escaped without a haircut, even those holding subordinated debt.

By contrast, in Cyprus the bail-out package, combined with capital controls, inflicted large losses on uninsured foreign depositors and bond-holders. Iceland's debt resolution initiative also stands in sharp contrast to the standard approach to banking crises. Relative to the size of its economy, Iceland faced the biggest banking failure in economic history. However, it has managed to restructure the banking system by letting some of the banks fail and bailing in private creditors, but sparing both taxpayers and domestic depositors. It has imposed capital controls to stem exit and passed an important part of the burden onto international creditors including bond-holders and depositors. It forced banks to write off debt for more than a quarter of the population and declared, in the face of a collapsing currency, loans indexed to foreign currencies illegal, thereby providing significant resources to households for a demand-led recovery.

Public discontent in the US and Europe with large-scale operations to rescue banks with public money after the 2008 crisis has forced authorities to move towards mandatory debt restructuring mechanisms for financial institutions, notably the so-called systemic or too-big-to-fail banks. Such mechanisms give statutory bail-in powers to banking authorities, often regulators, in order to speedily restructure banks by dictating the terms of recapitalization. In this respect it differs from contractual creditor-based recapitalization such as bonds with write-off or conversion features. It also bypasses lengthy legal processes entailed by general corporate bankruptcy codes and minimizes the role of the courts, even limiting the power of follow-up judicial reviews to reverse the resolution. It imposes, inter alia, elimination or significant reduction of the original shareholders, change of management, losses on creditors including uninsured depositors and bond-holders and conversion of debt to equity (see Zhou et al. 2012).[14]

[14] Two bankers, Calello and Ervin (2010), illustrate how a mandatory restructuring could have been done in the case of Lehman.

Unlike sovereign debt, statutory debt restructuring of financial institutions is now very much in vogue with official thinking, including the IMF (Zhou et al. 2012). In a report the FSB (2011) elaborated the Key Attributes of Effective Resolution Regimes for Financial Institutions, including mandatory bail-in powers, for the resolution of financial institutions without exposing taxpayers to loss. This was endorsed at the G20 Cannes summit in November 2011 and was followed by another report a year later intended to make the Key Attributes operational (FSB 2012). The Bank Recovery and Resolution Directive adopted by the European Parliament in May 2014 is designed to bring national resolution frameworks in the European Union in line with these Attributes. The Eurogroup has effectively agreed to formalize the bail-in applied in Cyprus in the single resolution mechanism of the Banking Union, with Germany taking the lead (Thomas 2014). The US has given powers to regulators to impose losses on creditors as part of the Dodd–Frank financial reform act. New rules based on a consultative document by the FSB (2014) were adopted by the G20 in the Australian summit on 16 November 2014. Each country will introduce its own legislation to put them into practice. They are criticized on grounds that rather than reining in the massive and risky derivatives markets, they prioritize the payment of banks' derivatives obligations to each other, ahead of everyone else, including not only public and private depositors but also the pension funds.[15]

Whatever all these would mean in practice for advanced economies—something that would not be known until the next big crisis—EDEs should not go back to 'business as usual' and socialize private liabilities in the event of corporate and banking crises with international dimensions. Rather, they should seek mandatory bail-in of creditors and uninsured depositors, both at home and abroad. They need to introduce statutory powers to restructure bank debt, in principle, on a 'going concern' basis, resorting to forced recapitalization using private rather than public money. They should also allow banks to fail, as needed, without cost to taxpayers. In all these respects, there are some useful lessons to be drawn from Iceland's restructuring. EDEs are now in a stronger position in resisting external pressures to bail out foreign creditors and large depositors than in past banking crises with international dimensions, given a wide international agreement on resolving them without exposing taxpayers to loss.

[15] See Brown (2014) who argues that pension funds are the target market for the so-called bail-in bonds—that is, special bonds that would automatically bail-in banks' creditors to increase the amount of capital that could be used at times of crises to recapitalize them without destabilizing the financial system. For a critique of bail-in bonds, see also Persaud (2013), and Durden (2014b).

5.4 Conclusions

As a result of their deepened integration into the international financial system, EDEs have become highly susceptible to global financial boom–bust cycles shaped mainly by policies in major advanced economies. This is a particular cause for concern because multilateral arrangements fail to impose adequate discipline over international financial markets and policies in systemically important countries which exert a disproportionately large impact on global conditions. They also lack effective mechanisms for orderly resolution of financial crises with international dimensions.

In all likelihood, EDEs will be facing strong destabilizing pressures in the years ahead as the US normalizes its monetary policy after flooding the world with dollars at exceptionally low interest rates for eight years. In weathering renewed instability, EDEs cannot always count on the more flexible currency regimes they came to adopt after the last bouts of crises or the reserves they have built from capital inflows or the reduced currency exposure of the sovereign. It is important that they, as well as the international community, avoid going back to business-as-usual in responding to a new round of instability, bailing out investors and creditors and maintaining an open capital account at the expense of incomes and jobs. They need to include many unconventional policy instruments in their arsenals to help lower the price that may have to be paid for the financial excesses of the past several years.

More importantly, EDEs need to rebalance the pendulum and rethink the depth and pattern of their integration into the international financial system, the liberalization of their capital accounts and the increased presence of foreigners in their domestic financial markets. They also need to rethink their participation in the international production system, particularly the pros and cons of the growing presence of foreign corporations in their markets for goods and services on terms and conditions shaped by major advanced economies which, in many respects, carry similar implications for stability, growth and development—an issue to be taken up in the next two chapters.

Part III

Foreign Direct Investment and Economic Development: Myths and Realities

6

Foreign Direct Investment

Its Nature and Impact on Capital Formation and Balance-of-Payments

The new millennium has seen a deepened integration of emerging and developing economies (EDEs) not only into the international financial system, but also into the international production system thanks to their increased openness to foreign firms. The growing presence of foreign investors and institutions in the financial markets of these economies, discussed in Chapter 3, has thus been accompanied by increased penetration of transnational corporations (TNCs), mostly but not only from advanced economies, in their markets for goods and services with the rapid liberalization of foreign direct investment (FDI) regimes. Two main considerations account for this; one financial, another developmental. First, in order to reduce their vulnerability to external financial shocks, governments in EDEs sought to shift from debt to equities in external financing on grounds that equity is more stable and less risky than debt. Second, after China's success in becoming an international hub for manufactured exports, hopes are increasingly pinned on participation in international production networks organized and controlled by TNCs for export-led industrialization.

However, the contribution of FDI to balance-of-payments and external financial stability, and growth and industrialization is highly contentious. Indeed FDI is perhaps one of the most ambiguous and least understood concepts in international economics. Common perceptions of FDI are confounded by several myths regarding its nature and impact on capital accumulation, technological progress, industrialization, and growth in EDEs. It is often portrayed as a long-term, stable, cross-border flow of capital that adds to productive capacity, helps meet balance-of-payments shortfalls, transfers technology and management skills, and links domestic firms with wider global markets. However, none of these are intrinsic qualities of FDI. Rather, policy in host countries plays a key role in determining the impact of FDI in these areas. A laissez-faire approach could not yield much benefit. Successful examples are found not necessarily among countries that attracted more FDI, but among those which used it in the context of national industrial policy designed to shape the evolution of specific industries through public interventions. This means that EDEs need adequate policy space vis-à-vis FDI and TNCs if they are to benefit from it. Still, the past two decades have seen a significant erosion of policy vis-à-vis TNCs. This is partly due to the commitments undertaken in the World Trade Organization (WTO). However, many of the more serious constraints are in practice self-inflicted through unilateral liberalization or bilateral investment treaties (BITs)[1] signed with advanced economies.

This and the following chapter revisit and review these contentious issues regarding the nature and impact of FDI, based on empirical evidence and historical experience. They examine if and under what conditions FDI can provide a stable source of external financing, supplement domestic resources, add to productive capacity and accelerate technological progress and industrial upgrading. This chapter starts with an examination of the concept of FDI as officially defined, measured, and reported in order to clarify what it is about. This is followed by a discussion of the impact of FDI on domestic capital formation, stability, and balance-of-payments. Chapter 7 examines the potential contribution of TNCs to technological progress in EDEs and the policies needed to secure positive spillovers from foreign firms, followed by a discussion of policy constraints brought about by multilateral and bilateral agreements and policy lessons drawn from post-war experience of EDEs.

6.1 What Is FDI?

In common discussions FDI is often meant to entail capital inflows from abroad and additions to productive capacity in host countries. However, the reality is a lot more complex and the concept is a lot more ambiguous than is commonly believed. An important part of FDI does not entail cross-border capital flows and it is very difficult to identify from existing statistics what FDI really comprises.[2] Indeed it is even difficult to make a sound judgement about the magnitude and evolution of FDI as statistics reported by two main official

[1] In this book BITs is used as a shorthand for all international agreements signed outside the multilateral system that contain provisions on foreign investment and investors, including free trade and economic partnership agreements.

[2] For an earlier account of some of the issues taken up here, see Woodward (2001).

sources of data, the IMF and UNCTAD, can differ significantly without any explanation for the reasons for such differences.[3]

OECD (2008) provides global standards for direct investment statistics consistent with the related concepts and definitions of 'Balance of Payments and International Investment Position Manual' of the IMF (2009). Direct investment is defined as a category of cross-border investment made by a resident in one economy (*direct investor*) with the objective of establishing a lasting interest in an enterprise (*direct investment enterprise*) that is resident in an economy other than that of the direct investor. The motivation of the direct investor is said to be a long-term, stable relationship with the direct investment enterprise to ensure a significant degree of influence on its management. The lasting interest and a significant degree of influence is said to be evidenced when the direct investor owns at least 10 per cent of the voting power of the direct investment enterprise. Ownership below 10 per cent is treated as portfolio equity investment.

Defined in this way, FDI comprises the initial equity transaction that meets the 10 per cent threshold and all subsequent financial transactions and positions between the direct investor and the direct investment enterprise. Thus, in addition to initial equity capital outflows from the home country, it includes reinvested earnings and intercompany debt flows.

The threshold of 10 per cent is totally arbitrary and there is no compelling reason why investment in 10 per cent ownership should be less fickle than investment in 9.9 per cent. Both the OECD and the IMF recognize that in practice influence may be determined by several other factors than the extent of ownership. However, they argue that 'a *strict application* of a numerical guideline is recommended to define direct investment' in order to secure international consistency and to avoid subjective judgements.[4]

In the official definition a direct investment enterprise is always a corporation and may also include public entities. However, contrary to a widespread perception, direct investors are not always TNCs. It could also be an individual or household, an investment fund, a government or an international organization or a non-profit institution. Certainly there are significant differences in the technology and managerial skills such diverse investors could bring to the host country. But readily available official statistics do not allow identifying them. This is one of the drawbacks of empirical studies linking aggregate FDI

[3] This was noted by Reisen (2016) in relation to FDI inflows to Africa in 2014 and 2015 in his piece 'Lies, Damned Lies, and FDI Statistics.' As noted in Section 6.5 (note 18), there are also large differences between UNCTAD and IMF statistics for the Chinese FDI flows and stocks. In this book the IMF country data are generally used because of their balance-of-payments consistency.

[4] OECD (2008: para 31). See also IMF (2009: para 6.13). Definition and measurement of FDI have changed considerably over time and varied across countries; see Lipsey (1999).

to various economic performance indicators in host countries such as fixed capital formation, productivity, and growth.

Every financial transaction after the initial acquisition of equity by the investor, that is, internal capital flows within firms, are also considered as direct investment. Thus, loans and advances from parent companies to affiliates are treated as part of direct equity rather than debt. Exceptions are made for loans between certain affiliated financial corporations, notably deposit taking corporations—international banks—on grounds that such debt is not so strongly connected to direct investment relationships. However, this may also be the case in non-financial enterprises since in practice it is not possible to identify the nature and effects of lending and borrowing between parents and affiliated corporations. Statistics do not generally give the terms and conditions of intra-company loans and advances (UNCTAD 2009a). They are known to fluctuate much more than equity capital. They are highly susceptible to changes in short-term business conditions and their inclusion as equity capital can cause large swings in recorded FDI flows. For instance in 2012 high levels of repayment of intercompany loans to parent companies by Brazilian affiliates abroad pushed total Brazilian FDI outflows to negative figures even though there was a net equity capital investment abroad of some $7.5 billion by Brazilian parent companies (UNCTAD WIR 2013).

While initial equity investment and intercompany loans constitute capital inflows to the host country, this is not the case for retained earnings. In FDI statistics these are imputed as being payable to the owners, to be reinvested as an increase in their equity. Thus, they are assumed to be used for lasting investment in the existing or new productive assets. In balance-of-payments they are first recorded as investment income payments in the current account and then as offsetting inflows of direct equity investment in the capital and financial account.

Retained earnings constitute a significant part of statistically measured FDI inflows. Historically, equity capital outflows and net debt from parent companies are relatively small parts of US outflows of direct investment while the rest comes from retained earnings. In the post-war period until the mid-1990s the latter accounted for no less than one half of US outward direct investment (Lipsey 1999). It was even higher in more recent years because of growth of the US outward FDI stock. In 2008, retained earnings constituted 60 per cent of outward FDI stock for non-bank affiliates of US non-bank corporations (see Table 6.1). Globally, in 2011 they accounted for 30 per cent of total FDI flows. This proportion was even higher for FDI in EDEs; in the same year, half of the earnings on FDI stock in EDEs were retained, financing about 40 per cent of total inward foreign direct investment in these economies (UNCTAD WIR 2013).

Clearly, when financed from earnings generated in host countries, FDI does not constitute an autonomous source of external financing. Given that

Table 6.1 Outward FDI and value of assets of US non-bank foreign affiliates (billions of US dollars)

	1989	2008
FDI (US parents)	**452**	**4376**
Equity	202	1638
Debt	25	130
Retained earnings	225	2608
Other US investors	**24**	**146**
Equity	1	3
Debt	22	138
Retained earnings	1	5
Net external finance from US sources[a]	**250**	**1909**
Net finance from US sources[b]	**476**	**4522**
Non-US finance	**761**	**11,910**
Equity	92	2741
Debt	567	4806
Retained earnings	102	4363
Value of assets of US affiliates[c]	**1237**	**16,432**

Note: [a] Equity and debt from US parents and other US investors
[b] FDI plus other US investors.
[c] Net finance from US sources plus non-US finance.

Source: 1989 figures from Feldstein (1994). 2008 figures are estimates from BOEA (2008) using the same method as Feldstein.

retained earnings constitute an important component of total recorded FDI, the notion that FDI is functionally indistinguishable from fresh capital inflows and represents a flow of foreign resources crossing the borders of two countries has no validity, as long noted by Vernon (1999). Equity and loans from parent companies account for a relatively small part of recorded FDI and an even smaller part of total foreign assets controlled by them.

This is illustrated in Table 6.1 for the majority-owned foreign non-bank affiliates of US non-bank corporations. Figures for 1989 are estimates at current cost given by Feldstein (1994) whereas those for 2008 are based on the 2008 benchmark survey of the US Bureau of Economic Analysis (BOEA 2008), using the same methodology as Feldstein (1994). In both years, FDI as defined in the balance-of-payments exceeds by a large margin not only equity and loans from parent companies, but also total net external finance from all US sources because of retained profits.[5] More importantly, the value of assets of US affiliates is significantly greater than net finance from US sources because of equity and debt from non-US sources and the share of non-US sources in

[5] Feldstein (1994) distinguishes among several definitions of outward FDI. The narrowest definition, net external finance from US sources, includes only outflows of equity and debt from US parents and other US sources. Net finance from US sources is a broader definition and includes, in addition, retained earnings due to US parents and other US investors. The broadest concept refers to total assets controlled by US parents, that is, value of assets of US affiliates, and includes, in addition, equity and debt finance from non-US sources and the share of non-US equity investors in retained earnings.

retained profits of majority-owned US affiliates. In 2008, total assets controlled by US affiliates were 8.6 times the net external finance from US sources (equity and debt from US parents and other US investors) and 3.8 times the stock of US outward FDI at current cost as conventionally defined (that is, including unrequited profits).

6.2 FDI and Capital Formation

As officially defined, FDI can take three main forms. The first is greenfield investment which involves creating a subsidiary from scratch with fresh capital by one or more non-resident investors. The second is cross-border M&A which relate to existing company structures. Cross-border mergers arise when resident and non-resident companies agree to combine into a single operation. Acquisitions involve the purchase of existing companies fully or partly by a non-resident company or a group of companies; that is, a transfer of ownership from residents to non-residents of 10 per cent or more of voting stock of an existing company. The third is the expansion of production capacity of existing firms partly or fully owned by non-residents through injection of fresh money, including loans from parent companies.

When FDI is in the form of acquisition of existing public or private assets, it has no direct contribution to domestic capital formation although changes in ownership can give rise to productivity gains and may be followed by new investment by the direct investor or may stimulate domestic investment that would not have otherwise taken place. Cross-border privatization could also add to domestic capital accumulation if the proceeds are used for investment. However, these all depend on several other factors, including host country policies. Moreover, such spillovers may also be generated by greenfield FDI. Thus, M&A cannot be treated at par with the other two components of FDI, which directly add to productive capacity in host countries.

These three categories of FDI are not separately identified in the existing statistics on FDI provided by the OECD and the IMF.[6] UNCTAD provides data on M&A as well as greenfield 'investment projects' from 2003 onwards which refer to capital expenditure planned by the investor at the time of the announcement. It is recognized that investment projects data 'can be substantially different from the official FDI data as companies can raise capital locally and phase their investments over time, and the project may be

[6] The fourth edition of OECD Benchmark Definition of FDI contains an updated benchmark definition and provides guidance on how to compile FDI by type and distinguish M&A (OECD 2008: 141–2). However, collection of data on FDI from member countries according to the new guidelines started only in September 2014, to be available not before the second quarter of 2015.

cancelled or may not start in the year when it is announced' (UNCTAD WIR 2014: 33, note 1). A comparison of reported FDI inflows with the sum total of M&A and greenfield projects shows considerable variations over 2003–13. For advanced economies, figures on total FDI exceed the sum total of the figures on greenfield projects and M&A for every year except 2005. For EDEs, this has been the case since 2010 and in some years the discrepancy is as high as 40 per cent of reported FDI figures. Given the global economic downturn after 2007, investment plans are unlikely to have been exceeded to the extent to account for the discrepancy. This strongly suggests that reported FDI figures contain items that may not really qualify as direct investment.

The existing statistical measures cannot always identify the use made of unrequited earnings and loans from parents. It is known that they are extensively used to accumulate record levels of cash and other liquid assets, rather than reinvested in productive capacity (UNCTAD WIR 2013). Certainly, any industrial or commercial enterprise needs to hold liquid capital in order to support its core activities for the production and marketing of goods and services. But it is very difficult to identify from official statistics the proportion of recorded equity capital held in such assets or whether they serve to support core activities rather than constitute an independent source of financial income and speculative capital gains.

All these difficulties in interpreting the reported FDI data as investment in productive capacity are also recognized by UNCTAD (WIR 2014: 149): 'FDI flows do not always translate into equivalent capital expenditures, especially where they are driven by retained earnings or by transactions such as mergers and acquisitions (M&As), although some M&A transactions such as brownfield investment in agriculture do result in significant capital expenditure. FDI can contain short-term, relatively volatile components, such as "hot money" or investments in real estate.'

The contribution of FDI to capital formation depends not only on whether it represents additional capital spending on productive capacity rather than transfer of ownership or portfolio investment, but also on its impact on domestic capital accumulation—that is, whether it crowds in or crowds out domestic investment. The impact can occur in various channels. FDI inflows attracted by privatization could allow public investment to be raised. Again, it can affect domestic investment by easing the balance-of-payments constraint. Whether FDI crowds in or crowds out domestic investors also depends on the externalities and spillovers generated by foreign firms. They can stimulate domestic investment if they help improve overall economic performance through linkages with the domestic industry and technological and managerial spillovers. For instance entry of foreign firms can promote additional investment by their local suppliers if they are connected. However, as discussed in the next chapter, such benefits are not automatic. In the absence of deliberate and effective policies to generate positive spillovers, financial and technological strengths of these firms can simply crowd out domestic investors.

The empirical evidence on the impact of FDI on aggregate domestic investment is inconclusive and the impact is often related to other variables including institutions and policy (Akyüz 2006; Morrissey and Udomkerdmongkol 2012; Farla et al. 2013). Results also differ across regions with East Asian EDEs mostly showing crowding-in while Latin America crowding-out.[7] Most of these studies do not distinguish between acquisition of existing assets and greenfield investment. One of the few studies examining the impact of M&A separately concludes that M&A-related FDI is not only less beneficial than greenfield investment, but has also adverse effect on accumulation and growth (Nanda 2009).

The impact of outward FDI on domestic investment in home countries is also ambiguous and the evidence is mixed. Outward investment may reduce investment at home if it is designed to shift the production base to low-cost locations abroad to supply world markets. It may also stimulate investment at home, for instance in capital goods industries to supply machinery and equipment for outward investment or in intermediate goods industries to supply inputs into production abroad. One of the first studies on this by Feldstein (1994) using data from the US for the 1970s and 1980s concluded that outbound FDI reduced domestic investment about dollar for dollar whereas inbound FDI raised domestic investment by the same magnitude. A more recent study on OECD countries using data from the 1980s and 1990s came to the same conclusion for the relation between aggregate domestic investment and outward FDI (Desai et al. 2005). However, when the analysis was confined to domestic and outward investment by TNCs, investment by US multinationals and their foreign affiliates appeared complementary; that is, higher levels of investment abroad by US affiliates are associated with higher levels of investment by parents at home.[8]

Research also suggests that the relation between domestic investment and outward FDI may be sector specific, with those with strong R&D components appearing to be complementary compared to efficiency seeking FDI (Goedegebuure 2006). With increased outward FDI from some major EDEs,

[7] Looking at Africa, Asia, and Latin America, Agosin and Machado (2005) finds that the impact of FDI on domestic investment is at best neutral in all regions, with Latin America showing crowding-out effect. See also Ernst (2005) on crowding out in the three largest economies of Latin America. The evidence provided by Mutenyo et al. (2010) suggests that FDI also crowds out private investment in sub-Saharan Africa.

[8] As the authors point out, this finding can be reconciled with the evidence on the economy-wide trade-off between outward FDI and domestic investment provided by Feldstein if investment abroad by US multinationals replaces activities previously undertaken by other firms in the US (Desai et al. 2005: 9).

Table 6.2 Investment and FDI (per cent of GDP)

	Investment[a]			FDI Inflows		
	1981–90	1991–2000	2001–13	1981–90	1991–2000	2001–13
World	24.4	23.4	23.6	0.64	1.71	2.29
AEs	24.3	23.2	21.3	0.65	1.57	1.90
EDEs	24.4	24.4	28.4	0.59	2.19	3.12

Note: [a] Includes inventories

Source: IMF WEO (2014b) and UNCTAD FDI database.

attention has recently turned to the impact of such investment on domestic capital accumulation in these economies. A study using aggregate domestic investment and outward FDI data from 121 countries, including both developing and transition economies, over the period 1990–2010 found that outward FDI in these countries had a negative effect on domestic investment (Al-Sadig 2013).

The rapid growth of global FDI in the past three decades appears to have led not so much to an acceleration of global capital accumulation as to a reallocation of production facilities, jobs and ownership across different countries. For the world economy as a whole, total FDI inflows as a proportion of GDP increased by more than three-fold since the 1980s while the investment ratio declined over the same period (see Table 6.2). During this period FDI inflows grew rapidly in both advanced economies and EDEs, but investment fell in the former while rising in the latter. In advanced economies in both the 1990s and 2000s, higher FDI inflows were associated with lower domestic capital accumulation. While the acceleration of FDI inflows to EDEs was associated with an increase in domestic investment in the new millennium, this was not the case in the 1990s.

In the 1990s privatization of public assets played an important role in the increase in FDI inflows, particularly in Latin America which received two-thirds of total FDI inflows to EDEs linked to privatization (UNCTAD TDR 1999). After a series of financial crises in EDEs starting in the mid-1990s, most forms of capital inflows, notably bank lending, fell sharply, but FDI kept up. An important factor was foreign acquisition of companies of EDEs hit by the crises. This happened particularly during the Asian crisis where massive flight of short-term capital and sale of foreign equity holdings were accompanied by a wave of FDI inflows in the form of foreign acquisition of Asian firms. Collapse of currencies and asset price deflation, together with the pressure from the IMF to abandon policies unfavourable to foreign ownership, created opportunities for TNCs to buy Asian companies at fire-sale prices (Krugman 2000). Indeed, cross-border M&A as a percentage of total FDI peaked during the recurrent crises in EDEs at the end of the 1990s and early

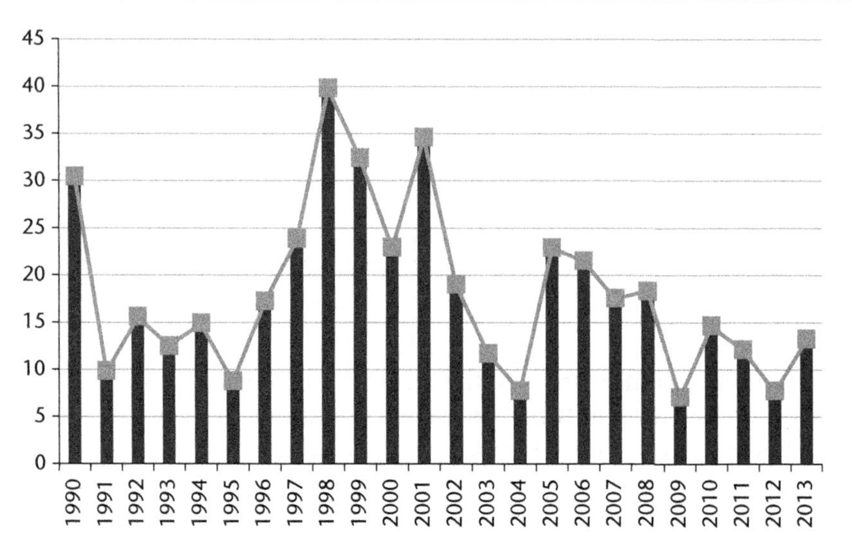

Figure 6.1 Share of cross-border M&A as per cent of total FDI inflows in developing countries (percentage)

Note: a: excludes China.

Source: UNCTAD WIR (2014).

2000s (see Figure 6.1). Foreign acquisitions at times of crises in host countries are driven mainly by non-financial acquirers targeting firms in the same industry, thereby concentrating market power in TNCs at the expense of national companies of EDEs (Alquist et al. 2013).

This suggests that the economic conditions that attract foreign enterprises may not always be conducive to faster capital formation and that the two sets of investment decisions may be driven by different considerations. Indeed, the generalized surge in FDI inflows to EDEs in the 1990s was not always associated with a concomitant increase in fixed capital formation. This is shown in Figure 6.2 in terms of the relation between changes in gross fixed capital formation (GFCF; that is, investment less changes in inventories) and FDI as a per cent of GDP in selected EDEs during the 1990s compared to the 1980s and during the 2000s compared to the 1990s. The data for the earlier period are from UNCTAD TDR (2003: Chapter IV) which are updated to the 2000s using the same database.

In Latin America in the 1990s there was a widespread association of increased FDI with reduced fixed capital formation; for the region as a whole FDI as a proportion of GDP was higher in the 1990s than in the 1980s by more than 1.7 percentage points, but the share of GFCF in GDP was lower by some 0.6 percentage points. In all major Latin American economies FDI as a proportion of GDP rose strongly while GFCF either stagnated or fell between the two periods. It is also notable that the inverse association between GFCF and FDI is found not only in countries where an important part of FDI was in the

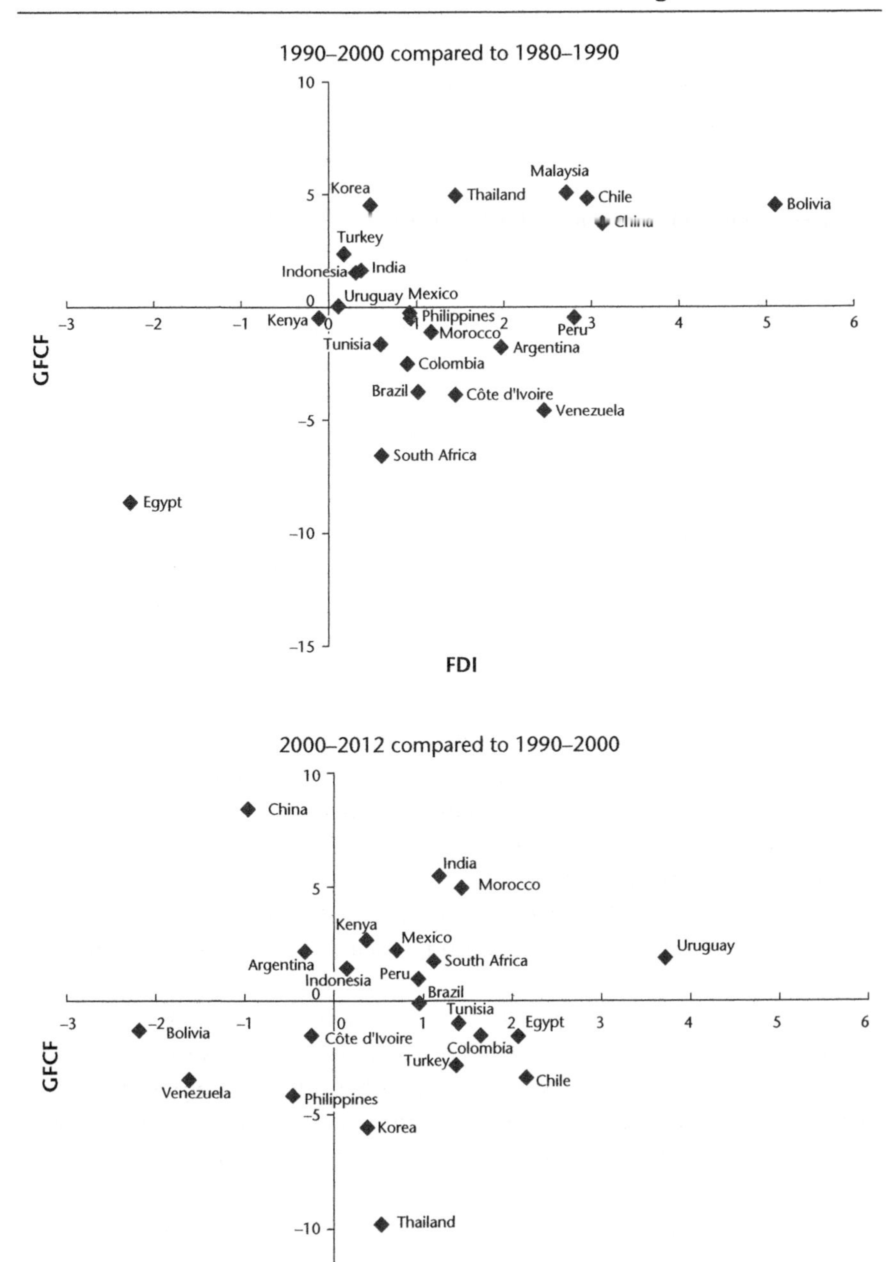

Figure 6.2 Changes in FDI inflows and domestic GFCF in selected emerging economies (percentage of GDP)

Source: UNCTADstat.

form of M&A, but also in Mexico where there was considerable greenfield investment stimulated by NAFTA. Again in several countries in Africa, including Côte d'Ivoire, Morocco, South Africa, and Tunisia, FDI and GFCF moved in opposite directions. By contrast in none of the rapidly growing East Asian NIEs was rising FDI associated with falling GFCF.

For the EDEs taken together both FDI inflows and fixed capital formation have been stronger in the new millennium, particularly until the crisis in 2008–09. However, in more than half of the EDEs which enjoyed a boom in FDI inflows, including Brazil, Korea, Turkey, and Thailand, GFCF fell or stagnated during 2000–12 compared to the 1990s. Indeed, several EDEs which enjoyed surges in both FDI and other types of capital inflows experienced falling or stagnant domestic investment rates and deindustrialization (Akyüz 2012; Naudé et al. 2013). In China FDI inflows as a per cent of GDP was lower than in the 1990s mainly because of contraction in its export markets after the crisis while GFCF increased sharply because of the policy response of the government with a massive investment package, discussed in Chapters 1 and 2. In India both FDI and GFCF were much stronger. Among the East Asian countries severely hit by the 1997 crisis, only Indonesia saw an increase in both FDI and GFCF in the 2000s compared to the 1990s while Malaysia experienced a sharp contraction in both.

Generally, FDI seems to follow rather than lead domestic investment. Evidence from a study on a large sample of countries over 1984–2004 indeed shows that lagged domestic investment has a strong influence on FDI inflows to the host economy (Lautier and Moreau 2012). On the other hand, FDI and non-FDI inflows are more closely connected than is commonly believed. This is partly because, like portfolio flows, part of FDI, property investment, is also driven by financial bubbles. Second, global liquidity conditions have an important impact on FDI because assets acquired by TNCs are often leveraged. As noted in Chapter 3 this is true not only for corporations from advanced economies but also from major EDEs. Financial cycles also exert a strong influence on profits of TNCs, which constitute an important source of FDI. As noted by the BIS (1998: 28) 'short-term movements in FDI flows are highly procyclical, mainly reflecting the influence of reinvestment of retained earnings'.

These influences have been particularly evident in the new millennium with FDI moving more closely with non-FDI inflows than with investment, particularly since the crisis (Figure 6.3). After the Asian crisis in 1997 until 2002, investment and non-FDI capital inflows followed a downward trend while FDI inflows kept up, thanks in part to fire-sale FDI in crisis-hit countries. After 2002, investment, FDI and non-FDI inflows all rose strongly until the Lehman turmoil. Investment kept up due largely to stimulus packages introduced in response to fallouts from the crisis. Inward FDI and non-FDI flows as

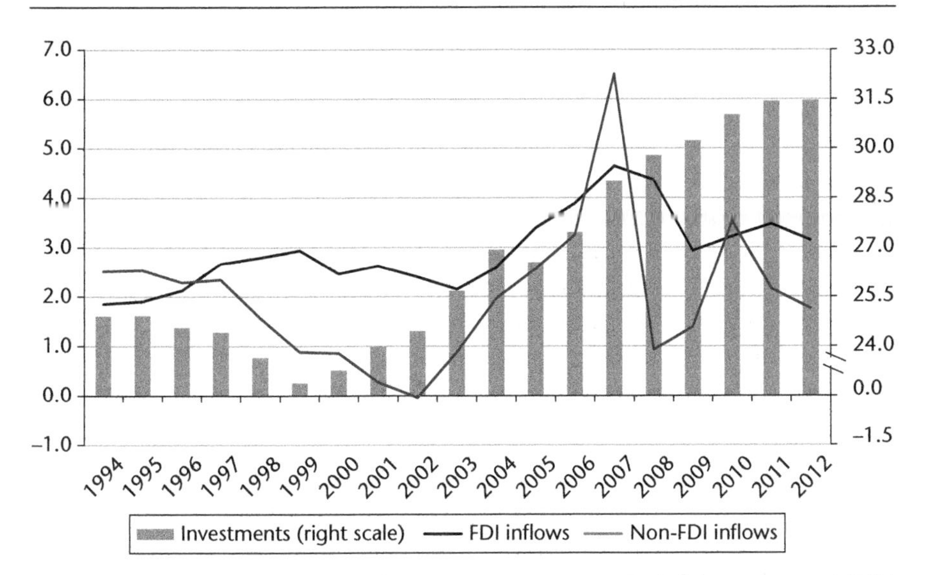

Figure 6.3 International capital inflows and investment in EDEs[a] (percentage of GDP)

Note: a: EDEs include emerging markets and developing countries as defined by the IMF. Investment includes inventories.

Source: IMF WEO Database and Balance of Payments Statistics, World and Regional Aggregates.

a per cent of GDP both fell sharply during 2008–09. They followed a similar path subsequently, recovering but remaining well below their pre-crisis levels.

6.3 Stability of FDI

It is widely held that FDI constitutes a stable source of finance for balance-of-payments shortfalls. On this view, because FDI is largely fixed in illiquid assets and reflects 'lasting interest' by the investor, the likelihood of direct investment to exit rapidly at times of deteriorations in global liquidity conditions and risk appetite is much more limited than other forms of capital inflows. In other words, 'it is bolted down and cannot leave so easily at the first sign of trouble' (Hausmann and Fernández-Arias 2000: 3). Consequently, it is argued, they do not pose a serious threat to macroeconomic and financial stability in EDEs.

This account is highly misleading. As noted in Section 6.1, profits as a major source of FDI tend to be highly volatile and pro-cyclical. Furthermore, certain features of FDI and TNCs can induce as much instability in balance-of-payments and domestic asset and credit markets as portfolio investment and investors. Finally, many of the changes in financial markets that have facilitated international capital movements have not only increased the mobility of FDI, but also made it difficult to assess its stability.

First, recorded FDI statistics do not always allow identifying the stability of its various components and hence the destabilizing impulses they may generate. While FDI inflows do not always involve inflows of financial capital, their exit always implies outflows of funds through the foreign exchange market as proceeds from sales are transferred abroad. By convention, retained earnings are recorded as additions to equity capital, but in reality they may well be used to acquire financial assets or repatriated as portfolio outflows. Further, financial transactions can accomplish a reversal of FDI. A foreign affiliate can borrow in the host country to lend the money back to the parent company or the parent can recall intercompany debt (Loungani and Razin 2001). More generally, what may get recorded as portfolio outflows may well be outflows of FDI in disguise:

> Because direct investors hold factories and other assets that are impossible to move, it is sometimes assumed that a direct investment inflow is more stable than other forms of capital flows. This need not be the case. While a direct investor usually has some immovable assets, there is no reason in principle why these cannot by fully offset by domestic liabilities. Clearly, a direct investor can borrow in order to export capital, and thereby generate rapid capital outflows (Claessens et al. 1993: 22).

Second, FDI inflows can undergo temporary surges as a result of discovery of large reserves of oil and minerals, widespread privatization, rapid liberalization, or favourable political changes. A glut in the foreign exchange market resulting from a one-off surge in FDI inflows could generate unsustainable currency appreciations in much the same way as surges in any other forms of capital inflows, contrary to the widespread fallacy that it is only short-term capital inflows that can lead to such an outcome. The impact on the currency could be particularly strong when FDI inflows involve acquisition of existing assets rather than greenfield investment since the latter involves imports of capital goods required to install production capacity.

Third, FDI includes components such as real estate investment that are often driven by speculative motivations and susceptible to sharp fluctuations. This has led the IMF (2009: 105) to suggest that '[b]ecause it may have different motivations and economic impact from other direct investment, if real estate investment is significant, compilers may wish to publish data on such investment separately on a supplementary basis'. Cross-border property acquisitions have no doubt played an important role in the increased volatility and gyration of property prices in the past two decades in several countries. Historical data on housing transactions in London shows significant foreign effect on house prices and volume of transactions (Badarinza and Ramadorai 2014). The recent recovery in house prices in London is predominantly due to growth in foreign demand (Property Wire 2014b). Foreign purchases played an important role in the build-up of the Spain property bubble in the run up to the crisis in 2008. Hopes are pinned once again on foreign demand for the recovery of the housing market in Spain as sales to foreigners increased almost 209 per cent in the 12 months ending in October 2014 with the share of foreigners hitting a new high of 13 per cent of the market (Taylor Wimpey 2014). In Turkey too foreign investment has been an important driver of the ongoing bubble in the property market (Property Wire 2014a).

Fourth, the 'lasting interest' the foreign direct investors are said to have with direct investment enterprise does not always translate into a long-term commitment of that enterprise to the host country. Investment in bricks and mortar can be highly footloose, particularly in fragmented production segments organized by TNCs as part of international production networks for manufactured products. It is less likely to happen when investment is resource-seeking in oil and minerals, but even then the discovery of more profitable reserves elsewhere could lead to migration of FDI. The emergence of lower cost locations for manufacturing production for global markets can result in shifts of location of production particularly when policies fail to lock TNCs into the economy with strong linkages to local firms and succeed in getting them to upgrade and move to higher echelons in the production chains they control. This is seen in East Asia, notably in Malaysia, where a number of plants producing electronics left for China as the latter emerged as a more attractive location for production for international markets (Ernst 2004). Again certain TNCs in electronics left Mexican maquiladoras for China and some other Asian countries, and Chinese inward FDI is found to have had a negative impact on FDI inflows to Mexico and Colombia, particularly after China joined the WTO (Zarsky and Gallagher 2008; García-Herrero and Santabárbara 2007). Much of the FDI in Ireland also appears to be footloose, encouraged by its entry to the EU and special incentives (Campa and Cull 2013).

Finally, as discussed in Chapters 3 and 4, foreign banks established in EDEs can be major conduits of destabilizing impulses from global markets. An important part of FDI into EDEs in the new millennium has been in the banking sector, including M&A and fully owned foreign subsidiaries. The share of foreign banks in the banking sector of these economies has more than doubled since the beginning of the decade. Contrary to the long-held orthodox view that they enhance the resilience of EDEs to external financial shocks, since the Eurozone crisis it is now widely recognized that the extensive presence of foreign banks can aggravate their financial fragility and vulnerability to financial shocks.

6.4 Contribution to Balance-of-payments: Net Transfers

Most EDEs, particularly those with chronic current account deficits and excessive dependence on foreign capital, regard FDI mainly as a source of external financing, rather than as an instrument of industrialization and development. In closing the external financing gap FDI is preferred to debt-creating inflows because it does not entail fixed obligations besides being more stable.

However, FDI can also result in considerable outflows in income remittances and hence exert pressure on the balance-of-payments in much the same way as debt obligations. A measure of this pressure is net transfers—that is, the difference between inflows of FDI and FDI-related payments abroad including profits, royalties, licence fees, wage remittances, and interest paid on loans from parent companies. This concept is akin to that of net transfers on debt obligations widely discussed during the Latin American debt crisis. If income transfers abroad exceed net inflows of FDI in any particular year, then the gap would have to be closed either by generating a current account surplus or using reserves or borrowing abroad.[9]

Generally, at the early stages of entry of TNCs, the stock of inward FDI tends to be small relative to new inflows. But over time inflows tend to fall relative to the stock. In other words, initially the growth rate of the FDI stock is likely to exceed the rate of return on it and transfers on FDI would be positive. However, as the stock of FDI increases, its growth rate tends to decline, eventually falling below the rate of return on existing FDI stocks, resulting in net negative transfers. Clearly, the higher the rate of return on foreign capital stock, the sooner the host country may face net negative transfers on FDI.

Countries with a long history of TNCs involvement, and hence a relatively large stock of foreign capital, tend to face negative transfers. A developing economy with abundant labour and good infrastructure such as China may start attracting large amounts of FDI for the production of labour-intensive manufactures for global markets, but over time FDI inflows are likely to level off as surplus labour gets exhausted and wages start rising. The emergence of low-cost locations can also lead to diversion of FDI, widening the gap between new inflows and income payments on foreign capital stock. Discovery of rich oil and mineral reserves can give rise to a strong surge in FDI which cannot be maintained over time. In such countries the growth rate of foreign capital stock can fall rapidly and negative net transfers can appear in a relatively short time after an initial surge in foreign investment. Again, a sudden opening up of an economy could lead to a one-off boom in FDI inflows.

The long-term trend in the growth rate of FDI stock in EDEs is downward, albeit showing large swings and boom-bust cycles (see Figure 6.4). This is clearly seen if periods of extreme instability are excluded. The average annual growth rate was around 14 per cent during the first half of the 1990s, before

[9] This holds whether or not profits are remitted since retained earnings are recorded as FDI inflows.

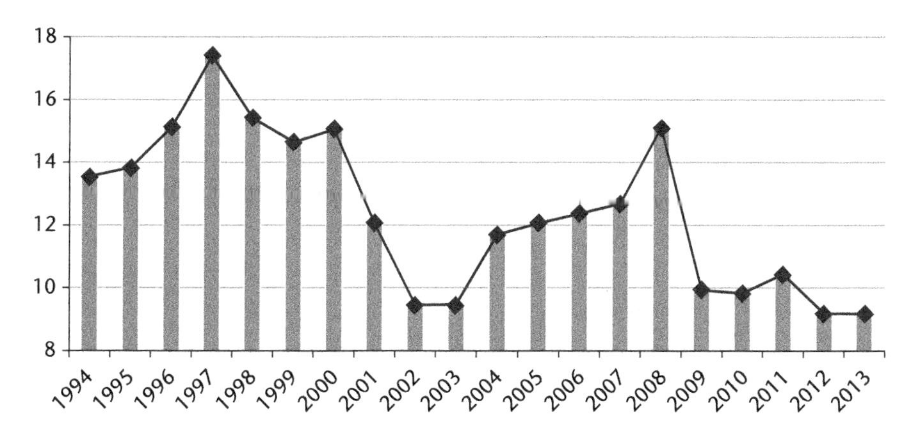

Figure 6.4 Inward FDI in EDEs: ratio of FDI flows to FDI stocks (Per cent)
Source: UNCTADstats.

Table 6.3 Net transfers on FDI in selected EDEs
Ratio of cumulative income payments to cumulative FDI inflows: 2000–13

Ranking	Country	Ratio		Country	Ratio		Country	Ratio
1	Algeria	3.09	**10**	Congo, Republic of	1.17	**19**	Colombia	0.83
2	Nigeria	2.09	**11**	Philippines	1.07	**20**	Zambia	0.73
3	Malaysia	1.73	**12**	Indonesia	1.06	**21**	China	0.52
4	Thailand	1.54	**13**	Chile	1.06	**22**	India	0.49
5	Singapore	1.43	**14**	Russian Federation	0.99	**23**	Brazil	0.43
6	Libya	1.38	**15**	Tunisia	0.95	**24**	Mexico	0.40
7	Côte d'Ivoire	1.31	**16**	Sudan	0.92	**25**	Kenya	0.39
8	Peru	1.21	**17**	Argentina	0.90	**26**	Egypt	0.39
9	South Africa	1.20	**18**	Korea	0.88	**27**	Turkey	0.18

Note: For 2000–04 data are based on BPM5 and for 2005–13 on BPM6.
Indonesia: 2003–13; Peru: 2007–13; Thailand: 2001–12; Algeria: 2005–13; Congo: 2000–07; Côte d'Ivoire: 2000–10; Libya: 2000–10; Singapore: estimates for 2002–12 based on national data; Sudan: 2002–13.
Source: IMF BOP.

the recurrent crises in EDEs. It fell to 11.3 per cent during 2002–07 and again to less than 10 per cent during 2010–13.

For EDEs as a whole, on average, annual inflows of FDI exceed income payments on FDI stocks. However, there are considerable inter-country variations. This is shown in Table 6.3 in terms of a comparison of cumulative income payments on the stock of FDI and cumulative inflows over 2000–13 for a number of EDEs, including major recipients of FDI.[10] In half of the

[10] Income payments on FDI in Table 6.3 include the item 'direct investment income' in the primary income account of the balance-of-payments which includes income on equity and investment fund shares and interest. Royalties and licence fees collected by foreign firms (now called 'charges for the use of intellectual property' in the balance-of-payments) and wage remittances by workers employed by them cannot be accounted for because they are recorded under separate entries in the balance-of-payments—see IMF (2009). Therefore, the figures in the

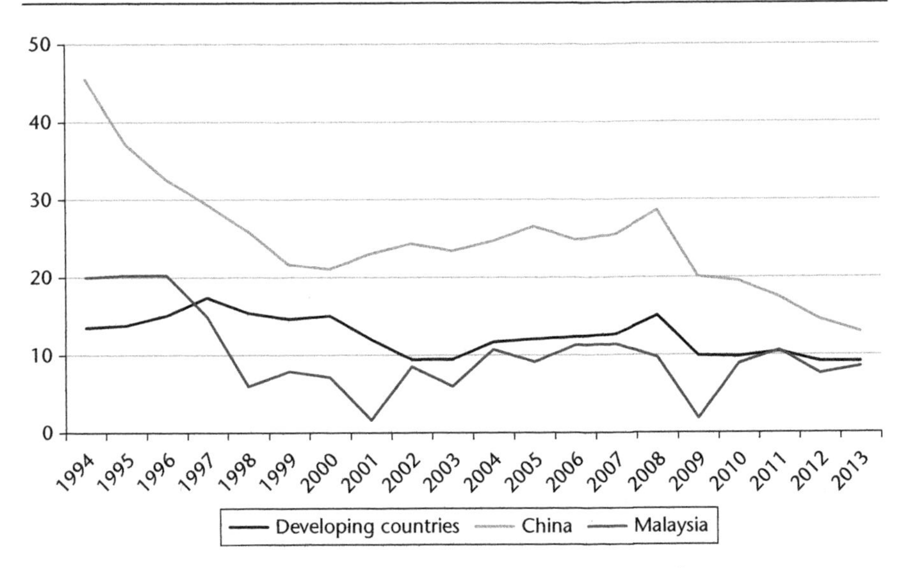

Figure 6.5 FDI inflows as a percentage of stocks
Source: UNCTADstats.

countries in the table, total income payments exceeded total new inflows over that period. Two African oil exporters top the list in terms of negative net transfers.[11] They are followed by three South East Asian countries that relied extensively on FDI from the early stages of their development. By contrast, the ratio of profits remittances to new inflows is low in countries which received large inflows of FDI relative to the initial stock in the more recent period, including Brazil, China, and Turkey.

Of countries with negative net transfers Malaysia has a long history of involvement with TNCs, often cited in the 1990s as an example of how to sustain rapid growth by attracting large inflows of export-oriented FDI. On both per capita basis and relative to GDP it had one of the largest FDI stocks and flows in the developing world in the 1990s (UNCTAD TDR 1997: Table 32). However, the momentum could not be kept up and the country experienced a sharp drop in FDI inflows in the new millennium (Figure 6.2) with the emergence of low-cost venues and the failure to upgrade rapidly while income transfers on FDI stock have kept up with full force.[12] In Malaysia manufactures no longer

table underestimate the net transfers on FDI. The same applies to FDI income payments for China in Table 6.4.

[11] According to Sumner et al. (2009: 3) in 'Sub Saharan Africa up to 90 per cent of FDI inflows are lost in profit repatriation.' However, since foreign firms in the primary sector are highly export-oriented, their current account impact, discussed in the subsequent section, is still positive.

[12] Malaysia also ran negative net transfers in the late 1980s, but in the 1990s FDI inflows accelerated significantly, exceeding income payments on the stock—see Woodward (2001: Chapter 11).

dominate export earnings if measured in value-added terms since they have much higher import contents than commodities (Akyüz 2012).

China, as a major recipient of FDI, still maintains a high level of FDI inflows as a proportion of its inward FDI stock, not only in comparison with Malaysia but also the rest of the developing world (see Figure 6.5). However, FDI inflows to China have been falling relative to the stock. This suggests that profit opportunities for foreign investors in labour intensive sectors and processes for production for markets abroad are being exhausted. To avoid a sharp drop in FDI inflows of the kind experienced by Malaysia, higher value-added sectors should become attractive to foreign investors and this depends largely on its success in industrial upgrading.

Some countries with negative net transfers such as Nigeria, Algeria, Malaysia, and Libya have had relatively large trade surpluses in recent years to help them to meet negative net transfers on FDI. But these surpluses have been falling rapidly with the end of the commodity boom, resulting in deterioration in the current account. In Malaysia and Nigeria the current account surplus fell from double digit figures during 2006–08 to 2–3 per cent in 2015. In Libya and Algeria, large surpluses of earlier years disappeared and these countries have started running large current account deficits. Most others with negative net transfers in Table 6.3 also run deficits on trade in goods and services. This means that they need to rely on reserves or borrow abroad or attract highly volatile portfolio inflows in order to balance their external accounts. If reserves prove inadequate and international lending and investment are cut back, they can then face liquidity problems because of large income outflows on the stock of FDI.

In addition to officially recorded income transfers, TNCs are known to be extensively involved in illicit financial outflows from EDEs through such practices as tax evasion, trade mispricing, and transfer pricing.[13] Some of these end up recorded in the balance-of-payments in the wrong places (as in the case of over-invoicing and under-invoicing) while others may not get recorded at all. Various estimates show that these account for the bulk of illicit outflows from EDEs (Johannesen and Pirttilä 2016). According to a recent report by a panel chaired by former president of South Africa, Thambo Mbeki, the continent has been losing $50–$60 billion per annum in illicit financial outflows in recent years (UNECA 2014). About 60 per cent of these originate from the activities of large foreign companies that operate in Africa mostly in sectors such as oil, precious metals and minerals, and ores. This is equal to three-quarters of FDI that the continent receives annually. If they are

[13] A factor contributing to tax avoidance is double taxation agreements promoted by countries such as Switzerland which often commit EDEs to low withholding tax rates in order to create more favourable conditions for their investors and in exchange for greater help in information for tracking tax evaders; see Bonanomi and Meyer-Nandi (2013).

added to recorded profit remittances by TNCs, then the region would go into the red in net transfers on FDI.

The figures in Table 6.3 also overestimate net transfers on FDI because of increased round-tripping whereby money departing a country through various channels comes back as FDI. In such a case the source of FDI would be the recipient country itself. This often happens when foreign investment benefits from various incentives, concessions, and guarantees compared to domestic investment or when it is possible to avoid high taxes by moving funds to low-tax countries with double taxation avoidance agreements and then moving them back as FDI. In countries with strict controls over resident outflows, outward transfers for round-tripping often occur through under-invoicing of exports. In such a case, what should normally be recorded in the current account as export earnings gets reported in the capital account as FDI inflows. In liberal capital account regimes, such FDI inflows are funded by capital outflows by residents so that there would be no net inflow into the recipient country.

There is significant evidence on round-tripping of capital from emerging economies to offshore financial centres (OFCs) and back as FDI. Round-tripping is known to account for an important proportion of FDI in several countries. For instance there is evidence of considerable round-tripping between India and Mauritius as the double taxation agreement between the two countries enables Indian businesses to avoid high Indian taxes by moving their funds to Mauritius and back again as FDI. Consequently, Mauritius accounted for 34 per cent of India's equity inflows from 2000 to 2015 even though its economic size does not reach 1 per cent of India (Sampath 2016). FDI round-tripping is also common in China. According to an early study, around 40 per cent of FDI into China originated in the country itself, with Hong Kong and Caribbean OFCs playing important roles in facilitating movement of funds (Xiao 2004). According to estimates given by a more recent study, in 2013, around 25 per cent of Chinese FDI abroad was round-tripped via Hong Kong, ending up reinvested into China as FDI (Garcia-Herrero et al. 2015). Similarly, for the same reason, for other BRIC countries too tax havens are known to have become more important sources of investment than major advanced economies—Cyprus for Russia and Netherlands for Brazil (Rovnick 2013).

6.5 Trade and Income Transfers by TNCs

A broader measure of the impact of FDI on balance-of-payments incorporates exports and imports of foreign-owned firms in addition to income transfers. The initial inflow of FDI for greenfield investment often entails imports of capital goods required to install production capacity but these are financed by the inflow of FDI. In fact, since part of the goods and services needed to install production capacity would be procured locally, the overall payment impact would be positive.

The subsequent impact of foreign firms on the trade balance depends not only on their imports and exports, but also their effect on the imports and exports in the economy as a whole through supply and demand linkages and macroeconomic channels. A full account of the impact of FDI on imports would require identification of not only direct imports by the firms concerned but also the indirect imports embodied in the goods and services locally procured. Foreign firms may also generate import substitution effects or can facilitate or impede exports by local firms. However, most empirical studies on the balance-of-payments impact of FDI do not explicitly account for such indirect effects and spillovers.

The debate on the balance-of-payments impact of FDI has often focussed on the distinction between traded and non-traded sectors. FDI in non-traded sectors clearly leads to a net outflow of foreign exchange because it does not generate export earnings (or import substitution) but entails imports and profit remittances. Services are traditionally considered as a non-tradeable sector. However, the tradability of services has been increasing rapidly. In the past three decades international trade in commercial services has grown faster than trade in goods. They have come to account for a sizeable proportion of export earnings of some EDEs such as India where FDI is found to have played a significant role in the expansion of services exports (Saleena 2013).

However, despite their increased tradability, an important part of services are still non-traded or little traded because they are impractical or too costly to trade, such as retail trade and banking, local transport, and public utilities. This implies that, ceteris paribus, a shift in the composition of FDI from primary and manufacturing sectors towards services could be expected to exacerbate its overall trade-balance impact. Indeed, such a shift had already started in the 1990s but accelerated in the new millennium. In the early 1990s services had accounted for some 45 per cent of total FDI inflows to EDEs, and this proportion averaged at almost 60 per cent during 2010–12 (see Figure 6.6). During the same period the share of manufacturing in total FDI inflows to EDEs fell from 36 per cent to 27 per cent while the primary sector enjoyed a small gain thanks to the commodity boom that started in the early years of the new millennium. If China is excluded, the increase in the share of services and the decline in manufacturing in FDI inflows to EDEs are much more pronounced.

On the other hand, the decline in the share of manufacturing in total FDI has been associated with a fundamental change in the nature of foreign investment in that sector. While earlier FDI flows into manufacturing were

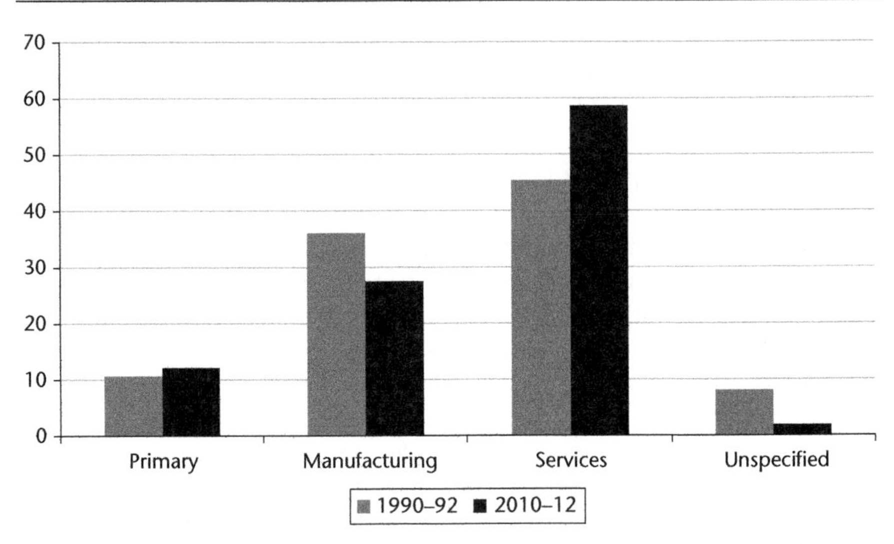

Figure 6.6 FDI inflows to EDEs by sector and industry: 1990–92 and 2010–12 (percentage of total FDI inflows)
Source: UNCTAD WIR (2014).

mainly motivated by attempts to overcome barriers to trade and involved establishing similar plants across countries, recently this horizontal production structure has been increasingly replaced by a vertical structure designed 'to slice up the value chain' through international production networks designed to supply not only local but also world markets. This shift in the composition of FDI in manufacturing is generally expected to improve its contribution to balance-of-payments because of its greater export orientation, but the outcome also depends on the import content of such production.

In discussing the impact of FDI on the current account, it would be more appropriate to distinguish between inward-oriented and outward-oriented FDI rather than traded and non-traded sectors. This applies to all sectors, primary, manufacturing, and services, though in different degrees. Inward-oriented foreign firms sell mainly in the domestic market while the principal outlets of outward-oriented TNCs are abroad. Foreign manufacturing firms established for tariff-jumping and market-seeking purposes fall into the former category and often entail more imports than exports. This is also true for most, though not all, foreign investment in services.

By contrast, foreign firms in natural resources such as those in most parts of Africa are generally outward oriented. Domestic sales constitute a very small proportion of their total production and they generate more exports than imports. Thus, their impact on the balance-of-payments tends to be positive. Firms linked to international production networks established and controlled by TNCs for supplying consumer manufactures to global markets are also outward oriented, but their domestic sales account for a greater proportion of total production than is typically the case for foreign firms active in primary sectors. Outward-oriented firms established in Export Processing Zones also sell a very large proportion of their production abroad.

Production by foreign firms is generally more import intensive than local firms. There is also evidence that wholly foreign-owned firms are more import intensive than joint venture firms. On the other hand, in countries closely integrated into the international production networks such as China and South East Asian EDEs and Mexico, the average import intensity or foreign value-added content of exports is higher than those which are not so closely connected to such networks, such as Brazil and most other Latin American countries, South Africa, India, Russia, and Turkey (Koopman et al. 2010; Koopman et al. 2012; Akyüz 2011d). In the former cases, an important part of the domestic value-added is absorbed by profits of TNCs, which often enjoy tax concessions. This proportion is estimated to have been around two-thirds of value-added in the Chinese export sector which is dominated by foreign firms (Akyüz 2011a).

The impact of fully inward-oriented foreign firms to the current account is negative while their contribution to GDP and GNI varies inversely with their imports and profits. Even when exports by inward-oriented firms meet their import bill, the impact on the current account would be negative because of profit remittances. To stop such firms from running current account deficits, it would be necessary to raise their exports without commensurate increases in the import content of production.

The contribution of outward-oriented foreign firms to GDP and GNI tend to be lower than that of inward-oriented firms because of their high import intensity. But their impact on the current account could be superior because of strong export orientation. This means that there may be no one-to-one correspondence between the export performance of TNCs and their contribution to domestic income. Indeed, some countries closely linked to international production networks in manufacturing are known to have increased their shares in world manufactured exports significantly without commensurate increases in their shares in world value-added in manufacturing. This happened in Mexico in the 1990s. After NAFTA, Mexico's share in world manufactured exports increased significantly while its share in world manufacturing value-added dropped. This happened because as high-export, low-value-added firms in maquiladoras expanded, the traditional industries with high value-added but low exports withered (UNCTAD TDR 2002; TDR 2003).

Often, outward-oriented foreign firms established in Export Processing Zones have little supply and demand linkages with the economy except through employment. They promise no significant dynamic benefits and their contribution to the current account is mainly confined to wage payments since such arrangements often include tax and tariff concessions. Their impact is quite similar to that of remittances from migrant workers abroad. However, since public investment would be required to establish a zone, the foreign exchange surplus generated by these firms may not justify the costs incurred.

The main policy challenge in EDEs closely connected to international production networks in manufactures in improving the contribution of foreign firms to the balance-of-payments, employment, and domestic value-added is to reduce the import content of their production rather than to increase their export-orientation. This would mean import substitution; that is, moving up in the value chain and replacing imported high-value parts and components with domestic production.

The impact of FDI on the current account naturally depends on the type of investment as well as the policies affecting import content and export-orientation of foreign firms. That FDI would have a negative impact in countries where it is concentrated in areas with little or no exports is incontrovertible. However, the discussions earlier in this chapter suggest that this may also be the case even in countries with strong presence of export-oriented foreign firms because of their high import intensity and profit remittances.

This appears to be the case in several South East Asian EDEs closely connected to international production networks in manufacturing. Jansen (1995) simulated a model for Thailand for 1987–91 to assess, inter alia, the impact of FDI on the balance-of-payments (see also UNCTAD WIR 1997). It is found that while FDI had a strong role in the expansion of exports, it also led to a sharp increase in imports as well as royalty and licence fees and profit remittances. About 90 per cent of all machinery and equipment used for foreign investment projects and 50 per cent of raw materials are estimated to have been imported. From the mid-1980s until 1991–92, exports as a per cent of GDP rose from 29 to 36 per cent while imports increased from 25 to 40 per cent. All these widened the current account deficit more than the increase in FDI inflows and contributed to the build-up of external debt that culminated in the 1997 crisis.

A study on Malaysia also estimated that the impact of foreign firms on the current account, including the initial imports associated with FDI inflows, was negative in every year during 1980–92 and FDI inflows could offset this in only four years (Eng 1998). According to another estimate, the FDI-related current account continued to be in the red also during 1993–96 (Woodward 2001). Putting all these together, it appears that throughout the entire period 1980–96, the impact of FDI on the current account in Malaysia was negative in every year and new FDI inflows matched or exceeded these deficits in only five years.

There is also evidence from other countries with significant presence of outward-oriented foreign firms in services and manufacturing sectors. India is one of them. As noted, FDI has played an important role in the rapid expansion of its services exports. Still, the overall impact of FDI on the Indian

Table 6.4 Foreign-funded enterprises in China (billions of US dollars)

	2000	2005	2006	2007	2008	2009	2010	2011	2012	2013
1. Imports	117.3	387.5	472.5	559.8	619.4	545.4	738.4	864.7	871.5	874.6
2. Exports	119.4	444.2	563.8	695.4	790.5	672.1	862.2	995.2	1022.6	1043.7
3. Trade balance	2.2	56.7	91.3	135.6	171.1	126.7	123.8	130.6	151.1	169.1
4. FDI income payments	20.2	47.6	49.5	61.9	72.6	105.9	159.6	204.5	171.8	206.4
5. Current account impact	–18.0	9.1	41.8	73.7	98.4	20.7	–35.8	–73.9	–20.7	–37.2
6. FDI inflows	38.4	111.2	133.3	169.4	186.8	167.1	273.0	331.6	295.6	347.8

Source: National Bureau of Statistics of China and IMF BOP.

current account appears to have been negative over 1997–2011 (Sarode 2012). Another estimate comes from Indonesia, one of the top recipients of FDI inflows among EDEs (Dhanani and Hasnain 2002). During 1990–96, FDI accounted for a quarter of manufacturing production in Indonesia. However, foreign firms imported 55 per cent of raw materials and intermediate goods; more than double that of domestic firms. Overall, FDI had a negative impact on the balance-of-payments and contributed to the persistent deficits in manufacturing due to its high propensity to import production inputs.

China's experience as a major recipient of export-oriented FDI reveals some interesting features and lessons for countries wanting to integrate closely into international production networks established and controlled by TNCs from advanced economies. The trade balance of foreign affiliates in China was negative throughout 1994–96 (UNCTAD WIR 1997: chapter II). Adding payments of direct investment income, this meant even a larger deficit in the current account. However, these were more than covered by new inflows of FDI as China had emerged as the largest recipient of FDI in the developing world in the 1990s. The trade deficits of foreign firms were due to those in non-processing trade since firms in processing exports generated larger surpluses as a result of declines in their import intensity.[14] However, the import intensity of these firms was still higher than that of local firms in processing trade—78 per cent compared to 66 per cent.

More recent research based on input–output data and accounting for indirect as well as direct import contents indicates that the average import intensity of Chinese exports has declined in the new millennium. In processing exports where foreign firms are dominant, China has been shifting from

[14] In China processing exports refer to a special category of goods produced by assembling and/or processing intermediate inputs that are exempted from tariffs because the final products are sold only in foreign markets.

simple assembly of foreign parts and components towards operations with greater domestic inputs, thereby raising their domestic value-added content. According to an estimate, the share of foreign value-added in China's processing exports fell from 79 per cent in 1997 to 62.7 per cent in 2007 and in its total manufactured exports from 50 to 40 per cent.[15]

This resulted in a significant improvement in the trade balance of foreign affiliates in China in the new millennium. Indeed, exports by foreign-funded firms, including wholly foreign-owned and joint venture firms, constantly exceeded imports after 2000 (Table 6.4). Income payments on direct investment also rose rapidly, but the trade surplus generated by foreign firms was large enough to finance these until 2010. Since that year, the current account balance of foreign affiliates in China turned to be negative with income payments exceeding the trade surplus generated by these firms. This implies that, unless the import intensity of foreign affiliates is reduced significantly, China could face growing current account deficits on their operations as income payments on the stock of FDI mount.[16]

As in the 1990s, FDI inflows have been strong enough to meet the foreign exchange shortfalls generated by foreign affiliates in China in recent years. However, closing the gap with more and more FDI inflows would be very much like Ponzi financing whereby existing liabilities are met by incurring new liabilities. It is true that currently China does not need new FDI inflows to pay for the existing ones. Despite growing income payments on FDI stock, China has been running a current account surplus thanks to an export surplus in the rest of the economy and the earnings on foreign assets. However, although it has a positive net international asset position, it has been in the red in investment income—since 2000, income paid by China on all foreign liabilities, including debt and equities, has exceeded the income received on all foreign assets held in every year except 2007–08 (SAFE 2015).

It is not clear if China can keep running surplus on its current account. Its surplus has already declined from a peak of 10 per cent of GDP in 2007 to less than 2 per cent in 2013–14. There is a wide agreement that China needs to increase the share of private consumption in GDP in order to sustain an acceptable pace of growth. If consumption starts rising faster than other components of aggregate demand, its trade surplus can shrink rapidly and may even fall below the net investment income payments abroad, thereby

[15] Koopman et al. (2012). According to a study by Upward et al. (2013) assessing the Chinese export boom during 2000–07 at the company and product level, the domestic content of Chinese exports increased from 53 to 60 per cent over 2003–06 thanks to newly entering firms which played a central role in the export boom.

[16] An earlier study on the dynamic effect of FDI on the balance-of-payments in China concluded that, as more companies come in, China's current account could turn from a surplus to a deficit; see Yao and Fan (2004).

leading to a deficit on the current account. Thus, a viable strategy for China would be to continue to reduce the import intensity of exports by foreign affiliates and reliance on TNCs.

Recent evidence suggests that import substitution in China's export industries has been continuing with full force since the crisis and this is a main factor in the slowdown in global trade. During 1995–2005 in volume terms world trade grew almost twice as fast as world income. Trade growth had already slowed down before the onset of the crisis. Since 2011 it has barely kept up with world income. It is argued that the changing relationship between world trade and income 'is driven primarily by changes in supply-chain trade in the two largest trading economies, the United States and China... [and] is reflected in a fall in the share of Chinese imports of parts and components in total exports, which decreased from its peak of 60 percent in the mid-1990s to the current [2012] share of about 35 percent' (Constantinescu et al. 2014: 40–1). Thus, in China, a larger proportion of effective demand, both domestic and foreign, is now met by domestic production rather than by imports as many activities that previously involved cross-border movement of goods are now taking place within national borders.[17]

The negative contribution of TNCs to balance-of-payments in EDEs is due not only to high import content of their production and exports, but also high rate of return on their investment. According to an estimate based on a detailed study of industrial firms, on the eve of the global financial crisis, the profit rate for private firms in China was 20 per cent (Lu et al. 2008). A similar estimate is given by Bai et al. (2006) who note that foreign firms have higher productivity and profitability than domestic firms. The rate of return on FDI is often calculated as direct investment income for the current year divided by the average FDI stock of the previous year and the current year. On this measure, using the total FDI liabilities and investment income given by the IMF, the average rate of return on FDI for 2010–13 in China would be just over 10 per cent.[18] The figure for EDEs as a whole was 11 per cent in 2012 with significant variations among regions; around 13 per cent in Africa and Asia, 8 per cent in the Middle East and 6.5 per cent in Latin America (Leke et al. 2014). An earlier estimate for a sample of EDEs put it

[17] Another factor affecting growth of trade is the composition of domestic demand. Consumption is typically a lot more import intensive than investment because an important part of it involves non-traded services (Akyüz 2011a). Thus, the general weakness of investment since the mid-2000s is another factor explaining the decline in growth of world trade relative to income, accentuated by China's shift from investment to consumption after 2010.

[18] However, if one used the inward FDI stock figures given by UNCTAD WIR (2016; Annex table 2) the rate of return on FDI in China would exceed 20 per cent since these figures are significantly lower than those reported by the IMF. The FDI stock figures given by UNCTAD WIR are in historical costs, ignoring price changes since the time when the investment was made. However, FDI inflows to China reported by the IMF are also significantly greater than those given by UNCTAD WIR (2016 Annex table 1).

close to 20 per cent (Lehmann 2002). More recently World Bank estimates put the rate of return on FDI at 24 per cent for Rwanda in 2013, and 87 per cent for Angola and 36 per cent for Nigeria in 2011 (World Bank 2014b; and Chen et al. 2015).

These rates are much higher than borrowing costs in international markets, particularly in recent years. It might thus be preferable to borrow the money and make the investment domestically rather than rely on FDI if local capabilities allow such investment to be made and run efficiently. It is true that income payments on FDI depend on the profitability of enterprises and, unlike debt, no payment would be involved unless profits are generated. But this also means that the host country would be writing a 'blank check' (Woodward 2001: 144) which could eventually entail significant transfer of resources.

However, FDI should not be judged on the basis of its balance-of-payments impact alone. It may yield significant other benefits, notably technological spillovers and positive externalities for the rest of the economy even when it has a negative contribution to the current account. Indeed, the potential contribution of FDI to industrialization and development in EDEs through technological spillovers and externalities is much more crucial than any positive contribution they may make to capital accumulation and balance-of-payments. However, as discussed in the next chapter, such benefits are not automatic and call for deliberate policies by host country governments.

7

FDI, Industrialization, and Development

Role of Policy

7.1 Technological Spillovers

TNCs from more advanced economies enjoy certain capabilities and own firm-specific tangible and intangible assets that distinguish them from their competitors. They take these assets to EDEs in which they invest, but they would be reluctant to pass their competencies on to local enterprises since that would reduce the rent they can earn. Furthermore, the competitive advantage they have can also damage local industry. Deliberate and carefully designed policies are needed both to prevent potential adverse effects of TNCs on the host economy and to promote positive spillovers. For this, it is important to identify correctly the capabilities of foreign firms, the channels through which they could stimulate growth and structural change, and the policies needed to deploy them.

There is a vast literature on the capabilities and competencies of TNCs from more advanced countries and the nature, channels, and effects of spillovers to the local economy in host countries (Kumar 2002; Malik et al. 2012; Narula and Driffield 2012; Giroud 2012; Forte and Moura 2013; Danakol et al. 2014). In this context, FDI is seen not so much as a flow of capital but as a flow of advanced technology and management skills—the two key determinants of their superior productivity. In addition, these firms also enjoy better access to global markets because of their close linkages. Exporting and international procurement are easier and less costly to them than to local firms. They often have the advantage of a brand image, and this helps them not only in marketing goods and services but also in attracting the best talents. They also enjoy easier access to international financial markets and better credit ratings and this gives them a significant cost advantage.

The main channels through which technological spillovers from TNCs to the economy of host countries occur include competition, imitation, demonstration, and labour turnover. However, the impact is not always benign. The high productivity and competition they bring could help improve the efficiency of local firms, but these can also block entry of these firms into high-value production lines or drive them out of business. They can prevent rather than promote infant-industry learning unless local firms are supported and protected by deliberate policies. Local firms can learn and imitate more easily when foreign firms establish forward and backward linkages with them rather than relying on linkages abroad. Domestic linkages are also essential for the integration of local firms in the global market. Foreign affiliates can have an important impact on industrial structure if they invest in relatively technology-intensive industries and relocate some of their R&D activities in host countries, but this may not be the most profitable option for them. Again, they can help improve the skill profile and the level of technical knowledge in the host country by employing and training local workers, but not so much when they focus on labour-intensive sectors or import labour along with capital.

For all these reasons there can be no generalization regarding the impact of FDI on capital formation, technological progress, economic growth, and structural change. Indeed there is no conclusive evidence to support the myth that FDI makes a major contribution to growth. This is emphatically put by Caves (1996: 237): 'the relationship between an LDC's stock of foreign investment and its subsequent economic growth is a matter on which we totally lack trustworthy conclusions'. What is established by most studies is that the impact of FDI depends on a host of other variables which are endogenous to the growth process. Positive spillovers from foreign firms can become significant only when there is already in place an appropriate level of local capabilities. Even then, policy in host countries plays a central role in generating the conditions needed to secure positive spillovers.

There is considerable diversity in the extent to which EDEs have been relying on FDI for industrialization and development. Successful examples are found not necessarily among EDEs that attracted more FDI, but among those which used it in the context of national industrial policy designed to shape the evolution of specific industries through intervention so as to accelerate industrialization and growth. In fact, extensive presence of foreign firms could well be a sign of weakness of indigenous capabilities.

Both cross-country and case studies show that in several instances performance requirements imposed on FDI made a positive contribution to various development objectives without having a major adverse impact on the FDI received.[1] East Asian EDEs have generally been more successful in attracting and using FDI for industrialization than countries at similar levels of development elsewhere.

[1] On theoretical issues involved and empirical evidence, see a number of essays in Kozul-Wright and Rowthorn (1998), Kumar (2005), and Rasiah (2005).

However, there is significant diversity among them in the extent to which they have relied on FDI as well as in the policies pursued.[2]

Among the first-tier newly industrializing economies (NIEs) Korea and Taiwan relied on FDI much less than Singapore and Hong Kong as well as the second-tier NIEs, notably China, Malaysia, and Thailand. As in Japan, they focused on promoting indigenous enterprises and local technological capabilities, using FDI only in targeted industries alongside other forms of technology transfer such as reverse engineering, import of capital goods, and technology licensing. They also used original equipment manufacturer (OEM) to encourage foreign firms to supply technological information and integrate local firms into international markets. Strong support was provided to R&D to help adapt and improve imported technology.

FDI regimes in Korea and Taiwan were restrictive and selective, and domestic policies were highly interventionist, particularly during the catching-up period. Licensing agreements were tightly controlled and imported technologies were closely screened to promote domestic learning. Local firms were nurtured to compete with TNCs and reduce dependence on them, particularly in Korea. Foreign ownership was restricted in certain sectors and joint ventures rather than wholly foreign owned enterprises were promoted. Local content agreements were extensively used not only for balance-of-payments reasons, but also to promote linkages with domestic suppliers and hence facilitate diffusion of technology and management skills. Managerial and technical assistance and training of engineers and technicians were part of the contracts with foreign companies, notably from Japan.

Although both Hong Kong and Singapore relied heavily on FDI, there were important differences in the policies pursued and hence the contribution of FDI to industrialization. While Hong Kong followed a laissez-faire policy towards FDI, Singapore targeted specific industries for promotion, using incentives and restrictions. In Hong Kong FDI helped to establish a low-skill industrial base, but brought little upgrading. Its lack of industrial depth and massive deindustrialization thus stand in sharp contrast with the rapid upgrading and industrial success of Singapore.

Among the second tier-NIEs, Malaysia and Thailand have followed a liberal approach towards FDI, allowing fully owned foreign subsidiaries. However, after an initial success in establishing assembly industries, they have not been able to develop a diversified manufacturing base and reduce their dependence on imported capital and intermediate goods. By contrast China's FDI regime has been more restrictive and policies highly interventionist. It started like Malaysia and Thailand, combining low-skilled assembly

[2] The account below draws on UNCTAD TDR (1994 and 1996).

activities with high-technology imported parts, but moved more vigorously in upgrading and reducing the foreign value-added in its production and exports, as noted above.[3] However, while it has moved faster than all late-industrializers over the past three decades, including the first-tier NIEs, it still has a long way to go to catch up with the productivity levels and industrial sophistication of indigenous firms not only in Japan but also in Korea (Zhu 2012).

7.2 Multilateral and Bilateral Constraints Over Investment Policy

The experience strongly suggests that policy interventions would be necessary to contain adverse effects of FDI on stability, balance-of-payments, capital accumulation, and industrial development and to activate its potential benefits. However, policy options in EDEs have been increasingly circumscribed in the past three decades as international capital and TNCs have gained more and more space to manoeuvre. There are two main sources of constraints over national policy in this area; multilateral rules and obligations in the WTO regarding investment policies, and commitments undertaken in investment and trade agreements signed with home countries of investors in EDEs. Although there is considerable diversity in the obligations contained in various BITs, the constraints they entail are becoming increasingly tighter than those imposed by the WTO regime.

There are two main sources of WTO disciplines on investment-related policies; the Agreement on TRIMs and specific commitments made in the context of GATS negotiations for commercial presence of foreign enterprises (the so-called mode 3) in the services sectors. In addition to these, a number of other agreements provide disciplines, directly or indirectly, on investment-related policies such as the prohibition of investment subsidies linked to export performance in the Agreement on Subsidies and Countervailing Measures.

The TRIMs agreement does not refer to foreign investment as such but to investment generally.[4] It effectively prohibits attaching conditions to investment in violation of the national treatment principle or quantitative restrictions in the context of investment measures. The most important provisions relate to prohibition of domestic content requirements whereby an investor is compelled or provided an incentive to use domestically produced rather than imported products, and to foreign trade or foreign exchange balancing

[3] Exports of South-East Asian NIEs, including Malaysia, Thailand, and Vietnam have higher import contents than exports of China; see Akyüz (2011a).

[4] This is provided by a subsequent interpretation by a panel on a TRIMs dispute; for a detailed discussion, see Das (1999: chap. 3) and Bora (2002).

requirements linking imports by an investor to its export earnings or to foreign exchange inflows attributable to investment. By contrast, in TRIMs or the WTO more broadly, there are no disciplines restricting beggar-my-neighbour investment incentives by recipient countries that are just as trade distorting. Such incentives provide effective subsidy to foreign investors and can influence investment and trade flows as much as domestic content requirements or export subsidies, particularly since a growing proportion of world trade is taking place among firms linked through international production networks controlled by TNCs (Kumar 2002).

The obligations under TRIMs may not affect very much the countries rich in natural resources, notably minerals, in their earlier stages of development. FDI in mineral resources is generally capital intensive and countries at such stages depend almost fully on foreign technology and know-how in extractive industries and lack capital good industries. Linkages with domestic industries are usually weak and output is almost fully exported. Domestic content of production by foreign companies is mainly limited to labour and some intermediate inputs. The main challenge is how to promote local processing to increase domestic value-added. However, over time, restrictions over domestic content requirements can reinforce the 'resource curse syndrome' as the country wants to nourish resource-based industries, to transfer technology to local firms and establish backward and forward linkages with them.

Restrictions over domestic content requirements are particularly important for investment in manufacturing in countries at intermediate stages of industrialization, notably in automotive and electronics industries—the two key sectors where they were successfully applied in East Asia. As noted, most industries of EDEs linked to international production networks have high import contents in technology-intensive parts and components while their domestic value-added mainly consists of wages paid to local workers. Raising domestic content would not only improve the balance-of-payments but also constitute an important step in industrial upgrading. Restrictions over domestic content requirements would thus limit transfer of technology and import-substitution in industries linked to international production networks.

However, TRIMs provisions leave certain flexibilities that could allow EDEs to make room to move in order to increase benefits from FDI. First, the domestic content of industrial production by TNCs is not independent of the tariff regime. Other things being equal, low tariffs and high duty drawbacks encourage high import content. Thus, it should be possible to use tariffs as a substitute for quantity restrictions over imports by TNCs when they are unbound in the WTO or bound at sufficiently high levels. Similarly, in resource-rich countries, export taxes can be used to discourage exports of unprocessed minerals and agricultural commodities as long as they continue to remain unrestricted by the WTO regime.

Second, as long as there are no commitments for unrestricted market access to foreign investors, the constraints imposed by the TRIMs agreement could be overcome by tying the entry of foreign investors to the production of particular goods. For instance a foreign enterprise may be issued a licence for an automotive assembly plant only if it simultaneously establishes a plant to produce engines, gearboxes, or electronic components used in cars. Similarly, licences for a computer assembly plant can be tied to the establishment of a plant for producing integrated circuits and chips. Such measures would raise domestic value-added and net export earnings of TNCs and would not contravene the provisions of the TRIMs agreement.

Third, export performance requirements can be used without linking them to imports by investors as part of entry conditions for foreign enterprises. This would not contravene the TRIMs agreement since it would not be restricting trade (Bora 2002: 177). Finally, the TRIMs regime does not restrict governments in demanding joint ventures with local enterprises or local ownership of a certain proportion of the equity of foreign enterprises. In reality, many of these conditions appear to be used widely by industrial countries in one form or another (Weiss 2005).

Since the TRIMs agreement applies only to trade in goods, local procurement of services such as banking, insurance, and transport can also be set as part of entry conditions of foreign firms in order to help develop national capabilities in services sectors. However, this would be possible as long as EDEs continue to have discretion in regulating access of TNCs to services sectors. The existing GATS regime provides considerable flexibility in this respect, including for performance requirements. However, the kind of changes in the modalities of GATS sought by advanced economies, including the prohibition of pre-establishment conditions and the application of national treatment, could shrink policy space in EDEs a lot more than the TRIMs agreement.[5]

The constraints exerted by most BITs signed in recent years on policy options in host countries go well beyond the TRIMs agreement because of wide-ranging provisions in favour of investors. There has been a proliferation of such agreements in recent years, with the number reaching 3304 at the end of 2015 (UNCTAD WIR 2016). Unlike earlier BITs, recent agreements give significant leverage to international investors. These include broad definitions of investment and investor, free transfer of capital, rights to establishment, the national treatment and the most-favoured-nation (MFN) clauses, fair and equitable treatment, protection from direct and indirect expropriation, and

[5] Cho and Dubash (2005) discuss the implication of adopting national treatment in GATs in relation to the electricity sector while Rasiah (2005) provides an illustrative account of it for policy space in Malaysia.

prohibition of performance requirements. Furthermore, the reach of BITs has extended thanks to the use of the so-called Special Purpose Entities which allow TNCs from countries without a BIT with the destination country to make the investment through an affiliate incorporated in a third-party state with a BIT with the destination country.[6] Many BITs also provide unrestricted arbitration, freeing foreign investors from the obligation of having to exhaust local legal remedies in disputes with host countries before seeking international arbitration. This, together with lack of clarity in treaty provisions, has resulted in the emergence of arbitral tribunals as lawmakers in international investment. These tend to provide expansive interpretations of investment provisions, thereby constraining policy further and inflicting costs on host countries (Bernasconi-Osterwalder et al. 2012; Eberhardt and Olivet 2012; UNCTAD TDR 2014).

While in TRIMs investment is a production-based concept, BITs generally incorporate an asset-based concept of investment whether the assets owned by the investor are used for the production of goods and services, or simply held with the prospect of income and/or capital gain. This is largely because BITs are fashioned by corporate perspectives even though they are signed among governments. Typically, agreements are prepared by the home countries of TNCs and offered to EDEs for signature. They include a broad range of tangible and intangible assets such as fixed-income claims, portfolio equities, financial derivatives, intellectual property rights, and business concessions, as well as FDI as officially defined by the OECD and the IMF. This implies that all kinds of assets owned by foreigners could claim the same protection and guarantees independent of their nature and contribution to stability and growth in host countries.

It also opens the door to mission creep. Investment agreements may be granted jurisdictions by tribunals over a variety of areas that has nothing to do with FDI proper, further circumscribing the policy options of host countries. Indeed, the expansive scope of investment protection in NAFTA has already given rise to claims that patents are a form of investment and hence should be protected as any other capital asset, thereby threatening the flexibilities left in the TRIPs Agreement and access to medicines (Correa 2013). Similarly, there have been claims by Argentinian bond-holders that such holdings should be protected as any other investment under the Italy–Argentina BIT, thereby intervening with the restructuring of sovereign debt (Gallagher 2012).

[6] For example if country A has no BIT with country B and a TNC from A wants to invest in country B, it can create an affiliate in country C with a BIT with country B and makes the investment through that affiliate in order to benefit from the BIT between B and C. This creates 'transit FDI' and leads to double-counting in reported FDI figures—see UNCTAD WIR (2014: Box I.1).

The combination of a broad, asset-based concept of investment and provisions for free transfer of capital seriously exposes host EDEs to financial instability by precluding controls over destabilizing capital flows. This is also recognized by the IMF. In its Institutional View on the Liberalization and Management of Capital Flows, the IMF (2012) notes that 'numerous bilateral and regional trade agreements and investment treaties... include provisions that give rise to obligations on capital flows' (para. 8) and 'do not take into account macroeconomic and financial stability' (para. 65) and 'do not allow for the introduction of restrictions on capital outflows in the event of a balance of payments crisis and also effectively limit the ability of signatories to impose controls on inflows' (Note 1, Annex III). The Fund points out that these provisions may conflict with its recommendation on the use of capital controls and asks its Institutional View to be taken into account in drafting such agreements.

Although the IMF's Institutional View focuses mainly on regulating capital inflows to prevent build-up of financial fragility, prohibitions in BITs regarding restrictions over outflows can also become a major handicap in crisis management. As discussed in Chapter 5, it is now widely agreed that countries facing an external financial crisis due to an interruption of their access to international capital markets, a sudden stop of capital inflows and rapid depletion of reserves could need temporary debt standstills and exchange controls in order to prevent a financial meltdown. However, such measures could be illegal under 'free transfer of capital' provisions of BITs.

Where rights of establishment are granted, the flexibilities in the TRIMs regarding entry requirements noted above would simply disappear. The national treatment clause in BITs requires host countries to treat foreign investors no less favourably than its own national investors and hence prevents them from protecting and supporting infant industries against mature TNCs and nourishing domestic firms to compete with foreign affiliates. It brings greater restrictions than national treatment in TRIMs because it would apply not to goods traded by investors but to the investor and the investment.

Further, provisions on expropriation and fair and equitable treatment give considerable leverage to foreign affiliates in challenging changes in tax and regulatory standards and demanding compensation. Especially the concept of indirect expropriation has led states to worry about their ability to regulate. The fair and equitable treatment obligation has also been interpreted expansively by some tribunals to include the right of investors to a stable and predictable business environment.

The large majority of outstanding BITs do not make any reference to performance requirements of the kind discussed above, but a growing number of them signed in recent years incorporate explicit prohibitions (Nikièma 2014). Some BITs go beyond TRIMs and bring additional prohibitions for performance requirements both at pre- and post-establishment phases. Others simply refer to TRIMs without additional restrictions. Still, this narrows the ability of governments to move within the WTO regime because it allows investors to challenge the TRIMs-compatibility of host country actions outside the WTO system. This multiplies the risk of disputes that host countries can face since corporations are much more inclined to resort to investor-state arbitration than the states do in the WTO system. The MFN clause could entail even greater loss of policy autonomy in all these areas, including performance requirements, by allowing foreign investors to invoke more favourable rights and protection granted to foreign investors in agreements with third-party countries.[7]

Only a few EDEs signing such BITs with advanced economies have significant outward FDI. Therefore, in the large majority of cases there is no reciprocity in deriving benefits from the rights and protection granted to foreign investors. Rather, most EDEs sign them on expectations that they would attract more FDI by providing foreign investors guarantees and protection, thereby accelerating growth and development. However, there is no clear evidence that BITs have a strong impact on the direction of FDI inflows. Econometric studies on the impact of BITs on FDI flows are highly ambivalent. The majority of studies find no link between the two (UNCTAD 2009b: Annex and UNCTAD TDR 2014: Annex to chapter VI). Similarly, survey data show that the providers of political risk or in-house counsel in large US corporations on investment decisions do not pay much attention to BITs (Yackee 2010).

BITs are neither necessary nor sufficient to bring significant amounts of FDI. Most EDEs are now wide open to TNCs from advanced economies through unilateral liberalization or BITs or Free Trade Agreements (FTAs), but only those vibrant economies with good physical and human infrastructure and a high level of domestic investment such as China have been getting the kind of FDI with significant developmental benefits and most of these countries have had no BITs with major advanced economies.

7.3 Conclusions: Policy Lessons

Unlike as maintained by the dominant corporate ideology, FDI is not a recipe for rapid and sustained growth and industrialization in EDEs. Contrary to widespread perception, it does not always involve flows of financial capital or real capital. Only greenfield investment makes a direct contribution to productive capacity and involves cross-border movement of capital goods,

[7] For a more detailed account of various provisions of BITs, their interpretation by tribunals and impact on policy space, see Bernasconi-Osterwalder et al. (2012).

but even then it may not add to aggregate capital formation because it may crowd out domestic investors. What is commonly known and reported as FDI contains speculative components and creates destabilizing impulses. The immediate contribution of FDI to balance-of-payments may be positive, but its longer-term impact is often negative because of high import content of foreign firms and high return on their investment. Finally, superior technology and management skills of TNCs create an opportunity for the diffusion of technology and ideas, but the competitive advantage of firms over newcomers in EDEs can also drive them out of business.

These do not mean that FDI does not offer any benefits to EDEs. Rather, policy in host countries plays a key role in determining the impact of FDI on industrialization and development. The discussions above suggest several policy lessons:

- encourage greenfield investment but be selective in terms of sectors and technology;
- encourage joint ventures rather than wholly foreign-owned affiliates in order to accelerate learning and limit foreign control;
- allow M&A only if there are significant benefits in terms of managerial skills and follow-up investment;
- do not use FDI as a way of meeting balance-of-payments shortfalls; the long-term impact of FDI on external payments is often negative even in EDEs attracting export-oriented firms;
- debt financing may be preferable to equity financing when there are no significant positive spillovers from FDI;
- FDI contains speculative components and generates destabilizing impulses, which need to be controlled and managed as any other form of international capital flows;
- no incentives should be provided to FDI without securing reciprocity in benefits for industrialization and development;
- performance requirements may be needed to secure positive spillovers including employment and training of local labour, local procurement, domestic content, export targets; and links with local firms;
- domestic firms should be nurtured to compete with TNCs;
- linking to international production networks organized by TNCS is not a recipe for industrialization; it could trap the economy in the lower ends of the value-chain.

Policy space in all these areas might be somewhat constrained by the WTO agreement on TRIMs, but it is still possible for EDEs to encourage positive spillovers without violating their commitments. Many of the more serious constraints are in practice self-inflicted through investment and free trade agreements. There are strong reasons for EDEs to avoid negotiating the kind of BITs promoted by advanced economies. They need to turn attention to improving their underlying economic fundamentals rather than pinning their hopes to BITs in attracting FDI. Where commitments undertaken in existing BITs seriously impair their ability to use FDI for industrialization and development, they can be renegotiated or terminated, as is being done by some EDEs, even if doing so may entail some immediate costs.

Conclusions

The preceding chapters have examined the deepened integration of emerging and developing economies (EDEs) into the international financial system in the new millennium and their changing vulnerabilities to external financial shocks. They have discussed the role that policies in advanced economies played in this process, including those that culminated in the global financial crisis and the unconventional monetary policy of zero-bound interest rates and quantitative easing adopted in response to the crisis, as well as policies in EDEs themselves.

In describing this integration the book has focused on gross foreign assets and liabilities and non-resident inflows and resident outflows and their composition, rather than net asset positions and net flows (current account balances). This is because a country's net external positions do not provide an adequate description of its vulnerability to swings in international capital flows and conditions in different layers of international financial markets. Even when assets match liabilities, they may belong to different economic actors and have different liquidity and maturity characteristics and currency denominations, and may not always be easily deployed to meet liabilities. Thus, the composition of assets and liabilities and the leverage of national balance sheets are key determinants of vulnerability to external financial shocks.

While net capital flows and current account balances in EDEs have manifested significant instability in the past three decades, non-resident inflows and resident outflows have never been negative. Consequently, gross international assets and liabilities have been rising not only in absolute terms but also relative to real economic activity as measured by GDP; that is, there is an ongoing process of international financial deepening, using the mainstream terminology. This process has resulted in unprecedented foreign presence in financial markets of EDEs through acquisition of domestic bonds and equities, and in the markets for goods and services through foreign direct investment (FDI). Consequently, international investors and transnational corporations, in both financial and non-financial sectors, have become key actors influencing economic conditions in EDEs.

In this process of integration, equity and bond markets in many emerging economies have become internationalized even to a greater extent than markets in some advanced economies, significantly increasing their susceptibility to global influences. In the same vein, there has been a visible increase in the presence of residents of several emerging economies in markets abroad as borrowers and investors. Domestic and foreign bonds and equities have become competing instruments in portfolios not only for investors in major advanced economies but also for the residents of EDEs. This has fundamentally altered the valuation dynamics of local securities in these economies.

This rapid growth in national balance sheets has also been accompanied by important changes in their composition, particularly on the side of liabilities. Equity liabilities have increased relative to debt; liabilities in debt securities have increased relative to international bank loans; private sector liabilities have increased faster than public sector liabilities; and sovereign external liabilities in local currencies have increased relative to those in reserve currencies. On the assets side the most important change is the rapid increase in official reserves, both in absolute terms and relative to privately held foreign assets. These are not just accumulated from current account surpluses that EDEs as a whole started running in the new millennium, but also from private capital inflows even in deficit countries. This stands in sharp contrast to the prognostications of mainstream theory that the need for international reserves should lessen as countries gained access to international financial markets. This is because while access to financial markets abroad has allowed building large amounts of external liabilities, it has also exposed countries to pro-cyclical behaviour of these markets and sudden stops and reversals in capital flows, thereby increasing the need to keep large amounts of reserves as self-insurance.

As a result of internationalization of finance in EDEs, the distinction between domestic and external debt has become increasingly fuzzy. The conventional *economic* (balance-of-payments) definition of external debt is based on residency while *legal* definition is based on governing law. External debt is often thought of as debt in foreign currency because of the inability of EDEs to issue debt to foreigners in local currency. However, this is no longer the case. It is no longer possible to clearly differentiate external and domestic debts in terms of their holders, currency denomination, or governing laws, and say that external debt is debt held by foreigners, denominated in foreign currencies, and subject to foreign jurisdiction. External debt economically defined now includes debt both in local and foreign currencies and is subject to both local and foreign jurisdiction, particularly for the sovereign. In the same vein, external debt legally defined now includes both local currency and foreign currency debt and holdings by both residents and non-residents. As a result, the debt that governments now owe to their own nationals can be part of external debt, denominated in foreign currency, and subject to foreign jurisdiction. Similarly, the debt owed to foreigners can be subject to local jurisdiction and denominated in local currency. These have significant implications for debt workouts, both de jure and de facto.

While a growing part of sovereign external debt in emerging economies has come to be issued locally in local currencies, non-financial corporate external debt has continued to be issued largely internationally under foreign jurisdiction and denominated in foreign currencies. Bank loans no longer constitute an important part of non-financial corporate external debt contracted in recent years, notably since the global crisis. This implies that non-financial corporations have become more susceptible to conditions in international bond markets than in international banking as was the case in earlier crises. On their part international banks have increasingly opted for local lending through their affiliates in EDEs instead of cross-border lending.

While the existing data and information provide a reasonably good picture of the depth and pattern of integration of EDEs into the global financial system, there are several gaps and inconsistencies. Statistics on external debt of EDEs, as conventionally defined, are not always accurate. There are no comprehensive data on non-resident holding of locally issued bonds and external debt statistics do not always include these holdings. By contrast, they often include internationally issued bonds held by residents even though these are not external debt as defined in balance-of-payments.

On the other hand, residency-based definition of assets and liabilities does not always adequately capture external vulnerabilities. Balance sheets defined on the basis of nationality may provide a better description. For instance, local lending in foreign currencies by foreign banks in EDEs funded abroad can create as much fragility as their cross-border lending even though, unlike the latter, it is not included in external debt. Again, borrowing by foreign subsidiaries of corporations in EDEs in international markets, including in off-shore centres, can expose them to significant risks. While they are not included in the conventional, residency-based balance-of-payments definition of external debt, they are included in corporate balance sheets.

Data problems are equally pressing for equity assets and liabilities, including portfolio and direct equity. Figures on foreign holding of portfolio equity are missing for many countries and those provided by the IMF underestimate such liabilities. FDI statistics reported by two main official sources of data, the IMF and UNCTAD, often differ significantly. Moreover, it is very difficult to identify from existing statistics what FDI really comprises—whether it adds to productive capital or consists of M&A, financial transactions linked to corporate reconfigurations, or simply portfolio flows.

Discussions of external vulnerability of emerging economies often focus on debt. Indeed, in the past two decades private debt has been the main reason in most emerging economies facing external financial and balance-of-payments crises. It is also likely to be the central factor in future bouts of instability because of massive international borrowing by non-financial corporations of several emerging economies since the onset of the crisis, attracted by exceptionally low interest rates. This debt is largely in dollars, often used for asset acquisitions and investment in property and commodities. It has also been associated with a rapid expansion of domestic credit. An important part of it is in bonds and unhedged. It is more difficult to restructure than bank loans because of dispersion of its holders. It entails exposure to both the exchange rate risk and hikes in dollar bond yields that may result from the normalization of monetary policy in the US, changes in expectations about future interest rates or a sudden turnaround in the global risk appetite.

Increased foreign acquisition of locally issued debt and the denomination of a greater proportion of sovereign external debt in local currencies have had the consequence of passing the exchange rate risk to non-resident lenders. However, this does not really eliminate the vulnerability of the sovereign to crises resulting from currency mismatches. In almost all crises which involved private sector borrowing abroad, an important part of private debt was socialized through government bail-outs, significantly raising sovereign debt. This was the case during the Southern Cone crisis in Latin America in the late 1970s and early 1980s and in East Asian and Turkish crises in the late 1990s and the early 2000s. Even the Latin American debt crisis of the 1980s involved a significant amount of private debt which subsequently became socialized. Again, there was extensive socialization of private debt during the recent Eurozone crisis. Thus, because of massive accumulation of corporate debt in dollars in recent years, public finances continue to be highly vulnerable to currency and debt crises.

Capital account liberalization is recognized to have resulted in a loss of autonomy in controlling policy rates in emerging economies, a phenomenon commonly described as impossible trinity—that is, inability of policy-makers to pursue simultaneously an independent monetary policy, control the exchange rate, and maintain an open capital account. In reality, the erosion of monetary policy autonomy is often greater than is typically portrayed by impossible trinity, as witnessed by the growing impact of policy rates in the US on short-term rates in emerging economies with flexible exchange rate regimes.

With closer integration of bond markets, there is now a significant loss of control over the whole spectrum of interest rates. The growing internationalization of sovereign debt of emerging economies, together with greater access of local investors to foreign debt securities, has served to link domestic debt markets closely with markets in reserve-currency countries and, like non-financial corporations, made the sovereign highly susceptible to conditions in bond markets abroad. It has reduced the capacity of local bond markets to act as a spare tyre and provide alternative channels of financing at times of stress in international debt markets. Increases in dollar bond yields could thus lead to hikes in long-term rates in emerging markets, creating difficulties in refinancing and servicing locally issued, local-currency sovereign debt. Adjustment to policy rates to counter such pressures cannot guarantee full control over long-term rates but would have undesirable consequences for the exchange rate and economic activity. Furthermore, since a growing share of domestically issued bonds is now held by foreign nationals, the sovereign may find its autonomy restricted de facto in restructuring such debt even if it is subject to local jurisdiction.

The combination of internationalization of sovereign debt and large-scale borrowing abroad by non-financial corporations has created destabilizing feedbacks between bond and currency markets of emerging economies. A sudden stop in capital inflows and sharp drop in the currency could trigger a rapid exit from local bond markets, pushing down prices and raising long-term domestic rates. In such conditions unhedged corporate debtors tend to rush in to buy dollars, accelerating the decline in the currency and the exit from bond markets. In the same vein, a rise in dollar bond yields can lead to sharp drops in local bond prices, triggering declines in the currency. Indeed the period since the onset of the global crisis has seen several episodes of simultaneous declines in currencies and bonds in emerging economies as a result of stress in international bond markets. There is very little the monetary authorities can do in defusing such shocks. When shocks are severe and durable, they may find it difficult to bring stability to currency and financial markets even if they were prepared to hike policy rates and sacrifice employment and growth.

In assessing external fragility, vulnerabilities associated with equity liabilities are often neglected. These have gained importance with the growing inflows into equity markets of emerging economies. Destabilizing feedbacks can also occur not only between bond and currency markets but also between equity and currency markets, particularly since portfolio equity flows are highly unstable and pro-cyclical. This was seen in the aftermath of the Lehman collapse in 2008 and during the taper tantrum in 2013. A bearish mood in major equity markets can lead to a rapid exit from emerging markets and trigger sharp declines in the currency, again aggravated by the response of unhedged debtors. Similarly, currency declines can prompt exit of foreign holders from equity markets.

Even the relative stability of direct investment is in doubt. FDI inflows tend to be pro-cyclical because retained profits as a main source of FDI can vary significantly with overall business conditions. An important part of recorded

FDI constitutes financial transactions linked to corporate reconfigurations and intra-company flows of finance and even hot money. Finally, outstanding FDI liabilities can generate balance of payments difficulties because income transfers are generally high compared to net exports generated by foreign companies even in countries where they are highly export oriented.

Economic orthodoxy proposes four basic lines of defence against vulnerabilities associated with growing integration of emerging economies into the global financial system. First, flexible exchange rate regimes are recommended in order to allow currency movements to absorb part of the capital account shocks. While exchange rate flexibility has a lot to commend compared to fixed rates, it is not a recipe to instability in capital flows. When capital surges continue for extended periods, flexible exchange rates can result in sustained appreciations and undermine industry. At times of rapid and sustained capital flight, on the other hand, they could lead to a free fall, deepening financial meltdown and economic contraction. Such exchange rate gyrations can be particularly damaging because of increased reliance on trade for industrialization and development.

The second line of defence is to maintain adequate foreign exchange reserves to prevent and mitigate balance-of-payments and currency crises and to provide international liquidity against sudden stops and reversals of capital inflows. However, in deficits EDEs with sizeable negative foreign asset positions, reserves are costly and cannot be expected to provide adequate protection against sustained capital outflows because they are piled up from capital inflows in the first place—that is, they are borrowed rather than earned from current account surpluses. They are costly both to the government and the nation as a whole because income earned on international reserves is typically much lower than the cost of foreign capital and the interest on government debt. Indeed, accumulating reserves from unsustainable capital inflows has little economic rationale—in effect, this would mean that the foreign money entering the economy is not used for any productive purpose but kept in low-yielding foreign assets as an insurance against its exit! Second, reserve accumulation does not prevent currency and maturity mismatches in private balance sheets, but can only provide public insurance for private risks. Finally, when inflows are also used to finance current account deficits and resident investments abroad, reserves accumulated are unlikely to match potential outflows. This would particularly be the case where reserves come from inflows into bond, equity, and deposit markets as well as short-term borrowing abroad.

Third, EDEs are also advised to use prudential regulations to contain destabilizing effects of capital flows on domestic financial markets. There can be little doubt such regulations appropriately extended to address the risks associated with capital flows through the banking system have a role to play. They could include more stringent rules for capital charges, loan-loss provisions, and liquidity and reserve requirements for capital account transactions in foreign currencies. But the preventive power of prudential regulations is highly contentious because markets constantly innovate to bypass them and they do not protect against macroeconomic shocks. In any case a large proportion of international capital flows now bypass the banking system, including borrowing by non-financial corporations in international bond markets and capital flows into domestic debt and equity markets.

Finally, capital controls are now added to the arsenal of orthodoxy to fight undesirable consequences of capital flows. As strong and sustained surges in capital inflows triggered by the ultra-easy monetary policy in advanced economies created widespread disruptions in emerging economies and many of them started looking for remedies, the IMF was compelled to reconsider its position on capital controls. The 'Institutional View' of the Fund discussed by the Board and supported by most Directors in 2012, however, brings no fundamental change to the long-held orthodox position regarding the benefits of free capital movements. It is simply recognized that there might be circumstances when capital movements need to be restricted. But measures introduced should be market-friendly and deployed only as a last resort—priority should be given to adjustment in monetary, fiscal, and exchange rate policies in managing unsustainable capital flows regardless of whether these policies are judiciously designed to attain stability and growth and debt and balance-of-payments sustainability. They should also be used on a temporary basis as countercyclical remedies to curb excessive flows. In practice such measures have not been effective in preventing build-up of fragilities described above because they are not designed to reduce the structural vulnerabilities resulting from deepened integration of emerging economies into the global financial system. The IMF advises countries with long-standing and extensive restrictions to liberalize in order to benefit from international capital movements and argues that a country could make progress towards greater liberalization before reaching all the necessary thresholds for financial and institutional development and doing so may spur progress in these dimensions. Concern was thus expressed during the discussions at the Executive Board that the 'Institutional View' could indeed become an instrument for opening up capital markets of emerging economies.

To sum up, policies and measures proposed by the mainstream would not be very effective in protecting EDEs sufficiently against destabilizing spillovers from global cycles. Nor are there adequate and effective global institutions and mechanisms for the prevention and effective management of financial crises with international origins and consequences. Several ideas have been advanced in the past three decades to reduce the likelihood of such crises and to contain their economic and social impact when they occur. These include: effective and even-handed multilateral surveillance over macroeconomic, financial, and exchange rate policies of major economies that exert a disproportionately large influence on global economic conditions; reform of the governance-related shortcomings in international financial institutions as a prerequisite for greater discipline over policies in systemically important economies; reform of the international reserves system so as to bring greater stability and reduce the influence of one or two countries over global monetary and financial conditions; multilateral regulation and oversight of systemically important banks and rating agencies; international recognition of the need for capital control measures in source as well as destination countries; international sanctioning of exchange controls and temporary debt standstills in countries facing liquidity crises, protection of such countries against creditor litigation, and adequate provision of international liquidity to support economic activity; and statutory debt workouts to apply the established principles of insolvency to sovereigns facing international debt crises. Although some of these issues have appeared from time to time on the international agenda, particularly after bouts of virulent crises, hardly any action has been taken to bring them to conclusion because of opposition of major advanced economies.

The absence of global institutions and arrangements in these areas makes it all the more important for EDEs to rethink their integration into the international financial system. One of the key lessons of the history of economic development is that successful policies are associated not with autarky or full integration into the global economy, but strategic and selective integration suitable to the stage of economic and financial development reached, seeking to use the opportunities that a broader economic space may offer, while minimizing the potential risks it may entail. This is more so in finance than trade and investment. In this area the pendulum has swung too far and would have to be rebalanced. Increased presence of foreign investors and financial institutions in domestic asset and credit markets of EDEs and unbridled access of their private non-financial corporations to international financial markets have made them highly vulnerable to global boom–bust cycles generated by policy shifts in major financial centres, notably the US. These cycles may recur with greater frequency and force in the years to come since monetary policy has remained the only game in town to regulate economic activity in these economies, but is incapable of sustaining growth on its own without creating asset and credit bubbles.

However, in the majority of EDEs, the trend has been in the opposite direction; to open domestic markets to international finance and to free their residents to be players in foreign markets as borrowers and investors. Finance-driven globalization has been oversold to the political elite in much of the global South. Despite common rhetoric about the demise of the

Washington Consensus, neo-liberal policies introduced since the mid-1980s have hardly been rolled back. On the contrary, as discussed in this book, the new millennium has seen acceleration of capital account liberalization and investment regimes in many EDEs, often unilaterally or as part of bilateral agreements with advanced economies. Many countries which suffered most from virulent crises in the 1990s and early 2000s have been among the fastest liberalizers. There is now a greater convergence of policy regimes among EDEs in international finance and investment than in the 1990s. More and more emerging economies are now willing to join the OECD and come under its capital account and investment regimes without having been able to achieve in any significant degree the industrial and financial maturity of the advanced members of the group.

The current depth and pattern of integration of EDEs into the global finance and investment regimes can have important consequences for their industrialization and development in the twenty-first century. Contrary to earlier optimism, finance-driven globalization has failed to bring about widespread and sustained economic convergence of the South with the North but produced increased inequality and instability. Inequality has been a major cause of stagnation in several major economies by depressing aggregate demand. It has also heightened instability by creating temptation for debt-driven expansions. Financialization and instability are major impediments to taking a long view which is essential for building dynamic industries for catch-up growth. Financial booms often favour short-term, speculative investment and leveraged asset acquisitions rather than the kind of investment needed for industrial development. This is seen in recent years when highly accommodating global financial conditions and sustained surges in capital inflows led to de-industrialization in many semi-industrialized countries with growth relying mainly on consumption, property, or commodity booms.

A hands-off approach to foreign direct investment has much the same consequences for industrialization and development as unrestrained finance. The interest of transnational corporations is not in passing their competencies to locals. Left alone, they cannot be expected to take a long view and act with a developmental perspective, helping build dynamically efficient industries to reap benefits in some distant, uncertain future. As discussed in Chapter 7, their contribution to industrialization and technological progress depends very much on deliberate policies that may compromise the goals they pursue. However, commitments undertaken in bilateral investment treaties with advanced economies have resulted in a considerable loss of policy autonomy in a broad area of public intervention, including international capital flows and access to domestic financial markets. Thus, dismantling such agreements may also be necessary to gain greater autonomy in financial policies.

Looking back to the past three decades since the birth of the globalization and the Washington Consensus ideology, hardly any developing country has been able to make significant progress in catching up with the productivity levels of advanced economies to replicate the earlier successes of Japan, Korea, and Taiwan in industrialization, with the single exception of China, which has been a successful outlier in managing its integration into the global economy in a selective and strategic manner. There would not be many more candidates for graduation to the ranks of advanced economies in the decades ahead if countries allow unfettered international finance and transnational corporations to drive their development.

References

Abramowicz, L. 2014. 'IMF Finds Flaw in Bond Industry as Exiting Funds Too Easy'. Bloomberg. 22 October. http://www.bloomberg.com/news/articles/2014-10-22/exiting-illiquid-bond-funds-is-too-easy-to-imf-as-fees-proposed. Accessed 10 January 2015.

ADB (Asian Development Bank). 2011. *Asia Capital Markets Monitor*. Asian Development Bank, Mandaluyong City, August.

Adler, G. and S. Sosa. 2011. 'Commodity Price Cycles: The Perils of Mismanaging the Boom'. IMF Working Paper 11/283. Washington, DC, December.

Adrian, T. and N. Liang. 2014. 'Monetary Policy, Financial Conditions, and Financial Stability'. Staff Report No. 690, Federal Reserve Bank of New York. New York, NY, September.

AFCG. 2013. 'Emerging Markets Debt: Local and Dollar Bonds Provide Different Routes to Returns'. *Viewpoints,* American Funds, Capital Guardian. February. https://www.google.ch/url?sa=t&rct=j&q=&esrc=s&source=web&cd=1&cad=rja&uact=8&ved=0CCgQFjAA&url=https%3A%2F%2Fserver.capgroup.com%2Fcapgroup%2Faction%2FgetContent%2Ffile%2FGIG%2FNorth_America%2FMarket_Insights%2FCapitals_Views%2FViewpoint_Dollar_Local.pdf&ei=6zRvU5L1E87T7AaiiIGgCg&usg=AFQjCNHGQC9Hl1edMGsp0CSbeM1t3gcV1g&bvm=bv.66330100,d.ZGU. Accessed 13 April 2014.

Agosin, M. R. and R. Machado. 2005. 'Foreign Investment in Developing Countries: Does it Crowd in Domestic Investment?' *Oxford Development Studies* 33 (2): 149–62.

Aiyar, S. and S. Jain-Chandra. 2012. 'The Domestic Credit Supply Response to International Bank Deleveraging: Is Asia Different?' IMF Working Paper No. 12/258. Washington, DC, October.

Aizenman, J. and J. Lee. 2005. 'International Reserves: Precautionary vs. Mercantilist Views, Theory, and Evidence'. IMF Working Paper No. 05/198. Washington, DC, October.

Akyüz, Y. 2002. 'Crisis Management and Burden Sharing'. In Akyüz, Y., ed. *Reforming the Global Financial Architecture: Issues and Proposals*. London: Zed Books.

Akyüz, Y. 2006. 'From Liberalization to Investment and Jobs: Lost in Translation'. Working Paper 74. Policy Integration Department, ILO. Also reprinted as TWN Global Economy Series 8. Penang, Malaysia.

Akyüz, Y. 2007. 'Debt Sustainability in Emerging Markets: A Critical Appraisal'. DESA Working Paper 61. November.

Akyüz, Y. 2008. 'The Current Global Financial Turmoil and Asian Developing Countries'. Inclusive and Sustainable Development No. 2, ESCAP. Bangkok. Reprinted in Akyüz, Y. 2014. *Liberalization, Financial Instability and Economic Development.* London: Anthem Press.

Akyüz, Y. 2011a. 'Export Dependence and Sustainability of Growth in China and the East Asian Production Network'. *China and World Economy* 19(1) (January): 1–23.

Akyüz, Y. 2011b. 'Capital Flows to Developing Countries in a Historical Perspective: Will the Current Boom End with a Bust?' South Centre Research Paper 37. March. Also in Akyüz, Y. 2012. *The Financial Crisis and the Global South. A Development Perspective*. London: Pluto Press.

Akyüz, Y. 2011c. 'Global Economic Prospects: The Recession May be Over but Where Next?' *Global Policy* (May): 127–137. Also in Akyüz, Y. 2012. *The Financial Crisis and the Global South. A Development Perspective*. London: Pluto Press.

Akyüz, Y. 2011d. 'The Global Economic Crisis and Asian Developing Countries: Impact, Policy Response and Medium-Term Prospects'. In Akyüz, Y., ed. *The Financial Crisis and Asian Developing Countries*. Penang: Third World Network.

Akyüz, Y. 2012. 'The Staggering Rise of the South?' South Centre Research Paper 44. March. Also in Akyüz, Y. 2014. *Liberalization, Financial Instability and Economic Development*. London: Anthem Press.

Akyüz, Y. 2015. 'Internationalization of Finance and Changing Vulnerabilities in Emerging and Developing Economies: The Case of Malaysia'. South Centre Policy Brief 20. August.

Akyüz, Y. and K. Boratav. 2003. 'The Making of the Turkish Financial Crisis'. *World Development* 31 (9): 1549–66.

Al-Sadig, A. J. 2013. 'Outward Foreign Direct Investment and Domestic Investment: the Case of Developing Countries'. IMF Working Paper 13/52. Washington, DC, February.

Al-Saffar, Y., W. Ridinger, and S. Whitaker. 2013. 'The Role of External Balance Sheets in the Financial Crisis'. Financial Stability Paper 24, Bank of England. London, October.

Alquist, R., R. Mukherjee, and L. Tesar. 2013. 'Fire-Sale FDI or Business as Usual?' NBER Working Paper 18837. February.

Altman, R. C. 2009. 'Globalization in Retreat'. *Foreign Affairs*. July–August. http://www.foreignaffairs.com/articles/65153/roger-c-altman/globalization-in-retreat. Accessed 18 May 2011.

Amadeo, K. 2013. 'What Was the Stimulus Package?' About.com US Economy. 10 September.

Anderson, P. R. D., A. C. Silva, and A. Velandia-Rubiano. 2010. 'Public Debt Management in Emerging Market Economies. Has This Time Been Different?' Policy Research Working Paper WPS5399, World Bank. Washington, DC, August.

Arslanalp, S. and T. Tsuda. 2014. 'Tracking Global Demand for Emerging Market Sovereign Debt'. IMF Working Paper No. 14/39. Washington, DC, March.

Atoyan, R., J. Manning, and J. Rahman. 2013. 'Rebalancing: Evidence from Current Account Adjustment in Europe'. IMF Working Paper 13/74. Washington, DC, March.

Avdjiev, S., Z. Kuti, and E. Takáts. 2012. 'The Euro Area Crisis and Cross-border Bank Lending to Emerging Markets'. *BIS Quarterly Review* (December): 37–47.

Backhouse, R. E. and M. Boianovsky. 2015. 'Secular Stagnation: The History of a Macroeconomic Heresy'. Version 1, preliminary draft of paper prepared for the Blanqui Lecture. Meetings of the European Society for the History of Economic Thought, Rome, 14 May. http://papers.ssrn.com/sol3/papers.cfm?abstract_id=

2602903. For a shorter version in Vox, 19 May 2015, see http://www.voxeu.org/article/secular-stagnation-history-heresy. Accessed 10 January 2016.

Badarinza, C. and T. Ramadorai. 2014. 'Home Away from Home? Foreign Demand and London House Prices'. Working Paper Series, Social Science Research Network. http://papers.ssrn.com/sol3/papers.cfm?abstract_id=2353124. Accessed 3 March 2015.

Bai, C., H. Chang-Tai, and Y. Qian. 2006. 'The Return to Capital in China'. *Brookings Papers on Economic Activity* 2: 61–88.

Ball, L. M. 2014. 'Long-Term Damage from the Great Recession in OECD Countries'. NBER Working Paper 20185. http://www.nber.org/papers/w20185. Accessed 10 August 2015.

Banerjee, R., J. Kearns, and M. Lombardi. 2015. '(Why) Is Investment Weak?' *BIS Quarterly Review* (March): 67–82.

Bastourre, D., J. Carrera, J. Ibarlucia, and M. Sardi. 2013. 'Common Drivers in Emerging Market Spreads and Commodity Prices'. BIS. 15 March. http://www.bis.org/search/?q=bastourre. Accessed 10 September 2013.

Bech, M. L. and A. Malkhozov. 2016. 'How Have Central Banks Implemented Negative Policy Rates?' *BIS Quarterly Review* (March): 31–44.

Bernanke, B. 2002. 'Deflation: Making Sure "It" Doesn't Happen Here'. Remarks. National Economists Club, Washington, DC, November 21. htpp://www.federalreserve.gov/newsevents/speech/2002speech.htm. Accessed 13 January 2013.

Bernanke, B. 2009. 'The Federal Reserve's Balance Sheet: An Update'. Federal Reserve Board Conference on Key Developments in Monetary Policy, Washington, DC, October 8. http://www.federalreserve.gov/newsevents/speech/bernanke20091008a.htm. Accessed 12 March 2013.

Bernanke, B. 2010. 'Federal Reserve's exit strategy'. Testimony before the Committee on Financial Services, U.S. House of Representatives. Washington, DC, February 10. http://www.federalreserve.gov/newsevents/testimony/bernanke20100210a.htm. Accessed 12 March 2013.

Bernanke, B. 2013. 'Monitoring the Financial System'. Speech at the 49th Annual Conference on Bank Structure and Competition sponsored by the Federal Reserve Bank of Chicago. Chicago, Illinois, May 10. http://www.federalreserve.gov/newsevents/speech/bernanke20130510a.htm. Accessed 12 May 2013.

Bernanke, B. S. 2015a. 'Why Are Interest Rates So Low, Part 2: Secular Stagnation'. Brookings. March 31. https://www.brookings.edu/blog/ben-bernanke/2015/03/31/why-are-interest-rates-so-low-part-2-secular-stagnation/. Accessed 15 February 2017.

Bernanke, B. S. 2015b. 'Why Are Interest Rates So Low, Part 3: The Global Savings Glut'. Brookings. April 1. http://www.brookings.edu/blogs/ben-bernanke/posts/2015/04/01-why-interest-rates-low-global-savings-glut. Accessed 12 April 2016.

Bernanke, B. S. 2015c. 'German Trade Surplus is a Problem'. Brookings. 3 April. http://www.brookings.edu/blogs/ben-bernanke/posts/2015/04/03-germany-trade-surplus-problem. Accessed 12 April 2016.

Bernanke, B. S. 2016. 'What Tools Does the Fed Have Left? Part 1: Negative Interest Rates'. Ben Bernanke's Blog, Brookings. 3 April. http://www.brookings.edu/blogs/ben-bernanke/posts/2016/03/18-negative-interest-rates. Accessed 12 April 2016.

Bernanke, B. S. and D. Kohn. 2016. 'The Fed's Interest Payments to Banks'. Brookings. 16 February. http://www.brookings.edu/blogs/ben-bernanke/posts/2016/02/16-fed-interest-payments-banks. Accessed 12 April 2016.

Bernasconi-Osterwalder, N., A. Cosbey, L. Johnson, and D. Vis-Dunbar. 2012. *Investment Treaties and Why They Matter to Sustainable Development: Questions and Answers*. Winnipeg, Canada: International Institute for Sustainable Development.

Birds, M. 2015. ' "The World is Still in Love with Debt" and There's $50 trillion More of It Since the Financial Crisis'. *Business Insider UK*. http://uk.businessinsider.com/baml-global-debt-has-rise-by-50-trillion-since-the-financial-crisis-2015-10. Accessed 12 January 2016.

BIS. 1998. *68th BIS Annual Report, 1st April 1997–31st March 1998*. Basel, 8 June.

BIS. 2010. 'The Global Crisis and Financial Intermediation in Emerging Market Economies'. BIS Paper No. 54. Basel, December.

BIS. 2013. 'International Banking and Financial Market Developments'. *BIS Quarterly Review* (September): 1–23.

BIS. 2014. *84th BIS Annual Report, 1st April 2013–31st March 2014*. Basel, June.

BIS. 2016. Quarterly Report. Basel, March.

Black, S. and A. Munro. 2010. 'Why Issue Bonds Offshore?' BIS Paper No. 52. Basel, July.

Blanchard, O. and D. Leigh. 2013. 'Growth Forecast Errors and Fiscal Multipliers'. IMF Working Paper 13/1. Washington, DC, January.

Blinder, A. S. and M. Zandi. 2010. 'How the Great Recession was Brought to an End'. http://www.economy.com/mark-zandi/documents/end-of-great-recession.pdf. Accessed 3 January 2013.

BNM (Bank Negara Malaysia). 2014. 'Economic and Financial Developments in the Malaysian Economy in the First Quarter of 2014'. *Quarterly Bulletin, First Quarter 2014*. http://www.bnm.gov.my/index.php?ch=en_publication&pg=en_qb&ac=90&lang=en&uc=2. Accessed 15 February 2017.

BOEA (Bureau of Economic Analysis). 2008. 'U.S. Direct Investment Abroad (USDIA): Operations of U.S. Parent Companies and Their Foreign Affiliates, Revised 2008 Statistics'. US Department of Commerce. http://www.bea.gov/international/usdia2008r.htm. Accessed 12 April 2015.

Bonanomi, E. B. and S. Meyer-Nandi. 2013. 'Swiss Double Taxation Agreements: Current Policy and Relevance for Development'. University of Bern, Word Trade Institute.

Bonizzi, B. 2013. 'Capital Market Inflation in Emerging Markets: The Case of Brazil and South Korea'. SOAS, University of London, London, September. http://mpra.ub.uni-muenchen.de/51255/. Accessed 12 March 2014.

Bora, B. 2002. 'Trade-Related Investment Measures'. In Hoekman, B., A. Mattoo, and P. English, eds. *Development, Trade and the WTO. A Handbook*. Washington, DC: World Bank.

Borio, C. and P. Disyatat. 2011. 'Global Imbalances and the Financial Crisis: Link or No Link?' BIS Working Paper 346. Basel, May.

Borio, C., E. Kharroubi, C. Upper, and F. Zampolli. 2015. 'Labour Reallocation and Productivity Dynamics: Financial Causes, Real Consequences'. BIS Working Paper 534. Basel, December.

Borio, C., R. McCauley, and P. McGuire. 2011. 'Global Credit and Domestic Credit Booms'. *BIS Quarterly Review* (September): 44–57.

Brooke, M., R. Mendes, A. Pienkowski, and E. Santor. 2013. 'Sovereign Default and State-Contingent Debt'. Financial Stability Paper 27, Bank of England. London, November.

Brown, E. 2014. 'New G20 Rules: Cyprus-Style Bail-Ins to Hit Depositors AND Pensioners' The Web of Debt Blog. 1 December. http://ellenbrown.com/2014/12/01/new-rules-cyprus-style-bail-ins-to-hit-deposits-and-pensions/. Accessed 3 December 2014.

Buch, C. M., K. Neugebauer, and C. Schröder. 2014. 'Changing Forces of Gravity: How the Crisis Affected International Banking'. ZEW Discussion Paper No. 14-006, Centre for European Economic Research. http://ftp.zew.de/pub/zew-docs/dp/dp14006.pdf. Accessed 26 May 2014.

Buiter, W. H. 2014. 'The Simple Analytics of Helicopter Money: Why It Works—Always'. *Economics*. The Open-Access, Open-Assessment E-Journal, Volume 4 (August). http://www.economics-ejournal.org/economics/journalarticles/2014-28. Accessed 18 April 2016.

Burda, M., H. P. Grüner, M. Hellwig, et al. 2012. 'In Support of a European Banking Union, Done Properly: A Manifesto by Economists in Germany, Austria and Switzerland'. http://voxeu.org/article/manifesto-banking-union-economists-germany-austria-and-switzerland. Accessed 2 March 2012.

Burger, J. D., F. E. Warnock, and V. C. Warnock. 2010. 'Emerging Local Currency Bond Markets'. NBER Working Paper 16249. August.

Calello, P. and W. Ervin. 2010. 'From Bail-out to Bail-in'. Economics focus. *The Economist*. 28 January. http://www.economist.com/node/15392186. Accessed 16 June 2014.

Campa, D. and R. Cull. 2013. 'Ireland's Foreign Direct Investment Sector: The Impact of a Hypothetical Irish Euro Zone Exit'. *Business and Economics Journal* 4(2):1–6.

Campos, C. F. S., D. Jaimovich, and U. Panizza. 2006. 'The Unexplained Part of Public Debt'. *Emerging Markets Review* 7(3): 228–43.

Caves, R. E. 1996. *Multinational Enterprise and Economic Analysis*. Cambridge and New York: Cambridge University Press.

Cecchetti, S. G. and E. Kharroubi. 2015. 'Why Does Financial Sector Growth Crowd Out Real Economic Growth?' BIS Working Paper 490. Basel, February.

Cerutti, E., G. Dell'Ariccia, and P. M. S. Martínez. 2005. 'How Banks Go Abroad: Branches or Subsidiaries?' Policy Research Working Paper 3753, World Bank. Washington, DC, October.

Cetorelli, N. and L. Goldberg. 2009. 'Globalized Banks: Lending to Emerging Markets in the Crisis'. Staff Report 377, Federal Reserve Bank of New York. New York, NY, June.

Cetorelli, N. and L. Goldberg. 2011. 'Global Banks and International Shock Transmission: Evidence from the Crisis'. *IMF Economic Review* 59(1): 41–76.

Chandra, M. 2010. 'Emerging Market Acquisitions in Developed Economies'. KPMG LLP. https://www.google.ch/url?sa=t&rct=j&q=&esrc=s&source=web&cd=1&cad=rja&uact=8&ved=0CCQQFjAA&url=https%3A%2F%2Fwww.kpmg.com%2FUS%2Fen%2FIssuesAndInsights%2FArticlesPublications%2FDocuments%2Femerging-market-

acquisitions.pdf&ei=P55cVIykIoTqOMCQgPAI&usg=AFQjCNEIi3OQcqvNAocKw59O-XciCNUdKlg&bvm=bv.79184187,d.ZWU. Accessed 7 October 2014.

Chen, G. and Y. Wu. 2014. 'Bank Ownership and Credit Growth in Emerging Markets During and After the 2008–09 Financial Crisis—A Cross-Regional Comparison'. IMF Working Paper 14/171. Washington, DC, September.

Chen, G., M. Geiger, and M. Fu. 2015. *Manufacturing FDI in Sub-Saharan Africa: Trends, Determinants, and Impact.* Washington, DC: World Bank Group.

Chen, R., G-M. Milesi-Ferretti, and T. Tressel. 2012. 'External Imbalances in the Euro Area'. IMF Working Paper 12/236. Washington, DC, September.

Cho, A. H. and N. K. Dubash. 2005. 'Will Investment Rules Shrink Policy Space for Sustainable Development? Evidence from the Electricity Sector'. In Gallagher, K., ed. *Putting Development First. The Importance of Policy Space in the WTO and International Financial Institutions*. London: Zed Books.

Choi, W. G., S. Sharma, and M. Strömqvist. 2007. 'Capital Flows, Financial Integration, and International Reserve Holdings: The Recent Experience of Emerging Markets and Advanced Economies'. IMF Working Paper 07/151. Washington, DC, July.

CIEPR (Committee on International Economic Policy and Reform). 2013. 'Revisiting Sovereign Bankruptcy'. Brookings. October. http://www.brookings.edu/research/reports/2013/10/sovereign-debt. Accessed 24 March 2014.

Claessens, S. and N. van Horen. 2012. 'Foreign Banks: Trends, Impact and Financial Stability'. IMF Working Paper No. 12/10. Washington, DC, January.

Claessens, S., M. Dooley, and A. Warner. 1993. 'Portfolio Capital Flows: Hot or Cool?' *World Bank Discussion Paper*, No. 228: 22. Washington, DC.

Claessens, S., D. Klingebiel, and S.L. Schmukler. 2001. 'FDI and Stock Market Development: Complements or Substitutes?' World Bank. December. http://www.google.ch/url?sa=t&rct=j&q=&esrc=s&source=web&cd=1&cad=rja&uact=8&ved=0CB0QFjAA&url=http%3A%2F%2Fwww.iadb.org%2Fres%2Fpublications%2Fpubfiles%2Fpubs-fdi-4.pdf&ei=1H1cVPmMCMi3OJ3xgfgH&usg=AFQjCNECYa4OZ8eKOGNe04BkZ_rB1byLWg. Accessed 7 October 2014.

Cohan, D. 2016. '"Too Big to Fail" Banks Thriving a Few Years after Financial Crisis'. *New York Times*. 22 January.

Colombo, J. 2014a. 'Why Southeast Asia's Boom Is A Bubble-Driven Illusion'. *Forbes*. 23 January. www.forbes.com/sites/jessecolombo/. Accessed 12 May 2014.

Colombo, J. 2014b. 'Why the Worst Is Still Ahead for Turkey's Bubble Economy'. *Forbes*. 5 March. www.forbes.com/sites/jessecolombo/. Accessed on 12 May 2014.

Colombo, J. 2014c. 'A Guide to South Africa's Economic Bubble and Coming Crisis'. *Forbes*. 19 March. www.forbes.com/sites/jessecolombo/. Accessed 12 May 2014.

Constantinescu, C., A. Mattoo, and M. Ruta. 2014. 'Slow Trade'. *Finance and Development* 51(4) (December). IMF, Washington, DC.

Coppola, F. 2016. 'It Was the Financial Crisis that Stopped Banks Lending, not Interest on Excess Reserves'. *Forbes*. 12 January. http://www.forbes.com/sites/francescoppola/2016/01/12/it-was-the-financial-crisis-that-stopped-banks-lending-not-interest-on-excess-reserves/#5b5a558866f7. Accessed 11 April 2016.

Cornia, G. A., J. C. Gómez-Sabaini, and B. Martorano. 2011. 'A New Fiscal Pact, Tax Policy Changes and Income Inequality: Latin America during the Last Decade'.

Working Paper No. 2011/70, United Nations University World Institute for Development Economics Research. November.

Correa, C.M. 2013. 'Investment Agreements: A New Threat to the TRIPS Flexibilities?' *South Bulletin* 72 (13 May): 23–5.

Cui, C. 2016. 'In Emerging Markets, Capital Controls Are Ratcheted Up to Stem Outflow of Funds'. *The Wall Street Journal*. January 21. https://www.wsj.com/articles/battered-emerging-markets-race-to-stem-outflows-1453410496. Accessed 8 May 2015.

Danakol, S. H., S. Estrin, P. Reynolds, and U. Weitzel. 2014. 'Foreign Direct Investment and Domestic Entrepreneurship: Blessing or Curse?' CEPR Discussion Paper 9793. January.

Das, B. L. 1999. The *World Trade Organisation. A Guide to the Framework for International Trade*. Penang: Third World Network.

de Bolle, M., B. Rother, and I. Hakobyan. 2006. 'The Level and Composition of Public Sector Debt in Emerging Market Crises'. IMF Working Paper No. 06/186. Washington, DC, August.

De Grauwe, P. 2010. 'Fighting the Wrong Enemy'. Vox. CEPR's Policy Portal. 19 May. http://www.voxeu.org/article/europe-s-private-versus-public-debt-problem-fighting-wrong-enemy. Accessed 24 September 2012.

Delikouras, S., R. F. Dittmar, and H. Li. 2013. 'Do Dollar-Denominated Emerging Market Corporate Bonds Insure Foreign Exchange Risk?' University of Michigan Ross School of Business, Ann Arbor, MI, November. http://www.google.ch/url?sa=t&rct=j&q=&esrc=s&source=web&cd=1&ved=0CCIQFjAA&url=http%3A%2F%2Fwebuser.bus.umich.edu%2Frdittmar%2FResearch_files%2FPapers%2FDelikouras_Dittmar_Li2013.pdf&ei=B8KVU777CKTN7Abnt4G4BQ&usg=AFQjCNEDfUj8u0ANdFeN05Axht-OgjuMmA&bvm=bv.68445247,d.ZGU. Accessed 4 March 2014.

Dell'Erba, S., R. Hausmann, and U. Panizza. 2013. 'Debt Levels, Debt Composition, and Sovereign Spreads in Emerging and Advanced Economies'. Working Paper 263, Centre for International Development, Harvard University. August.

Desai, M. A., C. F. Foley, and J. R. Hines. 2005. 'Foreign Direct Investment and the Domestic Capital Stock'. NBER Working Paper 11075. January.

Despain, H. G. 2015. 'Secular Stagnation. Mainstream Versus Marxian Traditions'. *Monthly Review* 67(4) (September).

Dhanani, S. and S. A. Hasnain. 2002. 'The Impact of Foreign Direct Investment on Indonesia's Manufacturing Sector'. *Journal of the Asian Pacific Economy* 7(1): 61–94.

Didier, T. and S. L. Schmukler. 2013. 'Financial Development in Latin America and the Caribbean: Stylized Facts and the Road Ahead'. Policy Research Working Paper 6582, World Bank. Washington, DC, August.

Dobbs, R., S. Lund, T. Koller, and A. Shwayder. 2013. 'QE and Ultra-low Interest Rates: Distributional Effects and Risks'. McKinsey Global Institute. November. http://www.mckinsey.com/global-themes/employment-and-growth/qe-and-ultra-low-interest-rates-distributional-effects-and-risks. Accessed 15 November 2013.

Dobbs, R., S. Lund, J. Woetzel, and M. Mutafchieva. 2015. 'Debt and (Not Much) Deleveraging'. McKinsey Global Institute. February. http://www.mckinsey.com/global-themes/employment-and-growth/debt-and-not-much-deleveraging. Accessed 12 September 2015.

Domanski, D., J. Kearns, M. Lombardi, and H. S. Shin. 2015. 'Oil and Debt'. *BIS Quarterly Review* (March): 55–65.

Doytch, N. 2013a. 'Does FDI Improve Financial Deepening of Host Country Stock Markets? Evidence from Sectoral FDI'. http://www.google.ch/url?sa=t&rct=j&q=&esrc=s&source=web&cd=2&ved=0CCQQFjAB&url=http%3A%2F%2Fworld-finance-conference.com%2Fpapers_wfc2%2F517.pdf&ei=0VFcVPWfPM2xPPqkgaAM&usg=AFQjCNETrvvr6NEkyJy2SyqDtC7zwZFm-g&bvm=bv.79184187,d.ZWU. Accessed 7 October 2014.

Doytch, N. 2013b. 'Determinants of Stock Market Development: A Brief Survey of Literature'. *Proceedings of the New York State Economics Association*, 66th Annual Meeting, Farmingdale, New York, October 4–5, Volume 6: 4–10. www.nyecon.net/nysea/publications/proceed/2013/Proceed_2013_p004.pdf. Accessed 7 October 2014.

Drummond, P. and E. X. Liu. 2013. 'Africa's Rising Exposure to China: How Large Are Spillovers through Trade?' IMF Working Paper No.13/250. Washington, DC, November.

Dufour, M. and O. Orhangazi. 2016. 'Growth and Distribution after the 2007–2008 US Financial Crisis: Who Shouldered the Burden of the Crisis?' *Review of Keynesian Economics* 4(2) (Summer): 151–74.

Durden, T. 2014a. 'Fed Prepares for Bond-Fund Runs, Looking at Imposing "Exit Fee" Gates'. Zero Hedge. 16 June. http://www.zerohedge.com/news/2014-06-16/fed-prepares-bond-fund-runs-looking-imposing-bond-exit-fees-gates. Accessed 3 July 2014.

Durden, T. 2014b. 'The G-20's Solution to Systemically Unstable, "Too Big To Fail" Banks: More Debt'. Zero Hedge. 23 August. http://www.zerohedge.com/news/2014-08-23/g-20s-solution-systemically-unstable-too-big-fail-banks-more-debt. Accessed 25 September 2014.

Durden, T. 2016. 'SocGen: "Now We Know Why the Fed Desperately Wants to Avoid a Drop in Equity Markets"'. Zero Hedge. 12 April. http://www.zerohedge.com/news/2016-04-12/socgen-now-we-know-why-fed-desperately-wants-avoid-drop-equity-markets. Accessed 18 April 2016.

Dünhaupt, P. 2013. 'The Effect of Financialization on Labor's Share of Income'. Working Paper 17/2013. Institute for International Political Economy. Berlin. http://www.ipe-berlin.org/index.php?id=working_papers&L=1#c829. Accessed 1 March 2016.

Ebeke, C. and Y. Lu. 2014. 'Emerging Market Local Currency Bond Yields and Foreign Holdings in the Post-Lehman Period—a Fortune or Misfortune?' IMF Working Paper No. 14/29. Washington, DC, February.

Eberhardt, P. and C. Olivet. 2012. *Profiting from Injustice. How Law Firms, Arbitrators and Financiers Are Fuelling an Investment Arbitration Boom.* Corporate Europe Observatory and the Transnational Institute, Brussels, November.

EC (European Commission). 2011. 'Public Finances in EMU 2011'. *European Economy* 3/2011. http://ec.europa.eu/economy_finance/publications/european_economy/2011/ee3_en.htm. Accessed 12 May 2013.

EC. 2015a. 'Completing Europe's Economic and Monetary Union. Completing the Banking Union'. 21 October. https://ec.europa.eu/priorities/publications/completing-banking-union_en. Accessed 2 December 2015.

EC. 2015b. 'Report on Public Finances in EMU, 2015'. Institutional Paper 014. December. http://ec.europa.eu/economy_finance/publications/eeip/ip014_en.htm. Accessed 1 March 2016.

ECB Eurosystem. 2016a. Interview with La Repubblica. Interview with Peter Praet, Member of the Executive Board of the ECB, conducted by Ferdinando Giugliano and Tonia Mastrobuoni on 15 March 2016 and published on 18 March 2016. http://www.ecb.europa.eu/press/inter/date/2016/html/sp160318.en.html. Accessed 18 April 2016.

ECB Eurosystem. 2016b. Introductory speech by Mario Draghi, President of the ECB, held at a panel on 'The Future of Financial Markets: A Changing View of Asia' at the Annual Meeting of the Asian Development Bank, Frankfurt am Main, 2 May. ECB Eurosystem. https://www.ecb.europa.eu/press/key/date/2016/html/sp160502.en.html. Accessed 4 May 2016.

Economist. 2016. 'The European Central Banks Fires Another Salvo'. 10 March. http://www.economist.com/news/business-and-finance/21694605-qe-gets-further-boost-euro-area-and-interest-rates-are-cut-further. Accessed 19 March 2016.

Eichengreen, B., R. Hausmann, and U. Panizza. 2003. 'Currency Mismatches, Debt Intolerance and Original Sin: Why They Are Not the Same and Why It Matters'. NBER Working Paper 10036. Cambridge, MA.

Elmas, B. 2010. 'Yabanci Portföy Yatirimlarinin IKMB'ye Etkisi: IMKB'de Endeks Bazli bir Calişma'. *İMKB Dergisi* 12(47): 1–18.

Eng, P. H. 1998. *Foreign Direct Investment. A Study of Malaysia's Balance of Payments Position*. Malaysia: Pelanduk Publications.

Ernst, C. 2005. 'The FDI—Employment Link in a Globalizing World: The Case of Argentina, Brazil and Mexico'. Employment Strategy Paper 17. Employment Strategy Department, ILO.

Ernst, D. 2004. 'Global Production Networks in East Asian Electronics Industry and Upgrading Perspectives in Malaysia'. In Yusuf, S., M. A. Altaf, and K. Nabeshima, eds. *Global Production Networking and Technological Change in East Asia*. World Bank and Oxford University Press: 89–158.

ERP. 2016. Economic Report of the President Together with the Annual Report of the Council of Economic Advisers. February. https://www.gpo.gov/fdsys/pkg/ERP-2016/pdf/ERP-2016.pdf. Accessed 17 March 2016.

Farla, K., D. de Crombrugghe and B. Verspagen. 2013. 'Institutions, Foreign Direct Investment, and Domestic Investment: Crowding Out or Crowding In?' UNU-Merit Working Paper 054. http://www.google.ch/url?sa=t&rct=j&q=&esrc=s&source=-web&cd=2&cad=rja&uact=8&ved=0CCgQFjAB&url=http%3A%2F%2Fwww.merit.unu.edu%2Fpublications%2Fwppdf%2F2013%2Fwp2013-054.pdf&ei=BGSEVKGG-GoGtUdWYgPAP&usg= AFQjCNEeqQ7oUajo78iC-k77CbDMNQcyWA&bvm=bv.80642063,d.d24. Accessed 12 September 2015.

Farooki, M. Z. and R. Kaplinsky. 2011. *The Impact of China on Global Commodity Prices*. London: Taylor and Francis.

Feldstein, M. 1994. 'The Effects of Outbound Foreign Direct Investment on the Domestic Capital Stock'. NBER Working Paper No. 4668.

Ferguson, N. 2013. 'Currency Wars Are Best Fought Quietly'. *Financial Times*, Opinion. 25 January. http://www.ft.com/intl/cms/s/0/cdc80aa0-6638-11e2-b967-00144feab49a.html#axzz2PDTzy8AU. Accessed 23 March 2013.

Fiechter, J., İ. Ötker-Robe, A. Ilyina, M. Hsu, A. Santos, and J. Surti. 2011. 'Subsidiaries or Branches: Does One Size Fit All?' Staff Discussion Note SDN 11/4, International Monetary Fund. Washington, DC, March.

Filimonov, V., D. Bicchetti, N. Maystre, and D. Sornette. 2013. 'Quantification of the High Level of Endogeneity and of Structural Regime Shifts in Commodity Markets'. UNCTAD Discussion Paper No 212. November.

Financial Times. 2012. 'Waiting for Growth. Bank of England Must Get Its Money into the Economy'. *Financial Times*, Editorial. 12 August.

Finger, R. 2016. 'Europe, Japan and the Fallacy of Negative Interest rates'. *Huffington Post Politics*. 11 March. http://www.huffingtonpost.com/richard-finger/europe-japan-and-the-fall_b_9434968.html. Accessed 3 April 2016.

Fitch Ratings. 2014. 'Bank Borrowing Drives Rise in Turkey's External Debt'. *Fitchwire*. 3 September. https://www.fitchratings.com/gws/en/fitchwire/fitchwirearticle/Bank-Borrowing-Drives?pr_id=863194. Accessed 5 September 2014.

Fitoussi, J-P. 2006. 'Diverging Tendencies of Competitiveness'. Briefing Paper 1. European Parliament Committee for Economic and Monetary Affairs. October.

Fontevecchia, A. 2013. 'Janet Yellen: No Equity Bubble, No Real Estate Bubble, and No QE Taper Yet'. *Forbes*. 14 November. http://www.forbes.com/sites/afontevecchia/2013/11/14/janet-yellen-no-equity-bubble-no-real-estate-bubble-and-no-qe-tapering-yet/. Accessed 23 November.

Forte, R. and R. Moura. 2013. 'The Effects of Foreign Direct Investment on the Host Country's Economic Growth: Theory and Empirical Evidence'. *The Singapore Economic Review* 58(3).

Foster, J. B. and Magdoff, F. 2009. *The Great Financial Crisis: Causes and Consequences*. New York: Monthly Review Press.

Fottrell, Q. 2015. 'Underwater American Homeowners Still Drowning in Mortgage Debt'. Market Watch. June 12. http://www.marketwatch.com/story/american-home-owners-still-drowning-in-mortgage-debt-2015-06-12. Accessed 8 January 2016.

Fox News. 2015. 'Fox News Poll: Voters Believe White House Incompetent, US Still in Recession and ISIS Has Moved Next Door'. 15 May. http://www.foxnews.com/politics/2015/05/15/fox-news-poll-voters-believe-white-house-incompetent-us-still-in-recession-and.html. Accessed 4 January 2016.

Frankel, J. A. 2006. 'The Effect of Monetary Policy on Real Commodity Prices'. NBER Working Paper 12713. December.

FRBNY (Federal Reserve Bank of New York). 2013. Foreign Portfolio Holdings of U.S. Securities as of June 30, 2012. Department of Treasury, New York, NY, April. http://www.google.ch/url?sa=t&rct=j&q=&esrc=s&source=web&cd=3&ved=0CCkQFjA-C&url=http%3A%2F%2Fwww.treasury.gov%2Fticdata%2FPublish%2Fshla2012r.pdf&ei=6gWPU_XiE8iv7QbVroHYCw&usg=AFQjCNGIgxuTDyKI3K5tlWRkG1SpN-p7g-w. Accessed 15 May 2014.

FRED. 2016. Federal Reserve Bank of St. Louis Economic Research. Home Ownership Rate for the United States. https://research.stlouisfed.org/fred2/series/RHORUSQ156N. Accessed 18 April 2016.

Freeman, R. B. 2010. 'What Really Ails Europe (and America): The Doubling of the Global Workforce'. *The Globalist*. March 5. http://www.theglobalist.com/what-really-ails-europe-and-america-the-doubling-of-the-global-workforce/. Accessed 18 January 2016.

Fried, D. B. 2013. 'An Empirical Analysis of the Currency Composition of Sovereign Borrowing'. Department of Economics, University of Virginia. 9 April.

FSB (Financial Stability Board). 2011. 'Key Attributes of Effective Resolution Regimes for Financial Institutions'. Basel, October. http://www.financialstabilityboard.org/publications/r_111104cc.pdf. Accessed 16 March 2014.

FSB. 2012. 'Recovery and Resolution Planning: Making the Key Attributes Requirements Operational'. Basel, November. http://www.financialstabilityboard.org/publications/r_121102.htm. Accessed 16 March 2014.

FSB. 2014. 'Adequacy of Loss-absorbing Capacity of Global Systemically Important Banks in Resolution'. Consultative Document, 10 November. http://www.financialstabilityboard.org/2014/11/adequacy-of-loss-absorbing-capacity-of-global-systemically-important-banks-in-resolution/. Accessed 3 December 2014.

Furceri, D. and P. Loungani. 2015. 'Capital Account Liberalization and Inequality'. IMF Working Paper 15/243. Washington, DC, November.

Gallagher, K. 2012. 'Mission Creep: International Investment Agreements and Sovereign Debt Restructuring'. IISD Investment Treaty News. January 12. http://www.iisd.org/itn/2012/01/12/mission-creep-international-investment-agreements-and-sovereign-debt-restructuring-3/. Accessed 13 June 2015.

García-Herrero, A. and D. Santabárbara. 2007. 'Does China Have an Impact on Foreign Direct Investment to Latin America?' 27 April. http://www.bis.org/search/?q=%22DOES+CHINA+HAVE+AN+IMPACT+ON+FOREIGN+DIRECT+INVESTMENT+TO+LATIN+AMERICA%3F%22&category=–&lang=–&mp=all&sb=0&adv=. Accessed 2 July 2015.

Garcia-Herrero, A., L. Xia, and C. Casanova. 2015. 'China's Outbound Foreign Direct Investment: How Much Goes Where After Round-tripping and Offshoring?' BBVA Working Paper 15/17. June. https://www.bbvaresearch.com/en/category/document-type/working-paper/. Accessed 2 July 2015.

Giles, C. 2013. 'IMF Changes Tune on Global Economic Assessment'. *Financial Times*. September 4.

Giles, C. 2016. 'Kuroda Calls for China to Tighten Capital Controls'. *Financial Times*. 23 January.

Giroud, A. 2012. 'Mind the Gap: How Linkages Strengthen Understanding of Spillovers'. *The European Journal of Development Research* 24(1): 20–5.

Gissurarson, H. H. 2016. 'The Rise, Fall and Rise of Iceland: Lessons for Small Countries'. Institute for Direct Democracy. 3 March. http://iddeurope.org/?p=880. Accessed 18 April 2016.

Goedegebuure, R. V. 2006. 'The Effects of Outward Foreign Direct Investment on Domestic Investment'. *Investment Management and Financial Innovations* 3(1): 9–22.

Goodhart, C., P. Pardeshi, and M. Pradhan. 2015. 'Workers vs Pensioners: The Battle of Our Time'. *Prospects*. November 12. http://www.prospectmagazine.co.uk/features/workers-vs-pensioners-the-battle-of-our-time. Accessed 3 April 2016.

Goodhart, C.A.E. and P. Erfurth. 2014. 'Monetary Policy and Long-term Trends'. Vox. 3 November. http://www.voxeu.org/article/monetary-policy-and-long-term-trends. Accessed 8 October 2015.

Griffith, J. 2012. 'Bipartisan Bill Pushes Shared Appreciation Principal Reductions'. Centre for American Progress. June 12. www.americanprogress.org/issues/housing/news/2012/06/12/11806/bipartisan-bill-pushes-shared-appreciation-principal-reductions/. Accessed 12 June 2013.

Gros, D. 2011. 'External versus Domestic Debt in the Euro Crisis'. 24 May. www.voxeu.org/article/external-versus-domestic-debt-euro-crisis. Accessed 2 March 2013.

Gruić, B. and P. Wooldridge. 2012. 'Enhancements to the BIS Debt Securities Statistics'. *BIS Quarterly Review* (December): 63–76.

Guscina, A., G. Pedras, and G. Presciuttini. 2014. 'First-Time International Bond Issuance—New Opportunities and Emerging Risks'. Working Paper No. 14/127, International Monetary Fund. Washington, DC, July.

Hake, M., F. López-Vicente, and L. Molina. 2014. 'Do the Drivers of Loan Dollarization Differ between CESEE and Latin America? A Meta-Analysis'. Documentos de Trabajo 1406, Banco de España. April.

Hale, G. B., P. Jones, and M. M. Spiegel. 2014. 'Home Currency Issuance in Global Debt Markets'. Economic Letter No. 24, Federal Reserve Bank of San Francisco. San Francisco, CA, August.

Hart-Landsberg, M. 2013. 'Lessons from Iceland. Capitalism, Crisis, and Resistance'. *New Left Review* 65(05) (October).

Hausmann, R. and E. Fernández-Arias. 2000. 'Foreign Direct Investment: Good Cholesterol?' Inter-American Development Bank Working Paper 417. Washington, DC.

Haworth, H. 2012. 'CAC'ed!: Implications of the Introduction of Collective Action Clauses into Eurozone Debt'. Securities Research and Analytics, Credit Suisse. 1 November. https://www.google.com.tr/url?sa=t&rct=j&q=&esrc=s&source=web&cd=3&cad=rja&uact=8&ved=0CC4QFjAC&url=https%3A%2F%2Fresearch-and-analytics.csfb.com%2FdocView%3Fdocid%3DkRuwxD&ei=WoH9U5GkDojPaPn7gvAG&usg=AFQjCNG-WodvL86G4jIuYLLxW1WL6gZpdTg&bvm=bv.74035653,d.d2s. Accessed 12 March 2013.

Hay, G. and N. Unmack. 2012. 'Breaking Views: Spain's Bank Rescue Is Part Bail-in, Part Bail-out'. *Reuters*. November 29. http://in.reuters.com/article/2012/11/29/idINL4N0991X420121129. Accessed 12 March 2013.

He, D. and R. N. McCauley. 2013. 'Transmitting Global Liquidity to East Asia: Policy Rates, Bond Yields, Currencies and Dollar Credit'. BIS Working Paper 431. Basel, October.

Hein, E. 2013. 'Finance-dominated Capitalism and Redistribution of Income: A Kaleckian Perspective'. Levy Economics Institute of Bard College Working Paper 746. January. http://www.levyinstitute.org/pubs/wp_746.pdf. Accessed 8 November 2015.

Hein, E. 2015. 'Secular Stagnation or Stagnation Policy? Steindl after Summers'. Levy Economics Institute of Bard College Working Paper 846. October. http://www.levyinstitute.org/pubs/wp_846.pdf. Accessed 8 November 2015.

Herndon, T., M. Ash and R. Pollin. 2013. 'Does High Public Debt Consistently Stifle Economic Growth? A Critique of Reinhart and Rogoff'. PERI Working Paper 322. University of Massachusetts, Amherst, April 15.

Higgins, A. 2013. 'Cyprus Bank's Bailout Hands Ownership to Russian Plutocrats'. *New York Times*. 21 August.

Hofmann, C. 2014. 'Sovereign-Debt Restructuring in Europe under the New Model Collective Action Clauses'. *Texas International Law Journal* 49: 383–441.

Hoggarth, G. and V. Saporta. 2001. 'Costs of Banking System Instability: Some Empirical Evidence'. *Bank of England Financial Stability Review*, June: 148–65.

ICMA (International Capital Market Association). 2014. Sovereign Debt Information: Standard Collective Action and Pari Passu Clauses for the Terms and Conditions of Sovereign Notes. August. http://www.icmagroup.org/resources/Sovereign-Debt-Information/. Accessed 12 September 2014.

IDB (Inter-American Development Bank). 2008. 'All That Glitters May Not Be Gold: Assessing Latin America's Recent Macroeconomic Performance'. Research Department, April.

IDB. 2014. 'Global Recovery and Monetary Normalization: Escaping a Chronicle Foretold?' *2014 Latin American and Caribbean Macroeconomic Report*. March.

Idzelis, C. and C. Torres. 2014. 'Fed Bubble Bursts in $550 Billion of Energy Debt: Credit Markets'. Bloomberg Business. December 11. http://www.bloomberg.com/news/articles/2014-12-11/fed-bubble-bursts-in-550-billion-of-energy-debt-credit-markets. Accessed 3 December 2015.

IIF (Institute of International Finance) 2014. Capital Flows to Emerging Market Economies, May.

IIF. 2015. Capital Flows to Emerging Market Economies, January.

IIF. 2016. Capital Flows to Emerging Market Economies, April.

ILO. 2011. *World of Work Report 2011—Making Markets Work for Jobs*. Geneva. www.ilo.org/wcmsp5/groups/public/—dgreports/—dcomm/—publ/documents/publication/wcms_166021.pdf. Accessed 8 March 2016.

ILO. 2015. *Global Wage Report 2014/15. Wages and Income Inequality*. Geneva. http://www.ilo.org/global/publications/books/WCMS_324678/lang–en/index.htm. Accessed 8 March 2016.

ILO/OECD. 2015. 'The Labour Share in G20 Economies'. Report Prepared for the G20 Employment Working Group, Antalya, Turkey, 26–7 February. www.oecd.org/g20/topics/employment-and-social-policy/The-Labour-Share-in-G20-Economies.pdf. Accessed 8 March 2016.

IMF. 1999. 'Involving the Private Sector in Forestalling and Resolving Financial Crises'. Washington, DC, April.

IMF. 2000a. 'Involving the Private Sector in the Resolution of Financial Crises—Standstills—Preliminary Considerations'. Washington, DC, September.

IMF. 2000b. 'IMF Executive Board Discusses Involving the Private Sector in the Resolution of Financial Crises'. Public Information Notice 00/80. Washington, DC.

IMF. 2002. 'Sovereign Debt Restructuring Mechanism—Further Considerations'. Washington, DC, August.

IMF. 2003a. 'Proposals for a Sovereign Debt Restructuring Mechanism (SDRM): A Factsheet'. Washington, DC, January.

IMF. 2003b. 'Sustainability Assessments—Review of Application and Methodological Refinements'. Washington, DC, June.

IMF. 2007. *Regional Economic Outlook: Western Hemisphere*. Washington, DC, November.

IMF. 2009. Balance of Payments and the International Investment Position Manual (BPM6). Washington, DC.

IMF. 2011. 'Assessing Reserve Adequacy'. Washington, DC, February.

IMF. 2012. 'The Liberalization and Management of Capital Flows: An Institutional View'. Washington, DC, November.

IMF. 2013a. World Economic and Financial Surveys. Fiscal Monitor. Washington, DC, April.

IMF. 2013b. 'Guidance Note for the Liberalization and Management of Capital Flows'. Washington, DC, 25 April.

IMF. 2013c. 'Sovereign Debt Restructuring—Recent Developments and Implications for the Fund's Legal and Policy Framework'. Washington, DC, 26 April.

IMF. 2013d. 'Greece: Ex Post Evaluation of Exceptional Access under the 2010 Stand-By Arrangement'. Country Report No. 13/156. Washington, DC, June.

IMF. 2013e. 'Assessing Reserve Adequacy—Further Considerations'. Policy Paper. Washington, DC, November.

IMF. 2014a. 'The Fund's Lending Framework and Sovereign Debt—Preliminary Considerations'. Washington, DC, June.

IMF. 2014b. 'Strengthening the Contractual Framework to Address Collective Action Problems in Sovereign Debt Restructuring'. Washington, DC, October.

IMF GFSR. 2012. *Global Financial Stability Report*. October. Washington, DC.

IMF GFSR. 2013a. *Global Financial Stability Report*. April. Washington, DC.

IMF GFSR. 2013b. *Global Financial Stability Report*. October. Washington, DC.

IMF GFSR. 2014. *Global Financial Stability Report*. April. Washington, DC.

IMF GFSR. 2015. *Global Financial Stability Report*. December. Washington, DC.

IMF WEO. 2007. *World Economic Outlook*. April. Washington, DC.

IMF WEO. 2008. *World Economic Outlook*. April. Washington, DC.

IMF WEO. 2011. *World Economic Outlook*. April. Washington, DC.

IMF WEO. 2012. *World Economic Outlook*. October. Washington, DC.

IMF WEO. 2013a. *World Economic Outlook*. April. Washington, DC.

IMF WEO. 2013b. *World Economic Outlook*. October. Washington, DC.

IMF WEO. 2014a. *World Economic Outlook*. April. Washington, DC.

IMF WEO. 2014b. *World Economic Outlook*. October. Washington, DC.

IMF WEO. 2015. *World Economic Outlook*. April. Washington, DC.

IMF WEO. 2016. *World Economic Outlook*. April. Washington, DC.

Jansen, K. 1995. 'The Macroeconomic Effects of Foreign Direct Investment: The Case of Thailand'. *World Development* 2(2).

Jaramillo, L. and A. Weber. 2013. 'Global Spillovers into Domestic Bond Markets in Emerging Market Economies'. IMF Working Paper No.13/264. Washington, DC, December.

Jaumotte, F. and C. O. Buitron. 2015. 'Inequality and Labor Market Institutions'. IMF Staff Discussion Note 15/14. Washington, DC.

Jeon, B. M. and J. Wu. 2013. 'Foreign Banks, Monetary Policy, and Crises: Evidence from Bank-Level Panel Data in Asia'. In Jeon, B. M. and M. P. Olivero, eds. *Global*

Banking, Financial Markets and Crises. International Finance Review series, vol. 14. Bingley, UK: Emerald Group Publishing Ltd, 91–113.

Jeon, B. M. and J. Wu. 2014. 'The Role of Foreign Banks in Monetary Policy Transmission: Evidence from Asia during the Crisis of 2008–9'. Working Paper 01/2014, Hong Kong Institute for Monetary Research. January. http://www.hkimr.org/uploads/publication/372/wp-no-01_2014-final-.pdf. Accessed 11 August 2014.

Jiménez, J. P. and J. C. Gómez-Sabaini. 2009. 'The Role of Tax Policy in the Context of the Global Crisis: Consequences and Prospects'. ECLAC LC/L.3037. Economic Commission for Latin America and the Caribbean, Montevideo, 19–20 May.

Johannesen, N. and J. Pirttilä. 2016. 'Capital Flight and Development. An Overview of Concepts, Methods, and Data Sources'. WIDER Working Paper 2016/95. August.

Jones, C. 2016. 'ECB Cash Giveaway to Banks Hit by Scepticism'. *Financial Times*. 18 March.

J.P. Morgan. 2013. 'Latin America: Financial Integration'. American Chamber of Commerce, Washington, D.C. Emerging Markets Research. 30 September. http://www.google.com.tr/url?sa=t&rct=j&q=&esrc=s&source=web&cd=1&cad=rja&uact=8&ved=0CBoQFjAA&url=http%3A%2F%2Fwww.aaccla.org%2Ffiles%2F2010%2F12%2FAmCham_Sep_2013_Latam_Werning.pdf&ei=SJ2-U53NKIHB7AaQ8IHICQ&usg=AFQjCNGXVuDr3Bb0fLgsLoKQcEiuDXGiuw&bvm=bv.70138588,d.ZGU. Accessed 15 March 2014.

Kaletsky, A. 2012a. 'How About Quantitative Easing for the People?' *Reuters*. 1 August. http://blogs.reuters.com/anatole-kaletsky/2012/08/01/how-about-quantitative-easing-for-the-people/. Accessed 2 March 2016.

Kaletsky, A. 2012b. 'Suddenly, Quantitative Easing for the People Seems Possible'. *Reuters*. 9 August. http://blogs.reuters.com/anatole-kaletsky/2012/08/09/suddenly-quantitative-easing-for-the-people-seems-possible/. Accessed 2 March 2016.

Keen, S. 2014. 'Secular Stagnation and Endogenous Money'. *Real-world Economics Review* Issue 66 (13 January). https://rwer.wordpress.com/comments-on-rwer-issue-no-66/secular-stagnation-and-endogenous-money/. Accessed 12 June 2015.

Keen, S. 2015. 'Bernanke-Summers Debate II: Savings Glut, Investment Shortfall, or Monty Python?' Real World Economics Review Blog. 9 April. https://rwer.wordpress.com/2015/04/09/bernanke-summers-debate-ii-savings-glut-investment-shortfall-or-monty-python/. Accessed 14 January 2016.

Keen, S. 2016a. 'Hey Joe, Banks Can't Lend Out Reserves'. Real-World Economy Review Blog. 22 February. https://rwer.wordpress.com/2016/02/18/hey-joe-banks-cant-lend-out-reserves-2/. Accessed 14 April 2016.

Keen, S. 2016b. 'Tilting at Windmills: The Faustian Folly of Quantitative Easing'. Real-World Economy Review Blog. 22 February. https://rwer.wordpress.com/2016/02/22/tilting-at-windmills-the-faustian-folly-of-quantitative-easing/#more-22677. Accessed 14 April 2016.

Keynes, J.M. 1971. 'Public Finance and Changes in the Value of Money'. In Keynes, J.M. *A Tract on Monetary Reform, The Collective Writings of John Maynard Keynes,* vol. IV, chap. 2. Cambridge: Cambridge University Press.

Koopman, R., W. Powers, Z. Wang, and S.-J. Wei. 2010. 'Give Credit Where Credit is Due: Tracing Value-Added in Global Production Chains'. NBER Working Paper 16426. September.

Koopman, R., Z. Wang, and S-J. Wei. 2012. 'Estimating Domestic Content in Exports When Processing Trade Is Pervasive'. *Journal of Development Economics* 99(1): 178–89.

Kozul-Wright, Richard and Robert Rowthorn, eds. 1998. *Transnational Corporations and the Global Economy*. Helsinki: UNU/WIDER.

Krueger, A. O. 2001. 'International Financial Architecture for 2002: A New Approach to Sovereign Debt Restructuring'. Address given at the National Economists' Club Annual Members' Dinner, American Enterprise Institute, Washington, DC, 26 November.

Krugman, P. 2000. 'Fire-Sale FDI'. In Edwards, S., ed. *Capital Flows and the Emerging Economies: Theory, Evidence, and Controversies*. University of Chicago Press: 43–59.

Krugman, P. 2013a. 'Bubbles, Regulation, and Secular Stagnation'. *The New York Times*. September 25. http://krugman.blogs.nytimes.com/2013/09/25/bubbles-regulation-and-secular-stagnation/?_r=0. Accessed 18 November 2013.

Krugman, P. 2013b. 'Secular Stagnation, Coalmines, Bubbles, and Larry Summers'. *The New York Times*, Opinion Pages. November 16. http://krugman.blogs.nytimes.com/2013/11/16/secular-stagnation-coalmines-bubbles-and-larry-summers/?_r=0#more-35994. Accessed 18 November 2013.

Krugman, P. 2015a. 'The Fiscal Future I and II'. *The New York Times*. 6–7 April. Reprinted in Other News. http://www.other-news.info/2015/04/the-fiscal-future-i-and-ii/. Accessed 18 January 2016.

Krugman, P. 2015b. 'Liquidity Traps, Temporary and Permanent'. *The New York Times*. November 2. http://krugman.blogs.nytimes.com/2015/11/02/liquidity-traps-temporary-and-permanent/. Accessed 18 January 2016.

Kumar, N. 2002. *Globalization and the Quality of Foreign Direct Investment*. New Delhi: Oxford University Press.

Kumar, N. 2005. 'Performance Requirements as Tools of Development Policy: Lessons from Developed and Developing Countries'. In Gallagher, K., ed. *Putting Development First. The Importance of Policy Space in the WTO and International Financial Institutions*. London: Zed Books.

Kutan, A., E. Ozsoz and E. Rengifo. 2012. 'Dynamics of Foreign Currency Lending in Turkey'. MPRA Paper No. 36214, Munich Personal RePEc Archive. January. http://mpra.ub.uni-muenchen.de/36214/. Accessed 12 January 2014.

Kuttner, R. 2013. *Debtors' Prison: The Politics of Austerity versus Possibility*. New York: Alfred A. Knopf.

Lambert, F. and K. Ueda. 2014. 'The Effects of Unconventional Monetary Policies on Bank Soundness'. IMF Working Paper No. 14/152. Washington, DC, August.

Lane, P. and G. Milesi-Ferretti. 2007. 'The External Wealth of Nations Mark II: Revised and Extended Estimates of Foreign Assets and Liabilities: 1970–2004'. *Journal of International Economics* 73(2): 223–50.

Lane, P. and G. Milesi-Ferretti. 2014. 'Global Imbalances and External Adjustment after the Crisis'. IMF Working Paper No. 14/151. Washington, DC, August.

Lapavitsas, C., A. Kaltenbrunner, G. Lambrinidis, D. Lindo, J. Meadway, J. Michell, J. P. Painceira, E. Pires, J. Powell, A. Stenfors, and N. Teles. 2010. 'The Eurozone between Austerity and Default'. RMF Occasional Report. September. www.researchonmoneyandfinance.org. Accessed 12 January 2013.

Lautier, M., and F. Moreau. 2012. 'An Empirical Criticism of the "FDI Development" Convention'. *Revista de Economia Contemporânea*. 16(3): 393–414.

Lavoie, M. and E. Stockhammer. 2012. 'Wage-led Growth: Concept, Theories and Policies'. Conditions of Work and Employment Series 41. ILO, Geneva.

Leduc, S., K. Moran, and R. J. Vigfusson. 2016. 'The Elusive Boost from Cheap Oil'. FRBSF Economic Letter. April 18. http://www.frbsf.org/economic-research/publications/economic-letter/2016/april/elusive-boost-from-cheap-oil-consumer-spending/. Accessed 23 April 2016.

Lefeuvre, E. 2015. 'The Looming Crisis'. Seeking Alpha. 24 April. http://seekingalpha.com/article/3099526-the-looming-liquidity-crisis. Accessed 2 December 2015.

Lehmann, A. 2002. 'Foreign Direct Investment in Emerging Markets: Income, Repatriations and Financial Vulnerabilities'. IMF Working Paper 02/47. Washington, DC, March.

Leke, A., S. Lund, J. Manyika, and S. Ramaswamy. 2014. 'Lions Go Global: Deepening Africa's Ties to the United States'. McKinsey Global Institute. August. http://www.mckinsey.com/global-themes/middle-east-and-africa/lions-go-global-deepening-africas-ties-to-the-united-states. Accessed 2 March 2015.

Leong, R. 2015. 'Profits at Big U.S. Banks Soar Since Crisis: New York Fed'. *Reuters*. October 7. http://www.reuters.com/article/us-usa-banks-marketmaking-idUSKCN0S11KS20151007. Accessed 8 January 2016.

Leubsdorf, B. 2016. 'Fed Sent Record $97.7 Billion in Profits to U.S. Treasury in 2015'. *The Wall Street Journal*. January 11. http://www.wsj.com/articles/fed-sent-record-97-7-billion-in-profits-to-u-s-treasury-in-2015-1452531787. Accessed 28 January 2016.

Lim, M.-H. and J. Lim. 2012. 'Asian Initiatives at Monetary and Financial Integration: A Critical Review'. South Centre Research Paper 46. Geneva, July.

Lipsey, R. E. 1999. 'The Role of Foreign Direct Investment in International Capital Flows'. In Feldstein, M. ed. International Capital Flows. NBER, Chicago University Press: 307–31.

Lord, J. 2013. 'EM Currencies: The Fragile Five'. Morgan Stanley Research. 1 August. *https://www.morganstanley.com/institutional/research/pdf/FXPulse_20130801.pdf* Accessed 30 October 2013.

Loungani, P. and A. Razin. 2001. 'How Beneficial Is Foreign Direct Investment for Developing Countries?' *Finance and Development* 38(2) (June). IMF, Washington, DC.

Lu, F., G. Song, J. Tang, H. Zhao, and L. Liu. 2008. 'Profitability of China's Industrial Firms (1978–2006)'. *China Economic Journal* 1 (1): 1–31.

Lutz, S. and M. Kranke. 2010. 'The European Rescue of the Washington Consensus? EU and IMF Lending to Central and Eastern European Countries'. The London School of Economics and Political Science 'Europe in Question' Discussion Paper No. 22/2010. London, May.

Lynn, M. 2016. 'Draghi May Have to Throw Money Out of a Helicopter'. *The Telegraph.* 7 March.

Magdoff, F. and J.B. Foster. 2014. 'Stagnation and Financialization. The Nature of the Contradiction'. *Monthly Review* 66(01) (May).

Malik, M. A. R., C. A. Rehman, M. Ashraf, and R. Z. Abbas. 2012. 'Exploring the Link between Foreign Direct Investment, Multinational Enterprises and Spillover Effects in Developing Economies'. *International Journal of Business and Management* 7(1) (January): 230–40.

Marcus, G. 2012. 'Consider the Small Nations Caught in the Central Bank Crossfire'. *Financial Times*. May 3.

McCauley, R. N., P. McGuire, and V. Sushko. 2015. 'Dollar Credit to Emerging Market Economies'. *BIS Quarterly Review* (December): 27–41.

McCauley, R. N., C. Upper, and A. Villar. 2013. 'Emerging Market Debt Securities Issuance in Offshore Centres'. *BIS Quarterly Review* (September): 22–3.

McLeay, M., A. Radia, and R. Thomas. 2014. 'Money Creation in the Modern Economy'. *Monetary Analysis Directorate Bank of England Quarterly Bulletin* 2014/Q1.

Minsky, H. P. 1977. 'A Theory of Systemic Fragility'. In Altman, E. I. and A.W. Sametz, eds. *Financial Crises*. New York: Wiley.

Miyajima, K., M. Mohanty, and T. Chan. 2012. 'Emerging Market Local Currency Bonds: Diversification and Stability'. BIS Working Paper 391. Basel, November.

Moody's. 2014. 'Turkish Lira Depreciation Credit Negative for Majority of Rated Turkish Corporates'. Global Credit Research. Dubai, 1 April. https://www.moodys.com/research/Moodys-Turkish-Lira-depreciation-credit-negative-for-majority-of-rated–PR_296142. Accessed 12 September 2014.

Morath, E. 2016. 'Six Years Later, 93% of U.S. Counties Haven't Recovered from Recession, Study Finds'. *The Wall Street Journal*. January 12. http://blogs.wsj.com/economics/2016/01/12/six-years-later-93-of-u-s-counties-havent-recovered-from-recession-study-finds/. Accessed 18 January 2016.

Morgan Stanley. 2014. 'Has This Been a "Good" Rally for EM? What if EM Central Banks Had Tightened Policy Instead?' The Global Macro Analyst, Morgan Stanley Research. London, 18 June. http://www.google.co.uk/url?sa=t&rct=j&q=&esrc=s&source=web&cd=4&cad=rja&uact=8&ved=0CDUQFjAD&url=http%3A%2F%2Fwww.morganstanley.com%2Finstitutional%2Fresearch%2Fpdf%2FGMA_20140618.pdf&ei=ihHiU7vgDK_64QSHuoGICA&usg=AFQjCNHoPGM44h2N_RhNgCBAPoBD8mFxeQ&bvm=bv.72197243,d.bGE. Accessed 12 July 2014.

Morrissey, O. and M. Udomkerdmongkol. 2012. 'Governance, Private Investment and Foreign Direct Investment in Developing Countries'. *World Development* 40(3):437–45.

Mutenyo, J., E. Asmah, and A. Kalio. 2010. 'Does Foreign Direct investment Crowd-out Domestic Private Investment in sub-Saharan Africa?' *The African Finance Journal* 12(1): 27–52.

Münchau, W. 2016. 'The European Central Bank Has Lost the Plot on Inflation'. *Financial Times*. 13 March.

Nanda, N. 2009. 'Growth Effects of FDI: Is Greenfield Greener?' *Perspectives on Global Development and Technology* 8(1): 26–47.

Narula, R. and N. Driffield. 2012. 'Does FDI Cause Development? The Ambiguity of the Evidence and Why It Matters'. *The European Journal of Development Research* 24(1): 1–7.

Naudé, W., A. Szirmai, and A. Lavopa. 2013. 'Industrialization Lessons from BRICS: A Comparative Analysis'. IZA Discussion Paper 7543. August. http://ftp.iza.org/dp7543.pdf. Accessed 5 February 2017.

Nikièma, S. H. 2014. 'Performance Requirements in Investment Treaties'. International Institute for Sustainable Development, Best Practice Series. December. http://www.iisd.org/library/best-practices-series-performance-requirements-investment-treaties. Accessed 3 April 2015.

O'Neill, J. 2001. 'Building Better Global Economic BRICs'. Global Economics Paper No. 66, Goldman, Sachs & Co. London. 30 November. http://www.goldmansachs.com/china/ideas/brics/brics-at-8/building-better-doc.pdf. Accessed 12 August 2014.

OECD. 2008. Benchmark Definition of Foreign Direct Investment. Fourth Edition. Paris.

OECD. 2015. *Economic Outlook*, Volume 2015, Issue 1. Paris.

OECD. 2016. Global Economic Outlook and Interim Economic Outlook. 18 February.

Onaran, O. and E. Stockhammer. 2016. 'The Policies for Wage-led Growth in Europe'. 22 February. http://www.feps-europe.eu/en/publications/details/364. Accessed 23 March 2016.

Oprita, A. 2013. 'IMF Warns on Emerging Markets Corporate Debt'. *Emerging Markets*. 17 April. http://www.emergingmarkets.org/Article/3192541/IMF-warns-on-emerging-markets-corporate-debt.html. Accessed 4 May 2013.

Osborne, H. and A. Monaghan. 2014. 'Bank of England Governor Warns of a Bubble as UK House Prices Rise 10.5%'. *The Guardian*. 15 July. http://www.theguardian.com/money/2014/jul/15/ons-uk-house-prices-may-london/print. Accessed 24 July 2014.

Öncü, T. S. 2015. 'People's Quantitative Easing. A Jeremy Corbyn Proposal'. *Economic and Political Weekly*, Vol L. No. 41 (October).

Palley, T. I. 2007. 'Financialization: What It Is and Why It Matters'. Working Paper 525. The Levy Economics Institute of Bard College. December. www.levyinstitute.org/pubs/wp_525.pdf. Accessed 11 January 2016.

Palley, T. I. 2012. *From Financial Crisis to Stagnation: The Destruction of Shared Prosperity and the Role of Economics*. Cambridge University Press. February.

Palley, T. I. 2013. Europe's Crisis without End: The Consequences of Neoliberal Run Amok. Macroeconomic Policy Institute (IMK) Working Paper, 111. March. Dusseldorf, Germany.

Palley, T. I. 2014. 'Explaining Stagnation: Why It Matters'. *Monthly Review Zine*.February 27. http://mrzine.monthlyreview.org/2014/palley270214.html. Accessed 15 March 2014.

Palley, T. I. 2016. 'Zero Lower Bound (ZLB) Economics: The Fallacy of New Keynesian Explanations of Stagnation'. Macroeconomic Policy Institute Working Paper 164. February. http://www.boeckler.de/pdf/p_imk_wp_164_2016.pdf. Accessed 28 April 2016.

Persaud, A. 2013. 'The Mirage of Bank "Bail-ins"'. Live Mint. 17 November. http://www.livemint.com/Opinion/fygDP8UCr86GmuT7Tw8GvI/Avinash-Persaud–The-mirage-of-bank-bailins.html. Accessed 25 November 2013.

Piketty, T., E. Saez, and S. Stantcheva. 2011. 'Taxing the 1%: Why the Top Tax Rate Could Be Over 80%'. Vox. 8 December. http://www.voxeu.org/article/taxing-1-why-top-tax-rate-could-be-over-80. Accessed 2 December 2013.

Pinto, L. 2014. 'Offshore Corporate Debt Raises Concern over Exposure Risks'. *International Valor*. São Paulo, 19 March. http://www.valor.com.br/international/news/

3484532/offshore-corporate-debt-raises-concern-over-exposure-risks#ixzz2wtUSe1Ak. Accessed 24 March 2014.

Pistor, K. 2012. 'Governing Interdependent Financial Systems: Lessons from the Vienna Initiative'. *Journal of Globalization and Development* 2(2): 1–25.

Polychronopoulos, A. and J. Binstock. 2013. 'An Emerging Asset Class: The Case for Emerging Markets Local Currency Debt'. White Paper, Research Affiliates. Newport Beach, CA, July. http://www.researchaffiliates.com/Production%20content%20library/2013_EM_Local_Currency.pdf. Accessed 8 April 2014.

Ponomarenko, A., A. Solovyeva, and E. Vasilieva. 2011. 'Financial Dollarization in Russia: Causes and Consequences'. BOFIT Discussion Paper 36/2011, Bank of Finland. Helsinki.

Pradhan, M., R. Balakrishnan, R. Baqir, G. Heenan, S. Nowak, C. Oner, and S. Panth. 2011. 'Policy Responses to Capital Flows in Emerging Markets'. Staff Discussion Note SDN/11/10, International Monetary Fund. Washington, DC, April.

Property Wire. 2014a. 'Real Estate Market in Turkey Expected to Be Healthy in 2015'. 3 December. http://www.propertywire.com/news/europe/turkey-real-estate-outlook-2/. Accessed 5 September 2015.

Property Wire. 2014b. 'International Demand for Prime Central London Property Remains Strong'. 5 December. http://www.propertywire.com/news/europe/london-prime-property-outlook-201412059901.html. Accessed 5 September 2015.

Psalida, L. E. and T. Sun. 2009. 'Spillovers to Emerging Equity Markets: An Econometric Assessment'. IMF Working Paper No. 09/111. Washington, DC, May.

Raffer, K. 1990. 'Applying Chapter 9 Insolvency to International Debts: An Economically Efficient Solution with a Human Face'. *World Development* 18(2): 311–13.

Rannenberg, A., C. Schoder, and J. Strasky. 2015. 'The Macroeconomic Effects of the Euro Area's Fiscal Consolidation 2011–2013: A Simulation-based Approach'. Research Technical Paper 03/RT/2015, Central Bank of Ireland.

Rasiah, R. 2005. 'Trade-related Investment Liberalization under the WTO: The Malaysian Experience'. *Global Economic Review* 43(4): 453–71.

Reinhart, C. 2016. 'The Post-Crisis Economy's Long Debt Hangover'. Project Syndicate. April 21. https://www.project-syndicate.org/print/debt-restructuring-needed-as-policy-option-by-carmen-reinhart-2016-04. Accessed 28 April 2016.

Reinhart, C. M. and K. S. Rogoff. 2010. 'Growth in a Time of Debt'. NBER Working Paper 15639.

Reinhart, C. M. and K. S. Rogoff. 2013. 'Financial and Sovereign Debt Crises: Some Lessons Learned and Those Forgotten'. IMF Working Paper 13/266. Washington, DC, December.

Reisen, H. 1998. 'Sustainable and Excessive Current Account Deficits'. Working Paper No. 132, OECD Development Centre. Paris, February.

Reisen, H. 2016. 'Lies, Damned Lies, and FDI Statistics'. *Shifting Wealth*. 30 March. http://shiftingwealth.blogspot.com.tr/2016/03/lies-damned-lies-and-fdi-statistics.html. Accessed 15 April 2016.

Reuters. 2012. 'IMF Chief Economist Says Crisis Will Last a Decade'. October 3. www.reuters.com/ assets/print?aid=USL6E8L34VH20121003. Accessed 6 October 2012.

Reuters. 2013. 'Too Few European Banks Have Been Wound Down—EBA's Enria'. 18 November. http://uk.reuters.com/article/2013/11/18/uk-europe-banks-idUKBRE9AH05X20131118. Accessed 19 November 2013.

Rogoff, K. 2015. 'Oil Prices and Global Growth'. Project Syndicate. December 14. https://www.project-syndicate.org/print/oil-prices-global-growth-by-kenneth-rogoff-2015-12. Accessed 3 January 2016.

Roubini, N. 2015. 'The Liquidity Time Bomb'. Project Syndicate. 31 May. https://www.project-syndicate.org/commentary/liquidity-market-volatility-flash-crash-by-nouriel-roubini-2015-05?barrier=true. Accessed 11 December 2015.

Roubini, N. and B. Setser. 2004. *Bailouts or Bail-ins? Responding to Financial Crises in Emerging Markets*. Washington, DC: Institute for International Economics.

Rovnick, N. 2013. 'Most Foreign Investment in BRICs Isn't Foreign At All—It's Tycoons Using Tax Havens'. *Quartz* (March 26). http://qz.com/#706493/alibabas-jack-ma-the-problem-with-counterfeits-is-theyre-better-quality-than-authentic-luxury-goods/. Accessed 12 May 2015.

Saez, E. 2015. 'Striking it Richer: The Evolution of Top Incomes in the United States' (updated with 2014 preliminary estimates). UC Berkeley, June 25. https://eml.berkeley.edu/~saez/saez-UStopincomes-2014.pdf. Accessed 15 March 2016.

SAFE (State Administration of Foreign Exchange). 2015. China's Balance of Payments Report 2014. http://www.safe.gov.cn/wps/portal/english/Data/BOP. Accessed 15 January 2016.

Saleena, N. J. 2013. 'Impact of FDI on Services Export: Evidence from India'. *Journal of Business Management & Social Sciences Research* 2(11): 34–8.

Sampath, G. 2016. 'The Hidden Wealth of Nations'. *The Hindu*. January 21. http://www.thehindu.com/opinion/lead/black-money-the-hidden-wealth-of-nations/article8130657.ece. Accessed 8 March 2015.

Sandbu, M. 2016. 'Beyond Minimum. Martin Sandbu's Free Lunch'. *Financial Times*. April 4. http://www.ft.com/intl/martin-sandbu-free-lunch. Accessed 4 April 2016.

Sarma, M. and A. Prashad. 2014. 'Do Foreign Banks in India Indulge in Cream Skimming?' Discussion Paper 14-01, CITD, School of International Studies, JNU. January. Delhi. http://www.jnu.ac.in/SIS/CITD/DiscussionPapers/DP01_2014.pdf. Accessed 12 March 2014.

Sarode, S. 2012. 'Effects of FDI on Capital Account and GDP: Empirical Evidence from India'. *International Journal of Business and Management* 7(8): 102–7.

Sastry, P. and D. Wessel. 2015. 'The Hutchins Center Explains: Quantitative Easing'. Brookings. 21 January. http://www.brookings.edu/blogs/up-front/posts/2015/01/21-how-does-qe-work-whats-it-accomplish-wessel. Accessed 5 June 2015.

Seguchi, M. 2012. 'Foreign Ownership of Japanese Stocks Drops'. *Wall Street Journal Online*. 20 June. http://online.wsj.com/news/articles/SB10001424052702304898704577478261427256918. Accessed 12 May 2014.

Sharf, S. 2015. 'Fed Sending $98.7 Billion of 2014 Profits to U.S. Treasury'. *Forbes*. 9 January. http://www.forbes.com/sites/samanthasharf/2015/01/09/fed-sending-98-7-billion-of-2014-profits-to-u-s-treasury/#328c12d22fe0. Accessed 8 July 2015.

Singh, K. 2010. 'Financial Crisis Conducive to Instability of Asia's Currency Markets: South Korea Imposes Currency Controls'. Global Research. 23 June. http://www.globalresearch.ca/financial-crisis-conducive-to-instability-of-asia-s-currency-markets-south-korea-imposes-currency-controls/19857. Accessed 25 June 2010.

Sinn, H-W. 2011. 'Germany's Capital Exports under the Euro'. Vox. 2 August. www.voxeu.org/article/germany-s-capital-exports-under-euro. Accessed 24 September 2012.

Snyder, M. 2016. 'Financial Crisis 2016: High Yield Debt Tells Us That Just About Everything Is About to Collapse'. Right Side News. 15 February. http://www.rightsidenews.com/us/economics/financial-crisis-2016-high-yield-debt-tells-us-just-everything-collapse/. Accessed 24 March 2016.

Sobrun, J. and P. Turner. 2015. 'Bond Markets and Monetary Policy Dilemmas for the Emerging Markets'. BIS Working Paper 508. Basel, August.

Stein, H. 2010. 'Financial Liberalization, Institutional Transformation and Credit Allocation in Developing Countries: The World Bank and the Internationalisation of Banking'. *Cambridge Journal of Economics* 34(2): 257–73.

Stein, J. C. 2013. 'Overheating in Credit Markets: Origins, Measurement, and Policy Responses'. Remarks at the research symposium sponsored by the Federal Reserve Bank of St. Louis, St. Louis, Missouri. www.federalreserve.gov/newsevents/speech/stein20130207a.pdf. Accessed 12 October 2013.

Stiglitz, J. and H. Rashid. 2016. 'What Is Holding Back the World Economy'. Project Syndicate. February 8. http://www.project-syndicate.org/print/whats-holding-back-the-global-economy-by-joseph-e–stiglitz-and-hamid-rashid-2016-02. Accessed 2 March 2016.

Stiglitz, J. E. 2013. 'Inequality Is Holding Back the Recovery'. *The New York Times* Opinionator. 19 January. http://opinionator.blogs.nytimes.com/2013/01/19/inequality-is-holding-back-the-recovery/. Accessed 3 March 2013.

Stockhammer, E. 2009. 'Functional Income Distribution in OECD Countries'. IMK Studies 5/2009. Duesseldorf, Germany. http://www.boeckler.de/imk_6456.htm?produkt=HBS-004499&chunk=3. Accessed 4 September 2012.

Stockhammer, E. 2012. 'Why Have Wage Shares Fallen? A Panel Analysis of the Determinants of Functional Income Distribution'. Conditions of Work and Employment Series No. 35. ILO, Geneva.

Summers, L. H. 2013. 'Policy Responses to Crises'. IMF Economic Forum, Washington, DC, 8 November. http://larrysummers.com/video/. Accessed 21 November 2013.

Summers, L. H. 2014. 'U.S. Economic Prospects: Secular Stagnation, Hysteresis, and the Zero Lower Bound'. *Business Economics*, Vol. 49, No. 2: 65–73. http://larrysummers.com/category/secular-stagnation/. Accessed 4 March 2016.

Summers, L. H. 2015a. 'On Secular Stagnation: Larry Summers Responds to Ben Bernanke'. Brookings. April 1. http://www.brookings.edu/blogs/ben-bernanke/posts/2015/04/01-larry-summers-response. Accessed 4 February 2016.

Summers, L. H. 2015b. 'Where Paul Krugman and I Differ on Secular Stagnation'. *The Washington Post.* November 2. https://www.washingtonpost.com/news/wonk/wp/2015/11/02/larry-summers-where-paul-krugman-and-i-differ-on-secular-stagnation/. Accessed 4 February 2016.

Summers, L. H. 2016. 'Secular Stagnation'. http://larrysummers.com/category/secular-stagnation/. Accessed 4 February 2016.

Sumner, A., E. Rugraff, and D. Sánchez-Ancochea. 2009. Introduction. In Rugraff, E., D. Sánchez-Ancochea, and A. Sumner, eds. *Transnational Corporations and Development Policy. Critical Perspectives*. New York: Palgrave Macmillan.

Taylor Wimpey. 2014. 'Spanish Property Prices up 1.15% in Third Quarter'. Taylor Wimpey Spain Home Blog. 12 October. http://taylorwimpeyspain.com/blog/. Accessed 4 March 2015.

Teulings, C. and R. Baldwin, eds. 2014. 'Secular Stagnation: Facts, Causes, and Cures'. A VoxEU.org eBook. CEPR Press. http://www.voxeu.org/content/secular-stagnation-facts-causes-and-cures. Accessed 14 February 2016.

Thomas, A. 2014. 'Germany OKs Plan to Make Creditors Prop Up Banks'. Market Watch. 9 July. http://www.marketwatch.com/story/germany-oks-plan-to-make-creditors-prop-up-banks-2014-07-09?link=MW_home_latest_news. Accessed 15 August 2014.

Tilford, S. 2015. 'German Rebalancing: Waiting for Godot?' Centre for European Reform. March. http://www.cer.org.uk/publications/archive/policy-brief/2015/germany-rebalancing-waiting-godot. Accessed 11 February 2016.

Toporowski, J. 2002. *The End of Finance: Capital Market Inflation, Financial Derivatives and Pension Fund Capitalism*. London: Routledge.

Tovar, C.E. 2005. 'International Government Debt Denominated in Local Currency: Recent Developments in Latin America'. *BIS Quarterly Review* (December): 109–18.

Truger, A. 2015. 'Cyclical Adjustment and the Remaining Leeway for Expansionary Fiscal Policies within the Current EU Fiscal Framework'. Working Paper, 20/2015, Institute for International Political Economy. Berlin.

Truman, E. 2002. 'Debt Restructuring: Evolution or Revolution?' *Brookings Papers on Economic Activity* 1: 341–6.

Turner, A. 2013a. 'Debt, Money and Mephistopheles: How Do We Get Out of This Mess?' Annual address, Cass Business School, 6 February. www.fsa.gov.uk/library/communication/speeches. Accessed 14 February 2013.

Turner, A. 2013b. 'Overt Monetary Finance and Crisis Management'. Project Syndicate. August 10. www.project-syndicate.org/print/overt-monetary-finance-and-crisis-management-by-adair-turner. Accessed 23 August 2013.

Turner, A. 2015. 'The Case for Monetary Finance—An Essentially Political Issue'. Paper presented at the 16th Jacques Polak Annual Research Conference, 5–6 November, International Monetary Fund.

Turner, P. 2012. 'Weathering Financial Crisis: Domestic Bond Markets in EMEs'. BIS Papers 63, Bank for International Settlements. Basel, January.

Turner, P. 2014. 'The Global Long-term Interest Rate, Financial Risks and Policy Choices in EMEs'. BIS Working Paper No 441. Basel, February.

UNCTAD. 2009a. *Training Manual on Statistics for FDI and the Operations of TNCs: Volume I. FDI Flows and Stocks*. United Nations publications, New York and Geneva.

UNCTAD. 2009b. 'The Role of International Trade Agreements in Attracting Foreign Direct Investment to Developing Countries'. UNCTAD Series in International Investment Policies for Development. Geneva.

UNCTAD. 2011. Regional Monetary Cooperation and Growth-Enhancing Policies: The New Challenges for Latin America and the Caribbean. United Nations publications, New York and Geneva.

UNCTAD. 2014. 'Argentina's "Vulture Fund" Crisis Threatens Profound Consequences for International Financial System'. UNCTAD. 24 June. http://unctad.org/en/pages/news-details.aspx?OriginalVersionID=783&Sitemap_x0020_Taxonomy=UNCTAD. Accessed 26 June 2014.

UNCTAD TDR. 1986. *Trade and Development Report.* Geneva: United Nations.

UNCTAD TDR. 1988. *Trade and Development Report.* Geneva: United Nations.

UNCTAD TDR. 1993. *Trade and Development Report.* Geneva: United Nations.

UNCTAD TDR. 1994. *Trade and Development Report.* Geneva: United Nations.

UNCTAD TDR. 1995. *Trade and Development Report.* Geneva: United Nations.

UNCTAD TDR. 1996. *Trade and Development Report.* Geneva: United Nations.

UNCTAD TDR. 1997. *Trade and Development Report.* Geneva: United Nations.

UNCTAD TDR. 1998. *Trade and Development Report.* Geneva: United Nations.

UNCTAD TDR. 1999. *Trade and Development Report.* Geneva: United Nations.

UNCTAD TDR. 2002. *Trade and Development Report.* Geneva: United Nations.

UNCTAD TDR. 2003. *Trade and Development Report.* Geneva: United Nations.

UNCTAD TDR. 2014. *Trade and Development Report.* Geneva: United Nations.

UNCTAD WIR. 1997. *World Investment Report.* United Nations publications, New York and Geneva.

UNCTAD WIR. 2013. *World Investment Report.* United Nations publications, New York and Geneva.

UNCTAD WIR. 2014. *World Investment Report.* United Nations publications, New York and Geneva.

UNCTAD WIR. 2016. *World Investment Report.* United Nations publications, New York and Geneva.

UNECA (United Nations Economic Commission for Africa). 2014. 'Track it! Stop it! Get it! Illicit Financial Flows: Why Africa needs to "Track it, Stop it and Get it"'. High Level Panel on Illicit Financial Flows from Africa. http://www.uneca.org/sites/default/files/PublicationFiles/illicit_financial_flows_why_africa_needs.pdf. Accessed 2 May 2015.

UNEP. 2013. *Recent Trends in Material Flows and Resource Productivity in Asia and the Pacific.* Bangkok.

United Nations. 2014. Towards the Establishment of a Multilateral Framework for Sovereign Debt Restructuring Processes: Revised Draft Resolution. General Assembly A/68/L.57/Rev.1, New York, 28 August. UNBISnet. http://unbisnet.un.org:8080/ipac20/ipac.jsp?session=1W113015H18N1.7012&profile=bib&uri=full%3D3100001 ~!1033741~!0&booklistformat=html&ri=1&bla_send_full_bib=true&aspect=subtab124&menu=search&view=items&page=0&group=0&term=A%2F68%2FL.57%2FRev.1&index=.UD&uindex=&aspect=subtab124&menu=search&ri=1&postmaster=United%20Nations%20Dag%20Hammarskj%EF%BF%BDld%20Library&subject=&emailaddress=yilmaz.akyuz@bluewin.ch&fullmarc=false. Accessed 18 September 2014.

Upward, R., Z. Wang, and J. Zheng. 2013. 'Weighing China's Export Basket: The Domestic Content and Technology Intensity of Chinese Exports'. *Journal of Comparative Economics* 41(2): 527–43.

van Horen, N. 2012. 'Branching Out: The Rise of Emerging Market Banks'. *The Financial Development Report*: 47–54. World Economic Forum, Geneva. http://www3.weforum.org/docs/WEF_FinancialDevelopmentReport_2012.pdf. Accessed 15 January 2014.

Van Rijckeghem, C. and B. W. di Mauro. 2013. 'Financial Deglobalization: Is The World Getting Smaller?' Development of Economics, Bogazici University. Istanbul, September. http://www.econ.boun.edu.tr/public_html/RePEc/pdf/201314.pdf. Accessed 14 August 2014.

Vernon, R. 1999. 'Review Article: United Nations Conference on Trade and Development World Investment Report 1997: Transnational Corporations, Market Structure and Competition Policy'. *Economic Development and Cultural Change* 47(2): 458–62.

Warren, E. 2013. 'Americans for Financial Reform and the Roosevelt Institute'. Speech delivered at the Roosevelt Institute, Washington, DC, November 12. www.warren.senate.gov/files/documents/AFR%20Roosevelt%20Institute%20Speech%202013-11-12.pdf. Accessed 14 November 2013.

Weeks, J. 2016. 'EU Stagnation Continues: Déjà Vu All Over Again'. Social Europe. 25 February. https://www.socialeurope.eu/2016/02/eu-stagnation-continues-deja-vu-all-over-again/. Accessed 28 February 2016.

Weisbrot, M. and H. Jorgensen. 2013. 'Macroeconomic Policy Advice and the Article IV Consultations: A European Union Case Study'. Center for Economic Policy Research, January.

Weisenthal, J. 2011. 'The Other Huge Lie about US Sovereign Debt'. *Business Insider*. 22 April. http://www.businessinsider.com/the-percentage-of-us-debt-held-abroad-2011-4. Accessed 16 March 2013.

Weiss, L. 2005. 'Global Governance, National Strategies: How Industrialized States Make Room to Move under the WTO'. *Review of International Political Economy* 12 (5): 723–49.

Wessel, D. 2015. 'Fiscal Drag Abates, and Budget Deal Will Reduce It Further'. Brookings Upfront. October 29. http://www.brookings.edu/blogs/up-front/posts/2015/10/29-fim-budget-deal-wessel. Accessed 1 February 2016.

Wessel, D. 2016. 'In CBO's Projections, a Growing Reason to Worry about the Federal Debt'. Brookings Opinion. http://www.brookings.edu/research/opinions/2016/03/30-cbo-projections-reason-to-worry-federal-debt-wessel. Accessed 14 April 2016.

West, J. 2014. 'Chiang Mai Initiative: An Asian IMF?' Asian Century Institute. 26 March. http://asiancenturyinstitute.com/economy/248-chiang-mai-initiative-an-asian-imf. Accessed 26 July 2014.

West, O., A. Rowley, and D. O'Neill. 2015. 'Spectre of Illiquidity Haunts Global Bond Markets Ahead of Fed Rate Hike'. *Emerging Markets*. 10 October. http://www.emergingmarkets.org/Article/3496401/Spectre-of-illiquidity-haunts-global-bond-markets-ahead-of-Fed-rate-hike.html. Accessed 11 January 2016.

Wharton Finance. 2016. 'Burdened by High Debt, European Banks Face a Reckoning'. March 2. http://knowledge.wharton.upenn.edu/article/burdened-by-high-debt-european-banks-face-a-reckoning/. Accessed 19 March 2016.

White, W. 2012. 'Ultra Easy Monetary Policy and the Law of Unintended Consequences'. Federal Reserve Bank of Dallas Globalization and Monetary Policy Institute

Working Paper No. 126. September. http://www.dallasfed.org/assets/documents/institute/wpapers/2012/0126.pdf. Accessed 8 February 2013.

White, W. 2013. 'Overt Monetary Financing (OMF) and Crisis Management'. Project Syndicate. June 12. www.project-syndicate.org/print/overt-monetary-financing–omf–and-crisis-management. Accessed 23 August 2013.

White, W. 2016. 'World Faces Wave of Epic Debt Defaults, Fears Central Bank Veteran'. Interview by The Telegraph, Ambrose Evans-Pritchard, in Davos. *The Telegraph*. 19 January. http://www.williamwhite.ca/media. Accessed 1 February 2016.

Wigglesworth, R. 2016. '"Helicopter Money" on the Horizon, Says Ray Dalio'. *Financial Times*. 18 February.

Wildau, G. 2016. 'China Steps Up Capital Controls to Stem Outflows'. *Financial Times*. January 8.

Wolf, M. 2013. 'The Case for Helicopter Money'. *Financial Times*. 12 February.

Wolf, M. 2016. 'Helicopter Drops Might Not Be Far Away'. *Financial Times*. 24 February.

Woodward, D. 2001. *The Next Crisis? Direct and Equity Investment in Developing Countries*. London and New York: Zed Books.

World Bank. 2003. Turkey. Country Economic Memorandum, World Bank. Washington, DC.

World Bank. 2013. Recent Developments in Local Currency Bond Markets (LCBMs). Washington, DC, October. www.g20.org/load/783687600. Accessed 8 November 2013.

World Bank. 2014a. *International Debt Statistics 2014*. Washington, DC.

World Bank. 2014b. 'Foreign Direct Investment Flows into Sub-Saharan Africa'. *Science, Technology, and Skills for Africa's Development*. Washington DC, March.

Worthington, S. 2016. 'Negative Interest Rates—Are There Any Positives?' The Conversation. 27 March. https://theconversation.com/negative-interest-rates-are-there-any-positives-56505. Accessed 11 April 2016.

Wray, L. R. 2013. 'Bow Down to the Bubble: Larry Summerian Endorses Bubbleonian Madness and Paul Krugman Embraces the Hansenian Stagnation Thesis'. New Economic Perspectives. 21 November. http://neweconomicperspectives.org/2013/11/bow-bubble-larry-summerian-endorses-bubbleonian-madness-paul-krugman-embraces-hansenian-stagnation-thesis.html. Accessed 22 November 2013.

Xiao, G. 2004. 'Round-Tripping Foreign Direct Investment and the People's Republic of China'. ADB Institute Research Paper 58. July. https://openaccess.adb.org/handle/11540/4165. Accessed 8 April 2015.

Yackee, J. W. 2010. 'Do Bilateral Investment Treaties Promote Foreign Direct Investment? Some Hints from Alternative Evidence'. *Virginia Journal of International Law* 51(2):397–442.

Yao, Zhi-zhong and He Fan. 2004. 'Will FDI Cause Balance of Payments Crisis?' *Economic Research Journal* (in Chinese) (November): 37–46.

Yellen, J.L. 2013a. 'A Painfully Slow Recovery for America's Workers: Causes, Implications, and the Federal Reserve's Response'. Remarks made at 'A Trans-Atlantic Agenda for Shared Prosperity', conference sponsored by the AFL-CIO, Friedrich Ebert Stiftung, and the IMK Macroeconomic Policy Institute,Washington, DC, 11 February.

http://www.federalreserve.gov/newsevents/speech/yellen20130211a.htm. Accessed 14 February 2013.

Yellen, J. L. 2013b. Speech at the 'Rethinking Macro Policy II', a conference sponsored by the International Monetary Fund, April 16, Washington, DC. Board of Governors of the Federal Reserve System. http://www.federalreserve.gov/newsevents/speech/yellen20130416a.htm. Accessed 19 April 2013.

Yeyati, E. L. and T. Williams. 2011. 'Financial Globalization in Emerging Economies; Much Ado about Nothing?' Policy Research Working Paper 5624, World Bank. Washington, DC.

Zarsky, L. and K. Gallagher. 2008. 'FDI Spillovers and Sustainable Industrial Development: Evidence from U.S. Firms in Mexico's Silicon Valley'. Discussion Paper 18, Working Group on Development and Environment in the Americas. April. http://www.ase.tufts.edu/gdae/Pubs/rp/DP18Zarsky_GallagherApr08.pdf. Accessed 12 April 2015

Zhou, J., V. Rutledge, W. Bossu, M. Dobler, N. Jassaud, and M. Moore. 2012. 'From Bail-out to Bail-in: Mandatory Debt Restructuring of Systemic Financial Institutions'. Staff Discussion Note SDN/12/03, International Monetary Fund. Washington, DC, April.

Zhu, X. 2012. 'Understanding China's Growth: Past, Present, and Future'. *Journal of Economic Perspectives* 26(4): 103–24.

Index

Introductory Note

References such as '178–9' indicate (not necessarily continuous) discussion of a topic across a range of pages. Wherever possible in the case of topics with many references, these have either been divided into sub-topics or only the most significant discussions of the topic are listed. Because the entire work is about 'EDEs', the use of this term (and certain others which occur constantly throughout the book) as an entry point has been restricted. Information will be found under the corresponding detailed topics.